A VISION OF EUROPE

A Vision of Europe

Franco-German Relations during the Great Depression, 1929–1932

CONAN FISCHER

OXFORD
UNIVERSITY PRESS

OXFORD
UNIVERSITY PRESS

Great Clarendon Street, Oxford, OX2 6DP,
United Kingdom

Oxford University Press is a department of the University of Oxford.
It furthers the University's objective of excellence in research, scholarship,
and education by publishing worldwide. Oxford is a registered trade mark of
Oxford University Press in the UK and in certain other countries

First Edition published in 2017

Published in the United States of America by Oxford University Press
198 Madison Avenue, New York, NY 10016, United States of America

British Library Cataloguing in Publication Data
Data available

Library of Congress Control Number: 2016946337

ISBN 978–0–19–967629–3

Preface

The interwar Great Depression demanded its price of international relations. The French Foreign Minister, Aristide Briand, presented a scheme for European unity at the League of Nations in May 1930 but, according to received wisdom, it was given short shrift by the key European powers, Germany included.[1] Briand's initiative might appear to have been the last gasp in the process of interwar European detente and Franco-German reconciliation that he had championed from 1925 in tandem with his German counterpart, Gustav Stresemann.[2] The latter's death in October 1929, an electoral breakthrough by the revanchist Nazi Party in the September 1930 German elections, and the impact of the Great Depression seemingly combined to put an end to their ambitions. The wider international climate was, it is claimed, similarly unpropitious as each major power promoted national economic self-interest above any collaborative solution to the crisis.

Some recent academic work is somewhat less pessimistic in its conclusions, however, demonstrating that the major powers persevered with efforts collectively to resolve the economic challenges of the Depression era, but that they did fall short.[3] It has even been argued that Franco-German rapprochement rested on more solid foundations than commonly believed and that enduring synergies, extending back over a century, have underpinned the current Paris–Berlin partnership.[4] However, at first sight the course of events suggests otherwise, for successive generations of French and Germans experienced the two World Wars of the earlier twentieth century as enemies. The Allied Commander-in-Chief, Marshal Ferdinand Foch, proved prescient when warning in 1919 that war between his French homeland and Germany would recur within a generation and it is not surprising that interwar Franco-German relations are generally seen as antagonistic and the four years of the Stresemann–Briand partnership as farsighted but exceptional. Furthermore, Karl Heinrich Pohl has most recently accentuated the ambivalence even of Stresemann's foreign policy.[5]

[1] See Ch. 3, Germany, France, and the Briand Plan, under heading 'The (Problematic) Launch of the Briand Plan'.

[2] Throughout the book I use both the adjectives 'Franco-German' and 'German-French'. It is revealing that the French spoke of 'Franco-German' matters, and the Germans of 'German-French'. My use of the terms reflects French and German usage respectively as the context demands. My own text favours the prevailing English-language usage of 'Franco-German'.

[3] Patricia Clavin, *Securing the World Economy: The Reinvention of the League of Nations, 1920–1946* (Oxford, 2013), chs. 2 and 3; Sylvain Schirmann, *Crise, cooperation économique et financière entre états européens 1929–1933* (Paris, 2000).

[4] Robert Frank, 'Le Paradoxe Franco-Allemand du siècle', in Robert Frank, Laurent Gervereau, and Hans Joachim Neyer (eds.), *Course au modern. France et Allemagne dans l'Europe des années vingt. 1919–1933* (Nanterre, 1992), 180.

[5] Karl Heinrich Pohl, *Gustav Stresemann. Biographie eines Grenzgängers* (Göttingen, 2015).

However, *A Vision of Europe* offers a less pessimistic evaluation of Franco-German relations after Stresemann, arguing that the mutual search for rapprochement was sustained for several years after his death until, during 1932, the challenges of the Great Depression and domestic political tensions in both countries finally disrupted the process. Neither side abandoned reconciliation without a fight; indeed the process of rapprochement culminated as late as September 1931 in a formal commitment to Franco-German economic union. This agreement was designed to pave the way towards a political partnership that would be located within a wider process of European integration, so offering the Briand Plan a fresh lease of life. It also drew inspiration from the early advocates of a progressive, transnational Catholicism, which sought to bridge the Franco-German divide by referring to a common spiritual heritage whose values would unite Europe's Christian and democratic societies against the challenges of Fascism and Bolshevism. If this particular pillar of Franco-German detente had been less in evidence while the Protestant, liberal Stresemann was in office, it proved vital during the final years of rapprochement.

Much of the resulting story will be unfamiliar or surprising to many readers, for the pattern and character of Franco-German relations during the Depression years have remained relatively neglected by historians to date and also misunderstood. The peace treaty and its aftermath have been extensively analysed and debated, while the Stresemann–Briand era has also attracted ample coverage that includes excellent biographies of the two foreign ministers. However, with one or two notable exceptions,[6] historians have had less to say and certainly less positive to say regarding the Depression years. The records of the French Foreign Office relating to the early 1930s were severely depleted by the loss and destruction of material during the Second World War, which has complicated and no doubt discouraged writing and research, while historians of Germany have confronted the more immediate matter of the implosion of Weimar and the Nazis' drive to power precisely during the Great Depression.

Franco-German rapprochement and thoughts of European integration during the early 1930s therefore appear at first sight to be unpromising research subjects, but when combined with the surviving French records, the extensive documentation held in the German Foreign Office archives tells a remarkable, if bitter-sweet story. This is not the place to pre-empt the narrative, but in brief French foreign policy was more imaginative and German foreign policy more constructive and collaborative than conventional wisdom has allowed. This book was completed in June 2016 just a day before the British referendum on whether to remain in the European Union. Readers will find some loose but striking parallels between the debates of the interwar era, which did draw in Britain, and those being fought out today, but this timing is entirely coincidental. The initial work on this project in

[6] For example, Franziska Brüning, *Frankreich und Heinrich Brüning. Ein deutscher Kanzler in der französischen Wahrnehmung* (Stuttgart, 2012); Schirmann, *Crise*.

2008 pre-dated the onset of the current British–EU crisis by several years; a crisis which few, if any, seriously anticipated at that time.

This book draws heavily on government and diplomatic documents and correspondence. The citations reflect the title of the documents as archived, which inevitably gives rise to some inconsistencies of form. It does however accurately reflect the vagaries of official cataloguing.

Acknowledgements

I am very grateful to the British Academy and the Elizabeth Barker Endowment for their invaluable financial support for my research programme in the German Foreign Office archives in Berlin, and to the School of History at the University of St Andrews for generously funding parallel research in the French Foreign Office archives at La Courneuve in Paris. I also owe a particular debt of gratitude to Volker Berghahn of Columbia University, New York, who was strongly supportive of this project from an early stage and who very generously provided me with accommodation in Berlin during a preliminary appraisal of German foreign policy records. It was thanks to this visit, in 2008, that I became convinced that the archives harboured an untold story that deserved to be told.

I am also deeply grateful to other colleagues and friends for a wide variety of support and assistance; in particular to Frank Müller, Stephen Tyre, and Andrew Williams at St Andrews; to Stanislas Jeannesson at the University of Nantes; to Tom Weber of the University of Aberdeen; and to Frank McDonough at Liverpool John Moores University. The archival staff in Paris and Berlin provided outstanding research support, among them François Falconet and Martin Kröger, while at Oxford University Press Christopher Wheeler was generously supportive while overseeing the commissioning of *A Vision of Europe*. Since then his successor Cathryn Steele has provided the judicious mix of encouragement and firmness needed to steer the book to conclusion, for which I am very grateful indeed.

If my daughters have flown the nest and so escaped the downside of life with two academic parents, my wife, Mary, has, again, been remarkably supportive and tolerant of the low-key but remorseless distraction and disruption of authorship. I am deeply grateful to her, as always.

Conan Fischer

Edinburgh
June 2016

Contents

List of Abbreviations xiii

1. **Tentative Beginnings: France, Germany, and Intimations of Rapprochement** 1
   Contrasting Perspectives 1
   The Opening Gambits 8

2. **From Thoiry to the Young Plan: Cautious Progress and the Death of Stresemann** 26
   Diplomatic Headwinds and Unofficial Initiatives 26
   The Grautoff Initiative 29
   Franco-German Relations on the Eve of the Hague Conferences 36
   The First Hague Conference 40
   Julius Curtius and the Second Hague Conference 50

3. **Germany, France, and the Briand Plan** 56
   The (Problematic) Launch of the Briand Plan 56
   Franco-German Exchanges 60
   Complications and Upsets 72
   The Rhineland Evacuation and Added Tensions 74
   The 1930 Reichstag Election: Challenges and Reassurance 77

4. **From Paris to Berlin: Official Visits and the Origins of the Franco-German Commission** 85
   Enduring Tensions and the Austro-German Customs Union 85
   Brüning in Paris 90
   The Catholic Connection 95
   Hopeful Signs: The Prussian Plebiscite and Economic Detente 106
   Preparations for the Berlin Ministerial Conference 110

5. **Berlin and the Creation of the Franco-German Commission** 123
   A Successful Conference 123
   Latour in Berlin 129
   Creating the Commission 131
   An Imminent Trade War and the Quota Issue 137
   Growing Discord in the Commission 141
   Political Instability and Diplomatic Stalemate 147

6. **Breakdown: The Stresemann Memoirs Scandal and Wounds that Failed to Heal** 151
A Difficult Climate 151
Alsatian Sensitivities 155
The Stresemann Memoirs Scandal 166
Impasse 176

Conclusion 185

Bibliography 189
Index 197

List of Abbreviations

AEG	Allgemeine Elektrizitäts-Gesellschaft (General Electric Company)
BVP	Bayerische Volkspartei (Bavarian People's Party)
DDP	Deutsche Demokratische Partei (German Democratic Party)
DNVP	Deutschnationale Volkspartei (German National People's Party)
DVP	Deutsche Volkspartei (German People's Party)
ILO	International Labour Organization
NSDAP	Nationalsozialistische Deutsche Arbeiterpartei (National Socialist German Workers' Party)
RDI	Reichsverband der Deutschen Industrie (National Confederation of German Industry)
SA	Sturmabteilung (Storm Section/Storm Troopers)
SPD	Sozialdemokratische Partei Deutschlands (Social Democratic Party of Germany)
UDE	Union douanière européenne (European Customs Union)
US	United States
USA	United States of America

1

Tentative Beginnings

France, Germany, and Intimations of Rapprochement

CONTRASTING PERSPECTIVES

Devastating warfare, economic crises, and a series of brutal dictatorial regimes may have characterized the history of Europe during the first half of the twentieth century, but there were times when it could seem otherwise. Memories persisted of a 'golden' decade that preceded the First World War, subsequently idealized as a time of stable expectations when even the summer weather could be counted upon if planning a riverside picnic. And once the bloodletting of the First World War had passed, the Western world came to enjoy a brief period of remission dubbed the 'roaring twenties' or 'jazz age', when a modicum of prosperity and efforts at social reform combined with radical changes in both popular and high culture.

The earlier period, up until 1914, marked the close of a 'long' nineteenth century of calculable progress that was swept away with the coming of war in 1914. There were to be backward-looking efforts to restore this idealized world, eulogized by the American President Warren G. Harding as a 'return to normalcy',[1] which included the restoration of gold-standard currencies as the supposed foundation stones of a solid and dependable social and international economic order. The jazz age was a very different matter. Alongside the polarizing impact of breakneck cultural and societal innovation which repelled the more conservatively minded, it was marked by a wave of conspicuous consumption funded by alarming levels of personal, corporate, and public debt. As has been said of the interwar American boom: 'In their appetite for immediate gratification, the consumers of the 1920s were devouring their future.'[2] A reckoning, in the form of the Great Depression, was not long in coming and the accompanying political upheaval as often as not came to include a conscious struggle between the traditional and the modern, whether, for example, in Nazism's selective rejection of the new, or in the struggle during the Spanish Civil War between an emancipating secular republicanism and a traditional social and moral order.

[1] Alan Sharp, *Consequences of the Peace: The Versailles Settlement: Aftermath and Legacy 1919–2010*, 2nd edn (London, 2015), 10.

[2] Edward Chancellor, *Devil Take the Hindmost: A History of Financial Speculation* (London, 1999), 197–8.

These complex patterns of upheaval left their mark on the conduct of international relations, which saw the victors of the First World War and their defeated foes respectively struggle to recover the advantages of a squandered past and harness diplomacy to deliver on the lavish, utopian promises made to their citizens during wartime. Post-war international relations could however equally be forward looking, seeking a fresh start for Europe and the wider world. Given that the conflagration of the Second World War followed hard on the heels of the First, these efforts might be dismissed as a sorry failure, but interwar diplomacy did notch up a series of positive achievements that anticipated key dimensions of the contemporary world, among them templates that subsequently served the cause of post-1945 European integration.

The 1919 peace settlement included provision for the creation of the League of Nations to act as the supranational executor of international affairs. This organization was the child of US President Woodrow Wilson's imagination, but he failed to secure ratification of the peace settlement in the American Senate and the resulting absence of the modern world's emergent superpower from the League set limits on its effectiveness. Initially dominated by Europe's imperial victor powers, it has often been written off as a failure.[3] Recently, however, it has been adjudged more sympathetically and credited for its innovative response to a number of challenges that transcended the competency of individual nation states. Among these achievements were the creation of a global Health Organization, which served as the direct predecessor of the United Nations' World Health Organization, and the International Labour Organization (ILO) whose work was also carried over into the United Nations after the Second World War. More generally, the League provided moral and institutional templates for the United Nations itself, as its successes and failures provided 'lessons of history' for the statesmen of a new era.[4]

Particular international crises, such as the 1929 Great Depression, also provided a combination of negative 'lessons' for the future, such as the widespread and ruinous imposition of protectionist trading policies, which contrasted with the more positive legacy of collaborative efforts to combat the slump that may have ultimately failed but, nonetheless, anticipated the economic multilateralism of the post-1945 era. These latter initiatives, it is claimed, also served as intimations of the present-day European Union, whether one looks to its successes or its particular traumas.[5]

Franco-German relations were at the heart of all this. French diplomacy sought above all else to secure the country against another German invasion, whilst German foreign policy prioritized elimination of the more onerous provisions of the 1919 peace settlement. Both countries, therefore, were confronted with the same fundamental choice, of either a reckoning with the other or achieving a

[3] For example, Patrick O. Cohrs, *The Unfinished Peace after World War I: America, Britain and the Stabilisation of Europe, 1919–1932* (Cambridge and New York, 2006), 46–67.

[4] Clavin, *Securing*; see also Patricia Clavin, 'Europe and the League of Nations', in Robert Gerwarth (ed.), *Twisted Paths: Europe 1914–1945* (Oxford, 2007), 325–54.

[5] Schirmann, *Crise*, back cover.

mutual reconciliation. During the immediate post-war years, confrontation—tellingly described as a latent state of war[6]—prevailed as each manoeuvred to revise the peace treaty in its own favour. As we shall see, there were simultaneous, but faltering, efforts on both sides to arrive at a more amicable settlement before, from 1925, the pursuit of rapprochement eventually gained the upper hand under the stewardship of the French and German Foreign Ministers of the day, Aristide Briand and Gustav Stresemann.[7] More recent work has tended to view these efforts sympathetically.[8] Briand's pioneering contribution to the cause of European peace and in particular his (ill-defined) plan for 'European federal union', which he submitted to the League of Nations in 1930, were celebrated by a major international conference held in Geneva in 1991.[9] Stresemann was traditionally regarded as a profoundly ambivalent figure, negotiating a tenuous divide between multilateral peacemaking and the pursuit of German national interests, but his recent biographers have treated him more positively, as a German patriot who regarded national interest and international harmony as interdependent.[10]

This reconciliation, of course, was temporary and *pace* Briand's scheme for European union, Stresemann's death in October 1929 is still generally taken to betoken the end of detente. Peter Krüger's magisterial history of Weimar Germany's foreign policy accordingly lends the post-Stresemann era short shrift as he devotes 506 pages to the first decade of the Republic, but summarizes and effectively dismisses the complex events of its final three years in an epilogue of 48 pages.[11] Changes in senior personnel at the Wilhelmstraβe (German Foreign Office) that occurred after Stresemann's death allegedly bore witness to this degradation of foreign policy. 'Committed opponents of the Locarno spirit and the Stresemann era', Krüger argues, took charge[12] and isolated the remaining supporters of detente.[13] Hans Mommsen reminds us that this process occurred within the context of a German republic that was on its last legs.[14] The final republican coalition government collapsed in March 1930 after an acrimonious and

[6] Gerd Krumeich and Joachim Schröder (eds.), *Der Schatten des Weltkriegs. Die Ruhrbesetzung 1923* (Essen, 2004).

[7] See Ch. 2.

[8] For an overview, Cohrs, *Unfinished Peace*, 259–86.

[9] Antoine Fleury (ed.), *Le Plan Briand d'Union fédérale européenne. Perspectives nationals et transnationales, avec documents. Actes du colloque international tenu à Genève du 19 au 21 septembre 1991* (Bern, 1998).

[10] Christian Baechler, *Gustave Stresemann (1878–1929). De impérialisme à la sécurité collective* (Strasbourg, 1996); Jonathan Wright, *Gustav Stresemann: Weimar's Greatest Statesman* (Oxford, 2002). Pohl, *Stresemann* is more equivocal, however.

[11] Peter Krüger, *Die Auβenpolitik der Republik von Weimar* (Darmstadt, 1985).

[12] Ibid., 513, 514. See also Eckart Conze, *Das Auswärtige Amt. Vom Kaiserreich bis zum Gegenwart* (Munich, 2013), 66.

[13] Peter Krüger, 'Der abgebrochene Dialog. Die deutschen Reaktionen auf die Europavorstellungen Briands in 1929', in Antoine Fleury (ed.), *Le Plan Briand d'Union fédérale européenne. Perspectives nationales et transnationales, avec documents. Actes du colloque international tenu à Genève du 19 au 21 septembre 1991* (Bern, 1998), 300–1; see also Martin Vogt, 'Die deutsche Haltung zum Briand-Plan im Sommer 1930. Hintergründe und politisches Umfeld der Europapolitik des Kabinetts Brüning', in Fleury (ed.), *Plan Briand*, 324–5.

[14] For wider detail, Hans Mommsen, *Die verspielte Freiheit. Der Weg der Republik von Weimar in den Untergang 1918 bis 1933* (Frankfurt-am-Main, 1990), 226ff.

intractable dispute over how best to balance the budget and the resulting elections in September saw an upsurge in support for the National Socialists that left them as the second-strongest party in a fragmented parliament. A republican majority remained mathematically possible, but the Social Democrats (SPD) could still not reach agreement with their erstwhile liberal coalition partners over how to address the burgeoning budget deficit, added to which the President and his entourage had no wish to see the SPD back in government in any case.

Germany's conservatives argued that the Weimar system was incapable of addressing the deepening economic crisis that had followed the 1929 Wall Street Crash and aspired to reform the constitution so as to strengthen the executive at the expense of parliament.[15] In late 1930 President Hindenburg appointed a centre-right minority government, led by the Catholic Centre Party politician Heinrich Brüning, and granted him emergency decree powers under Article 48 of the constitution. This Article was originally intended to protect the young and vulnerable republic against counter-revolutionary forces, but now the same law was being exploited by the very people it had been designed to repel. Not surprisingly, this development is widely seen as the first step down a slippery slope which saw parliamentary democracy first displaced by an increasingly authoritarian form of rule and thereafter by Nazism.[16] In October 1931 Brüning also took on the foreign policy portfolio and here too his performance has often been judged negatively. Krüger is withering as he concludes that Brüning took risks in the hope that 'it would turn out alright on the day [*daß es gut ginge*]'.[17] Furthermore, he continues, this brinkmanship left Berlin unresponsive to French overtures as Germany went all out to secure an end to reparations and soon enough resolved to adopt an unyielding line at the 1932 International Disarmament Conference in pursuit of its long-standing ambition to secure 'equal rights' with the other major powers. To this extent, Hitler's foreign policy may have come to harbour much more radical longer-term objectives, but on taking power he was able from the outset to reinforce and entrench initiatives that had been launched by his immediate predecessors.

Not surprisingly, this has served to inform a pessimistic interpretation of German diplomatic practice during the Depression years that reinforces the image of the Stresemann era as an interlude in Weimar's history of failure. The legacy of Locarno, it is argued, evaporated and the award of the Nobel Peace Prize to Briand, Stresemann, and their British counterpart Austen Chamberlain for their contribution to the detente of the mid-1920s came to appear hollow and founded on illusory hopes. The effects of this twilight era extended of course well beyond France and Germany as the all-too-fleeting optimism of the later 1920s was extinguished and premonitions of catastrophe grew ever more insistent.[18] When

[15] Among the more influential contemporary theorists, Carl Schmitt, *The Crisis of Parliamentary Democracy*, trans. Ellen Kennedy (Cambridge, MA, 1988).

[16] Mommsen, *Verspielte Freiheit*, 226ff; see also Heinrich August Winkler, *Weimar 1918–1933. Die Geschichte der ersten deutschen Demokratie*, 2nd edn (Munich, 1994), chs. 13–15.

[17] Krüger, *Außenpolitik*, 515.

[18] See, for example, in the British case, Richard Overy, *The Morbid Age: Britain between the Wars* (London, 2009).

Western European statesmen picked up the pieces after the Second World War and Konrad Adenauer and Charles de Gaulle signed the Franco-German Friendship Treaty in 1963, there was little or no acknowledgement of the precedent set by Briand and Stresemann,[19] nothing of the struggle for detente conducted during the early 1930s by Heinrich Brüning and his colleagues in the German Foreign Office which will form an important part of our story. Perhaps it was too easy to dismiss Stresemann as an ambivalent figure whose career marked a temporary relaxation in the tenor of German revisionism at best, while Brüning was unable to avoid the charge of complicity in the collapse of the Weimar Republic.

Turning to France, if the Third Republic was in significantly better shape than Weimar, Briand's personal legacy appeared similarly ambivalent, for his collaboration with German counterparts later became conflated with the subsequent appeasement of Hitler during the 1930s by London and Paris, or even, with the benefit of a good dose of hindsight, with the dark years of Vichy. Briand, after all, had concluded his career in 1931/32 as a member of Pierre Laval's Cabinet and his choice of Georges Suarez to pen his biography proved equally unfortunate. Like Laval, Suarez later threw in his lot with Vichy and both were executed after the liberation.[20]

However, it is possible to view the Franco-German rapprochement of the interwar era, or even aspects of pre-1914 relations, in a different light. Franco-German economic relations, it transpires, were founded as much on fundamental synergies as on confrontation, an enduring factor that after 1945 informed the process of Franco-German reconciliation within the wider framework of (West) European integration.[21] The French historian Robert Frank has been particularly bold, maintaining that throughout the twentieth century a deep-seated and positive relationship existed between France and Germany. 'In fact,' he argues, 'despite the drama of the two world wars, things have developed as if the natural trajectory of the past century has led to rapprochement, to entente and a special relationship between France and Germany.'[22] So strong was this relationship, Frank maintains, that not even the twelve years of Hitlerism could destroy it. This argument might appear heroic at best, possibly based more on wisdom after the event than on the force of documentary evidence, for due to losses during the Second World War important elements of France's Foreign Office records are missing, leaving it a struggle to reconstruct the whole story.[23]

[19] Jacques Bariéty, 'Aristide Briand. Les raisons d'un oubli', in Antoine Fleury (ed.), *Le Plan Briand d'Union fédérale européenne. Perspectives nationales et transnationales, avec documents. Actes du colloque international tenu à Genève du 19 au 21 septembre 1991* (Bern, 1998), 1–2.

[20] Ibid., 2–4.

[21] Jacques Bariéty, *Les Relations franco-allemandes après la Première Guerre Mondiale. 10 novembre 1918–10 janvier 1925. De l'exécution à la negotiation* (Paris, 1977). For pre-1914 intimations of this same process: Raymond Poidevin, *Les Relations économiques et financiers entre la France et l'Allemagne de 1898 à 1914* (Paris, 1969); Klaus Wilsberg, *'Terrible ami—aimable ennemi'. Kooperation und Konflikt in den deutsch-französischen Beziehungen 1911–1914* (Bonn, 1998).

[22] Frank, 'Paradoxe', 180.

[23] Ministère des relations extérieures, *Les Archives du Ministère des relations extérieures depuis des Origines. Histoire et guide suivis d'une étude des sources de l'histoire des affaires étrangères dans les dépôts parisiens et départementaux* (Paris, 1984), 187–98.

Nonetheless, it is a proposition which finds some support in this current work, with its focus on the Depression years, 1929–32. The surviving French Foreign Office records need not be exploited in isolation, but can be viewed in tandem with the extensive and thematically organized German Foreign Office documentation relating to interwar Franco-German relations. The very organization of these German records says much on the structure of a complex relationship, but can trip the unwary or the impatient. The obvious first port of call is found in ten bulky folders covering '[French] political relations with Germany' during the years 1929–32.[24] They offer extensive coverage of contentious issues such as frontier revision, reparations, and disarmament where Franco-German relations generally remained obdurately difficult. This negative impression has informed mainstream historical interpretations of the period and also strongly influenced the general tenor of the edited volumes of documents on German foreign policy,[25] themselves an important source for historical scholarship. However, the Wilhelmstraße extracted a mass of documentation from its original records, which it then filed separately, including a strikingly extensive collection covering the years 1929–32 labelled 'Efforts to bring about German-French détente'.[26] This consists of eleven thick folders complemented by an additional folder labelled 'Franco-German rapprochement',[27] but this is by no means the end of the story. Nine further folders cover ministerial visits during 1931 by Brüning to Paris and by Laval and Briand to Berlin,[28] which are of particular significance here. Five more detail cultural collaboration between the two neighbours,[29] four document the activities of a private industrial pressure group (the Mayrisch Committee) that was dedicated to the promotion of closer Franco-German collaboration,[30] while four deal with the German reception of Briand's 1930 European Union plan.[31] There are further collections, in particular the documents that relate to the work of individual diplomats (*Handakten*), which include among other things[32] valuable detail on economic relations,[33] and also records of the Foreign Minister's speeches, meetings, and related activities.[34] Most of this diverse collection of material, again, relates to the pursuit of detente, or to the ultimate reasons for its failure. All in all, therefore,

[24] Politisches Archiv des Auswärtigen Amts (AA), Politische Beziehungen zu Deutschland, Signatur R (R) 70501–10.

[25] *Akten zur deutschen auswärtigen Politik 1918–1945. Serie A: 1918–1925*, ed. Hans-Georg Fleck et al. (Göttingen, 1982–93); *Serie B: 1925–1933*, ed. Hans Rothfels et al. (Göttingen, 1966–83).

[26] AA, Bestrebungen zur Herbeiführung einer deutsch-französischen Verständigung, R70534–44.

[27] AA, Deutsch-Französische Verständigung, R28263.

[28] AA, Gegenseitige Besuche führender Staatsmänner, R70567–70; Handakten hierzu (Friedberg), R70571–4; Pressestimmen zum französischen Gegenbesuch in Berlin, R70575.

[29] AA, Die deutsch-französische Gesellschaft (Grautoff) und deren Veröffentlichungen, R70550–4.

[30] AA, Die deutsch-französische Studienkommission sowie Gründung eines französischen wirtschaftlichen und politischen 'Comité d'Entente international' (Comité Fougère) und eines deutschen Gegenkomitees, R70576–9.

[31] AA, Bund der Vereinigten Staaten von Europa (Briand-Memorandum), R28629–31; Ges. Seeliger: Briand Memorandum, R105491.

[32] See bibliography and individual references for greater detail.

[33] AA, Ges. Eisenlohr, R105386–8.

[34] AA, Reden, Interviews und Aufsätze des Reichsministers, R27994–8.

the bulk of German documentation relating to France during the years 1929–32 concerns rapprochement rather than confrontation. This simple measurement of *Aktenmeter* (shelving metres of archival files) is not in itself conclusive, but with this copious evidence to hand there is clearly a story here worthy of serious investigation.

And as the surviving records in Paris confirm, France remained equally wedded to the pursuit of detente with Germany, regarding Brüning and his Foreign Minister, Julius Curtius, as men with whom they could do business. Curtius had previously played a significant role in the 1929 Young Plan renegotiation of Germany's reparations liabilities, and was regarded by Paris as Stresemann's understudy, who, far from seeking confrontation with France, remained dedicated to the policies of his late mentor.[35] For his part, Brüning understood rapprochement with France from a Catholic perspective, which saw him wedded to the idea of a Europe resting on Christian ideological foundations that, in essence, anticipated elements of post-1945 Christian Democracy. In this regard Brüning, as a Catholic politician, could offer France something Protestant liberal politicians with their historic attachment to the German national state could not or would not.[36]

Therefore, despite some important changes in senior German diplomatic personnel, and despite significant upsets, the Quai d'Orsay (French Foreign Office) continued ultimately to trust Berlin and maintained an intimate and positive relationship with Germany into the spring of 1932. Paris always fretted over the threat posed by the German right and especially over its trenchant repudiation of Franco-German detente, but Brüning was considered a bulwark against this rising tide of nationalist opinion, which, like all tides, would ebb in due course. Berlin was reassured that Brüning's use of emergency powers in the conduct of government was perfectly acceptable to Paris, for the alternatives hardly bore thinking about. Implausible though it remained, the fall of Brüning might conceivably see the Austrian revanchist demagogue Adolf Hitler being offered a role in Germany's government.

This line of argument cuts across received wisdom, for it dates the demise of Franco-German rapprochement three years or more after the death of Stresemann. And as will be seen, this pursuit of rapprochement rested squarely on economic collaboration, yet in the shadow of the 1929 Wall Street Crash, which is seen with justification as the trigger for an upsurge in economic nationalism across the globe.[37] A succession of upsets did, indeed, serve to complicate the pursuit of Franco-German rapprochement, but both sides responded by intensifying their efforts to circumvent such obstacles rather than by abandoning rapprochement. Some recent work has dedicated greater attention to efforts at collaborative economic diplomacy during these troubled years,[38] efforts which saw France and Germany propose to meet the challenges of the Great Depression on a bilateral and

[35] See Ch. 2 under 'Julius Curtius and the Second Hague Conference', 50–3.

[36] See Ch. 4 under 'Brüning in Paris' and 'The Catholic Connection'.

[37] See, for example, Patricia Clavin, *The Great Depression in Europe, 1929–1939* (Basingstoke, 2000), 166.

[38] Clavin, *Securing*; Schirmann, *Crise*.

ultimately on a continental basis. This agenda was never going to be prejudiced on a whim, given its centrality to the wider pursuit of detente. It was only during the spring of 1932 that the recourse to economic nationalism finally intruded on this Franco-German project, just as the damage was compounded by a publishing scandal which inflicted massive if gratuitous damage on German-French relations. But before turning to the events of the Depression years, it is important to outline, in brief, the origins of the thinking and forces that underpinned and sustained rapprochement.

THE OPENING GAMBITS

German heavy industry came to consume far more iron ore during the early twentieth century than its domestic mines could hope to supply, leaving the country's blast furnaces overly reliant on imported Swedish ore. The vast iron ore fields of neighbouring France offered an attractive and geographically convenient alternative, prompting the Thyssen heavy industrial conglomerate, among others, to build stakes in the mines of French Lorraine and Normandy. In the latter case it only secured a deal in 1912 after hard-fought negotiations which centred on whether ultimate control of this strategic asset would rest in French or German hands. On the face of it, the bargain struck left Thyssen a minority partner in the Societé des Hauts Forneaux de Caen (The Caen Blast Furnaces Corporation) with French board members in the majority, while its operations were financed in large measure by French merchant bankers. However, August Thyssen, founder and owner of the eponymous German firm, was no stranger to transnational business ties for he had interests across Europe and also overseas, for example in South America and India. Practicalities alone saw him espouse the vision of a 'European trading economy, free from national political rivalries', while the French Director of the Hauts Forneaux, Louis Le Chatelier, held comparable views and looked beyond business relations to a future where Franco-German economic cooperation would serve to mend wider relations between the two hereditary enemies. He praised Thyssen's personal role in this process, observing that a deal had been struck in Normandy 'thanks to the lofty ideals of M. August Thyssen who, in his own words, hoped that the agreements concluded between ourselves "form the foundation stone of a lasting accord and contribute to the improvement of relations between our two countries"'.[39] August Thyssen's son, Fritz, echoed his father's sentiments during a visit to Normandy in 1912, anticipating (quixotically) that Franco-German economic integration would henceforward render war between the two former enemies obsolete.

Thyssen and Le Chatelier were, of course, hard-headed businessmen, who soon enough clashed as the latter attempted to extend French influence within their joint venture, but the commercial alliance held and there was little discernible political

[39] Quoted in Wilsberg, *Terrible ami*, 234–5.

fallout. As the French Foreign Minister of the day, Stéphen Pichon, remarked, 'We have no interest in lending a political character to an affair which is entirely private and commercial in nature.'[40] Thyssen's activities were in fact typical of the age as a string of German mining, metallurgical, and chemical companies set up in France, thanks in large measure to some 16 billion francs of capital provided by French investment houses.[41] Meanwhile, French counterparts, including the glass manufacturer St Gobain and the cross-border, but essentially French, de Wendel metallurgical combine, reciprocated by investing in Germany. This two-way process was not lost on opinion formers in the French media, with the journalist Auguste Pawlowski remarking that: 'we have interests in German mines. The Germans have the same in French mines. What could be fairer?'[42] Or as the nationalist journalist Louis Bruneau concluded: 'One must grant each activity... its due and so recognize with complete justice that M. Thyssen's are truly prodigious.'[43]

Franco-German business collaboration extended beyond their domestic economies into their respective empires and beyond. The Berlin to Baghdad railway was a case in point, and although the German military weighed its importance in strategic terms, its financing, building, and operation proceeded as a multinational venture, which included significant French participation. Thus the German Ambassador at Constantinople contradicted his military colleagues, concluding that its rationale was economic and its political function was to promote great power detente.[44] Wider trade between France and Germany also blossomed, for consumer preference could trump cross-border political tensions or hereditary enmity and very few businessmen welcomed talk of war or the distraction of a fiscally disruptive arms race. As the influential Ruhr magnate, Hugo Stinnes, warned, war would constitute 'an immense financial and economic catastrophe with dangerous social possibilities'.[45]

However, none of this could wish away the series of crises that continued to punctuate Franco-German relations. The scars inflicted on France by its defeat in the 1870–1 Franco-Prussian war had only partly healed and during the early twentieth century these sensitivities were heightened by an erratic, sometimes confrontational, German foreign policy. The German Emperor, Wilhelm II, used his constitutional powers to make a series of provocative, ill-advised interventions in international diplomacy, for example during a dispute over the status of Morocco, which flared up in 1905 and again in 1911. Germany had significant business interests there and favoured the country remaining independent with an 'open door' trading policy, whereas France sought to annex the country for economic and strategic reasons, while offering Spain the port of Tangier as a sweetener. If Germany's stance might appear the more enlightened by twenty-first-century

[40] Quoted in Wilsberg, *Terrible ami*, 236.

[41] Raymond Poidevin, 'Le Nationalisme économique et financier dans les relations franco-allemandes avant 1914', *Revue d'Allemagne et des pays de langue allemande*, 28, 1 (1996), 63–70.

[42] Quoted in Wilsberg, *Terrible ami*, 258.

[43] Quoted ibid., 223.

[44] Hew Strachan, *The First World War*, vol. I: *To Arms* (Oxford, 2003), 667.

[45] Quoted in Gerald D. Feldman, 'Hugo Stinnes and the Prospect of War before 1914', in Manfred F. Boemeke, Roger Chickering, and Stig Förster (eds.), *Anticipating Total War: The German and American Experiences 1871–1914* (Cambridge, 1999), 90.

standards, imperialism was, of course, *à la mode* at the time and, as noted, the confrontation was badly handled by Berlin. Matters reached a nadir during the 1911 crisis when Britain openly backed France while Berlin's allies, Italy and Austria-Hungary, sat on their hands and left Germany isolated.

The situation was eventually defused in talks between the French Ambassador at Berlin, Jules Cambon, and the German Foreign Minister, Alfred von Kiderlen-Wächter, which saw France secure Morocco, but in turn compensate Germany with a slice of territory in the French Congo. The impetus for this deal had originated in Paris where, in June 1911, the Radical politician Joseph Caillaux was appointed Prime Minister. He sought finally to repair Franco-German relations, not as an idealist, but from an acute awareness of the military threat a belligerent Germany would always pose for France.[46] As for the Moroccan crisis, he was determined to uphold French colonial interests in Africa and elsewhere, but simply responding to the German challenge with force was a game France might all too easily lose. The Entente Cordiale, reached with Britain in 1904, had resolved a series of colonial disputes between London and Paris and so paved the way to a more amicable relationship overall. This included military and diplomatic cooperation and it seems that Caillaux envisaged reaching a comparable accord with Germany. He therefore authorized Cambon to offer Berlin the prospect of a comprehensive Franco-German accommodation, explaining that: 'It will be a question of wide-ranging discussions designed to iron out the greatest possible number of difficulties between Germany and ourselves, which currently divide us at various points on the globe'[47] and, as a past (and future) Finance Minister, Caillaux appreciated that domestic economic synergies were central to any such initiative. He was, however, forced to resign as Prime Minister in January 1912 after it transpired that his negotiations with Germany had outstripped any brief agreed in parliament or with the French President and his departure brought to an end the active pursuit of rapprochement with Berlin. His successor, Raymond Poincaré, was prepared to maintain correct relations across the Vosges, but believed that the best guarantee of national security lay in the Franco-Russian alliance, which included military guarantees, and in the Franco-British entente.

When war did break out in the summer of 1914 powerful voices in Berlin and Paris were quick to articulate far-reaching war aims in their respective quests for long-term military and material security. German ambitions focused on Russian Poland and the Baltic states but also the iron ore fields of French Lorraine, while France coveted Germany's Rhineland, which, apart from its strategic significance, contained key industrial assets, including its war industries.[48] It was left to isolated

[46] Apart from Germany's armaments programme, French perceptions of German bellicosity were reinforced by publications such as Friedrich von Bernhardi, *Germany and the Next War*, trans. Allen H. Powles (London, 1914). See also Heinrich August Winkler, *Der lange Weg nach Westen*, vol. I: *Deutsche Geschichte vom Ende des Alten Reiches bis zum Untergang der Weimarer Republik* (Munich, 2002), 326.

[47] Quoted in Wilsberg, *Terrible ami*, 49.

[48] The classic works on Germany were: Fritz Fischer, *Germany's Aims in the First World War* (London, 1967); Fritz Fischer, *War of Illusions: German Policies from 1911–1914* (London, 1975); and

individuals to promote the cause of Franco-German reconciliation. They included Walther Rathenau, from 1915 Chairman of the German electrical engineering giant AEG, who before the war had advocated a broad Central European trading bloc, located within a multilateral global economy, to enable Germany to offset its industrial and manufacturing exporting strengths against its need for imported raw materials.[49] Rathenau came to oversee the procurement of raw materials for the German war economy, but he doubted the value of annexing French territory, instead arguing that it was essential to reach a speedy and conciliatory peace with Paris, for 'occupation and the transfer of property in France would be more trouble than they were worth'.[50] As the war ground on into 1917, exacting an ever-burgeoning toll in human life and material wealth to no apparent end, Caillaux agitated for a compromise peace with Germany. However, he came to cut a relatively isolated figure as the Prime Minister of the day, Georges Clemenceau, dropped any thought of compromise and pressed for outright victory. Caillaux's efforts saw him arrested in early 1918 and in 1920 eventually convicted for treason, before being rehabilitated and resuming his political career in 1925. More typical of this belligerent age were Gustav Stresemann and Aristide Briand, who may have been destined to serve as the godfathers of Franco-German rapprochement during the mid- and later 1920s, but were convinced wartime annexationists, committed to all-or-nothing victory. Thus Briand envisaged Germany being contained to the east of the Rhineland, asserting that: 'In our view Germany can no longer have any presence beyond the Rhine; the organization of these territories, their neutrality and their initial occupation should be resolved in inter-Allied negotiations.'[51]

On the face of it the Allied military victory in November 1918 left France well placed to secure its future. The armistice terms compelled Germany to evacuate Alsace-Lorraine and accept an Allied occupation of the Rhineland within a matter of weeks, well before the actual peace conference opened. However, inter-Allied relations deteriorated rapidly as each victor power pursued its particular interests. The United States President, Woodrow Wilson, envisaged a new world order where democratic nation states would articulate common interests and arbitrate their differences within a League of Nations, but idealism aside, the United States had ended up as the principal financier of the Allied war effort. The Americans now made clear that

for a briefer, longer-term overview, Fritz Fischer, *From Kaiserreich to Third Reich: Elements of Continuity in German History* (London, 1986). For France: David Stevenson, 'French War Aims and Peace Planning', in Manfred Boemeke, Gerald Feldman, and Elizabeth Glaser (eds.), *The Treaty of Versailles: A Reassessment after 75 Years* (Cambridge, 1998), 107; Jacques Bariéty, 'France and the Politics of Steel, from the Treaty of Versailles to the International Steel Entente, 1919–1926', in Robert Boyce (ed.), *French Foreign and Defence Policy, 1918–1940: The Decline and Fall of a Great Power* (London, 1998), 30ff; Hans-Ludwig Selbach, *Katholische Kirche und französische Rheinlandpolitik nach dem Ersten Weltkrieg* (Cologne, 2013), 21–89; Georges-Henri Soutou, 'La France et les marches de l'est, 1914–1919', *Revue historique*, 578 (1978), 387.

49 Volker R. Berghahn, *Quest for Economic Empire: European Strategies of German Big Business in the Twentieth Century* (Providence, RI, 1996), 9.

50 Quoted in Hartmut Pogge von Strandmann (ed.), *Walther Rathenau: Industrialist, Banker, Intellectual, and Politician. Notes and Diaries 1907–1922*, trans. Caroline Pinter-Lacraft (Oxford, 1985), 185.

51 Quoted in Selbach, *Katholische Kirche*, 31.

they expected these loans to be repaid in instalments, and while Britain could countenance this arrangement, as long as its own debtors paid up, France could not. French ministers faced having to explain to their citizens that victory notwithstanding, the war had effectively bankrupted the country and in some desperation they looked to the sequestration of German assets in order to square the circle. It was already understood that Germany would pay restitution for damage to Allied civilian property and assets, which stood to benefit France and Belgium in particular, but less so Britain. British civilians had been fed a diet of wartime propaganda that portrayed the German enemy as wicked, even bestial, and in the first post-war, 'khaki', elections it quickly became clear that voters expected a fair share of the spoils of war.[52] London therefore argued for the widest possible definition of compensation-worthy assets, including war pensions, and French negotiators responded in kind, arguing that if the United States was not prepared to regard its financial sacrifice as equivalent to France's massive blood sacrifice, then the 'Boche' would have to pay.

Fantastical numbers were floated by French ministers, at least in part to shock the Americans into scaling down inter-Allied liabilities. However, it took a heroic leap of imagination to believe that the Germans could honour their own war debt as well as a good measure of the Allies'. The French Finance Minister, Louis Klotz, estimated his country's wartime damages at £5.36 billion, but the British economist, John Maynard Keynes, estimated that Paris might legitimately claim £800 million.[53] It also transpired that while Britain and the United States would countenance the transfer of Alsace and the Moselle (German Lorraine) to France without the inconvenience of a plebiscite, they were opposed to further French territorial gains at Germany's expense. It was left to the French Prime Minister, Georges Clemenceau, doggedly to extract what he could from his Allies without estranging them and so leaving his country isolated and vulnerable to a German war of revenge. After hard bargaining it was agreed that the Rhineland would be occupied by Allied troops for a term ranging from five years in the north to fifteen in the south, while the Saar territory with its extensive coalfields and metallurgical industry was placed at France's disposal (under League of Nations sovereignty) until 1935, when a plebiscite would determine its final status. Even so, the post-war map of Europe stood to contain a France of just 40 million people against a more youthful Germany of 60 million (as well as 6 million German Austrians who were agitating for union with Germany itself). As the French Minister of Commerce, Étienne Clémentel, gloomily observed, France faced decline, as a trading nation, a financial centre, and in terms of population. It would be squeezed between the 'Anglo-Americans' and a Central European economy dominated by the great industrial combines of an 'incorrigibly malevolent' Germany.[54]

Paris had one further card to play. During the war the French Foreign Ministry had maintained a 'press and propaganda bureau' in the Swiss capital, Bern.[55] Led

[52] John Maynard Keynes, *The Economic Consequences of the Peace* (London, 1920), 131, 133.

[53] Ibid., 119.

[54] Stevenson, 'French War Aims', 96.

[55] Gaby Sonnabend, *Pierre Viénot (1897–1944). Ein Intellektueller in der Politik* (Munich, 2005), 95 note 262.

by François-Émile Haguenin, its primary task was to monitor German domestic opinion, but during 1916 and 1917 it also served to sound out Germany on the possible terms of a compromise peace. Haguenin knew the country well, having taught before the war as a Professor of Romance Languages at the Friedrich-Wilhelm-University in Berlin, and by the same token he was also something of a known quantity to the German authorities. In March 1919 he travelled secretly to Berlin on behalf of the Quai d'Orsay to float the idea of Franco-German cooperation. Would the German Foreign Office, he enquired, consider pursuing a common European economic policy with France, rather than looking to the United States? Berlin, however, believed that America rather than France offered the best prospects for a moderate peace settlement and suspected Paris of trying to drive a wedge between Germany and the USA. At the very least, Haguenin was told, Paris needed to make its offer public, but France could no more afford to alienate the USA (and Britain) than could Germany. No doubt with an eye to happier pre-war days, when the outlook for Franco-German economic collaboration had looked much more hopeful, Haguenin regretted Berlin's lack of interest and 'stressed again that Germany and France were economically interdependent; henceforth he would seek to establish private economic accords [between the two countries]'.[56] Thereafter he was appointed head of France's Bureau of Economic and Social Affairs in Berlin, but died in 1924, shortly before Stresemann and Briand launched a sustained effort to bring about Franco-German rapprochement.

When the peace settlement was presented to the Germans in May 1919 for comment rather than negotiation, and then in June for signature in slightly amended form, it was met with a toxic combination of anger and despair. Whether German leaders and wider opinion had genuinely come to terms with the reality of defeat is a moot point, but there were also clear discrepancies between Woodrow Wilson's magnanimous, publicly stated war aims and the final peace terms. The scale of territorial losses to Poland was excessive in German eyes, but the reparations clauses triggered particular outrage. National recovery, Berlin had hoped, would be secured by way of economic recovery (war-debt notwithstanding) realized through even-handed participation in an open and liberal global economic order. But nothing of the kind was now on offer. Instead the Allies presented Berlin with a hefty interim reparations bill which included the surrender of German-owned assets in Alsace and the Moselle as well as in Allied and neutral countries, of intellectual property, of shipping and railway rolling stock, and even of livestock and other farming produce from a country teetering on the brink of famine.[57] The Allies, however, were unable to agree among themselves on a final bill, instead delaying a definitive settlement until 1921. In effect the German signatories to the peace treaty were being asked to put their names to a blank cheque.

[56] Peter Krüger, *Deutschland und die Reparationen 1918/19. Die Genesis des Reparationsproblems in Deutschland zwischen Waffenstillstand und Versailler Friedenschluß* (Stuttgart, 1973), 137.

[57] Conan Fischer, *The Ruhr Crisis, 1923–1924* (Oxford, 2003), 60–1; see also Conan Fischer, 'The Human Price of Reparations', in Conan Fischer and Alan Sharp (eds.), *After the Versailles Treaty: Enforcement, Compliance, Contested Identities* (London, 2008), 81–95.

With a treaty too benign to guarantee French security and too severe to secure German goodwill, Clemenceau was left to console himself that the defeated enemy would default and provide France and its allies with a pretext to impose further sanctions, in the form of an extended occupation of western Germany.[58] Meanwhile German leaders complied with the peace terms grudgingly, doing just enough, they hoped, to avert these Allied sanctions. The final reparations bill followed in early 1921 and at 132 billion gold marks it was significantly less severe than French negotiators had proposed, but in German diplomats' eyes it remained beyond their country's means. By March there was stalemate, at which point Britain gave the nod to an indefinite Franco-Belgian military occupation of three major industrial centres on the Rhine and Ruhr (Düsseldorf, Duisburg, and Ruhrort) and the establishment of a temporary customs barrier between the Allied-controlled Rhineland and unoccupied Germany. Weeks of political upheaval in Berlin followed and precipitated a change of government, leaving a centre-left coalition led by Joseph Wirth to secure ratification of the Allied terms in parliament. Wirth made it plain that he was acting under duress and proposed buying time by meeting the existing terms while trying to revise the reparations schedule.

However, despite this dialogue of the deaf, there were figures in the business and political worlds on both sides of the Rhine who, perhaps with an eye back to the synergies that had characterized pre-war Franco-German economic relations, looked to repair the damage inflicted by the war and, for that matter, the peace settlement which had served to fragment the previously integrated mining and metallurgical industries of France, Germany, and the Low Countries. Wirth's predecessor as Chancellor, Konstantin Fehrenbach, had already floated the idea of meeting reparations obligations to France 'in kind', in the form of coal, coke, timber, and even labour; resources amply available in Germany, even as Berlin struggled to raise the gold-based cash sums demanded by the existing reparations schedule. This initiative came to nothing at the time, but the concept was dusted down in June 1921 by Wirth's Minister for Reconstruction, the industrialist Walther Rathenau, who found a willing negotiating partner in France's Minister for the Liberated Regions, Louis Loucheur. The latter envisaged the creation of Franco-German joint ventures to rehabilitate the devastated countryside and towns of northern France. As successful businessmen, both with an expertise in the electrics industry, the two politicians shared much in common and also appreciated that Franco-German collaboration offered sufficient economies of scale to compete with the United States' burgeoning commercial strength.[59]

Several months of negotiation culminated in the Wiesbaden Agreement of 7 October, but despite its endorsement by the French Premier, Aristide Briand,[60]

[58] Stevenson, 'French War Aims', 100. See also Soutou, 'Marches de l'est', 387; Anna-Moniker Lauter, *Sicherheit und Reparationen. Die französische Öffentlichkeit, der Rhein und die Ruhr (1919–1923)* (Essen, 2006), 54.

[59] See also Adam Tooze, *The Deluge: The Great War and the Remaking of the Global Order* (London, 2015), 12–13.

[60] Jacques Bariéty, 'Aristide Briand et la sécurité de la France en Europe, 1919–1932', in Stephen A. Schuker and Elizabeth Müller-Luckner (eds.), *Deutschland und Frankreich. Vom Konflikt zur Aussöhnung. Die Gestaltung der westeuropäischen Sicherheit, 1914–1963* (Munich, 2000), 124.

the accord failed to stick. Opposition politicians in Germany denounced reparations in any shape or form while within French industrial circles, many of whom had willingly collaborated with their German counterparts before the war, there was little enthusiasm for a second German economic penetration of their home markets. Instead French businessmen looked to investment opportunities for themselves east of the Rhine, abetted to a degree by the French High Commissioner in the Rhineland, Paul Tirard.[61] Furthermore, France's entente partner, Britain, feared that this bilateral Franco-German arrangement might undermine the wider reparations settlement and compromise British interests. On 10 November the *Sydney Morning Herald* reported that Sir John Bradbury, the Principal British Delegate to the Reparations Commission, had protested that:

> The burdens which Germany undertakes towards France under the Wiesbaden agreement (providing for certain payments in material and goods) cannot be borne without prejudice to the execution of her treaty obligations. Germany doubtless will plead her new obligations to France as a ground for the reconsideration of her position regarding reparations generally. The agreement, therefore, will become an alteration favouring France detrimentally to other Allies.[62]

At the very least, he concluded, France would need to compensate its fellow creditors accordingly.[63] The British Prime Minister, David Lloyd George, responded by proposing to his French counterpart, Aristide Briand, the launching instead of a multilateral European recovery programme and, although he did not specifically repudiate the Wiesbaden Agreement, Briand concurred. This recovery programme informed the agenda of the conference on security, economic reconstruction, and reparations held in Genoa in April 1922, but unforeseen developments there brought Franco-German relations to the brink of collapse.

Poincaré had succeeded Briand as French Prime Minister in January 1922, for Briand's willingness to discuss the reconstruction of Europe with Britain and with German involvement had deprived him of support in parliament from the centre-right Bloc National.[64] Although Briand had never questioned the need to enforce the Versailles Settlement, Poincaré took an ostensibly tougher line and prioritized enforcing the existing reparations agreement over any possible revision, at least as long as the United States (and Britain) continued to demand the honouring of inter-Allied war debts. And his well-rehearsed scepticism regarding German good faith seemed to be confirmed when, during the Genoa Conference, Soviet Russia and Germany signed a separate agreement in the neighbouring town of Rapallo. This regulated their bilateral trade relations and cancelled all claims arising from the war and the Russian Revolution. It was essentially defensive in nature and rumours of an imminent reconciliation between the Russians and Allies, to include Soviet involvement in the Allied war debts and reparations regime, had spurred Berlin to

[61] Conan Fischer, *Europe between Democracy and Dictatorship, 1900–1945* (Oxford, 2011), 153.
[62] 'Reparations. Wiesbaden Agreement. British Objections', *The Sydney Morning Herald* (10 November 1921), 7 (http://trove.nla.gov.au/newspaper/article/15979751).
[63] Ibid. [64] Bariéty, 'Aristide Briand et la sécurité', 124.

pre-empt the Allies and close its own deal, which had already been some months in the making. However, a shocked Poincaré interpreted the Rapallo Treaty as a clandestine military alliance. French plans for the occupation and exploitation of the Ruhr District were dusted down and lent added urgency when, during August, efforts by Paris to reach a fresh agreement with Britain on war debts and reparations failed comprehensively.[65] Meanwhile, events in Germany had already compounded tensions when, on 24 June, right-wing extremists murdered Walther Rathenau, who had been appointed German Foreign Minister on 31 January. For all of the furore over his part in the Rapallo Accord, he was widely respected at home and abroad as a stabilizing force within the embattled Weimar Republic, and his violent death served further to destabilize the domestic political climate, while doing nothing for foreign confidence in the currency and Berlin's creditworthiness. Finally, on 30 August, as a famine reminiscent of the darkest days of the war gripped Germany's cities, Wirth announced a unilateral suspension of cash payments to the reparations account, declaring to a sombre Reichstag that 'The entire nation understands the slogan "bread first, then reparations".'[66]

However, if the main thrust of French policy towards Germany was decidedly confrontational, there were also renewed efforts during the latter half of 1922 to forge a more collaborative relationship, which owed a fair deal to Loucheur and Rathenau's earlier initiative. The mood in French industrial circles had now softened as doubts over the Wiesbaden Agreement were replaced by the conviction that, sooner or later, they would have to rebuild ties with their inherently stronger German counterparts. Initial French soundings were followed during August by negotiations between the influential Ruhr industrialist, Hugo Stinnes, and the French senator and industrialist, Louis de Lubersac, who also served as President of the General Confederation of Cooperatives of the Devastated Areas. By 4 September they had agreed a programme of reparations deliveries 'in kind', which, Stinnes appreciated, would play well for his own industrial holdings, but he also understood that rapprochement between the business communities of France and Germany offered a path to more tolerable Franco-German relations generally. The Stinnes–Lubersac Agreement did attract official support on both sides of the Rhine, in Germany's case not least because Stinnes sat in parliament for the centre-right DVP (German People's Party) whose leader, Gustav Stresemann, supported these exploratory efforts to mend Franco-German relations.

Stresemann had been an outspoken annexationist during the war itself, but after Germany's defeat he quickly changed his tune. As early as 1919 he had come to regard the Franco-German relationship as essentially symbiotic, being 'convinced . . . that France could not recover without financial and economic assistance from Germany and French appreciation of this interdependence would compel it to moderate its demands'.[67] However, he also recognized the unprecedented degree of power that France exercised in post-war Europe and understood that Paris was more predisposed to wielding the stick than offering the carrot when it came to

[65] Fischer, *Ruhr Crisis*, 21–5. [66] Quoted in Fischer, 'Human Price', 86–7.
[67] Baechler, *Stresemann*, 316; see also Wright, *Stresemann*, 1.

relations with a latently powerful Germany. He therefore supported the Stinnes–Lubersac Agreement less as an economic arrangement which may have held advantages for Germany and more as 'a means of setting in train a political entente between France and Germany . . . Rapprochement between French and German heavy industry', he reasoned, 'would prove incompatible with a French policy of sanctions and ultimatums, or with maintaining the occupation [of German territory] at its current level.'[68] In the event the initiative came to nothing, for Poincaré rejected the offer on 21 October as too little, too late. In November 1922 he sanctioned a French (and Belgian) occupation of Germany's heavy industrial heartland in and around the Ruhr District, which left the immediate prospects for further diplomacy very bleak indeed.

The French Premier refined his plans during December as the Reparations Commission established a technical German default in the delivery of telegraph poles and cut timber. This default served to provide Paris with a legal pretext for the projected invasion, but as Sir John Bradbury remarked: 'History had recorded no such political use of wood since the Greeks built a horse outside Troy.'[69] Poincaré nonetheless continued to insist, spuriously,[70] that the reparations defaults posed an elemental risk to France's economic well-being, lobbying the press to this effect, and insisting in public that the Ruhr occupation was 'a straightforward police operation' designed to secure undelivered reparations vital to the 'national interest'.[71] This, however, simply served to obscure the enormity of his ambitions. Poincaré sought a thoroughgoing revision of the peace settlement in France's favour and dared to anticipate that 'by March or April Germany will fall to pieces',[72] adding that '[they] were no longer discussing payments, France had to develop a political plan'.[73]

On 11 January French and Belgian troops began their occupation of the Ruhr. The history of this invasion has been amply documented elsewhere,[74] but, in brief, a new German government, led by the respected Hamburg businessman, Wilhelm Cuno, with Frederic von Rosenberg as his Foreign Minister, proved unequal to the

[68] Quoted in Baechler, *Stresemann*, 312. For general discussion: Baechler, *Stresemann*, 312–13, 323 note 232; Gerald Feldman, *The Great Disorder: Politics, Economics and Society in the German Inflation, 1914–1924* (Oxford, 1993), 460–5; Stanislas Jeannesson, *Poincaré, la France et la Ruhr (1922–1924). Histoire d'une occupation* (Strasbourg, 1998), 110.

[69] Paraphrased in Otto Friedrich, *Before the Deluge: A Portrait of Berlin in the 1920s* (London, 1974), 123.

[70] Jeannesson, *Poincaré*, 138.

[71] Lauter, *Sicherheit*, 310–11, 313.

[72] Jeannesson, *Poincaré*, 116.

[73] Georges-Henri Soutou, 'Vom Rhein zur Ruhr: Absichten und Planungen der französischen Regierung', in Gerd Krumeich and Joachim Schröder (eds.), *Der Schatten des Weltkriegs. Die Ruhrbesetzung 1923* (Essen, 2004), 66.

[74] Fischer, *Ruhr Crisis*; Jeannesson, *Poincaré*; Barbara Müller, *Passiver Widerstand im Ruhrkampf. Eine Fallstudie zur gewaltlosen zwischenstaatlichen Konfliktaustragung und ihren Erfolgsbedingungen* (Münster, 1996); Elspeth Y. O'Riordan, *Britain and the Ruhr Crisis* (Basingstoke, 2001); Michael Ruck, *Die Freien Gewerkschaften im Ruhrkampf 1923* (Frankfurt-am-Main, 1986); Hans Spethmann, *Zwölf Jahre Ruhrbergbau. Aus seiner Geschichte von Kriegsanfang bis zum Franzosenabmarsch 1914 bis 1925, iii. Der Ruhrkampf 1923 bis 1925 in seinen Leitlinien* (Berlin, 1929); Hans Spethmann, *Zwölf Jahre Ruhrbergbau. Aus seiner Geschichte von Kriegsanfang bis zum Franzosenabmarsch 1914 bis 1925, iv. Der Ruhrkampf 1923 bis 1925. Das Ringen um die Kohle* (Berlin, 1930).

challenges of the day. Rosenberg had held a succession of senior posts in the German Foreign Office, but was unable to resolve the crisis through diplomatic means, while Cuno's domestic policy tended towards the reactive as his government latched on to a grass-roots campaign of passive resistance on the Rhine and Ruhr, organized in essence by the trade unions. This campaign certainly obstructed French efforts to exploit the industrial assets of the region and also cut across plans effectively to sunder it from Germany, but at the cost of a collapse in German economic activity and a crisis in public finances that created profound social chaos and unprecedented levels of hyperinflation.[75] On 13 August Cuno's government fell, to be replaced by a broad-based coalition led by Gustav Stresemann, who also served as Foreign Minister. Stresemann and his ministers were clear from the outset that the passive resistance campaign had run its course and adopted a twin-track strategy which sought an interim accord with France as a prelude to multilateral diplomacy aimed at securing a longer-term, international resolution of the crisis.

On 3 September Stresemann proposed to the French Ambassador at Berlin, Pierre de Margerie, that Germany mortgage elements of its heavy industry to raise reparations payments, alongside closer Franco-German industrial ties and a reconsideration of the scope and volume of deliveries in kind. De Margerie was sympathetic and knew that Stresemann's efforts to reach a settlement by addressing legitimate French concerns enjoyed strong support from senior German diplomats.[76] However, his political masters in Paris were less keen, for the imminent collapse of German passive resistance appeared to offer outright victory on Poincaré's terms. Ultimately the French Premier 'had no wish to negotiate with the German government; it was to be overwhelmed by the domestic crisis and Germany would become prey to the forces of disintegration',[77] and nothing changed after Stresemann called an unconditional halt to the passive resistance campaign on 26 September. On 27 September Poincaré warned his civilian and military commanders on the Rhine and Ruhr to refuse any concessions, insisting that 'we cannot relinquish any of the assets we are seizing, nor abandon any of the positions we have taken'.[78] As Stanislas Jeannesson concludes, the Prime Minister saw no reason to do otherwise, for 'French long-term ambitions were in the process of coming to fruition. The domestic crisis which buffeted the Reich from late September did not create these ambitions; it simply expedited their realization.'[79]

Poincaré had enjoyed widespread domestic support throughout the crisis, but the French left was always critical and was latterly joined by Radical politicians who

[75] See Feldman, *Disorder*, 631–736.

[76] Fischer, *Ruhr Crisis*, 226–7; Peter Krüger, 'Carl von Schubert und die deutsch-französischen Beziehungen', in Stephen A. Schuker and Elizabeth Müller-Luckner (eds.), *Deutschland und Frankreich. Vom Konflikt zur Aussöhnung. Die Gestaltung der westeuropäischen Sicherheit, 1914–1963* (Munich, 2000), 73–96.

[77] Quoted in Peter Krüger, *Versailles. Deutsche Außenpolitik zwischen Revisionismus und Friedenssicherung*, 2nd edn (Munich, 1993), 116. See also Baechler, *Stresemann*, 354, 356–7.

[78] Quoted in Jeannesson, *Poincaré*, 298. See John F.V. Keiger, *Raymond Poincaré* (Cambridge, 1997), 303–4 for a very different interpretation.

[79] Jeannesson, *Poincaré*, 303. See also Marc Trachtenberg, *Reparation in World Politics: France and European Diplomacy 1916–1923* (New York, 1980), 311–14.

became increasingly uneasy over France's international isolation, as the crushing of passive resistance came at the price of British and American goodwill.[80] It also fuelled the elemental brutality of a struggle which saw the occupiers use famine as a weapon against recalcitrant civilian communities.[81] Seasoned politicians and diplomats argued that the time had come for France to reach a negotiated settlement from an undoubted position of strength and before it estranged its key allies still further. As the veteran diplomat Paul Cambon argued: 'All of public opinion is convinced that sooner or later the current conflict between France and Germany will have to end; it is vital that France is not held responsible should these hopes not be realized.'[82] He found supporters at the political heart of the French Third Republic as the President, Alexandre Millerand, and also the Allied wartime commander Marshal Foch, proposed rewriting the peace and reparations settlement through French and German diplomatic channels on terms not vastly different from Stresemann's proposals. Reparations from the Ruhr would be secured by the creation of a Franco-German economic bloc which would regulate deliveries in kind as well as the exchange of German coke for French iron ore and see French participation in German coal mining companies.[83] The French Ironmasters' Federation (Comité des Forges) offered their German counterparts a similar deal during late August, involving an exchange of shares between Lorraine's ironmasters and the Ruhr's coal producers to recreate the integrated heavy industrial economy of the pre-war years, when French iron ore and Ruhr coke had fed the blast furnaces of Western Europe. This arrangement also echoed the Wiesbaden and Stinnes–Lubersac Agreements in as far as it proposed a transnational commercial arrangement in place of the politically predicated 1921 reparations regime. Startled German industrial chiefs lacked the authority unilaterally to strike such a deal, but insisted that in any case it would have to await the evacuation of the Ruhr District.[84] However, as we have seen, Poincaré was in no mood for a magnanimous compromise settlement and threatened to resign if his political colleagues forced the issue.

From early October, therefore, Stresemann sought an international settlement of the Ruhr occupation and wider reparations crisis. A group of Ruhr industrialists, led by Hugo Stinnes, again proposed a Franco-German deal based on the thoroughgoing integration of French and German heavy industry, but Stresemann (from November 1923 serving as Foreign Minister in a Cabinet led by the Catholic politician Wilhelm Marx) was adamant in rejecting such notions. Marx's government succeeded in floating a new and stable currency underwritten by the Bank of

[80] For British reactions, O'Riordan, *Britain*, esp. chs. 4–6. See also Cohrs, *Unfinished Peace*, 100–15.

[81] On famine, Conan Fischer, 'Soziale Verwerfungen im Ruhrkampf durch Hunger und Evakuierung', in Gerd Krumeich and Joachim Schröder (eds.), *Der Schatten des Weltkriegs. Die Ruhrbesetzung 1923* (Essen, 2004), 149–67.

[82] Quoted in Jeannesson, *Poincaré*, 294.

[83] Charles Reibel, 'Une grand occasion manqué, le premier drame de la Ruhr', *Écrits de Paris*, 55 (1949), 24–31.

[84] Conan Fischer, 'Scoundrels without a Fatherland? Heavy Industry and Transnationalism in Post-First World War Germany', *Contemporary European History*, 14, 4 (2005), 454.

England and seeing off a succession of domestic insurrections, including Hitler's notorious Munich Putsch that briefly threatened the existence of the German Republic. Stresemann was now determined to prevent anything cutting across the work of two international Experts Committees, one chaired by an American banker, Charles Dawes, the other by a British politician and banker, Reginald McKenna, that had begun their work in December 1923. In essence their remit was to establish Germany's financial and economic condition and, therefore, its capacity to pay reparations. Such international mediation, Stresemann insisted, offered Germany far more than could the hard line consistently promoted by Poincaré.

Last-gasp efforts by the French authorities to retain the initiative variously by promoting a motley band of Rhineland separatists, seeking a direct reparations delivery deal with Ruhr industry, and securing British support for an indefinite Allied occupation of the Ruhr District also ultimately came to nothing.[85] On 9 April the Experts Committees reported their findings which proposed a revised reparations schedule, renegotiable after five years, but on condition that 'Germany's economic sovereignty is restored. Its operation will be proportionately postponed if there is a delay in effecting that restoration.'[86] With this, French efforts unilaterally to establish a special, dependent status for the Rhineland were effectively doomed, despite an eleventh-hour attempt by Poincaré to distinguish between the restoration of German economic unity and France's military presence in the Ruhr. Thereafter, on 11 May, French parliamentary elections saw him voted out of office and succeeded on 13 June by a centre-left coalition led by the Radical politician, Édouard Herriot. The new Premier was less strident in his assertion of French interests and, with a new international reparations conference scheduled to open in London on 16 July, accepted the essentials of the Dawes Report. However, he was not initially prepared to relinquish all of his predecessor's gains and further ambitions.

The composition and agenda of the London Conference confirmed that, for the time being at least, the promotion of bilateral Franco-German relations was a dead letter. Although the United States President and Secretary of State stayed away, the USA had brokered the creation of the Experts Committees and, in Dawes, provided the convener of the key committee. Now, the US ambassador at London, Frank Kellogg, played an intimate role alongside a British delegation which included the country's first Labour Prime Minister, Ramsay MacDonald. He had formed a minority government in January with Liberal support, which was markedly less sympathetic to France than its Conservative predecessor. Herriot therefore found himself confronted by nominal allies who sought an equitable solution to the Ruhr and reparations crises, rather than a deal that explicitly favoured France. His allies also understood that Stresemann and the German government had staked their immediate future on the outcome of this multilateral mediation. Things might have ended badly, for the French Premier struggled to prepare thoroughly for talks and his penchant for tearful outbursts left 'some sessions . . . more opera than

[85] Fischer, *Ruhr Crisis*, 243–89.

[86] Quoted in Carl Bergmann, *The History of Reparations* (Boston and New York, 1927), 254.

conference',[87] but the senior diplomats who accompanied him to London were hard-headed realists. Jacques Seydoux, who served as Director of Commercial Relations in the French Foreign Office, consistently harboured doubts regarding Germany's ultimate intentions and bona fides,[88] but appreciated that the Ruhr adventure had created financial difficulties for France as well as Germany and that an acceptable reparations agreement took precedence over a French presence in the Ruhr. He also welcomed US involvement in European affairs, which reinforced the need for French moderation towards Germany. Philippe Berthelot, the Permanent Secretary in the Foreign Office, felt similarly and by 6 August, when a German delegation was admitted to the conference, a compromise deal was in the offing. Accepting the Germans as equal negotiating partners remained a bitter pill for the French delegation, leaving Herriot looking 'as though he were having a tooth drawn',[89] but a deal was struck. The French Premier conceded a full evacuation of the Ruhr District within a year; in return Germany accepted a new reparations schedule, which came with the considerable sweetener of a US loan to Berlin of 800 million gold marks.

The Dawes Plan began the process of transforming Germany from defeated enemy into a rehabilitated participant in the international order. Acceptance by Berlin, the then Chancellor Wilhelm Marx observed, formed part of a step-by-step policy 'that appeared slowly but surely to lead towards our goal',[90] by which of course he meant the full restoration of German sovereignty. This search for equal rights (*Gleichberechtigung*) continued to serve as the leitmotiv of German policy throughout Stresemann's tenure as Foreign Minister,[91] but he understood that Berlin could ill afford to indulge in overt revisionism given the sensitivities of the French political right, who as often as not formed part of the governing coalition in Paris. However, patient negotiation that included the espousal of measured collaboration was no less problematic, for any engagement with the peace settlement infuriated German nationalists within and outwith parliament.

Furthermore, although the immediate crisis had now been resolved, France's deep-seated security fears remained undiminished, while as Marx intimated Germany's search for international rehabilitation had made relatively modest progress. Paris began to explore the possibility of creating a new security framework whereby the League of Nations would impose fresh sanctions on Germany should Berlin breach the disarmament clauses of the Versailles Treaty. British scepticism saw this proposal come to nothing, but as Berlin prevaricated over disarmament the Allies agreed to delay their scheduled military evacuation of the northern Rhineland.

87 Anthony Adamthwaite, *Grandeur and Misery: France's Bid for Power in Europe 1914–1940* (London, 1995), 105.

88 Stanislas Jeannesson, 'L'Europe de Jacques Seydoux', *Revue historique*, 299, 1 (1998), 139, 141.

89 Adamthwaite, *Grandeur*, 105. See also Cohrs, *Unfinished Peace*, 182–3.

90 *Akten der Reichskanzlei. Weimarer Republik. Die Kabinette Marx I und II, 30 November 1923 bis 3 Juni 1924. 3 Juni 1924 bis 15. Januar 1925*, ed. Karl Dietrich Erdmann, Hans Booms, and Gunter Abramowski (Boppard am Rhein, 1973), here *II*, Nr 282, Besprechung mit den Staats- und Ministerpräsidenten der Länder. 19 August 1924, 977.

91 Wright, *Stresemann*, 416–17; see Pohl, *Stresemann*, 316–17 for a more equivocal appraisal.

Stresemann feared that a new Franco-British military accord might now follow and sought to pre-empt this in early 1925 by proposing that the European powers, including Germany, should offer and in turn receive collective guarantees by way of a Rhineland security agreement. In other words, in search of its own rehabilitation Berlin was prepared to address the concerns of its primary adversary, France. This initiative also offered London a means of securing European stability by reconciling its obligations to France with its support for the rehabilitation of Germany.

In the event, it coincided with an equally fundamental change in French strategy towards Germany as Paris prioritized efforts to secure a substantive improvement in bilateral Franco-German relations. This policy was in large measure sustained by Aristide Briand who in April 1925 was appointed Foreign Minister by the incoming Radical Premier, Paul Painlevé. Briand appreciated that the passage of time was not working in France's favour, for a low birth rate and widespread domestic opposition to compulsory military service necessitated a more defensive military posture. Furthermore, France's public finances remained stretched and the imminent restoration during 1925 of German customs sovereignty (as provided for in the Treaty of Versailles) promised to end the artificial advantage Paris had hitherto enjoyed in the two countries' trading relations. As far as the trade question went, French diplomacy looked to an emerging network of Franco-German private business cartels to provide a way forward. Their existence had been temporarily derailed by the war and its aftermath, but now they offered regulated partnership in place of a race to the bottom. As we shall see, Paris soon enough accorded them a more ambitious role within official efforts to build a Franco-German economic alliance, seen as the first step on a road to European economic union. Beyond helping to secure wider Franco-German relations, this initiative was designed to address further, deep-seated economic challenges by sustaining the continent's well-being in the face of superpower competition, be it American or Soviet.[92]

Briand was to remain Foreign Minister in a succession of Cabinets, until his final illness forced him to resign in early 1932, and his enduring presence lent a degree of coherence and continuity to French foreign policy despite the potential disruptiveness of the repeated changes in government that plagued the Third French Republic. For his part Stresemann was constantly forced to balance the pursuit of international detente against the pressures of domestic government, but one attempt to appease the nationalist right by allowing the Prussian Crown Prince Wilhelm to return as a private citizen in October 1923 from exile in the Netherlands had been poorly received in Paris. Nonetheless, he continued to exploit his own relationship with the Prince to garner parliamentary support from more moderate nationalists, but this strategy came back to haunt Weimar some years after his death. In 1925 he had penned a particularly frank letter to the Prince which, on the face of it, presented German diplomacy as little more than an exercise in subterfuge, designed to restore the country's great-power status at the expense of

[92] See Ch. 4 under 'Brüning in Paris', 95.

a credulous France. This letter became public knowledge in early 1932 and as we shall see, the impact on French opinion was to be devastating.[93]

That crisis was for the future, but matters were further complicated in early 1925 when the German President, Friedrich Ebert, died of appendicitis. Ebert, a Social Democrat, had been one of the founding fathers of the Weimar Republic, but the ensuing election saw the country's wartime military commander, Paul von Hindenburg, returned as President. Hindenburg was careful to work within the parameters of the constitution, but his election said much for the popular mood. His ultimate ambition to amend the constitution on more authoritarian lines soon enough became apparent, added to which his name was included on France's list of wanted war criminals.

Nonetheless, the Locarno Conference, held in October 1925, secured agreement on a new multilateral European security pact that confirmed the post-war territorial boundaries in Western Europe. If Germany had voluntarily renounced any claim to Alsace-Lorraine, or the small pockets of territory lost in 1919 to Belgium, the fact that Britain and Italy acted as international guarantors to this agreement protected German territory against any future French intervention as much as they protected France against Germany. Briand pushed for comparable guarantees for Poland's and Czechoslovakia's borders with Germany, but Stresemann managed to secure a looser agreement for these two French allies, consisting of non-binding arbitration agreements that lacked British or Italian guarantees and so leaving sufficient wiggle room for an eventual negotiated revision of the country's eastern frontiers.[94] Locarno also provided for German membership of the League of Nations, which it subsequently joined on 10 September 1926. In Stresemann's eyes this marked another significant step in the incremental diplomatic rehabilitation of Germany and understood that any amendments to Germany's frontiers would likely be brokered through the League. For his part Briand alluded to the League's role as the upholder of the Paris Peace Settlement and understood Berlin's membership to represent acceptance of the post-war international order.

The French and German parliaments ratified the Locarno accords, although both Foreign Ministers were given a rough ride by nationalist parliamentarians. The German right remained implacably opposed to reparations or the wider peace terms, modified or not, while French conservatives' elemental mistrust of Germany remained largely undiminished. However, if the concessions made by both sides rankled with nationalists, Stresemann and Briand focused on the positive, including intimations of Franco-German economic cooperation within the cadre of an emergent European union. 'Do you believe', Briand declared to sceptical deputies, 'that I went to that conference, where I had to meet the German ministers, devoid of emotion?... I went, they came, and we spoke European.'[95] Stresemann also alluded to the European dimension when stressing the need for 'a peaceful

93 See Ch. 6 under 'The Stresemann Memoirs Scandal'.

94 See Wright, *Stresemann*, 527, map 2; Pohl, *Stresemann*, 261–6.

95 Quoted in Bariéty, 'Aristide Briand', 8; see also Zara Steiner, *The Lights that Failed: European International History 1919–1933* (Oxford, 2005), 583–4.

Germany at the centre of a peaceful Europe', invoking the economic dimension of Locarno, which provided fresh US loans for Paris and Berlin. This, he continued, offered the prospect of a Europe where 'it might . . . be possible to solve political problems by economic means'.[96] His stance was eminently compatible with the trajectory of wider Franco-German economic relations, for during 1925 Berlin and Paris concluded a trade arbitration agreement which was to pave the way to a comprehensive bilateral trade treaty in 1927. This normalization of commercial relations was accompanied by the revival of a series of international industrial and business cartels, which as often as not had French and German enterprises at their core.[97] This process was regarded by contemporaries as integral to political rapprochement[98] as it fostered nuts-and-bolts cooperation and built trust without needing directly to confront the outstanding flashpoints of high diplomacy.

The diplomats themselves took note. In the immediate aftermath of Locarno, Bariéty observed, 'Briand's *Chef de Cabinet*, Alexis Léger, informed the Germans that France sought industrial ententes with Germany in order to develop cooperation and a "United States of Europe".'[99] Léger was to replace Seydoux in 1926 as Director of Political and Commercial Affairs in the Quai d'Orsay and was markedly more Germanophile than his predecessor, or for that matter Berthelot.[100] He shared Briand's conviction that Stresemann's diplomacy represented a fundamental departure in Germany's approach to external relations and that his espousal of negotiation and reciprocity in the conduct of international affairs offered France a realistic prospect of enduring security.

This thaw in relations was further strengthened in the aftermath of Germany's admission to the League of Nations at Geneva, when Briand and Stresemann met for private talks in the neighbouring French village of Thoiry. During their open and wide-ranging discussions a personal chemistry and enduring friendship developed which came to characterize Franco-German relations during the later 1920s.[101] And as we shall see, even during the years following Stresemann's sudden death in October 1929, during negotiations further to reduce reparations payments, Briand and his colleagues remained convinced that the late German statesman's efforts continued to serve as the Pole Star that guided Berlin's relationship with Paris.[102]

This relationship was, then, intended to secure a comprehensive settlement of bilateral differences as the first step on the road to a wider European union. Related

[96] Quoted in Wright, *Stresemann*, 342, 344. See also Krüger, 'Carl von Schubert', 95.

[97] See, for example, AA R70503, K240519–27, a) Vereinbarungen zwischen den beiderseitigen Industrien, undated, individual entries 1925–30.

[98] Clemens August Wurm, 'Internationale Kartelle und die deutsch-französischen Beziehungen 1924–1930: Politik, Wirtschaft, Sicherheit', in Stephen A. Schuker and Elizabeth Müller-Luckner (eds.), *Deutschland und Frankreich: vom Konflikt zur Aussöhnung. Die Gestaltung der westeuropäischen Sicherheit, 1914–1963* (Munich, 2000), 97–115.

[99] Bariéty, 'Politics of Steel', 43.

[100] Élisabeth Du Réau, *L'Idée d'Europe au XXe siècle. Des myths aux réalités* (Paris, 2008), 99.

[101] See for example Ch. 6 under 'The Stresemann Memoirs Scandal', 166–76.

[102] See Ch. 2 under 'Julius Curtius and the Second Hague Conference', 50–3.

joint efforts to combat the slump were understood in both capitals to reinforce the primary aim of reintegrating Germany within the international community in a non-confrontational manner. When French and German statesmen and diplomats, most with painful memories of conflict and confrontation, in 1931 signed an agreement in Berlin to initiate the process of Franco-German economic integration, each side dared believe, as we shall see,[103] that they had cracked the conundrum of how to reconcile the vital interests of the other with their own and so provide for enduring peace on the continent of Europe and a place for the old continent in a world of emerging global superpowers.

This story combined vaulted ambition with ultimate failure so decisive as to consign it to near oblivion. This failure will also require a detailed explanation, looking to the inherent tensions as well as the extraneous forces that derailed the efforts of the official power brokers. Yet failure aside, French and German leaders had pursued their cause with a dogged determination and imagination. It seems more than curious that their sustained efforts have attracted a few, usually dismissive lines at best, an omission this book seeks to redress.

[103] See Ch. 5 under 'A Successful Conference', 127–9; 'Latour in Berlin', 129–31; and 'Creating the Commission', 131–2.

2

From Thoiry to the Young Plan

Cautious Progress and the Death of Stresemann

DIPLOMATIC HEADWINDS AND UNOFFICIAL INITIATIVES

In September 1926 Germany took its seat in the League of Nations. Describing the Germans as 'a great people which has its qualities and its faults',[1] Briand anticipated and welcomed the prospect of Berlin playing a positive part in Geneva. 'Germany', he continued, 'will certainly find itself obliged to adapt in order to play a role there. And France believes that Germany does have a role to play in Europe and the world.'[2] Private talks followed between Briand and his German counterpart, Gustav Stresemann, in the French village of Thoiry, which was just a stone's throw from Geneva and the League's headquarters. The two statesmen had already forged a trusting working relationship, and now sought to resolve the outstanding bones of contention between Germany and the victor powers. An Allied military evacuation of the Rhineland well ahead of schedule and the immediate return of the Saarland to Germany, without the plebiscite originally timetabled for 1935, would be matched by a substantial, early reparations payment by Berlin. France was the main beneficiary of reparations and planned to use this cash to support its currency, which was depreciating alarmingly. The repurchase of Eupen and Malmédy from Belgium by Germany, with Brussels' knowledge and consent, was also on the table at Thoiry, even though this cut across the mutual guarantee at Locarno of Germany's existing western borders. However, all these proposals came to nothing and the rapprochement process began to lose momentum. The complexities of the Thoiry reparations deal proved insuperable and even obsolete as Paris managed to stabilize its currency without outside help. Furthermore there was little enthusiasm in France for any speedy military evacuation of western Germany, still less for a premature surrender of the Saarland and its heavy industrial enterprises.

Diplomatic progress may have slowed perceptibly after Thoiry, but the formation and growth of transnational cartels continued unabated, so extending the plethora of Franco-German commercial partnerships. This process included an International Steel Cartel that brought together West European heavy industrial enterprises whose pre-1914 operations had been particularly closely integrated.

[1] Achille Elisha, *Aristide Briand. La paix mondiale et l'union européenne* (Groslay, 2003), 248.
[2] Ibid., quoted from 250.

One might hesitate to idealize the hard-headed business logic that underpinned this cartel, for the immediate commercial interests of major heavy industrialists in Belgium, Luxembourg, Germany, the Saarland, and France were uppermost.[3] The Steel Cartel's prime mover, the Luxembourg industrialist Émile Mayrisch, kicked any thought of a European customs union into the long grass as he declared that when all was said and done a 'worldwide' (!) union would be easier to create than a European one,[4] and the cartel itself quickly ran into difficulty once its participants' interests began to diverge. Nonetheless, transnational commercial agreements required and in turn promoted a measure of international political harmony and French diplomacy remained wedded to the idea of exploiting business unions to further political union. This line of thinking would inform Franco-German negotiations over Briand's proposals in 1930 for a European union and then subsequently assume particular importance for relations between Paris and Berlin during the autumn of 1931.[5]

Meanwhile, plans for European union and Franco-German rapprochement continued to be advanced by other unofficial pressure groups, whose membership frequently overlapped. This could take the form of 'cultural demobilization' or the 'disarmament of hatred', as promoted by Marc Sangnier's Democratic International, which rebuilt and added to a network of cross-border personal friendships that had been severed by the war.[6] Other Franco-German youth groups, such as the later Sohlberg Circle, distinguished their membership from the 'Verdun generation',[7] and as John Horne observes, 'cultural demobilization (or its absence) determined what type of peace it would be'.[8] The Pen Club promoted lectures by French writers in Germany and vice versa, Thomas Mann included, while Count Coudenhove-Kalergi's Pan-Europa Movement, founded in 1923, was particularly influential. Its patron, himself with an Austrian noble father and Japanese mother, argued that the French search for security and Germany's quest for equal rights could only be reconciled within the process of European integration,[9] and offered a forum for liberal businessmen, academics, cultural figures, and European-minded politicians to exchange views and mobilize support for their cause. Although senior

[3] Charles Barthel, 'Émile Mayrisch et le pacte international de l'acier des années 1920', *Journal of European Integration History*, 1 (2006), 43–65.

[4] Ibid., 65.

[5] See Ch. 4 under 'Hopeful Signs: The Prussian Plebiscite and Economic Detente', 107–10 and 'Preparations for the Berlin Ministerial Conference', 115–18.

[6] Gearóid Barry, *The Disarmament of Hatred: Marc Sangnier, French Catholicism and the Legacy of the First World War, 1914–1945* (Basingstoke, 2012), 6.

[7] Karen Fiss, *Grand Illusion: The Third Reich, the Paris Exposition, and the Cultural Seduction of France* (Chicago, IL, 2009), 22. Fiss, however, observes the altered pro-Nazi role played by the Sohlberg Circle during the Third Reich.

[8] John Horne, 'Demobilising the Mind: France and the Legacy of the Great War, 1919–1939', *French History and Civilisation: Papers from the George Rudé Seminar*, 2 (2006), here quoted in Barry, *Disarmament*, 209, 250, note 3.

[9] Martin Posselt, 'Die deutsch-französischen Beziehungen und der Briand-Plan im Spiegel der Zeitschrift *Paneuropa*, 1927–30', in Antoine Fleury (ed.), *Le Plan Briand d'Union fédérale européenne. Perspectives nationales et transnationales, avec documents. Actes du colloque international tenu à Genève du 19 au 21 septembre 1991* (Bern, 1998), 35.

French diplomats were ambivalent about and even suspicious of its 'Germanophile and aggressive Eurocentric tendencies',[10] even as the Wilhelmstraße was concerned by its 'Francophile' leanings,[11] it was too important an organization for officialdom to ignore. Its conferences and seminars attracted financial backing and public endorsement from continental governments, including Paris and Berlin, and in 1927 Briand became its Honorary President. Elsewhere, Émile Mayrisch showed a more idealistic side as his Luxembourg home, the Château de Colpach, became a meeting point from 1920 for prominent figures dedicated to Franco-German rapprochement, including André Gide, Walther Rathenau, and also Coudenhove-Kalergi. In 1926 Mayrisch and the French Republican-Socialist politician, Pierre Viénot, founded the Franco-German Study Committee or *Comité Franco-Allemand d'Information et de Documentation* (dubbed the Mayrisch Committee), which advocated and sought to promote Franco-German collaboration within an increasingly integrated Europe. With offices in Paris and Berlin its membership included prominent businessmen from either side of the Rhine, as well as senior civil servants and figures from the educational and cultural worlds. Close contact was maintained with the French and German Foreign Offices, both of which regarded the Committee's activities as complementary to the central objectives of official policy.[12]

Intervention by other enthusiastic amateurs could, however, prove profoundly unhelpful, including well-publicized efforts by the German businessman, Arnold Rechberg, to forge a French, British, and German tripartite military alliance directed against the Soviet Union. Rechberg was essentially well-meaning and for a time the French security services even perceived him as a stalking horse for official German policy.[13] His unwavering commitment to Franco-German rapprochement would eventually land him in the Nazi concentration camp at Dachau, but his earlier initiatives came to require repeated damage limitation by increasingly exasperated diplomats and politicians on both sides of the Rhine.[14] In March 1929 the German Ambassador at Paris, Leopold von Hoesch, had to reassure his Soviet counterpart that Germany unequivocally disowned Rechberg's efforts to enlist France in an anti-Soviet war.[15] In September the French Prime Minister, Raymond Poincaré, was also forced to deny any part in Rechberg's schemes,[16] but

[10] Ibid., 39. [11] Ibid., 47.

[12] For documentation on its activities in official records, AA Die deutsch-französische Studiumkommission (R70576–7). For specific examples: AA R70576 H027005–9, Auswärtiges Amt II Fr. 2526, Aufzeichnung. Signed Friedberg, Berlin, 26 Aug. 1931; AA R70576 H027035–6, zu II Fr. 2553. Ang.2. Aufzeichnung, Berlin, 8 Sept. 1931.

[13] Archives du Ministère des affaires étrangères (MAE), Correspondence Politique et Commerciale 1914 à 1940 Tome 1. Série Z. Europe: Allemagne (Z) 392, 173–5, Le Ministre de l'Interieur (Direction de la Sûreté Générale) à M. Le Ministre des Affaires Étrangères Paris. Paris, 22 May 1929.

[14] See, for example, MAE Z393, 26 (front and back), Note. Prétendues negotiations entre 'nationalistes' français et allemands. 28 Sept. 1929.

[15] AA Die Bemühungen des Arnold Rechberg (R70562–4), here R70562 H025356–7, Telegramm, Nr. 237 vom 23/3. Signed Hoesch, Paris, 23 Mar. 1929.

[16] AA R70562, 'Poincaré über seine Besprechungen mit Arnold Rechberg', *Wolff's Telegraphisches Büro (W.T.B.)*, 80—Nr. 1946, Berlin, 25 Sept. 1929.

the Wilhelmstraße found the amateur diplomat hard to control.[17] Finally, in May 1931, he was given a dressing-down by an exasperated Gerhard Köpke, Head of Section II (the Western Desk):

> I emphasized to Herr Rechberg that I could not discuss with him, a private person, the foreign policy objectives, aims, and ambitions of the National Government. I also stressed to Herr Rechberg in no uncertain terms that I regarded his private foreign policy initiatives not merely as useless, but as positively damaging.[18]

However, the most significant thing about the whole affair was French and German determination not to allow the deluded enthusiast to disrupt relations between the two countries, with politicians and diplomats cooperating to limit any damage. As Stresemann reported in March 1929, after Rechberg had first presented his plans to anyone in Paris who would listen: 'I placed Rechberg's extraordinary scheme in context. Briand declared that he had not received Rechberg . . . He personally regarded him as a nutcase.'[19]

THE GRAUTOFF INITIATIVE

But whatever the challenges thrown up by misguided amateurs, and more significantly by swathes of the intellectual and cultural world that were openly hostile to the interwar order,[20] cultural collaboration continued to be supported at the highest official level.[21] A publishing venture by the well-regarded literary historian and Romanist Otto Grautoff was particularly favoured by French and German officials, even if the project quickly ran into major financial difficulties. In late 1926 Grautoff proposed to launch two journals dedicated to mutual reconciliation, the *Deutsch-französische Rundschau* in Germany and the *Revue d'Allemagne et des pays de langue allemande* in France, in order to compensate for the relative lack 'of genuinely informative books in either country concerning the other'.[22] He envisaged prominent French contributors engaging a wide German readership on French cultural, economic, and business affairs and German contributors doing

[17] AA R70563 H025433–4, Auswärtiges Amt II Fr 573. Signed Bülow, 14 Feb. 1931.

[18] AA R70563 H025474–5, Bemerkungen zu den Privatbrief des Herrn Arnold Rechberg an mich vom 16. Mai, zu II Fr 1538. Signed Köpke, Berlin, 19 May 1931.

[19] AA R70562 H025351, Telegramm Del. Nr. 11 vom 6/3. Signed Stresemann, Geneva, 6 Mar. 1929.

[20] See, for example, Michel Trebitsch and Hans Manfred Bock, 'L'Image du voisin. Opinions et rencontres', in Robert Frank, Laurent Gervereau, and Hans Joachim Neyer (eds.), *La Course au moderne. France et Allemagne dans l'Europe des années vingt, 1919–1933* (Paris, 1992), 29.

[21] AA Politische Beziehungen zu Deutschland (R70501–10), here R70503 K240536–40, Herrn Dir. v. Friedberg. Signed Krümmer, undated, filed late Nov. 1930.

[22] AA Die deutsch-französische Gesellschaft (R70550–4), here R70550 H022790, Aufzeichnung über den Plan einer Zeitschrift für Frankreich- und Deutschlandstudium. Signed Schwendemann, Geneva, 21 Sept. 1926.

the same in France, in the hope that bilateral rapprochement would ultimately contribute to a process of European integration.[23]

However, if Grautoff could readily come up with the names of prospective supporters and contributors,[24] his planning involved a fair deal of wishful thinking and even deception.[25] The Chairman of the National Confederation of German Industry (RDI), Ludwig Kastl, complained to the Foreign Office that: 'Although there is a strong interest here in Franco-German rapprochement, none of our members is prepared to join Grautoff's proposed committee. I personally agree and have communicated with Dr Grautoff accordingly.' The problem, Kastl continued, was that Grautoff 'was apparently playing off interested parties in Berlin against those in Paris'. He made exaggerated claims in Paris regarding the level of funding for, and degree of progress of, the German publication, and the same in Berlin regarding the French publication. 'He flags up a list of personalities', Kastl continued, 'who have allegedly signed up for the German Management Committee—but in reality these are just nominations.'[26] The Mayrisch Committee refused to touch Grautoff for similar reasons, with the Director of its Paris Bureau, Gustav Krukenberg, complaining to Berlin that the would-be editor had greatly exaggerated progress on the journals in Germany to receptive officials at the Quai d'Orsay. This, Krukenberg concluded, left his own organization in a false position; he could only recommend that Berlin should translate Grautoff's claims into something resembling reality.[27] Not that the Mayrisch Committee itself now agreed to offer any support,[28] arguing that it 'was more important to gain influence in the mainstream daily press'.[29]

In the final analysis the future of the project came down to money and Grautoff turned for support to the French Embassy in Berlin and to the German diplomat, Karl Schwendemann, who was then serving as a Press Officer at the League of Nations in Geneva. The French Ambassador and also the Quai d'Orsay proved consistently supportive,[30] while Schwendemann shared Grautoff's interest in using the printed media to promote cultural rapprochement with France.[31] Schwendemann was aware that the project 'was receiving intensive support from the French Embassy [at Berlin]', which threatened to transform the *Deutsch-französische Rundschau* into 'an

[23] Hans Manfred Bock, 'Weimarer Intellektuelle und das Projekt deutsch-französischer Gesellschaftsverflechtung', *Themenportal Europäische Geschichte*, http://www.europa.clio-online.de/site/lang__de/ItemID__107/mid__12188/40208766/Default.aspx, 2.

[24] AA R70550 H022824–5, Streng vertraulich! Unsigned, undated, filed autumn 1926.

[25] See AA R70550 H022837–40, Abschrift. Signed Krukenberg, Paris, 17 Dec. 1926.

[26] AA R70550 H022936–9, Reichsverband der Deutschen Industrie. Signed Kastl, Berlin, 25 Jan. 1927; quotes on 22938.

[27] AA R70550 H022837–40, Abschrift. Signed Krukenberg, Paris, 17 Dec. 1926.

[28] AA R70551 H023041 (3pp.), Konzept, Nr. II Fr. 4597. Unsigned, Berlin, 12 Nov. 1927.

[29] AA R70551 H023189–90, Reichsverband der Deutschen Industrie. Signed Kastl, Berlin, 16 Jan. 1928.

[30] MAE Affaires Administratives Diverses (Z602–3), here Z603, 89, Affaires Étrangères, Télégramme à l'Arrivée, No 235. Signed Margerie, Berlin, 18 May 1929; AA R70551 H023004–5, St.S. Aufzeichnung. II Fr. 2953. Unsigned, Berlin, 14 Jul. 1927.

[31] AA R70550 H022789–92, Aufzeichnung über den Plan einer Zeitschrift für Frankreich- und Deutschlandstudium. Signed Schwendemann, Geneva, 21 Sept. 1926.

instrument of French cultural propaganda steered by the French Embassy and quite possibly secretly funded by the Quai d'Orsay'.[32] He noted that Paris was already conducting a skilful international charm offensive under the rubric '*faire aimer la France*',[33] but nonetheless remained convinced of the inherent value of the project.[34] He advised the head of the Foreign Office Press Section, Otto Kiep, to 'commit unreservedly to the principle of reciprocity, that is to say the simultaneous launch in Paris of a German affairs journal and in Berlin of a French affairs journal', with both jointly endorsed by Stresemann and Briand, and generously funded.[35]

The Wilhelmstraβe subsequently devoted a considerable amount of time and effort to the venture, which restyled itself in December 1927 as the German-French Association or Deutsch-französische Gesellschaft,[36] but Grautoff's idealism was not equalled by his organizational or financial abilities. In May 1927 he briefed Rudolf Count Waldbott von Bassenheim of the Wilhelmstraβe's French Division on developments, claiming that while the French-published *Revue d'Allemagne* was ready to launch, the Quai d'Orsay was increasingly dismayed by the lack of progress on the *Deutsch-französische Rundschau*.[37] Grautoff claimed to have assembled a committee of a dozen or more grandees from the business world to expedite matters and had secured a publisher for the journal, but there was, apparently, still no money. His publisher estimated yearly production costs at 60,000 marks and did not anticipate any profits for at least three years; a financial guarantee was needed to cover these initial three years of publication which, Grautoff intimated, might be met by the Foreign Office.[38] The Wilhelmstraβe hesitated,[39] and given the lack of interest of the Mayrisch Committee in the whole project, the diplomats concluded there was little prospect of any private investment.[40] However, it appears that the German business community did eventually come up with the money[41] without the records offering an explanation for this change of heart. The *Revue d'Allemagne* appeared in November 1927, with essays by Rainer Maria Rilke and Edmond Vermeil among others,[42] and was complemented by monthly editions of the *Rundschau* from January 1928.[43] The new journal won acclaim from the liberal daily, the

[32] AA R70550 H022786–8 (esp. 787), Auswärtiges Amt, Presseabteilung der Reichsregierung. Signed Schwendemann, Geneva, 24 Sept. 1926.
[33] AA R70550 H022792, Aufzeichnung über den Plan einer Zeitschrift für Frankreich- und Deutschlandstudium. Signed Schwendemann, Geneva, 21 Sept. 1926.
[34] AA R70550 H022789–92, ibid.
[35] AA R70550 H022790, ibid.
[36] AA R70551 H023186, Gesellschaft der Deutsch-französischen Rundschau. Signed Grautoff, Berlin, 22 Dec. 1927.
[37] AA R70550 H022962, Gesellschaft der Deutsch-französischen Rundschau. Signed Grautoff, Berlin, 2 May 1927.
[38] AA R70550 H022962–3, ibid.
[39] AA R70551 H023012–13, Gesellschaft der Deutsch-französischen Rundschau. Signed Grautoff, Berlin, 20 Sept. 1927.
[40] AA R70551 H023041ff, Konzept Nr. II Fr. 4597. Unsigned, Berlin, 12 Nov. 1927.
[41] AA R70552 H023325–6, Aufzeichnung, II Fr. Unsigned, 25.X.28.
[42] AA R70551 H023070, *Revue d'Allemagne et des pays de langue allemande*, No. 1, Paris, Nov. 1927.
[43] AA R70551 H023197, Deutsch-Französische Gesellschaft, Herrn Geheimen Legationsrat von Bülow. Signed Grautoff, Berlin, 22 Jan. 1928.

Berliner Tageblatt,[44] and its prospects were further enhanced when the Wilhelmstraβe subscribed to 200 copies of the *Rundschau* each month.[45]

Weeks later Grautoff published a questionnaire in the journal which canvassed views on his personal scheme for wide-ranging collaboration between the French and German cultural, media, and business worlds. In a premonition of current European arrangements and practice, he envisaged systematic exchanges of university students and lecturers, as well as school teachers, the placement of French interns with German newspapers and vice versa, and employee exchanges within the financial, commercial, and industrial sectors.[46] However, at this point the limits of cultural reconciliation were laid bare, for his efforts to elicit responses from the German Chancellor, Wilhelm Marx, his French counterpart Raymond Poincaré, or from Aristide Briand, failed.[47] The German refusal was informed partly by the parallel French refusal and partly by a belief that for all the efforts to forge detente, serious differences remained between the two countries which left Grautoff's scheme offering too many hostages to fortune. The Foreign Office briefed the Chancellor's office accordingly, concluding that:

> In our view political relations between France and Germany have yet to stabilize sufficiently to allow a positive response to Dr Grautoff's questionnaire. Our relationship with France is currently subject to such a degree of volatility as to preclude us sanctioning unreservedly a mutual exchange of citizens from each and every profession and branch of the economy. Given the current position our answer must therefore be that political relations between the two countries must be normalized before we can usefully embark on a more intensive cultural rapprochement.[48]

Such thinking was, however, regarded as too sensitive for the public domain and officials simply informed Grautoff that Marx would not be completing the questionnaire.[49]

Despite this scepticism and the primacy accorded to political reconciliation, the Wilhelmstraβe remained convinced that Grautoff's newspapers served a useful purpose and subscribed to 1,000 copies monthly of the *Revue d'Allemagne*, 'the orientation of which accords with our foreign policy objectives'.[50] From late 1928 the journal was placed in German diplomatic missions, 'particularly overseas', and

[44] AA R70551, 'Deutsch-Französische Rundschau. Und Revue d'Allemagne', *Berliner Tageblatt*, 179, 15 Apr. 1928.

[45] AA R70771, H023196, zu II Fr. 360 Ang. III, initialled, Berlin, 24 Apr. 1928.

[46] AA R70551, H023202–3, Abschrift zu Rk. 2297. Deutsch-Französische Gesellschaft (E.V.), Herrn Reichskanzler Dr Marx, Enquête. Signed Grautoff, Berlin 8 Mar. 1928.

[47] AA R70551 H023202, Abschrift zu Rk. 2297. Deutsch-Französische Gesellschaft (E.V.), Herrn Reichskanzler Dr Marx. Signed Grautoff, Berlin 8 Mar. 1928; R50551, H023206, zu II Fr. 1224. Auf das gefl. Schreiben vom 14. d. M.—Rk 2297. Unsigned, Berlin, 1 May 1928.

[48] AA R70551 H023204–5, Konzept II Fr. 1224. Unsigned, Berlin, 16 Mar. 1928.

[49] Ibid.

[50] AA R70552 H023325–6, Aufzeichnung, zu II Fr. Unsigned, 25.X.28. See also: R70552 H023347–8, Deutsch-Französische Gesellschaft. Signed Grautoff, Berlin, 12 Nov. 1928; R70552 H023248–50, Abschrift. Auswärtiges Amt, Nr. II Fr. 2142. Signed V. Bülow, Berlin, 18 May 1928; R70552 H023383–4, zu II Fr. 4943, 4965, 5007, An Herrn Gesandtschaftsrat Kühn, Paris, Deutsche Botschaft. Sig. illeg., Berlin, 28 Dec. 1928.

circulated to prominent foreigners, all with a view to demonstrating 'that there is a strong movement within the French intelligentsia that regards Germany as an equal in international affairs and does not begrudge it its recovery'.[51] However, despite attracting 800 subscribers by October, the *Rundschau* remained financially vulnerable and its French partners continued to insist that the *Revue* could only continue in partnership with its German counterpart. Berlin increased its monthly *Rundschau* subscription to 300 copies[52] and turned again to the business community for cash.[53] In late October 1928 Köpke organized a meeting of senior Foreign Office officials, the *Rundschau's* staff, and sympathetic businessmen in an effort finally to put the journal on a sound footing. The Wilhelmstraße continued to prioritize rapprochement with France and Grautoff's publishing venture, he explained, had become a bellwether of this relationship:

> [Köpke] began by stressing that the collapse of the *Rundschau* for want of French or German financial support could have consequences which, at the present time, must be avoided at all costs. In the interests of overall relations with France the Foreign Office attached great importance to the continued publication of the journal.[54]

Warm words were spoken and budgetary strategies aired, but significant challenges remained. Discussion turned to meeting the projected deficit for 1929 of 62,500 marks, whether through increased sales, a fresh appeal to the Mayrisch Committee this time to take the journal under its wing, or through further subsidies. The Wilhelmstraße pledged 10,000 marks for the coming year,[55] but Grautoff found the business world less forthcoming and during early November had to beg Köpke and his colleague Bernhard von Bülow to provide the *Rundschau* with further financial guarantees.[56] He also indulged in a fresh bout of amateur diplomacy, reportedly trying to incite the French Ambassador at Berlin to intervene in support of the *Rundschau*, before the Mayrisch Committee did finally come up with 30,000 marks, supplemented by smaller sums from elsewhere. The journal was secured for a further year.[57] Paris sought to match this commitment, with the Quai d'Orsay's Press Office subscribing to 100 copies monthly of the *Rundschau*, erroneously believing that this equalled Berlin's subscription to the *Revue* rather than the actual 1,000.[58]

Grautoff himself maintained a high profile among the supporters of Franco-German reconciliation. In May 1929 he and the German-French Society were received in Paris by the left-leaning pacifist organization, Amitiés internationales,

[51] AA R70552 H023325, zu II Fr, Aufzeichnung. Unsigned, 25.X.28.
[52] AA R70552 H023277, e.o. II Fr 3164, Aufzeichnung. Sig. illeg., Berlin, 23 Jul. 1928.
[53] AA R70552 H023326, zu II Fr, Aufzeichnung. Unsigned, 25.X.28.
[54] AA R70552 H023353–4, Aufzeichnung. Unsigned, Berlin, 29 Oct. 1928.
[55] AA R70552 H023353–7, Aufzeichnung. Unsigned, Berlin, 29 Oct. 1928.
[56] AA R70552 H023341–2, Deutsch-Französische Gesellschaft. Signed Grautoff, Berlin, 8 Nov. 1928; R70552 H023347, Deutsch-Französische Gesellschaft. Unsigned, Berlin, 12 Nov. 1928.
[57] AA R70552 H023383–4, zu II Fr. 4943, 4965, 5007, An Herrn Gesandtschaftsrat Kühn, Paris, Deutsche Botschaft. Sig. illeg., Berlin, 28 Dec. 1928.
[58] AA R70552 H023397, Ministère des Affaires Étrangères. Service d'Information et de Presse. Sig. illeg., Paris, 15 Feb. 1929.

which attracted an impressive guest list of authors, academics, parliamentarians, and diplomats, including the German Cultural Attaché, Joachim Kühn, to the event. As the reception drew to a close, Grautoff and the French war hero, Colonel Yves Picot, embraced, to warm and 'sincere' applause, lending substance to Amitiés' motto, '*Comprenons nous les uns les notres*' (Let us learn to understand one another). Picot's commitment to reconciliation was particularly significant; badly disfigured, he had founded a veterans' association specifically for French soldiers who had been mutilated in the fighting, the Gueules Cassées, who had little emotional reason to show any fondness for Germans. The media reception from newspapers of the political centre and democratic left in both countries was warm and positive, with *L'Oeuvre* urging the protagonists of peace to take advantage of this 'fair wind',[59] and the *Berliner Tageblatt* concluding that: 'Our peoples are interdependent; we must understand and help one another, we must be Europeans for the well-being of Europe.'[60] Weeks later Köpke learned that the German-French Society had engaged in a programme to bring together French and German children as pen-pals, with some 1,000 corresponding by early July.[61]

Both of Grautoff's journals continued to be funded on a hand-to-mouth basis through 1929, and the *Rundschau*'s 1,800 subscribers fell well short of the 3,000 needed to break even.[62] The industrialist Otto Wolff came up with 3,000 marks for the *Rundschau*,[63] but German and French diplomats struggled to square the financial circle. The Cultural Director at the Quai d'Orsay confirmed that French interest in the two journals 'was exceptionally strong' and that the Education Ministry had lobbied French universities to take the *Rundschau*. The number of French public subscriptions consequently rose from 25 to 150 and the Director promised to see if French libraries might also take the journal.[64] This came at a cost for, as Kühn reported, the *Rundschau's* cover price was double that of the *Revue d'Allemagne*, which itself was significantly dearer than competing French journals.[65] Meanwhile, by October 1929, Germany's deteriorating public finances led the Foreign Office to weigh up the political importance of Grautoff's journals against their cost. Grautoff lobbied hard, stressing the wide cultural reach achieved by the German-French Society, with a Presidium that included Konrad Adenauer, Otto Dix, Albert Einstein, André Gide, Henri Lichtenberger, Thomas Mann, Albert Thomas, and Otto Wolff, and with an equally distinguished list of contributors.[66]

[59] AA R70552, Pariser Reise Mai 1929: 'Le bon vent', *L'Oeuvre*, 25.V.29; see also Pariser Reise: 'Brillante reception aux Amitiés internationales en l'honneur de la Société franco-allemande', *L'ere nouvelle*, 25 May 1929.

[60] AA R70552, '"Wir müssen einander verstehen." Ein Bankett der Friedenswilligen', *Berliner Tageblatt*, 25.V.29.

[61] AA R70552 H023435, Deutsch-Französische Gesellschaft. Sig. illeg., Berlin, 3 Jul. 1929.

[62] For example: AA R70552 H023429, II Fr. 1696. Aufzeichnung. Sig. illeg., Berlin, 29 May 1929; R70552 H023471–2. Signed Willy Sundheimer, Berlin, 8 Oct. 1929.

[63] AA R70552 H023431, Erhard Deutelmoser, B. Nr. 1711A. Signed Deutelmoser, Berlin-Wilmersdorf, 26 May 1929.

[64] AA R70552 H023442–4, Deutsche Botschaft Paris. Unsigned, Paris, 5 Jul. 1929.

[65] AA R70552 H023445, Deutsche Botschaft Paris, P.S. Unsigned, Paris, 5 Jul. 1929.

[66] AA R70553 H023496, 23500–5, Deutsch-Französische Gesellschaft e.V., Herrn Ministerialdirigent Dr von Bülow. Signed Grautoff, Berlin, 8 Nov. 1929.

The Wilhelmstraβe reassured Grautoff that his efforts remained highly appreciated,[67] but settled on a financial compromise. The *Revue d'Allemagne* appeared more valuable as an instrument of soft diplomacy and its funding was maintained, while support for the *Rundschau* was cut[68] in January 1930 from 300 copies to 50.[69]

Little changed thereafter. Grautoff took umbrage at these official economies, but raised sufficient cash from private donors to maintain his journals and organize a series of supporting meetings and conferences.[70] The Wilhelmstraβe continued to scrape together what little financial support it could, while appealing again to private benefactors, notably in industry, to donate to the German-French Society. Among these industrialists was Robert Bosch of the eponymous engineering and electrics combine,[71] himself a partisan of Franco-German rapprochement.[72] But all this effort served as little more than life support, leaving Grautoff's ventures teetering above a financial abyss. In March 1931 the Society found itself 24,000 marks in deficit and by June it could no longer pay secretarial salaries or the rent on its premises.[73] Köpke's officials offered a small subsidy of 5,000 marks for 1932,[74] but in August the Wilhelmstraβe observed that:

> The chaotic financial situation confronting the German-French Society has occupied the Foreign Office for years . . . But, unfortunately, Dr Grautoff fails to appreciate the need for ordered finances. So long as he has a role in the Society's financial management there is no prospect of matters being resolved. The Foreign Office has repeatedly supported the Society. However, it has had to conclude that so long as the personal situation remains unchanged any further support would be useless.[75]

It demanded a thorough reorganization of the Society,[76] but one such effort had already come to nothing in 1931[77] and nothing changed during 1932. The Society staggered on as diplomats struggled to square Grautoff's undoubted value as an instrument of Franco-German rapprochement with the financial *misère* of the whole venture. In November Berlin stumped up another 1,000 marks to cover

[67] AA R70553 H023538–9, Auswärtiges Amt, II Fr 3668. Signed Bülow, Berlin, 25 Nov. 1929.

[68] AA R70553 H023511–12, Abschrift! Auswärtiges Amt. Nr. II Fr 3182. Signed Köpke, Berlin, 15 Oct. 1929.

[69] AA R70553 H023516–17, zu II Fr 3668. Unsigned, Berlin, 29 Jan. 1930.

[70] AA R70553 H023532–3, Reinkonzept. II Fr. 3782. Signed Bassenheim, Berlin, 29 Mar. 1930; R70553, 'La Deutsche-Französische gesellschaft' [*sic*]. *La Volonté*, 4 Feb. 1930; R70553 H023596–8, Zu II Fr. 1394. Signed Köpke, Berlin, ? Jun. 1930.

[71] AA R70554 H023829, Aufzeichnung, Auswärtiges Amt II Fr. 725. Unsigned, Berlin, 7 Mar. 1931.

[72] Rolf Becker and Joachim Scholtyseck, *Robert Bosch und die deutsch-französische Verständigung. Politisches Denken und Handeln im Spiegel der Briefwechsel* (Stuttgart, 1957).

[73] AA R70554 H023829, Aufzeichnung, Auswärtiges Amt II Fr. 725. Unsigned, Berlin, 7 Mar. 1931.

[74] AA R70554 H024015, Vermerk, II Fr. 709. Unsigned, Berlin, 9 Mar. 1932; R70554 H024016, Auswärtiges Amt. P. Geb. 65, Auf das Schreiben vom Leg. Rat Kühn an Geheimrat v. Friedberg vom 26.2. Signed v. Kaufmann, Berlin, 30 Mar. 1932.

[75] AA R70554 H024051–2, St.S. zu II Fr 2603, An den Herrn Staatssekretär in der Reichskanzlei. Signed St.S., Berlin, 13 Aug. 1932.

[76] AA R70554 H024053, ibid.

[77] AA R70554 H023981–4, Aufzeichnung, zu II Fr. 1656. Unsigned, Berlin, 2 Jun. 1931.

the most pressing bills,[78] while Grautoff's publisher, the Verlag Walther Rothschild, met outstanding contributors' fees for 1932 and agreed a business plan for 1933.[79] This, of course, proved irrelevant, for Hitler was appointed Chancellor just weeks later with consequences for Franco-German relations (and the publisher) that are well understood.

FRANCO-GERMAN RELATIONS ON THE EVE OF THE HAGUE CONFERENCES

Returning now to the world of high diplomacy, the 1924 Dawes Plan had provided for the renegotiation (and possible amelioration) of the reparations settlement after five years. In September 1928 the League of Nations agreed an agenda for these talks which were subsequently held in the Netherlands city of The Hague during August 1929 and January 1930. The first round decided the sums to be paid and the distribution of these payments, the second the modalities of the new reparations regime. Both sessions were chaired by the American businessman and lawyer Owen D. Young, who had co-authored the Dawes Plan in 1924 and now saw his own name attached to a significantly more moderate reparations settlement, the Young Plan. The first Hague Conference also provided for a full Allied military evacuation of the Rhineland by June 1930, so clearing the southern, French-occupied Mainz sector five years ahead of the schedule set at Versailles.

The wider diplomatic climate was ripe for such a deal, although tensions remained between supporters and opponents of rapprochement in both Germany and France. Briand was always clear that the plethora of private initiatives dedicated to European integration and rapprochement could influence the atmosphere surrounding international diplomacy, but could not themselves deliver substantive change. It was down to European governments to forge the necessary agreements[80] and in June 1929 he briefed Stresemann on his own European agenda, stressing that it was 'more ambitious than the latter possibly assumed'.[81] He envisaged Germany, France, and Britain underpinning a system of European economic and financial cooperation, insisting that:

> European cooperation of this sort is necessary, since developments in the individual European states can only be regarded with great concern. Dependence on the United States of America continues to grow. Europe must strengthen itself, something that is also in America's interest when all is said and done.[82]

Among other things, renewed agreement on the reparations question offered the Americans a sporting chance of recovering their wartime loans to the Allies and while

[78] AA R70554 H024107–9, Frau Erna Grautoff, zu II Fr 3855. Signed D., Berlin, 22 Nov. 1932.

[79] AA R70554 H024182, Erhardt Deutelmoser, B. Nr. 6192A, Betr.: Deutsch-Französische Gesellschaft. Signed Deutelmoser, 5 Jan. 1933.

[80] AA Bund der Vereinigten Staaten von Europa (R28630–1), here R28630 D702910–13, quote on 912, Telegramm Nr. 715 v. 15/7. Signed Hoesch, Paris, 15 Jul. 1930.

[81] AA R70501, Abschrift II Fr 2001, 20 Jun. 1929.

[82] Ibid.

these loans themselves were not his concern, Stresemann otherwise agreed, making his feelings clear in the Reichstag just days later. He dismissed the vacuous and isolationist rhetoric of the Nationalist (DNVP) leader, Alfred Hugenberg, observing that with the rise of the New World, European nation states could choose to collaborate, or go under: 'A time will come when from economic necessity French, German and perhaps other European economies must seek a common way to maintain themselves in the face of a competition to which they are not equal.'[83]

Briand too continued to encounter fierce and politically complex parliamentary opposition. As Hoesch observed in a confidential memorandum to Stresemann, the governing coalition led by Raymond Poincaré was by no means the natural bedfellow of Briand's rapprochement policy:

> The right wants to sustain Poincaré, but desires no part of his foreign policy, whereas the left is perfectly happy with the Cabinet's foreign policy, but does not wish to sustain Poincaré in office. This paradoxical situation gives rise currently to the extremely tortuous, contradictory, and inhibited evolution of French policy, which can produce surprises of a particularly unpleasant kind.[84]

In other words, while Stresemann faced criticism from the opposition benches, Briand's adversaries included senior figures in France's right-leaning coalition government. 'The Minister', Hoesch continued, 'has never before been so outspoken on the difficulties created for his policy by reactionary elements in the Cabinet and on the government benches.'[85] Furthermore, these right-wingers did not even spare Poincaré himself, whom they regarded as a political soulmate who had sold out on one issue after another; particularly on reparations and the continued occupation of the southern Rhineland. 'It cannot be denied', Briand observed, 'that the Prime Minister, who constantly strives to be seen by all as the patriotic defender of French rights, is far from untroubled by these accusations.'[86]

An incident had occurred in May 1929 that was characteristic of this complex relationship. Poincaré visited the Verdun fortress of Douaumont and made a speech scarcely calculated to soothe troubled wartime memories, prompting Hoesch to comment that:

> It is regrettable that Poincaré repeatedly feels constrained to harp on in his speeches about wartime events. In this particular case he completely unnecessarily . . . soured the comradely atmosphere engendered by French assistance following the forced landing of a Zeppelin airship [near Toulon on 16 May].[87]

Briand agreed, reassuring the German Ambassador that: 'He had made it absolutely clear to Poincaré . . . that he disapproved of his repeated references to wartime

83 Quoted in Wright, *Stresemann*, 476.

84 AA Deutsch-Französische Verständigung, R28263k D517324–8, here 327, Telegramm Nr. 561 vom 3.7. Signed Hoesch, Paris, 3 Jul. 1929.

85 AA R28263k D517324–8, here 324, Telegramm Nr. 561 vom 3.7. Signed Hoesch, Paris, 3 Jul. 1929.

86 Ibid., here 326.

87 AA Politische Beziehungen Frankreich-Deutschland (R30181 a/b–182 a/b), here R30181b E430280, Telegramm, Nr. 398 vom 24.5. Signed Hoesch, Paris, 24 May 1929.

events, which after all were at least ten years in the past.' He even accused the Premier of conduct unworthy of his office, conduct which only served to reopen old wounds and 'was not at all well received by the public'.[88] But polemics aside, Briand and Hoesch could agree that Poincaré's stance, for instance on the question of German war guilt, had mellowed, to the point where relatively little of substance now divided him from his Foreign Minister.[89] And the fact that Briand was prepared to relay an account of this altercation with his Prime Minister to the German Foreign Office said much about the relationship between the French and German polities at the time of the Hague Conferences.

In the event, the stress of office seems to have taken its toll on Poincaré's health and on 29 July 1929, shortly before the first Hague Conference opened, Briand took over as Prime Minister while also retaining his Foreign Ministry portfolio. He was replaced in turn on 3 November by André Tardieu in whose Cabinet he continued as Foreign Minister. Tardieu had served as Georges Clemenceau's right-hand man at the Paris Peace Conference and thereafter had called for a tough Allied line to ensure German compliance with the peace terms. However, his views on Franco-German relations became increasingly dovish with time, demonstrating again how far down the road to rapprochement key figures on the French right were prepared to travel. On Sunday 10 November 1929 he turned up unannounced to visit Hoesch, who happened to be elsewhere, before the two men finally met on Wednesday 13 November to discuss the prospects for Franco-German rapprochement in considerable detail. Tardieu was anxious to reassure and as Hoesch reported:

> The Prime Minister presented his personal views on rapprochement in detail. He accepted that up till now he had been regarded in Germany with suspicion as one of the authors of the Versailles Treaty and as someone who had strongly criticized the Allies' half-hearted [treaty enforcement] during the immediate post-war period. He would not deny his past record, but wished to stress that from the beginning of the Stresemann era he had come increasingly to identify with the policy of rapprochement and had come of his own volition to support Briand's foreign policy. He believed that German-French rapprochement offered many further interesting possibilities and he was therefore determined to continue along this road.[90]

He continued that only a right-oriented French Cabinet could hope to expunge the remaining legacies of the war, by engaging 'patriotic circles' in the process, whereas any left-oriented Cabinet would be destroyed by popular opposition if it attempted such a thing. Hoesch was less sure and remained troubled by the presence in Tardieu's Cabinet 'of several personages from the far right, who are bound to act as a ball and chain [on the rapprochement process]'. Tardieu could only agree.[91]

[88] AA R30181b E430280–1, Telegramm, Nr. 398 vom 24.5. Signed Hoesch, Paris, 24 May 1929.
[89] Ibid.
[90] AA R70501 K240291–6, here 292, Telegramm Nr. 1111 vom 14/11. Signed Hoesch, Paris, 14 Nov. 1929.
[91] Ibid., here 293.

Beyond the complexities of (French) parliamentary politics, German behaviour could also impinge on Franco-German relations. Weeks before the first Hague Conference opened, the tenth anniversary of the signing of Versailles (28 June) fell due. French diplomats in Bavaria were disturbed when the German National People's Party (DNVP) organized a series of rallies to condemn the 'war guilt lie' and oppose the payment of reparations on any terms.[92] Comparable reports also arrived in Paris from its missions in Koblenz and Hamburg.[93] In the latter city churches were to fly flags at half mast on the day of the signing, their bells to toll at the precise moment the treaty was signed.[94] Meanwhile, schools in Hessen were instructed to mark this 'national day of mourning', and 'pronounce on the origins, significance and consequences of the Versailles Treaty'. Bavarian pupils (including those in the French-occupied Palatinate) were to be instructed 'not only on the economic and political consequences of the Versailles Treaty, but in particular on the war guilt question'.[95] The French Ambassador, Pierre de Margerie, complained to Köpke that such actions were 'regrettable and particularly inopportune; the French government regards the perpetuation of revanchist thinking and of hatred among young people as highly undesirable and incompatible with the spirit of rapprochement between our two countries'.[96]

Even Köpke, a partisan for Franco-German rapprochement, could not resist observing that: 'People in France should have more sympathy for any national day of mourning, where for a whole generation Paris marked the anniversary of the Treaty of Frankfurt [1871] by draping the statue of Strasbourg in black.'[97] However, he was at pains to confirm that the national government was doing everything possible to calm the public mood, adding that the Prussian government was having nothing to do with the whole schools business.[98] De Margerie had already reassured Paris that the German government was cold-shouldering rallies and demonstrations of any kind, and that the President, Paul von Hindenburg, had refused an invitation to a major nationalist rally in Berlin.[99] Similarly, demonstrations in the Allied-occupied Rhineland, where feelings on the Treaty ran high, were boycotted by national and

[92] MAE Z382 43 here back, Legation de la République Française en Bavière. Signed André d'Ormesson, Munich, 30 Apr. 1929.

[93] MAE Z382 46–7, Haut Commissariat de la Republique Française dans les Provinces du Rhin, Objet: Manifestations projetées en Allemagne, pour le 28 Juin contre le Traité de Versailles. Signed Tirard, Koblenz, 13 May 1929; Z382 53, Consulat Général de France à Hambourg, Communiqué à Berlin. Signed Saugon, Hamburg, 21 May 1929; Z382 90 (3pp.), Le Ministre des Affaires Étrangères, Telegramme. Signed B, Paris, undated, stamped Poste Berlin 22 Juin 1929.

[94] MAE Z382 96 (front), Consulat Général de France à Hambourg, Communiqué à Berlin. Signed Véquaud, Hamburg, 24 Jun. 1929.

[95] AA R70501 K240258–9, Aufzeichnung, Ausw. Amt. II Fr. 2097. Signed Köpke, Berlin, 25 Jun. 1929; MAE Z382 43 (back), Légation de la République Française en Bavière. Signed André d'Ormesson, Munich, 30 Apr. 1929.

[96] AA R70501 K240260, Aufzeichnung, Ausw. Amt. II Fr. 2097. Signed Köpke, Berlin, 25 Jun. 1929.

[97] AA R70501 K240261, ibid.

[98] AA R70571 K240260–1, ibid.; but cf. MAE Z382 74, E.L./S. No A—5.678. Le traité de Versailles . . . les Écoles Allemandes. Unsigned, Paris, 11 Jun. 1929.

[99] MAE Z382 64–5, Affaires Étrangères. Telegramme à l'Arrivée, No 282. Signed Margerie, Berlin, 11 Jun. 1929.

Prussian officials.[100] The German government's own declaration on the Treaty was brief, designed, de Margerie reported, 'to head off any inopportune demonstrations',[101] and was as much forward as backward looking:

> Germany signed the Treaty without thereby accepting that the German people started the war. This reproach refuses to leave our people in peace and undermines trust between the nations. We join all Germans in rejecting the assertion that Germany was solely responsible for the war, and we are fully confident that the future belongs to the idea of a real peace, which is not based on injunctions, but solely on agreement, conviction, and the good faith of free peoples, enjoying equal rights.[102]

Such an agreement, Berlin concluded, would address the need for international cooperation to secure 'the economic prosperity of all Europe'.[103]

THE FIRST HAGUE CONFERENCE

Turning now to the Hague Conferences themselves, the French authorities were aware from the outset that reparations continued to rankle across Germany's political spectrum. If injured *amour propre* inflamed right-wing, nationalist protests, more practical considerations worried the republican German government, which was finding it increasingly difficult to balance its budget. The Social Democratic Chancellor, Hermann Müller, complained to de Margerie that the French press was exaggerating German prosperity and the country's capacity to pay reparations,[104] continuing that the post-war assumption that 'the Boches would pay for everything' hardly stood up to serious scrutiny. Instead, Müller claimed, reparations had fuelled the 1923 German hyperinflation and a massive destruction of domestic capital.[105] But despite the ruinous impact of this hyperinflation on the country's economic health, the Dawes Plan had assumed that Germany's economy would be back on a 'normal' footing when the time came to review the reparations settlement in 1929.[106] In early 1929 Seymour Parker Gilbert, the Allied Agent General for Reparations, argued that this was indeed the case and was optimistic that Germany's reparations obligations could be commercialized with little difficulty.[107]

[100] MAE Z382 168–71, Haut Commissariat de la République Française dans les Provinces du Rhin, No. 3740 A.T.R.P. Signed Tirard, Koblenz, 2 Jul. 1929.

[101] MAE Z382 102–3, Affaires Étrangères. Telegramme à l'Arrivée, No 321. Signed Margerie, Berlin, 25 Jun. 1929.

[102] MAE Z382 126–7, Affaires Étrangères. Telegramme à l'Arrivée, No 335. Signed Margerie, Berlin, 28 Jun. 1929.

[103] Ibid.

[104] MAE Z496 1, Affaires Étrangères. Telegramme à l'Arrivée. Signed Margerie, Berlin, 2 Jan. 1929.

[105] MAE Z496 6, Déclaration du Chancelier Hermann Müller au Service de presse social démocrate (*Leipziger Neueste Nachrichten*, 25/26 décembre 1928). Unsigned, 2 Jan. 1929.

[106] MAE Z496 98–9, Affaires Étrangères. Telegramme à l'Arrivée, No 67. Signed Margerie, Berlin, 8 Feb. 1929.

[107] MAE Z496 62, Affaires Étrangères. Telegramme à l'Arrivée, No 33. Signed Claudel, Washington, 21 Jan. 1929.

The German authorities remained less sure. The Economics Minister, Julius Curtius, reminded the Foreign Press Association in Berlin that the country's agricultural sector was in crisis,[108] while the Bavarian Minister President, Heinrich Held, declared in his state parliament that:

> I cannot refrain from expressing my great surprise regarding Parker Gilbert's assessment of German economic life. His report is quite simply a grotesque caricature of reality... The crisis in our agricultural sector, the massive debts we owe abroad, the misery faced by our rentier class, all these in themselves should have served to prevent any attentive observer of our [economic] situation from publishing such an erroneous report.[109]

Nothing had changed when the Allied and German reparations experts opened preliminary negotiations in Paris in March 1929. The individual Allied powers focused on securing an optimal share of the spoils,[110] while the Governor of the German National Bank, Hjalmar Schacht, viewed 'Germany's capacity to make payments' as fundamental.[111]

This dialogue of the deaf elicited negative press coverage on both sides of the Rhine, with German reporters decrying the Allies' proposals as worthy of the ultra-nationalist and monarchist Action française,[112] while French newspapers played up the difficulties surrounding the negotiations in general and asserted (erroneously) that the talks had all but collapsed. German diplomats protested to de Margerie that overblown pessimism served no one's interests,[113] but Schacht himself did Germany few favours when he tabled revisionist demands, to include the recovery of lost German colonies and the return to Germany of the Polish Corridor, as a quid pro quo for future reparations payments.[114] However, Schacht's role at the talks was purely advisory and most certainly did not extend to formulating German foreign policy. Stresemann was furious,[115] Germany's republican press erupted in outrage,[116] and Berlin was left to pour a great deal of oil on very troubled waters.[117]

108 MAE Z496 98, Affaires Étrangères. Telegramme à l'Arrivée, No 67. Signed Margerie, Berlin, 8 Feb. 1929.

109 MAE Z496 74 (front), M. d'Ormesson, Ministre de France en Bavière à M. le Ministre des Affaires Étrangères. Unsigned, Munich, 11 Jan. 1929.

110 MAE Z496 128–9, Le Directeur Politique, Note, Minute. Unsigned, 8 Mar. 1929; Z496 141–2, Le Directeur Politique, Note, Minute. Unsigned, 28 Mar. 1929.

111 MAE Z496 149, Affaires Étrangères. Telegramme à l'Arrivée, No 142. Signed Margerie, Berlin, 30 Mar. 1929.

112 MAE Z496 159, Affaires Étrangères. Telegramme à l'Arrivée, No 169. Signed Margerie, Berlin, 15 Apr. 1929.

113 MAE Z496 165, Affaires Étrangères. Telegramme à l'Arrivée, No 176. Signed Margerie, Berlin, 19 Apr. 1929.

114 MAE Z496 166, Affaires Étrangères. Telegramme à l'Arrivée, No 175. Signed Margerie, Berlin, 19 Apr. 1929.

115 MAE Serie Y Internationale (Y)41 155–6, Affaires Étrangères. Telegramme à l'Arrivée, No 789–90. Signed Margerie, Berlin, 18 Dec. 1929.

116 MAE Z496 188–93, Affaires Étrangères. Telegramme à l'Arrivée, No 181–6. Signed Margerie, Berlin, 21 Apr. 1929.

117 MAE Z496 166–7, Affaires Étrangères. Telegramme à l'Arrivée, No 175–6. Signed Margerie, Berlin, 19 Apr. 1929.

A second, equally maladroit intervention by Schacht would follow in January 1930 during the second round of the reparations conference.

There were other bones of contention. During their 1926 Thoiry meeting, Briand and Stresemann had mooted an early evacuation of Allied troops from the Rhineland, and the return of the Saarland to Germany well ahead of, and without, the plebiscite scheduled for 1935. Neither proposal had come to fruition then, but both ideas resurfaced in June 1929 during a meeting in Madrid of the League of Nations Council. Briand spoke in private to Stresemann of 'a kind of liquidation of the war', to include a Rhineland evacuation and some form of economic deal on the future of the Saar.[118] Stresemann hoped that such agreement would serve to pre-empt political advances by the German nationalist right, including Hitler's NSDAP, having earlier warned the British Ambassador at Berlin that the Rhineland question was driving people back to the DNVP and threatening to 'end . . . the spirit of Locarno'.[119] Leading French newspapers understood that German foreign policy had to strike a balance between what was rational and realizable in the world of international diplomacy and the need to appease the powerful nationalist current in German public opinion. However, they were less happy about the Saar, with the liberal *Journal des débats* warning that any deal on the territory was strictly off the agenda.[120]

Despite Briand's tentative offer, this proved an accurate enough reflection of official policy, for while the French and Germans had agreed on a Rhineland evacuation by early July, Paris baulked at any deal on the Saar and was able to elicit British support. France insisted that the Rhineland and Saar occupations rested on totally different legal foundations, continuing that: 'Nothing is more important than leaving the German government in absolutely no doubt about this even before the conference opens',[121] to receive the reassuring reply that: 'His Majesty's Government doubt whether it would serve any useful purpose to include the retrocession of the Saar on the agenda.'[122] Meanwhile Briand warned Hoesch during an otherwise relaxed discussion 'unequivocally of the danger for the German government of heading into a cul-de-sac'.[123] The legal, procedural, and political difficulties surrounding any initiative on the Saar were insuperable, he continued, with even the rapprochement-minded French Socialists determined that the people of the Saar be allowed to exercise their right to self-determination in 1935 through a plebiscite.[124] On the following day Stresemann adopted a slightly different tack,

[118] Wright, *Stresemann*, 474. [119] Ibid., 476.

[120] AA Reden, Interviews und Aufsätze des Reichsministers (R27994–8), here R27994 164–70, esp. 164–5, 167, Telegramm Spezialdienst Nr. 7764. Signed Wertheimer, Paris, 22 Jun. 1929; see also R27994 263–5, 'Neue Rede Stresemanns', *Berliner Tageblatt*, 25 Jun. 1929.

[121] MAE Y38 60–1, Aide Mémoire pour l'Ambassade d'Angleterre, Copie. Unsigned, 2 Jul. 1929.

[122] MAE Y38 107, Aide Mémoire, Copie. Signed Foreign Office S.W.1, 2 Jul. 1929; see also Y41 138–9, République Française, Ministère des Affaires Étrangères, Direction des Affaires politiques et commerciales. Unsigned, Paris, 3 Dec. 1929.

[123] MAE Y38 45–50, here 48, Audiences du Ministre, Ambassadeur d'Allemagne. Unsigned, 1 Jul. 1929.

[124] Ibid., here 49.

suggesting to de Margerie that whatever the obstacles to an early agreement, the way might be cleared for a deal that transformed the Saar into a locus for structured, long-term Franco-German cooperation.[125] He subsequently floated this notion publicly during an interview with Jules Sauerwein, a senior correspondent with the Paris newspaper, *Le Matin*,[126] but without eliciting a positive reaction from French counterparts.

A cack-handed German press campaign regarding the Saar followed during late July, which was dismissed by de Margerie as 'a mixture of intimidating behaviour and seemingly enticing offers'.[127] French diplomacy continued to insist that German claims were based on a profoundly erroneous interpretation of the relevant clauses of the Versailles Treaty,[128] but neither side wished to sacrifice their wider relationship to the Saar question and they even made a low-key effort to resolve the question. Bilateral Franco-German negotiations on the Saar, independent of the Hague Conference, opened during October, but without Briand seeking approval from a parliament which was already divided enough over the Young Plan.[129] The talks themselves created more problems than the Saar was worth, were inconclusive, and eventually were suspended in July 1930.[130] A maladroit attempt during November 1929 by the Centre Party's leader, Ludwig Kaas, again to link the Saar question with the reparations conference only resulted in Hoesch having to assure Briand that, 'Monsignor Kaas's speech was simply the personal view of a German parliamentarian, was in no way associated with the German government, and could not be interpreted in any way as reflecting official German opinion.'[131]

The Saar was not the only territorial issue under debate. In February 1929 the retired senior French diplomat and economist, Jacques Seydoux, a confirmed sceptic when it came to Germany's bona fides,[132] had created a storm of indignation in Germany, but also consternation in Paris, when writing in the mass circulation *Petit Parisien* that a transfer of East Prussia to Poland was desirable. He was speedily retired from the French section of the rapprochement-minded Franco-German Study Committee,[133] under

[125] MAE Y38 59, Affaires Étrangères. Telegramme à l'Arrivée, No 356. Signed Margerie, Berlin, 2 Jul. 1929.

[126] AA R27994 283, 'Was Stresemann erwartet. "Jetzt muβ das Fazit gezogen warden"', *Vossische Zeitung*, 318, 9 Jul. 1929.

[127] MAE Y38 226–30, here 228, Affaires Étrangères. Telegramme à l'Arrivée, No 427–31. Signed Margerie, Berlin, 31 Jul. 1929.

[128] Ibid.

[129] AA R30181b E430282–7, here 282, 284–6, Telegramm Nr. 1058 vom 5/11. Signed Hoesch, Paris, 5 Nov. 1929.

[130] AA R27996 E223669–71, Interview vom R M für *Saarbrücker Zeitung*, R.M. 74, 17 Jan. 1930; R27997 48a, 'Curtius über die Saarverhandlungen. Rede in Karlsruhe', *Vossische Zeitung*, 327, 14 Jul. 1930.

[131] MAE Y41 124–5, here 125, Audiences du Ministre. M. von Hoesch, Ambassadeur d'Allemagne. Unsigned, 19 Nov. 1929.

[132] Jeannesson, 'Europe de Jacques Seydoux', 141.

[133] AA R70534 H019145–6, Aufzeichnung, II Fr. 726. Signed Bassenheim, Berlin, 1 Mar. 1929; R70534, Jacques Seydoux, 'Notre Politique Extérieure. La Pologne ressuscitée et l'Allemagne', *Petit Parisien*, 24 Feb. 1929; R70534, 'Seydoux propagiert Vergröβerung Polens', *Der Tag*, 48, 24 Feb. 1929; R70534, 'Seydoux am Pranger', *Berliner Börsen-Zeitung*, 94, 25 Feb. 1929.

cover of his genuinely poor health,[134] and each unhelpful individual intervention of this kind was more than countered by the advocates of collaboration. Thus the former (and future) Prime Minister, Édouard Herriot, spoke on Franco-German rapprochement when addressing the Lesezirkel Hottingen in Zürich, a venerable literary association which had also played host to a string of Germany's most distinguished authors. Shortly before his visit he stressed to the *Petit Parisien* the importance of privately negotiated trade agreements between the various branches of French and German industry, as a counterweight to American competition.[135] In Hottingen, however, he focused on the cultural foundations of rapprochement—the latter a necessity that rested 'on the things shared in common between German and French culture, particularly in art and literature'.[136] He then recounted meetings with the former German Chancellor Wilhelm Marx and with Gustav Stresemann, before praising the Prussian Minister of Culture, Carl Heinrich Becker, for his tireless efforts in the cause of international rapprochement.[137]

There were also fresh institutional initiatives. In June 1928, for example, Briand and the Socialist politician Joseph Paul-Boncour became joint honorary conveners of a newly formed Franco-German liaison committee of French parliamentarians which was chaired by the senator and former Cabinet minister Yves Le Trocquer. The committee lobbied energetically for the creation of a German counterpart and after some delay, and with some prodding from the German Embassy in Paris,[138] these efforts bore fruit in March 1929. The German liaison committee contained members of the Liberal, Catholic, and Social Democratic parties and was chaired by the influential Catholic elder statesman Joseph Wirth. Warm words were exchanged as Wirth assured Le Trocquer that: 'Our work will be dedicated to the lofty goal of rapprochement between our two nations and we have every reason to hope it will contribute to the resolution of misunderstandings and the elimination of error.'[139] Within weeks newspapers reported on the first personal exchanges between these committees[140] and Le Trocquer took space in the socialist-leaning *La Volonté* to associate Franco-German rapprochement with European unification. He quoted the historian and journalist Lucien Romier that: 'Europe is too fragmented

[134] AA R70534 H019149, Deutsche Botschaft Paris, A. 761. Unsigned, Paris, 25 Feb. 1929; R70534 H019150, Deutsche Botschaft Paris, A 866. Signed Hoesch, Paris, 4 Mar. 1929; R70534 H019151, Pressenotiz, zu 866. Unsigned, 1 Mar. 1929.

[135] AA R70534 H019201–3, Deutsches Generalkonsulat Zürich, D. 1. Signed Heilbron, Zurich, 27 May 1929; R70534, 'M. Édouard Herriot parlera dimanche à Zurich du rapprochement franco-allemand', *Petit Parisien*, 29 May 1929.

[136] AA R70534 H019201–3, here 202, Deutsches Generalkonsulat Zürich, D. 1. Signed Heilbron, Zurich, 27 May 1929.

[137] Ibid., here 202–3.

[138] For example, AA R70534 H019156, Telegramm Nr. 104 vom 7.2. Signed Hoesch, Paris, 7 Feb. 1929; response in R70534 H019157–9, Ausw. Amt II Fr. 491. Unsigned, Berlin, 8 Feb. 1929.

[139] AA R70534 H019165–6, here 166, Entwurf eines Briefes des Deutsch-Französischen Parlamentarischen Comités an Herrn Le Troquer [*sic*] . . . Signed Dr Wirth, 21 Mar. [1929]; see also R70534 H019194, Deutsche Botschaft Paris, ? 1095. Signed Hoesch, Paris, 26 Mar. 1929.

[140] AA R70534, 'Kleinarbeit für die Verständigung', *Vossische Zeitung*, 248, 29 May 1929; R70534, 'Der Besuch des Freiherrs v. Rheinbaben in Paris', *Wolff's Telegraphisches Büro*, Nr. 1067, Berlin, 1 Jun. 1929.

and if the European market does not organize itself more energetically, American products will soon enough inundate the old continent' (evidently a recurrent theme at the time), continuing that this process depended on Franco-German reconciliation for we will 'not create a European entente . . . without sincere cooperation between France and Germany'.[141] It was, therefore, not without reason that the journalist Albert Dubarry could claim in June 1929 that Franco-German relations stood on the cusp of a breakthrough,[142] or as the senior Social Democratic parliamentarian, Rudolf Breitscheid, concluded at a press conference in Paris:

> I hope and believe that the day is near, on which all the states of Europe appreciate that only their union, under the aegis of the League of Nations, can guarantee our old world a prosperous and peaceful future. It is up to France and Germany, nations that complement one another in so many ways, to provide an example through the definitive liquidation of their historic differences and through the pursuit of a fruitful policy based on agreement.[143]

Preparations for the first Hague Conference, if anything, served to strengthen the positive dimensions of the diplomatic relationship between Paris and Berlin, whilst those between Paris and London deteriorated, sometimes almost to the point of crisis. The first Franco-British squalls involved negotiations, rather late in the day, over where to hold the talks. The French authorities favoured a neutral location for the conference, possibly in the Swiss city of Lucerne, but in Britain the newly elected minority Labour government was still finding its feet and so pressed for London. Stresemann had already assured Poincaré and Briand of German support, but Berlin also expressed sympathy for the British position. Briand summoned Hoesch to the Quai d'Orsay for an explanation and was relieved when the German Ambassador reassured him that the sympathy offered to London was one thing, but that 'in reality the choice of a city in a neutral country, such as Lucerne, as suggested by MM. Poincaré and Briand during their talks with M. Stresemann, still accorded with the German government's own preferences'.[144] Discussions then turned to the timing of the conference and other procedural issues before, again, running into the sand over the Saar question. Briand could only advise Germany to desist from making unacceptable demands which threatened to sour the wider negotiations.[145]

Meanwhile the British Foreign Secretary, Arthur Henderson, transmitted by way of Belgium a second proposal which involved locating the conference in Bournemouth. Would this idea, the Belgians enquired of Paris, be acceptable to the [French] Republic?[146] Apparently not, for on the following day Philippe Berthelot,

141 AA R70534, Albert Dubarry, 'Au service de l'Allemagne', *Volonté*, 11 Jun. 1929.

142 AA R70534, H019214, Deutsche Botschaft Paris, A 2046. Signed Kühn, Paris, 11 Jun. 1929.

143 AA R70501, 'Déclarations de M. Breitscheid', *Le Temps*, 6 Jul. 1929.

144 MAE Y38 45–50, here 46, Audiences du Ministre, Ambassadeur d'Allemagne. Unsigned, 1 Jul. 1929.

145 MAE Y38 45–50, here 50, Audiences du Ministre, Ambassadeur d'Allemagne. Unsigned, 1 Jul. 1929.

146 MAE Y38 99, Affaires Étrangères, Télégramme à l'Arrivée, No 188. Signed Maurice Herbette, Brussels, 11 Jul. 1929.

Permanent Secretary at the Quai d'Orsay, telegraphed the French Embassy in Brussels that 'the proposal to replace London with Bournemouth does not address the situation'.[147] Relations with Britain continued to deteriorate as Henderson asked Aimé de Fleuriau, French Ambassador at London, whether France's opposition to London as locus of the conference masked a deeper problem. The centre-right French coalition appeared so hostile to the new Labour government, Henderson continued, 'that public opinion and the press, as well as he himself, are beginning to wonder whether its opposition to holding the conference in London marked the beginning of the end of the Franco-British entente'.[148] Fleuriau's reassurances did little to placate Henderson[149] who went on to lambast the Ambassador 'with a naive frankness':[150]

> He and his colleagues were treated with the mistrust reserved for newcomers by the old [French] allies of [Labour's] domestic adversaries. However misplaced it might be, such mistrust is difficult to overcome and, as always, rests on a question of form. Whatever we might say [Fleuriau observed], our persistent refusal to countenance London is interpreted here as denoting a change in our attitude to Great Britain and this change is put down to the advent of the Labour Government. It would take a great deal of effort, [Henderson warned], to repair the damage, something that did not augur well for the conference.[151]

Berthelot was unmoved, informing Fleuriau that although France might originally have considered London as a favour to Ramsay MacDonald's new administration, this was now impossible. Newspaper interviews by MacDonald and Henderson had given offence, while the general attitude of the British press against the backdrop of deepening Franco-British disagreement over the modalities of the Rhineland evacuation coupled with the current state of French public opinion made any accommodation by Paris 'very difficult'.[152] The British authorities floated Brussels as a compromise, but Stresemann could not countenance the Belgian capital, where wartime memories remained raw.[153] Finally, Lord Tyrrell, British Ambassador at Paris, suggested The Hague, a neutral capital (as favoured by France) which was also reasonably convenient for the British delegation. Britain asked France to use its good offices to secure Belgian approval, but in Belgian eyes Dutch wartime trade with Germany had prolonged the conflict and post-war Belgian–Dutch relations remained poor. French diplomats prevaricated, merely advising Brussels that they had no formal grounds for objecting to The Hague, before promising that if the

[147] MAE Y38 120, Affaires Étrangères, Télégramme au depart, Ambassadeur français Bruxelles. Signed Berthelot, Paris, 12 Jul. 1929.

[148] MAE Y38 115, Affaires Étrangères, Télégramme à l'Arrivée, No 328. Signed Fleuriau, London, 12 Jul. 1929.

[149] Ibid., 116.

[150] MAE Y38 118, Affaires Étrangères, Télégramme à l'Arrivée, No 329. Signed Fleuriau, London, 12 Jul. 1929.

[151] Ibid.

[152] MAE Y38 130, Affaires Étrangères, Télégramme au depart, Ambassadeur français Londres, 588. Signed Berthelot, Paris, 15 Jul. 1929.

[153] MAE Y38 152, Affaires Étrangères, Télégramme à l'Arrivée, No 392. Signed Margerie, Berlin, 21 Jul. 1929.

Belgians could set aside their objections they would host the proposed Bank for International Settlements (established to manage future reparations and other international payments) in compensation.[154] In the event the Bank was headquartered in the Swiss city of Basel.

Berlin, de Margerie informed Paris, had greeted the resolution of this spat 'with great relief', accompanied by 'a favourable impression of France's attitude to the issues that make up the conference agenda'.[155] However, Berlin was more nervous about British intentions as it transpired that London intended to challenge the proposed distribution between the Allies of reparations, perhaps in part to fund measures designed to cut high domestic unemployment rates.[156] It was not just a question of money. The British Chancellor of the Exchequer, Philip Snowden, was deeply Francophobic, a man, Bernard Oudin remarks, whose 'abrupt and brutal' demeanour 'would make life a misery for the other delegates, and for the French in particular'.[157] Efforts by the French Finance Minister, Henri Cheron, to defend France's corner were brushed aside by Snowden as 'grotesque and ridiculous',[158] all part of a Franco-British dispute which boded ill for the wider conduct of the conference and contrasted with the relatively serene relationship between Paris and Berlin.[159] Further disagreement arose over the form German payments would take, whether in kind (largely coal) or in cash. The former method was of some advantage to Germany and was acceptable to France, not least because the process promised to create increasingly intimate links between French and German industry, but London feared that this reparations coal would come to displace Britain's own coal exports.[160] Things reached the point where the United States feared that an isolated and truculent Snowden might undermine the whole conference. Thus the 'World' section of the *Washington Post* concluded ironically on 15 August that: 'Mr Snowden's outburst will undoubtedly have the effect of bringing about a Franco-German rapprochement and an even earlier evacuation of the Rhineland.'[161] However, Germany's Social Democratic and trade union leaders in the occupied Rhineland began to fear that if The Hague Conference faced collapse, this might disrupt the

[154] MAE Y38 171–2, Ministère des Affaires Étrangères, Télégramme, à Londres 671, à Bruxelles 350. Signed B, Paris, date stamped 25 Jul. 1929; Y38 173–4, Affaires Étrangères, Télégramme au depart, Ambassadeur Français Bruxelles 353-354-355, Londres 672-673-674. Signed Berthelot, Paris, 25 Jul. 1929.

[155] MAE Y38 176, Affaires Étrangères, Télégramme à l'Arrivée, No 406. Signed Margerie, Berlin, 26 Jul. 1929.

[156] MAE Y39 176, Affaires Étrangères, Télégramme à l'Arrivée, No 497. Signed Claudel, Washington, 15 Aug. 1929.

[157] Bernard Oudin, *Aristide Briand. La paix. Une idée neuve en Europe* (Paris, 1987), 521.

[158] Ibid.

[159] MAE Y38 176, Affaires Étrangères, Télégramme à l'Arrivée, No 406. Signed Margerie, Berlin, 26 Jul. 1929; see also Y39 98, Affaires Étrangères, Télégramme à l'Arrivée, No 468. Signed Margerie, Berlin, 9 Aug. 1929; Y39 138–9, Affaires Étrangères, Télégramme à l'Arrivée, No 29/30. Signed Massigli, The Hague, 12 Aug. 1929.

[160] MAE Y39 140–3, Affaires Étrangères, Télégramme à l'Arrivée, No 27/28. Signed Massigli, The Hague, 12 Aug. 1929.

[161] MAE Y39 176, Affaires Étrangères, Télégramme à l'Arrivée, No 497. Signed Claudel, Washington, 15 Aug. 1929.

schedule for the Allied evacuation of the region[162] and as the dispute rumbled on into late August[163] they urged Labour Party contacts in London to persuade Snowden to moderate his demands.[164] After some eleventh-hour brinkmanship by Snowden,[165] a deal was finally struck on 28 August which reduced Germany's total reparations liability by some 20 per cent, from 132 billion gold marks to 112 billion, and allowed considerable flexibility in payments according to the state of German economic health.

From this shrinking cake it proved possible to meet 75 per cent of British demands,[166] but only against the backdrop of simultaneous and acute Franco-British disagreement over the timing and execution of the Rhineland evacuation. The military occupation of the region rested on inter-Allied agreements which, in French eyes, demanded that any changes to its terms be multilateral. On 19 August, however, Briand learned from Henderson that orders had already been given for a unilateral British military withdrawal from German territory. This, and orders to British commanders 'not to discuss the modalities of the evacuation... with their French counterparts',[167] flew in the face of existing conventions and of precedent, with Briand warning that 'the situation might force him to draw the appropriate conclusions'.[168] London insisted that the Rhineland evacuation was an exceptional case and in no way compromised the wider entente,[169] but within twenty-four hours it transpired that Britain planned to withdraw not only its troops, but also, simultaneously, its High Commissioner for the Rhineland. Yet again, the multilateral character of the Allied presence in the Rhine territories was being called into question for, Paris warned: 'The withdrawal of the British High Commissioner signifies that the occupation no longer attaches to Britain, so undermining the treaty and creating serious difficulties for ourselves if the Germans decide to contest the legality of the Commission after the withdrawal of British troops.'[170] 'Should the British persevere with this attitude,' the senior French diplomat, René Massigli, warned, 'we will inevitably be compelled to reach the conclusion that [London] actively seeks to bring to an end Franco-British political cooperation.'[171] Thereafter, following tense negotiations between Stresemann and the Allies on the timing of the evacuation,[172] Henderson and Snowden agreed to

[162] MAE Y40 112, S.C.R. 2/II, Reseignement, Très bonne source, 20 Aug. 1929.

[163] MAE Y40 106, Délégation britannique, 2 Lange Hout Straat. Signed Philipp Snowden, The Hague, 26 Aug. 1929.

[164] MAE Y40 112, S.C.R. 2/II, Reseignement, Très bonne source, 20 Aug. 1929.

[165] MAE Y40 106, Délégation britannique, 2 Lange Hout Straat. Signed Philipp Snowden, The Hague, 26 Aug. 1929.

[166] MAE Y40 131, Affaires Étrangères, Télégramme à l'Arrivée, No 84. Signed Berthelot, The Hague, 28 Aug. 1929.

[167] MAE Y39 239–41, here 240, Démarche auprès de Sir Eric Phipps. Unsigned, The Hague, 20 Aug. 1929.

[168] Ibid., here 240–1. [169] Ibid., here 241.

[170] MAE Y40 6, A.S. du maintien en Rhenenie d'un Haut Commissaire britannique. Unsigned, The Hague, 21 Aug. 1929.

[171] Ibid., 6–7.

[172] MAE Y40 32–3, Affaires Étrangères, Télégramme à l'Arrivée, No 61. Signed Massigli, The Hague, 22 Aug. 1929; see also Wright, *Stresemann*, 481–2; and MAE Y40 84–6, H. Paper No. 4,

retain a British High Commissioner until 31 May 1931 'at the latest' in return for further concessions on reparations.[173]

However, the French authorities continued to fear for the future of the Entente Cordiale, as Ramsay MacDonald's Cabinet prioritized repairing the transatlantic relationship between Britain and the United States.[174] A report by the influential American Whaley-Eaton News Service, which was circulated by the Quai d'Orsay to its major embassies, served to underline the wretched state of Franco-British relations, claiming that: 'Shortly before M. Snowden left for The Netherlands, a resolution was adopted at a [British] Cabinet meeting effectively to end the Entente Cordiale with France, in as far as this entente still existed at all.'[175] On arrival in The Hague, the report continued, Snowden declared that 'he did not have any particular friends, still less allies, on the continent, and that the Entente Cordiale must be considered dead and buried, both in spirit and in law'.[176] A well-informed British source had to conclude that: 'From this perspective, as perhaps from many others, we are isolated in Europe. This situation is typical and shows yet again that only Anglo-American supremacy can secure world peace. This is the main lesson to be drawn from Mr Snowden's stormy speech in The Hague.'[177] 'Under the circumstances', Whaley-Eaton concluded, 'one can no longer believe that Mr Snowden is bluffing, for he is backed by the entire British Cabinet. An agreement [at The Hague] will demand tact and an extension of the negotiating period, before British claims come eventually be accepted in their entirety.'[178] The contrast with Franco-German relations was not lost on American journalists. Shortly after the successful conclusion of the first conference, the French Embassy in Washington informed Briand that 'a remarkable article by M. Edwin Masse . . . reports that the success of The Hague Conference is due above all to your Excellency's generosity of political spirit, supported by M. Stresemann. Beautifully written as usual, this article promises to influence profoundly the American public.'[179]

However, it was no secret that the nationalist right in Germany planned, through parliament and through a referendum, to propose rejection not just of the Young Plan, but of the entire reparation settlement. As we shall see, this catastrophist stance garnered scant support either in parliament or from the public,[180] but for the moment the French Ambassador at Berlin fretted over the underlying political mood in the country. The tone of German press comment on The Hague

Copy No. 16. The Hague Conference, August 1929. Report of the Political Commission. Signed Arthur Henderson, 29 Aug. 1929.

[173] MAE Y40 79–80, Affaires Étrangères, Télégramme à l'Arrivée, No 77. Signed Coulandre, The Hague, 25 Aug. 1929.

[174] Robert W. D. Boyce, 'The Briand Plan and the Crisis of British Liberalism', in Antoine Fleury (ed.), *Le Plan Briand d'Union fédérale européenne. Perspectives nationales et transnationales, avec documents. Actes du colloque international tenu à Genève du 19 au 21 septembre 1991* (Bern, 1998), 134.

[175] MAE Y41 96, Whaley-Eaton Service, La fin de l'entente cordiale, 27 Aug. 1927 [*sic*] but filed in folder dated 1 September to 31 December 1929.

[176] Ibid. [177] Ibid. [178] Ibid., at 97.

[179] MAE Y40 189, Affaires Étrangères, Télégramme à l'Arrivée, No 540. Signed Claudel, Washington, 31 Aug. 1929.

[180] See Ch. 2 under 'Julius Curtius and the Second Hague Conference', 53.

conference was mercurial, but more often than not negative and critical, particularly when it came to territorial and military matters such as the Rhineland evacuation or the future of the Saar.[181] De Margerie warned against 'exaggerating the significance of press reports when ascertaining the mood of a country', but noted the close links between Germany's political parties and particular newspapers which lent press comment authority and substance.[182] He was particularly concerned that this hostility extended far beyond the usual suspects on Germany's political right to include major republican newspapers:

> For now one can only state, with regret, that the concessions made by France in the cause of peace and the European order have not been accepted by the majority of non-nationalist German newspapers, other than as an insufficient and excessively tardy contribution to the full re-establishment of the circumstances that favoured Germany before 1914.[183]

Perhaps, de Margerie observed, this hostile comment was directed more against the German government than against France, but that in turn betrayed the hostile popular pressure that confronted German diplomacy. He went on to observe that Stresemann had even felt constrained during an interview with the liberal *Berliner Tageblatt* to threaten 'to refuse in future any official communication with newspapers "which attack state power through the spreading of false news"'.[184]

JULIUS CURTIUS AND THE SECOND HAGUE CONFERENCE

By the time de Margerie's report was logged in Paris, Stresemann had died, on 3 October, of a devastating stroke. He and Briand had come to personify Franco-German rapprochement and the wider cause of European peace; it remained to be seen whether Julius Curtius, Stresemann's successor as Foreign Minister, would be equal to the task of sustaining a policy which had enemies as well as friends on either side of the Rhine. Perhaps with the benefit of hindsight, and knowing that Hitler would be appointed German Chancellor in little more than three years, many historians have come to regard Stresemann's death as marking the demise of a relatively short-lived era of European detente.[185] The deteriorating world economy was already creating difficulties for international diplomacy while in Germany a series of other setbacks seemed to compound the damage. March 1930 saw Hermann Müller's SPD-led ruling coalition fall apart, whilst in mid-1930 the Permanent Secretary at the Wilhelmstraße, Carl von Schubert, who had given invaluable service to the cause of detente as Stresemann's right-hand man, was

[181] MAE Y41 105–14, Republique Française, Ministère des Affaires Étrangères. La presse allemande et les resultants de la Haye. Unsigned, Paris, 15 Oct. 1929.

[182] Ibid., 105. [183] Ibid., 113. [184] Ibid., 114.

[185] See, for example, Franz Knipping, *Deutschland, Frankreich und das Ende der Locarno-Ära 1928–1931. Studien zur internationalen Politik in der Anfangsphase der Weltwirtschaftskrise* (Munich, 1987), 220.

removed from his post and replaced by Bernhard von Bülow. Bülow was not opposed to rapprochement between Germany and the western Allies as such, but viewed it as one among several possible strategies, which included promoting German interests in the Baltic and in South-Eastern Europe.[186]

Meanwhile the new Chancellor, Heinrich Brüning, failed to assemble a stable parliamentary coalition and called early elections for September 1930. This unscheduled poll allowed German voters their say in the middle of a devastating economic crisis and, not surprisingly, the established parties (with the exception of the Catholic Centre and its Bavarian affiliate) were punished as almost a fifth of voters turned to the belligerent and hyper-nationalist Nazi Party. The Reichstag remained as polarized as ever, forcing Brüning to seek decree powers from the President, a process which left parliament increasingly marginalized and which is widely regarded as marking the beginning of the end for Weimar.[187] Peter Krüger's excoriation of German foreign policy under Brüning[188] extends to Curtius and Bülow who are characterized as enemies of the Locarno spirit, while the surviving advocates of rapprochement, among them Hoesch, are presented as little more than voices in the wilderness.[189]

However, it will transpire that rapprochement with France remained central to German foreign policy until mid-1932.[190] France's commitment to the process over this period was equally strong,[191] and the appointment of Julius Curtius as Stresemann's interim successor was widely welcomed in Paris for securing continuity in Franco-German relations. A close confidante of Stresemann, he had already participated in the first Hague Conference as the German Economics Minister and, like his mentor, belonged to the centre-right, liberal German People's Party (DVP). The gulf separating his foreign policy from the aspirations of the German right was profound and earned him a vitriolic reception from nationalists in parliament. Stresemann had felt obliged to play to this nationalist gallery and Curtius had to do the same, although with less panache and in the less propitious circumstances of an upsurge in Nazi parliamentary strength and self-confidence.[192]

De Margerie anticipated these problems from the outset,[193] but agreed that Curtius stood as a worthy successor to Stresemann:

> The appointment of M. Curtius as Minister of Foreign Affairs has generally been well received. It seemed natural that M. Stresemann's acting successor be someone well

[186] David E. Kaiser, *Economic Diplomacy and the Origins of the Second World War: Germany, Britain, France, and Eastern Europe 1930–1939* (Princeton, NJ, 1980), 27–30.

[187] Classic account in Mommsen, *Verspielte Freiheit*, chs. 7–13.

[188] See Ch. 1 under 'Contrasting Perspectives', 3–4.

[189] Krüger, *Außenpolitik*, 513–14, 518–19; Krüger, 'Abgebrochene Dialog', 300–1; Vogt, 'Deutsche Haltung', 324–5.

[190] See Chs. 4 and 5.

[191] Ibid.

[192] Andreas Rödder, *Stresemanns Erbe. Julius Curtius und die deutsche Außenpolitik 1929–1931* (Paderborn, 1996), 14–15, 27ff, 78–9, 93. See also Wright, *Stresemann*, 517–18.

[193] MAE Z382 240–3, here 243, Affaires Étrangères, Télégramme à l'Arrivée, No 539. Signed Margerie, Berlin, 9 Oct. 1929.

> versed in his thinking, an influential member of his party, and someone who in personal terms as well as in terms of his experience is particularly well placed to secure the adoption and execution of the Young Plan.[194]

The French Ambassador continued that Curtius' work at the Economics Ministry had already played a central role in the promotion of closer Franco-German relations, adding that: 'M. Curtius, just fifty-two years old, has studied in Paris, lived a long time in Baden, close to our frontier, and speaks our language.'[195] If Stresemann's personal contribution to German foreign policy had been definitive, Schubert was quick to reassure de Margerie that his 'policy has struck such deep roots and accords with current imperatives to such a degree as to rule out any possible change',[196] and upon meeting Curtius the French Ambassador was struck by the similarity between his choice of language and Schubert's. 'My discussion with him could only be construed as an unequivocal commitment to a continuing policy of rapprochement', de Margerie reported, although Curtius conceded to the Ambassador that the troubled domestic political climate was doing him few favours.[197]

On 4 November 1929 President Hindenburg confirmed Curtius' appointment as Foreign Minister, to the general satisfaction of his largely republican Cabinet colleagues and the particular satisfaction of French diplomats. De Margerie reported that:

> It almost appears that the late [Stresemann] wished to groom his successor by sharing with him his own private thoughts. We can only welcome a choice which, if it cannot guarantee the survival of Stresemann's distinctly personal 'style' and his unrivalled prestige among the parties and within the nation, will at least assure us that the key thinking underpinning his foreign policy will continue.[198]

The Ambassador's colleagues in Paris agreed and were impressed by Curtius' maiden parliamentary speech as Foreign Minister. Berthelot instructed de Margerie 'to inform Dr Curtius that I very much appreciated in its entirety his first Reichstag speech as Foreign Minister. The occasion reassured me without a shadow of doubt that he is determined to align himself with the policy initiated and pursued by M. Stresemann.'[199] Curtius replied in like manner, appreciating Berthelot's kind words and stressing 'his unshakable determination to continue with and develop by every means at his disposal the policy which attaches in name to Your Excellency and M. Stresemann'.[200]

Curtius delivered on these high expectations as he negotiated the second round of Hague talks during January 1930 and then on 12 March secured the two-thirds

[194] Ibid., here 240. [195] Ibid., here 241.

[196] MAE Z382 246, Affaires Étrangères, Télégramme à l'Arrivée, No 543. Signed Margerie, Berlin, 12 Oct. 1929.

[197] Ibid., 248.

[198] MAE Z382 251, Affaires Étrangères, Télégramme à l'Arrivée, No 611. Signed Margerie, Berlin, 4 Nov. 1929.

[199] MAE Z382 263, Affaires Étrangères, Télégramme au départ, No 966. Signed Berthelot, Paris, 10 Dec. 1929.

[200] MAE Z382 264, Affaires Étrangères, Télégramme à l'Arrivée, No 771. Signed Margerie, Berlin, 15 Dec. 1929.

parliamentary majority required for ratification of the Young Plan. Efforts by the collected nationalist right to derail the whole process by parliamentary and extra-parliamentary means failed miserably. Their proposed 'Law against the Enslavement of the German People', which called for the repudiation of the entire reparations and peace settlement, attracted scant parliamentary support while a national referendum calling for the same outcome saw a pitiful electoral turnout of 14.9 per cent. Republican voters simply stayed at home, so leaving the turnout far short of the 50 per cent required by the constitution for the result of any such referendum to stand. The participation of the Nazis in this charade granted them invaluable exposure and even political respectability, but their twelve Reichstag deputies could barely influence the wider political process. Under the circumstances, the resignation of Hermann Müller as Chancellor on 27 March and the departure of the SPD from government (in a stand-off over the financing of social insurance) were especially unfortunate. The ensuing Reichstag elections in September 1930 only served, unnecessarily, to gift the Nazis an unanticipated mass constituency and a parliamentary platform for their assault on the Republic.

But for the moment these political storm clouds remained on the horizon. The second session of The Hague Conference during January saw Curtius make a point of honouring everything agreed by Stresemann at the first session,[201] but this could not soothe French anxiety over the modalities of reparations payments and provision of a guarantee mechanism should Germany default.[202] Tough negotiations followed.[203] Schacht was, this time, an official member of the German delegation, but remained an unwelcome presence for German ministers as he sought to trespass, stridently, on areas of parliamentary authority.[204] His official remit was confined to discussions concerning the new Bank for International Settlements, particularly the provision of capital from national central banks,[205] but he could not resist making further political demands, prompting Philippe Berthelot to demand of Curtius a speedy initiation of reparations transfers:

> During our discussion this morning I explained to M. Curtius that the placement of the first tranche was fundamentally important and that only this placement would reassure the French public that the Plan was a living reality. I added that the Schacht

201 MAE Y41 183, Affaires Étrangères, Télégramme à l'Arrivée, No 836. Signed Margerie, Berlin, 1 Jan. 1930.

202 AA R70501, Deutsche Botschaft Paris, A. 4695, 1–11. Inhalt: Kammerdebatte über die auswärtige Politik. Signed Hoesch, Paris, 28 Dec. 1929; R70501, Telegramm Paris, Nr. 278 vom 20/3, 1–3. Signed Hoesch, Paris, 20 Mar. 1930.

203 MAE Y42 50–4, Affaires Étrangères, Télégramme à l'Arrivée, No 26–30. Signed Berthelot, The Hague, 11 Jan. 1930.

204 MAE Y41 162, Affaires Étrangères, Télégramme à l'Arrivée, No 826. Signed Margerie, Berlin, 28 Dec. 1929; Y41 183–4, Affaires Étrangères, Télégramme à l'Arrivée, No 836. Signed Margerie, Berlin, 31 Dec. 1929.

205 MAE Y41 165, Affaires Étrangères, Télégramme à l'Arrivée, No 819. Signed Margerie, Berlin, 28 Dec. 1929; Y41 169, Affaires Étrangères, Télégramme à l'Arrivée, No 823. Signed Margerie, Berlin, 30 Dec. 1929; Y42 92, Affaires Étrangères, Télégramme à l'Arrivée, Retransmission d'un télégramme de Berlin No 14. Signed Coulandre, The Hague, 16 Jan. 1930.

> incident had made this guarantee all the more indispensable for us, from a psychological as much as from a practical perspective.[206]

Schacht's pronouncements also triggered Social Democratic efforts to remove him as expeditiously as possible from The Hague[207] and clip his wings,[208] but his indiscretions had no lasting impact. Although some nationalist newspapers latched onto Schacht's outburst, de Margerie could report that: 'the German press as a whole has adopted a more favourable tone than during past years in comparable circumstances'.[209] Days later, on 23 January 1930, the Ambassador informed the Quai d'Orsay that the German Cabinet had unanimously approved the Young Plan, as had the President.[210] Parliamentary approval was expected, and came, within a matter of weeks, for the prospect of reduced annuities and the expeditious liberation of the Rhineland left acceptance a no-brainer.

The Young Plan itself had a short life. Germany had only in 1928 finally made up the economic ground lost during the Great War and still struggled to cover its import bills, let alone service the reparations account. De Margerie warned in February 1930 that the scale of the economic misery in Germany had engendered a profound polarization of society, the destruction of a secure middle class, and circumstances 'which leave it impossible to foresee when matters might improve'.[211] Germany's foreign policy, he observed, was increasingly the prisoner of domestic developments, which left 'the Reichstag debates on the Young Plan merely marking the first stage of this critical era'.[212] Not that this would have particularly surprised his colleagues in Paris. Well before the ink was dry on The Hague reparations settlement the initial shock of the Wall Street Crash of October 1929 had been succeeded by an unprecedented global financial and economic crisis. If France with its massive gold reserves managed to ride out the storm until late 1931, most major economies were swiftly overwhelmed. The USA's gross national product was to fall by 60 per cent and by 1932 a third of America's industrial workforce was registered as unemployed. Thousands of American banks (small, local affairs in the main) collapsed, fuelling a terror in national and international banking as investors and depositors started a run on allegedly insecure institutions, and countries. Central European banks toppled like skittles and as lenders started a run on the Bank of England, Britain was forced to abandon the gold standard and renege on a series of international financial obligations. Brüning shared in the disbelief and shell-shock of world leaders, reflecting that: 'The realisation slowly dawned that the world [was]

[206] MAE Y42 90, Affaires Étrangères, Télégramme à l'Arrivée, No 47. Signed Berthelot, The Hague, 16 Jan. 1930.

[207] MAE Y42 96, Affaires Étrangères, Télégramme à l'Arrivée, No 52. Signed Coulandre, The Hague, 17 Jan. 1930.

[208] MAE Y42 92, Affaires Étrangères, Télégramme à l'Arrivée, Retransmission d'un télégramme de Berlin No 14. Signed Coulandre, The Hague, 16 Jan. 1930.

[209] MAE Y42 120, Affaires Étrangères, Télégramme à l'Arrivée, No 12. Signed Margerie, Berlin, 20 Jan. 1930.

[210] MAE Y42 157, Affaires Étrangères, Télégramme à l'Arrivée, No 14. Signed Margerie, Berlin, 23 Jan. 1930.

[211] MAE Z761 7–17, 1er Février 1930. Quote on 12.

[212] Ibid. Quote on 17.

facing a situation without parallel in history.'[213] Germany's economic downturn was every bit as savage as the USA's and during mid-1931 the country's entire banking system was forced to close its doors. In June 1931 the US President, Herbert Hoover, secured international agreement to declare a moratorium on international debt payments, reparations included, so effectively removing a cornerstone of the post-1918 peace settlement.

However, Franco-German relations remained workmanlike through 1930 and 1931. A balance always needed to be struck between national interest and international reconciliation, even if the latter was frequently perceived as the means to the former. Despite the various points of contention outstanding from the war and the peace settlement, French and German diplomacy—supported by a network of private and quasi-official cultural, economic, and political associations—therefore continued to prioritize rapprochement. The altercations between London and Paris during The Hague Conferences may have had their counterpart in a Franco-German dialogue of the deaf over the future of the Saar region, but the time had long passed when the Entente Cordiale simply confronted its defeated enemy. The resulting prospect of a further improvement in Franco-German relations was to prove particularly important during mid- and later 1930 as Aristide Briand presented proposals for European union to the League of Nations. Britain was to prove unenthusiastic, whereas Germany, contrary to much received historical wisdom, was prepared to engage constructively with Briand and offer the prospect of European unification organized around a Paris–Berlin axis.

[213] Quoted in Clavin, *Great Depression*, 110.

3

Germany, France, and the Briand Plan

THE (PROBLEMATIC) LAUNCH OF THE BRIAND PLAN

The Young Plan agreement went some way towards reconciling Germany's quest for 'equal rights' with France's need for 'security' within a pacified Europe, but if anything the international climate had become more challenging towards the end of the 1920s. The world economy looked increasingly fragile as income from agricultural and mineral products fell, while an unsustainable credit bubble supported the United States' domestic market.[1] A series of disputes soured international relations, among them growing US concern that its Allies would never repay their war loans, a stand-off between France and Italy over the respective size of their navies, and Polish–German border tension which strained the wider peace settlement.

However, in May 1927 the League of Nations had sponsored a World Economic Conference with a remit to cut international tariffs and stimulate global economic activity. It failed to deliver, as a British commitment to universal free trade confronted a more regulated continental approach, championed by France in particular. In British eyes this smacked of protectionism, but Paris and London disagreed more on means than on ends.[2] Paris sought to exploit the growing network of European bilateral trade treaties, which detailed tariffs sector by sector, product by product, to create regional trade blocs, which, with time, would merge into a European customs union. In the meantime a growing continental network of private producer cartels offered a practical route to deeper integration.[3] However, with the Atlantic powers sceptical at best, France's efforts to transform the Conference into a permanent world economic government were equally doomed to failure.[4]

French economic diplomacy was, as noted,[5] driven partly by the realization that the war had gravely weakened the European economy to the advantage of the United States of America. Washington's post-war protectionist trade policy served to buttress its new-found pre-eminence and the emergent Soviet Union, with its

[1] Chancellor, *Devil Take*, 191–225. [2] Boyce, 'Briand Plan', 132.

[3] Elisha, *Aristide Briand*, 30, 73–5.

[4] Eric Bussière, 'Les Aspects économiques du projet Briand. Essai de mise en perspective. De l'Europe des producteurs aux tentatives régionales', in Antoine Fleury (ed.), *Le Plan Briand d'Union fédérale européenne. Perspectives nationales et transnationales, avec documents. Actes du colloque international tenu à Genève du 19 au 21 septembre 1991* (Bern, 1998), 78–9.

[5] Bariéty, 'Aristide Briand et la sécurité', 124; see also Ch. 1 under 'The Opening Gambits', 12, 14.

vast unrealized potential, threatened to compound the problem. In French eyes European powers could no longer compete individually in world markets, leading Paris to propose a collective response through the pooling of European resources.[6] As a means to this end, the Quai d'Orsay collaborated with the French bureau of a prominent pressure group, the European Customs Union (UDE). Led by the former Cabinet Minister Louis Loucheur, the UDE advocated a regional trading union founded on existing Franco-German trade agreements, supported by the expanding network of private business cartels. The resemblance to official French policy was unmistakable and, beyond German interest, the scheme attracted Belgian and Dutch businesses that were heavily dependent on trade with their larger neighbours and were already participating in many of these cartels.[7]

It was, therefore, no accident that Briand's efforts to secure the peace in Europe and address the continent's geopolitical decline focused initially on the economy. A confederal 'European Union' under French moral leadership would form around a Franco-German axis, offering Berlin an outlet for its foreign policy ambitions while simultaneously enabling the Old World to withstand American economic power.[8] Although Stresemann had no wish to alienate the United States, a key market for German business and the main financier of German public debt, he proved sufficiently receptive when Briand sounded him out in June 1929 for the French statesman to announce his plans to the press on 10 July.[9] Weeks later, on 9 September, Briand canvassed the League of Nations, where his case was complemented by two reports from the League's own Economic Bureau. These advocated a united European economy to serve as a counterweight to the huge, integrated American domestic market, and the League duly agreed to sponsor a French-led consultation on European union.[10] Franco-German relations were at the heart of all this and as Briand declared to the League: 'We overcame all obstacles at The Hague; tomorrow the last remaining difficulties in German-French relations will disappear; closer collaboration will be possible; polemical exchanges can cease, in the name of the greater good of peace.'[11]

On 1 May 1930, Briand finally circulated formal proposals to the twenty-six European members of the League of Nations, but despite France's earlier focus on economic integration, 'political union' was suddenly the order of the day. It seems that Briand feared firstly that Britain, with its global and imperial trading links, would shy away from an economic model that London viewed as essentially

[6] Bussière, 'Aspects économiques', 76; Boyce, 'Briand Plan', 133.

[7] Laurance Badel, 'Les Promoteurs français d'une union économique et douanière de l'Europe dans l'entre-deux-guerres', in Antoine Fleury (ed.), *Le Plan Briand d'Union fédérale européenne. Perspectives nationales et transnationales, avec documents. Actes du colloque international tenu à Genève du 19 au 21 septembre 1991* (Bern, 1998), 18–19, 23–4; Bussière, 'Aspects, économiques', 80–4; Wurm, 'Internationale Kartelle', 111–12; Elisha, *Aristide Briand*, 73–4.

[8] Adamthwaite, *Grandeur*, 132.

[9] Bariéty, 'Aristide Briand', 11, 16.

[10] Bussière, 'Aspects, économiques', 86–9; Andrea Bosco, 'The British Foreign Office and the Briand Plan', in Antoine Fleury (ed.), *Le Plan Briand d'Union fédérale européenne. Perspectives nationales et transnationales, avec documents. Actes du colloque international tenu à Genève du 19 au 21 septembre 1991* (Bern, 1998), 347.

[11] Quoted in Elisha, *Aristide Briand*, 303.

continental, alien, and potentially anti-American,[12] and secondly that smaller countries might baulk at the prospect of economic domination by the great powers.[13] Political union was designed to take the line of least resistance, being defined sufficiently vaguely to avoid offending anyone.[14] Member states were to retain 'unconditional sovereignty and full political independence', making no more than a moral commitment in principle to the concept of European union.[15] As Briand explained to Leopold von Hoesch, the German Ambassador at Paris, his proposals 'did not represent any French ideal, instead being a compendium of the various ideas advanced',[16] and his prioritization of political union reflected his belief that European governments would need first to engage politically to realize any collective economic agenda.[17]

However, if the French Foreign Minister imagined he would avoid trouble, the reaction of one European government after another left him disappointed. Rome was unenthusiastic[18] while London and Berlin, the key players, feared that Briand's proposals would duplicate or even undermine the League of Nations. Britain certainly acknowledged the USA's economic pre-eminence,[19] but neither country wished to confront the United States; indeed the British Foreign Minister, Arthur Henderson, warned Briand to avoid any such confrontation,[20] even though the USA introduced its own swingeing trade tariff hikes in June 1930, the Smoot–Hawley Tariffs. The *Deutsche Wirtschafts-Zeitung*, organ of the Federation of Chambers of Commerce, warned that Germany could not afford to isolate itself from global markets,[21] and for Britain these trading links were all the more important. Officials feared that the destructive centrifugal impact of regional trading blocs, extending to the Americas and East Asia, could doom the British Empire. Although the Smoot–Hawley Act arguably left Briand's proposals as the only (European) game in town, London was determined to see his plan subordinated to League of Nations authority, where a Committee of Enquiry for European Union 'did little more than keep the project alive for the sake of appearances'.[22] In mid-August Sir Arthur Salter, Chief of the League's Economic Section, still dared hope that Britain would come to back Briand,[23] but the reality was already

[12] Bosco, 'British Foreign Office', 349–50; Boyce, 'Briand Plan', 132–4. However, cf. P. J. V. Rollo, 'Britain and the Briand Plan: The Common Market that Never Was', Inaugural Lecture, University of Keele, 6 Dec. 1972, 16, where Rollo notes that the Foreign Office was surprised at the 'volte face in subordinating economic to political union'.

[13] Oudin, *Aristide Briand*, 551–2.

[14] Boyce, 'Briand Plan', 139.

[15] Bosco, 'British Foreign Office', 348.

[16] AA R28630 D702910–13, quote on 912, Telegramm Paris, Nr. 715 v. 15/7. Signed Hoesch, Paris, 15 Jul. 1930.

[17] Ibid.

[18] See, for example, MAE Y645 135, Affaires Étrangères, Télégramme à l'Arrivée, No 527. Signed Margerie, Berlin, 16 Jun. 1930.

[19] Tooze, *Deluge*, 463–4.

[20] Rollo, 'Britain', 13.

[21] MAE Y645 105–6, Ambassade de France à Berlin, Direction Politique et Commerciale, No 445. Signed P. de Margerie, Berlin, 27 May 1930.

[22] Boyce, 'Briand Plan', 139–43, quote from 142.

[23] MAE Y653 19, 'La Fédération Européenne. "L'Angleterre devrait adherer au plan de M. Briand"', *Petit Journal*, date stamped 13 Aug. 1930.

otherwise. The German Ambassador at London, Friedrich Sthamer, reported on 6 June that according to a 'well-informed source' the British Government would wish the Plan well, 'but reject it as incompatible with the structure of the British Empire'.[24] The official British reply did just this and the *Daily Telegraph* reflected mainstream British press opinion when pouring cold water on a plan which it dismissed as impracticable:

> and would only unleash intercontinental rivalry. Our position as a European power on the one hand and a member of the British community of nations on the other would become untenable. Therefore the sentimental and nebulous evocation of a united Europe which underlies this concept proves to be fraught with danger . . . The British official reply marks the final word on this unhappy project which, no doubt, will soon be consigned to oblivion.[25]

The Radical French newspaper, *L'Ere nouvelle*, singled out the British response as exceptionally negative, for while most European powers had reservations, Britain alone, it claimed, had rejected the Briand Plan in principle. Detached from the continent, the paper continued, 'British policy seeks to create an Anglo-Saxon order at the expense of the European order.' Perhaps time would eventually convince Britain of the error of its ways, but the first practical steps towards European integration would now be taken regardless.[26]

London might passively support a process of integration on the continent, French commentators observed, but as something distinct from essential British interests, which focused on the Empire and the Atlantic.[27] As if in retrospective confirmation of this, Winston Churchill took space in the liberal German financial daily, the *Berliner Börsen-Courier*, in January 1931 to elaborate on the fundamentals of Britain's foreign policy. He observed that British reserve was not the only challenge to the Briand Plan, for international reaction, he claimed, had been generally negative. The older countries were determined to defend their vital interests, while the emergent states of Central and Eastern Europe baulked at compromising their newly won independence. As for Britain's future role, he continued:

> We wish Pan-Europeanism well, but remain non-committal. We have numerous ties with Europe and we are a significant European power. We conduct a great deal of trade with Europe and a thriving and peaceful Europe is central to our essential interests. But we also move in other circles which are of greater substantive and emotional significance for us. These include the British Empire . . . and the wider English-speaking world . . . all of this preventing Britain joining a European Union unconditionally, even while being unable to isolate itself entirely from the same.[28]

[24] AA R28630 D702733, Telegramm Nr. 320 v. 6./6. Signed Sthamer, London, 6 Jun. 1930.

[25] MAE Y652 57, 'La réponse britannique . . . ', *Daily Telegraph*, 18 Jul. 1930; see also Y652 141, 'Le projet de Fédération européenne. Une opinion anglaise', *Journal des Débats*, date stamped 7 Aug. 1930. *The Times* was similarly hostile: Rollo, 'Britain', 19; see also 20.

[26] MAE Y652 79, 'Éditorial', *Ere nouvelle*, date stamped 24 Jul. 1930.

[27] AA R28630 D702884–5, Telegramm Nr. 672. Signed Hoesch, Paris, 7 Jul. 1930; see also Bosco, 'British Foreign Office', 357.

[28] AA R28631, 'Die Vereinigten Staaten von Europa. Vom The Rt. Hon. Winston Churchill', *Berliner Börsen-Courier*, date stamped 11 Jan. 1931.

Perhaps, with time, the influential French journalist Jules Sauerwein speculated, Britain might come to see the economic attractions of a reorganized Europe, but 'we know that British thinking does not evolve particularly quickly'.[29] In the event, the official British reply welcomed the notion of European cooperation in principle, but alluded to the range of complications that precluded unconditional British participation in such a project.[30]

FRANCO-GERMAN EXCHANGES

So, with no meaningful support forthcoming from London, and with Italy, in French eyes, gripped by 'feverish ambition' and a 'delusive persecution mania',[31] Paris would have to look elsewhere. The diplomatic thaw of the Stresemann era and the ongoing expansion of Franco-German business and trading links pointed towards a possible Franco-German axis, but not if Briand persisted in prioritizing political union. Curtius was disappointed at the Plan's relatively perfunctory discussion of economic issues, and suspected that Paris wished to conclude an 'eastern Locarno' agreement, designed to set the borders of Eastern and South-Eastern Europe in stone. This challenged 'most fundamental' German foreign policy objectives,[32] for it would prejudice any revision of its contested eastern frontiers[33] and stymie any prospect (however distant) of an Austro-German union.[34] Vienna was similarly alarmed by this and proposed a coordinated German and Austrian response to the Plan,[35] a request which did engender ongoing consultation between the two capitals and a German desire not to cut across Austrian wishes.[36] As we shall see, this Austro-German collaboration was to culminate in early 1931 in proposals for a customs union between the two countries, a development not well received in Paris.[37] In the meantime, Curtius was equally anxious to avoid compromising Germany's links with the United States

[29] AA R28630 D702884–5, Telegramm Nr. 672. Signed Hoesch, Paris, 7 Jul. 1930.

[30] AA R28630 D702914–16, Telegramm Nr. 393 v. 15/7. Signed Sthamer, London, 15 Jul. 1930; R28630, 'Die vorläufige englische Antwort auf das Europa-Memorandum', *Wolff's Telegraphisches Büro*, 81, Nr. 1440, 18 Jul. 1930.

[31] AA R28630 D702884–6, quote on 885, Telegramm Nr. 672. Signed Hoesch, Paris, 7 Jul. 1930; R28630 D702910–13, here 913, Telegramm Nr. 715 v. 15/7. Signed Hoesch, Paris, 15 Jul. 1930; MAE Y645 135, Affaires Étrangères, Télégramme à l'Arrivée, No 527. Signed Margerie, Berlin, 16 Jun. 1930.

[32] AA Handakten-Samml. Ges. Seeliger, Briand Memorandum (R105491), Auswärtiges Amt, Vbd. 1530. Signed Curtius, 31 May 1930, 3.

[33] AA R105491, Auswärtiges Amt, Vbd. 1530. Signed Curtius, 31 May 1930, 1–2.

[34] AA R28630 D702730–2, Abschift im Auszug aus einer unter dem 31. Mai d.J. aus Wien an den Österreichischen Gesandten in Berlin ergangenen Instruktion (offenbar Zirkularerlaß). Unsigned, 31 May 1930.

[35] AA R28630 D702852. Signed Bülow, Berlin, 1 Jul. 1930.

[36] AA R28631 D702964–70, here 965–6, Aufzeichnung betr. Studienausschuss für die Europäische Union, Vbd. 3650. Signed Köpke, Berlin, 11 Dec. 1930; R28631 D 702984–9, here 984, Abschrift, Vbd. 3679. Signed Curtius, Berlin, 20 Dec. 1930.

[37] See Ch. 4 under 'Enduring Tensions and the Austro-German Customs Union', 87–8.

and Soviet Union, and since Britain was cool on the whole European idea,[38] avoid anything that prejudiced relations with London.[39] However, despite these reservations, German policy aimed at a bilateral accommodation with France and here, Curtius believed, the Plan's economic clauses did offer a way forward:

> The serious conflicts of interest and reservations on the political side demand that we examine particularly carefully the possibilities offered by purely economic issues, transport links, and social and cultural cooperation between European states. Indeed it is difficult not to see why, major political considerations aside, an effort should not be made to forge European rapprochement issue by issue. This has already been achieved, albeit with qualified success, at the Tariff Truce Conference in Geneva. It is therefore to be desired that we table concrete proposals, or at least suggestions, in order to chalk up some successes in the current political environment.[40]

On 31 May he canvassed other Ministries on the Briand Plan, focusing on economic issues and asking his colleagues to identify any such areas which they considered ripe for international agreement. Where appropriate, he suggested, they might draw lessons from the March 1930 Tariff Truce Conference, organized by the League of Nations, in order 'to clarify our overall objectives'.[41]

When inter-ministerial discussions followed on 19 June, the draft submissions of the Economics and Labour Ministries proved particularly detailed and largely positive. The Economics Ministry noted the profound disruption and distortion of European markets caused by the 1919 frontier settlements as a plethora of newly independent small states guarded their individual national interests. 'The 1927 World Economic Conference', the Ministry continued, 'alluded to the exaggerated economic nationalism and the economic consequences arising from the new European border settlements and established that this exaggerated nationalism and territorial upheaval had resulted in a counter-productive duplication of industrial plant and insufficient specialization between individual European states.'[42] These problems were now being compounded by a devastating and intensifying world economic crisis, the Ministry observed, and it could only agree with its French colleagues 'that efforts be made through a "progressive liberalization and simplification in the movement of goods, capital and people" across Europe to achieve "a rational ordering of production and European trade"'.[43] The Ministry envisaged a future in which Europe operated a single labour market with unrestricted personal freedom of movement, buttressed by the coordination of national social insurance systems and the cross-border regulation of wage rates.[44] It did warn against compromising Germany's multilateral trading interests through any onerous external continental tariff, against duplicating any global regulatory agreements,

38 For a further example, AA R28630 D702749–50, 614/6. Signed Schubert, Berlin, 13 Jun. 1930.

39 AA R105491, Auswärtiges Amt, Vbd. 1530. Signed Curtius, Berlin, 31 May 1930, 4.

40 Ibid., 3–4. 41 Ibid., 4–6.

42 AA R105491, zu Vbd. 1873/30, Vertraulich! Unverbindlicher Referentenentwurf. Unsigned, undated, filed with June 1930 papers.

43 Ibid., 2. 44 Ibid., 6.

and against prejudicing the powers of the League of Nations,[45] but remained convinced that the Briand Plan 'can be supported unreservedly in its essentials'.[46]

The Labour Minister's views were similar. He observed that the League of Nations' International Labour Organization (ILO) was functioning well and should not be undermined, but continued that 'this reservation aside, I can only welcome the notion of European solidarity with regard to social policy, whether on a multilateral or bilateral basis, and whether within or outwith the ILO'.[47] The Ministry looked to supranational collective wage bargaining in Europe, the elimination of obstacles to the free movement of labour across the continent, and the coordination of welfare systems and labour laws, all with a view to simplifying the practicalities of working abroad.[48] 'The contents of the (Briand) Memorandum', the Minister concluded, 'are clearly directed towards this same goal; to this extent it can be supported unreservedly in its essentials.'[49]

However, the remaining Ministries were divided. The Chief of the Army Command, General Kurt von Hammerstein-Equord, a liberal and supporter of the Weimar Republic, signed off the Defence Ministry's response which argued that the Briand Plan 'sought to secure French hegemony in Europe'.[50] 'All in all,' it concluded, 'from the perspective of national defence these proposals can only be considered more closely following a completely even-handed, rather than one-sided, process of disarmament.'[51] The Agricultural, Communications, Justice, and Occupied Territories Ministries were similarly unenthusiastic, whilst the Finance and Interior Ministries sided with the Economics and Labour Ministries in arguing for a positive response,[52] all of this leaving the Foreign Office to square the circle.

On 13 June the former Permanent Secretary at the Wilhelmstraβe, Carl von Schubert, discussed Briand's proposals with the British Ambassador at Berlin, Sir Horace Rumbold, who confessed that London was currently too preoccupied with India to reach a definitive view of the Briand Plan. Schubert conceded that discussion of the Plan in Berlin was also proving 'very difficult' and repeated that German leaders remained concerned that Britain might exclude itself from any union, and that Briand's scheme did seem to challenge the 'processes of the League of Nations'. Nonetheless, although doubts remained regarding its political clauses, he viewed the Plan as 'essentially positive in the final analysis'.[53] This, of course, would require France once again to prioritize economic collaboration. Cautiously at first, both sides began to put out feelers and on the following day Leopold von

[45] Ibid., 7–9. [46] Ibid., 9.

[47] AA R105491, Abschrift Vbd. 1803, Der Reichsarbeitsminister, Betrifft: Memorandum der Französischen Regierung über die Organisation einer europäischen Bundesordnung. Signed Dr Stegerwald, Berlin, 18 Jun. 1930, 2.

[48] Ibid., 2–9. [49] Ibid., 9.

[50] AA R28630 D702741–3, quote on 741, Abschrift Vbd. 1733, Der Reichswehrminister. Signed v. Hammerstein, Berlin, 12 Jun. 1930.

[51] Ibid., quote on 743.

[52] AA R28630 D702772–7, Vbd. 1813, Aufzeichnung über die Ressortbesprechung vom 19. Juni 1930 über das französische Europa-Memorandum. Unsigned, Berlin, 19 Jun. 1930.

[53] AA R28630 D702749–50, 614/6. Signed Schubert, Berlin, 13 Jun. 1930.

Hoesch held lengthy but informal discussions with the French Trade Minister, Pierre-Étienne Flandin. The Minister wished to prioritize political integration, having previously argued that, 'European economic union would only be possible when all outstanding political problems had been settled.' However, Hoesch declared the prospects for a political compact as next to hopeless, and continued that, 'Europe's economic problems appear to me too acute to permit any further delay in efforts to reach economic agreement.'[54] He feared that a tariff war was imminent and since Flandin agreed, their thoughts turned to resolving this particular challenge. The Trade Minister rehearsed French interest in exploiting and extending private cartel agreements to achieve a customs union in Western Europe, which might include France, Germany, Belgium, and Switzerland. Hoesch was struck by the (predictable) parallels between Flandin's thinking and official French policy and was convinced that the tariff question provided an opening for further negotiation; was 'the [further] conduct of such discussions of interest [to Berlin]?' he asked.[55]

Guidance was not long in coming. On 16 June Köpke briefed Germany's European missions, and also the Embassies in Washington and Tokyo that while the Cabinet had yet to agree on its formal response, diplomats could communicate that:

> We view positively the notion of European collaboration, but wish to avoid at all costs anything that undermines the League of Nations and our relations with non-European countries, as well as Russia. France's subordination of economic issues to the political creates unnecessary delay in the vital task of providing emergency relief for the economy. The question of [economic versus political] prioritization should therefore be put to one side. We do not reject the discussion of political issues, but do reject French proposals that would result in the consolidation of the status quo laid down at the Paris Peace Conference.[56]

Köpke continued that German policy would focus on the immediate resolution of specific economic issues, such as tariff policy, delaying decisions on the organizational structure of a European union until its competencies had been agreed.[57] Comparable reassurances were given to the French Ambassador at Berlin.[58]

On 19 June, Bernhard von Bülow, who had replaced Schubert as Permanent Secretary at the Wilhelmstraße on 2 June, opened an inter-ministerial conference convened to resolve the issues originally flagged up by Curtius on 31 May.[59] As we saw, ministerial submissions had varied from the positive to the decidedly negative, but when Bülow asserted at the outset that Germany 'would assume a positive

[54] AA R28630 D702758–60, quote on 758–9, Telegramm Nr. 584 vom 14/6. Signed Hoesch, Paris, 14 Jun. 1930.

[55] Ibid., quote on 760.

[56] AA R28630 D702765, Abschrift zu Vbd. 1752. Ang. I., Telegramm. Signed Köpke, Berlin, 16 Jun. 1930.

[57] Ibid.

[58] MAE Y645 135, Affaires Étrangères, Télégramme à l'Arrivée, No 527. Signed Margerie, Berlin, 16 Jun. 1930.

[59] See Ch. 3 under 'Franco-German Exchanges', 61.

stance' to the Briand Plan, subject to the familiar reservations regarding the League of Nations and relations with the extra-European world,[60] he in effect predetermined the direction of travel. He continued that the political dimensions of the Briand Plan threatened to impose strategic constraints on German foreign policy, but it would be left to the Cabinet to respond to this issue. For the moment, he declared, the economic dimension needed to be prioritized over the political and to this end the meeting should 'confine itself to positive proposals, which will equip us to play a substantive role in forthcoming [international] negotiations and thereafter in the [League of Nations] Committee of Enquiry'.[61]

However, this was easier said than done, for the views of individual Ministries continued to range from enthusiastic to openly hostile. Global regulation appeared preferable to European in international financial transactions, postal and telecommunications services, air travel, or agricultural policy. However, European integration was favoured when it came to economic, financial, and labour issues.[62] Midway through these discussions Bülow was 'called away', and handed the chair to his deputy Gerhard Köpke[63] who was a known supporter of Franco-German rapprochement. Köpke briskly brought the discussions to a close, noting that while four Ministries (in addition to the Foreign Office) had identified opportunities for European cooperation, 'the remaining Ministries were unable to offer any suggestions'.[64] He went on to propose that the Economics Ministry and Foreign Office flesh out the details of the official German response between them; no one thought to disagree.[65] In a tardy, but measured, response to Curtius' original enquiry, the new President of the Reichsbank, Hans Luther, saw particular opportunities in the liberalization of European capital transfers: 'an area where France could contribute very effectively to European communal life, particularly by easing the contradictions in the heart of Europe'.[66]

Briand met Hoesch on 25 June to continue discussions and the Ambassador reassured him that while deliberations were ongoing in Berlin, he believed 'a complete rejection [of the Plan] was out of the question'.[67] Curtius said as much in the Reichstag on the same day,[68] and Hoesch repeated the Minister's view that with economic issues so pressing, it seemed ill-advised to become bogged down in a reordering of European political affairs, adding that the exclusion of Russia from the process also appeared unwise. Briand was receptive, agreeing that 'economic

[60] AA R28630 D702772, Vbd. 1813, Aufzeichnung über die Ressortbesprechung vom 19. Juni 1930 über das französische Europa-Memorandum. Unsigned, Berlin, 19 Jun. 1930.

[61] Ibid., D702772–4, quote on 773–4.

[62] Ibid., D702772–6; for financial transactions see R28630 D702841–3, Abschrift (Vbd. 2018), Der Präsident des Reichsbank-Direktoriums Nr. I 7162. Signed Luther, Berlin, 27 Jun. 1930.

[63] AA R28630 D702776, Vbd. 1813, Aufzeichnung über die Ressortbesprechung vom 19. Juni 1930 über das französische Europa-Memorandum. Unsigned, Berlin, 19 Jun. 1930.

[64] Ibid., D702777. [65] Ibid.; cf. Vogt, 'Deutsche Haltung', 326.

[66] AA R28630 D702841–3, quote on 842, Abschrift (Vbd. 2018), Der Präsident des Reichsbank-Direktoriums Nr. I 7162. Signed Luther, Berlin, 27 Jun. 1930.

[67] AA R28630 D702828, Telegramm Nr. 626 v. 26/6. Signed Hoesch, Paris, 26 Jun. 1930.

[68] MAE Y645 143–4, Ambassade de France à Berlin, Direction des Affaires Politiques et Commerciales Europe, No 528. Signed P. de Margerie, Berlin, 26 Jun. 1930.

problems appeared particularly acute, whilst he fully appreciated that the framing of a European Charter would require considerable time'.[69] He was, however, less willing to accord Russia anything beyond a consultative role in any negotiations.[70] He insisted that France had no desire to secure 'a hegemonial position' in Europe, portraying his own role as nothing more than a facilitator and midwife of a pan-European agenda.[71] British reserve, he continued, was certainly a problem, but its 'position was exceptional and its opinion was, therefore, less crucial than that of a leading continental power'.[72]

Briand having tipped the wink, French diplomacy continued to seek common ground with Berlin on the European question. The French Press Attaché at Berlin, Oswald Hesnard, sounded out Curtius on 3 July, who again stressed that economic rather than political collaboration was called for.[73] This was echoed by the editor of the authoritative *Deutsche Diplomatisch-Politische Korrespondenz*, Edgar Stern-Rubarth, himself a partisan for European collaboration. His journal served effectively as a mouthpiece for the Wilhelmstraβe, and Stern-Rubarth now dwelt at length on international support for the prioritization of economic integration. The Quai d'Orsay itself, he noted, had just hosted a conference of the pressure group, European Customs Union, which declared 'that the establishment of a European customs union is the prerequisite for a stabilization and reordering of Europe'. Belgian and Dutch foreign ministers concurred, he continued, so reinforcing Germany's own case.[74] A commensurate French response was not long in coming. The senior political correspondent of the authoritative French newspaper, *Le Matin*, Jules Sauerwein, reported at length on 7 July on the overall prospects for European union, writing off the significance of the smaller states and doubting Britain's commitment to the Briand Plan, before turning to Germany.[75] Dismissing the country's radical right as fantasists without a credible political agenda, he concluded that 'the continuation of Stresemann's [foreign] policy amounts to German collaboration with France'. Sauerwein, who enjoyed intimate contacts with the Quai d'Orsay, set out in detail the nature of such collaboration, which, he believed, 'despite all the incidents and upsets [meant] that Germany will stand alongside us to rebuild Europe'.[76] The industrialists and agrarians east of the Rhine, he argued, fully understood that France alone was in a position to offer them financial assistance, and that France alone could broker a more lenient reparations settlement, grant a relaxation of restrictions on German armaments, and secure land links between East Prussia and the rest of Germany. But it was the economic question he regarded as decisive, concluding that: 'If markets are liberalized and if the future

[69] Ibid.

[70] AA R28630 D702828–30, here 829, Telegramm Nr. 626 v. 26/6. Signed Hoesch, Paris, 26 Jun. 1930.

[71] Ibid., here 829–30. [72] Ibid., here 830.

[73] AA R28630 D702858–60, RM 1013, Niederschrift über eine Besprechung mit Herrn Professor Hesnard. Signed Curtius, Berlin, 3 Jul. 1930.

[74] MAE Y645 157–8, Ambassade de France à Berlin, Direction des Affaires Politiques et Commerciales Europe, No 561. Signed P. de Margerie, Berlin, 4 Jul. 1930.

[75] AA R28630 D702884–6, Telegramm Nr. 672. Signed Hoesch, Paris, 7 Jul. 1930.

[76] Ibid., D702886.

appears brighter then I believe the voice of reason will prevail in Germany. In that case there would be no major obstacles to a European economic entente.'[77]

The German Cabinet remained to be fully convinced, leading Curtius to declare ironically that some of his colleagues wished to give the Briand Plan 'a first-class funeral',[78] words often taken, mistakenly, to reflect literally his own views.[79] But in the event Curtius stuck to his original agenda, by prioritizing economic over political factors, negotiating privately with France to this end, and achieving collective support in Cabinet for his strategy. Days before the official German reply was dispatched to Paris, Pierre de Margerie, French Ambassador at Berlin, was briefed 'by a well-placed official' that: 'Although it contains some objections and reservations, the German government's response . . . will adopt a positive line.'[80] On 11 July the reply was forwarded to Paris, translated there into French on the 12th, and handed to the French authorities on the 14th.[81] German diplomats in Paris were instructed by Curtius to stress 'Germany's positive attitude to European collaboration' and emphasize Berlin's determination to avoid any rupture with Paris over issues where the two governments currently disagreed. The Foreign Minister continued that the Briand Plan's prioritization of the political had demanded a German response, but that: 'We have in this regard, and I wish to stress this unequivocally, held entirely to the direction of our foreign policy to date.'[82]

The reply itself, just five and a half single-spaced pages long, therefore amounted to qualified support for Briand's proposals. Noting the urgent need for deeper European cooperation, Curtius welcomed the French initiative, but warned against any rupture with the extra-European world, or with European powers (specifically the Soviet Union and Turkey) which did not currently belong to the League of Nations. The German note discussed Briand's prioritization of a political compact relatively briefly and in general terms, but Curtius rehearsed his fear that France wished to entrench the geopolitical status quo and so stymie Germany's search for change. 'Equal rights', particularly with regard to security and armaments, and also eastern border arrangements remained central to German policy,[83] objectives which, he knew, were finding increasing support in the American press.[84] On a decidedly more positive note, Berlin had much to say on economic issues, identifying the

[77] Ibid. [78] Rödder, *Stresemanns Erbe*, 116–17; see also Wright, *Stresemann*, 484–5.

[79] See, for example, Krüger, *Außenpolitik*, 529; Vogt, 'Deutsche Haltung', 325; Elisha, *Aristide Briand*, 75.

[80] MAE Y645 159–60, Affaires Étrangères, Télégramme à l'Arrivée, No 581. Signed Margerie, Berlin, 7 Jul. 1930.

[81] AA R28630 D702894, RM 187, Zeittafel für die Antwort auf das Briand-Memorandum. Unsigned, undated, filed before 11 July 1930; R28630 D702896, Vbd. 2061, Germadiplo Paris Nr. 461. Signed (R.M.) Curtius, Berlin, 11 Jul. 1930.

[82] AA R28630 D702896–7, Vbd. 2061, Germadiplo Paris Nr. 461. Signed (R.M.) Curtius, Berlin, 11 Jul. 1930.

[83] AA R28630 D702899–902, Antwort der Deutschen Regierung auf das Memorandum der Französischen Regierung vom 1. Mai 1930 über die Organisation einer europäischen Bundesordnung. Unsigned, Berlin, 11 Jul. 1930.

[84] AA R28630 D702908, Telegramm Nr. 305 v. 14/7, Anschluβ 215. Signed Prittwitz, Washington, 15 Jul. 1930.

agricultural crisis and trade liberalization as most pressing, and regarding the engagement of the private sector in any recovery plan as vital.[85]

Greater detail, the reply stated, could await formal discussions at the League of Nations in September,[86] but for Briand's proposals to have any chance of success there, Franco-German political differences needed to be squared in advance. On 15 July Briand warned Hoesch that the political content of the German reply was problematic, continuing: 'One must appreciate that the current European order is founded on treaties, and to put amendment of these treaties up for discussion would precipitate the dismemberment rather than the unification of Europe.'[87] Hoesch assured him that German aims were less radical, observing that: 'Alongside the provisions which delineate the current European status quo, the treaties also contain clauses which open the way for evolutionary change. Germany is therefore not stepping outwith the parameters of the treaties when it evokes and supports the concept of evolution.'[88] Briand appeared somewhat reassured, even observing that Article 19 of the Versailles Treaty offered a route to such evolution,[89] preferably as part of a process of European collaboration. However, he warned Berlin not to make such 'evolution' a precondition for German participation in the process of European integration.[90] As their discussion drew to a close Briand declared himself reasonably satisfied with the wider international reception of his plan, Italy's response excepted. As Hoesch reported:

> He concluded with further sarcastic remarks regarding the Italian reply, which contrasted somewhat with the tone of other countries' responses. He asked himself whether the Italians, if they wished to toy with revision of the existing European order, stopped to consider whether they should surrender wartime gains achieved at other countries' cost.[91]

With the mood suitably lightened, Hoesch could report to Berlin that: 'All in all Briand's response to our reply was essentially positive', a result which owed something to the verbal clarification he had provided.[92] During subsequent, wide-ranging discussions with Philippe Berthelot, Permanent Secretary in the Quai d'Orsay, Hoesch requested a further meeting with Briand, to discuss the modalities of European union and to place Franco-German collaboration at its heart. 'It is clear', the German Ambassador declared, 'that France and Germany will be able to reach agreement on economic questions and that will be a major achievement; everyone will follow.'[93]

[85] AA R28630 D702899–905, Antwort der Deutschen Regierung auf das Memorandum der Französischen Regierung vom 1. Mai 1930 über die Organisation einer europäischen Bundesordnung. Unsigned, Berlin, 11 Jul. 1930.

[86] Ibid., D702905.

[87] AA R28630 D702910–11, Telegramm Nr. 715 v. 15/7. Signed Hoesch, Paris, 15 Jul. 1930.

[88] Ibid., D702911.

[89] Ibid.; see also HMSO, *The Treaty of Peace between the Allied and Associated Powers and Germany* (London, 1928), Article 19, 31.

[90] AA R28630 D702911, Telegramm Nr. 715 v. 15/7. Signed Hoesch, Paris, 15 Jul. 1930.

[91] Ibid., D702913. [92] Ibid.

[93] MAE Y645 209, Note du Secrétaire Général, 31 Jul. 1930.

Hoesch was less sure how public opinion would receive developments and in particular how the French press would respond to the German reply. Briand reassured him that the French government would make every effort to secure friendly media coverage[94] and was able to deliver on this promise. The Quai d'Orsay's Press Office displayed just a touch of reserve when evaluating 'the German reply as satisfactory, making an appropriate contribution to the further development of the idea of Europe'.[95] Foreign Office officials in Paris responded to German press enquiries in similar vein. French papers sympathetic to Briand's foreign policy tailored their message accordingly, playing down German geopolitical ambitions as a previously known quantity. As *Le Matin* remarked, these political issues, and also neutral countries' aversion to European integration, meant that: 'European collaboration should be initially pursued through economic cooperation, where there are real prospects of achieving substantial and useful results.'[96] In other words, newspapers close to the French government were now arguing that the Germans had a point when prioritizing economic union. If France's right-wing press adopted a more sceptical tone, Hoesch was satisfied. Nothing could be taken for granted, he warned Berlin, but:

> Given the large circulation of the moderate journals mentioned above, and considerably smaller readership of the nationalist press, one can conclude that a clear majority of the French public, on reading their newspapers, will have gained a relatively positive impression of the German reply's content.[97]

The same could be said for readers of German newspapers, for on 17 July de Margerie reported a remarkably positive consensus in the German press. The liberal *Berliner Tageblatt*, he wrote, claimed that 'M. Stresemann would not have replied any differently and that the German Note "had created a united front extending from the Socialists on the left to the Hugenberg camp [on the right]".' Conservative and especially Catholic papers added that territorial revision and multilateral disarmament needed to be part and parcel of any final settlement, but the Social Democratic organ, *Vorwärts*, focused on the economy. Much remained to be done, the newspaper declared, so it was 'amazing that for all this effort to reconcile the peoples of Europe, governments continue to divide them through the imposition of ever higher customs barriers'. 'One expects with good reason', *Vorwärts* concluded, 'that economic entente will see a notion of solidarity and a sense of security come to fruition.'[98]

However, when Briand's proposals came up for discussion at the League of Nations on 8 September, British obfuscation[99] saw them consigned, after just three hours of discussion, to the long grass of a 'Committee of Enquiry into the European Union'. It was to report in 1931 to a plenary session of the entire League of Nations

[94] AA R28630 D702911–13, Telegramm Nr. 715 v. 15/7. Signed Hoesch, Paris, 15 Jul. 1930.

[95] AA R28630 D702917–18, Telegramm Nr. 719 v. 16/7. Signed Hoesch, Paris, 16 Jul. 1930.

[96] Ibid., D702918. [97] Ibid., D702920.

[98] MAE Y645 187–9, quotes on 188–9, Affaires Étrangères, Télégramme à l'Arrivée, No 640. Signed Margerie, Berlin, 17 Jul. 1930.

[99] For example, MAE Y652 141, 'Le projet de Fédération européennne. Une opinion anglaise', *Journal des Débats*, stamped 7 Aug. 1930.

and so provide a basis for further discussion.[100] This may have accorded with a near-universal wish not to cut across the competences of the League itself, but more or less guaranteed a lack of speed and focus in framing and implementing any concrete proposals for European integration. Even so, Curtius remained upbeat when addressing the League on 16 September, where he promoted economic collaboration as the pathway to European union. The conservative *Deutsche Allgemeine Zeitung* adjudged his ideas as relatively vague, but saw in them 'nothing less than the thought of a Franco-German customs union and a Franco-German customs parliament'.[101] Well-informed German readers would recall the important role played by the nineteenth-century German Customs Union (Zollverein) in the process of German unification. And in a withering attack on economic protectionism, *Le Matin* familiarized its French readership with this particular dimension of German history. There was only one response to British and American protectionism, the paper insisted, 'and that is to smash the customs barriers that separate Germany, Belgium, Italy, Switzerland and all Europe's nations'.[102] Turning to nineteenth-century Germany, the paper continued:

> There was a time, and not long ago, when right across Germany, a traveller, or merchandise, going from Prussia to Saxony, from Bavaria to Württemberg, or from Hanover to Baden, had to endure a series of vexatious and costly formalities. The Germans wisely recognized this as a huge error. So they founded the Zollverein, or customs union, meaning that economic unity preceded German political unity. We must, in the same way, create a European Zollverein as a prelude to European political unity.[103]

The conservative *Figaro* was less convinced, accusing Briand of forgetting where his loyalties should lie: 'Of which country is M. Briand the Foreign Minister, of France or the Reich?', continuing that 'M. Briand celebrates for having merited Germany's trust. Is he absolutely sure he has preserved that of France?'[104] However, as seen above, reservations of this sort in the French nationalist media were more than offset by positive coverage elsewhere.

The Quai d'Orsay's files also contain a number of private and very personal responses to Briand's project. A citizen of Frankfurt-am-Main composed the musical score and penned the libretto for a 'Pan-European March',[105] while the German-Jewish war veteran, Herbert Sulzbach, who after 1945 was to strive for German–British reconciliation, wrote of his respect and admiration for 'la Grande

[100] AA R28631, 'Henderson siegt über Briand. Nur drei Stunden Europa-Konferenz', *Vossische Zeitung*, 424, 9 Sept. 1930; R28631, 'Briands Paneuropa-Dunst. Europäische Konferenz ergebnislos verlaufen—Die gesamte Frage der Vollversammlung des Völkerbundes überwiesen—Englands Veto', *Der Tag*, 9 Sept. 1930; R28631 D702951–2, Telegramm Nr. 48, Kzl. Nr. 2202. Signed Weizsaecker, Geneva, 16 Sept. 1930.

[101] AA R28631, 'Gefahr einer Illusion. Der Gedanke einer deutsch-französischen Zollunion', *Deutsche Allgemeine Zeitung*, 433, 17 Sept. 1930.

[102] MAE Y652 15, Charles Richet, 'Les États-unis d'Europe. L'unité commerciale doit préluder à l'unité économique', *Le Matin*, 3 Oct. 1930.

[103] Ibid.

[104] MAE Y653 120, 'Bulletin du Jour. Dors-tu content . . . ?', *Le Figaro*, 18 Sept. 1930.

[105] MAE Y655 151, Brosende, *Pan-Europa Marsch (Volksausgabe)*, 20 May 1930.

France' and its advocacy of Franco-German friendship. 'That is why', he continued, 'you will also help our democracy and republican government, so that [your] policy will endure and culminate in the United States of Europe.'[106] American opinion varied, with the *Christian Science Monitor* depicting Briand sowing the seeds of a United States of Europe on fertile soil,[107] but the *New York American* was more critical, publishing a cartoon (forwarded to Paris by a disgruntled German resident in the United States) portraying a dismembered Germany and Austria being invited to join a Europe presided over by the victor powers, to which they replied, 'First give us back our arms and legs.'[108] On balance, however, American opinion was sympathetic, with the French diplomat, Jules Henry, reporting to Briand that: 'It is widely recognized that your project cannot be directed against the United States, which stands to benefit economically.'[109] Quite so, and in November an enterprising Montana high school student, Dorothea A., wrote to Briand seeking additional material for her essay on his United States of Europe project.[110]

However, despite largely favourable public opinion, the diplomatic wheels of the League of Nations ground fine and slowly. Briand was confirmed as Chair of the Committee of Enquiry on 23 September; the Secretary General of the League, Sir Eric Drummond, was nominated as Secretary and as the only other member of the Committee. Any further decisions would await the first full meeting of this Committee, which was scheduled for January 1931.[111] However, Curtius noted 'a remarkable U-turn' in French policy since the summer 'with emphasis shifting from political to economic issues',[112] a stance which certainly complied with German wishes, but created problems of a different kind. As Köpke observed:

> The Committee of Enquiry's mandate is confined to pursuing its investigations and, as far as possible, submitting any substantive proposals to the General Assembly. Briand's Europe has not therefore as yet been established, and will assume concrete form at the earliest during the League's plenary session in the autumn of 1931. [But] if the Committee of Enquiry drafts substantive proposals regarding European economic issues, then this would presume the creation of the European Union. The German delegation could then be accused of returning from Geneva committed to a new European institution.[113]

[106] MAE Y655 94, Monsieur le Ministre Aristide Briand. Signed Herbert Sulzbach, Berlin-Wilmersdorf, 24 Dec. 1929.

[107] MAE Y655 46 (back), 'Fertile Soil', *The Christian Science Monitor*, Boston, Friday ? Sept. 1930.

[108] MAE Y656 260, 'Come, let us be Brothers!' *New York American*, 29 Aug. 1930, plus covering letter. Signed H.B., New York City, 29 Aug. [1930].

[109] MAE Y645 219, Affaires Étrangères, Télégramme à l'Arrivée, No 462. Signed Jules Henry, Washington, 11 Sept. 1930.

[110] MAE Y657 94–5, 'Dear Sir, As a member of a modern history class . . . '. Signed Dorothea A., Bonner, Montana, 12 Nov. 1930.

[111] AA R28631 D702954–5, Telegramm Nr. 98, Kzl. Nr. 2288. Signed Weizsaecker, Geneva, 23 Sept. 1930.

[112] AA R28631 D702984–9, quote on 985, Abschrift. Vbd. 3679 II. Signed Curtius, Berlin, 20 Dec. 1930.

[113] AA R28631 D702964–70, quote on 968, Vbd. 3650, Aufzeichnung betr. Studienausschuss für die Europäische Union. Signed Köpke, Berlin, 11 Dec. 1930.

The French Prime Minister, André Tardieu, had, perhaps inadvertently, complicated matters further through a speech on 13 November to the Chamber of Deputies. In an effort to soothe the ruffled feathers of the French political right (on which his government depended for its majority), he insisted that the prioritization of economic over political integration in no way prejudiced France's vital interests. Indeed, he continued, economic integration created a twofold barrier, against Bolshevism but also against 'various revisionist campaigns'.[114] This in turn prompted Curtius to reiterate Germany's commitment to amending the peace settlement, by evolutionary means.[115]

Days later, Briand and Hoesch met to take stock of developments. Briand was exceptionally conciliatory, adjudging Germany's latest proposals 'as more or less according with French thinking'[116] and appeared happy to see the Committee of Enquiry take shape step by step over time. Turning to specific issues he declared France ready to admit non-League members to discussions in the fullness of time, but still feared that Russia might turn up determined 'to toss grenades into the gradually emerging European [entity]'. Without wishing explicitly to exclude political matters from the agenda, Briand confirmed that economic issues were now paramount and particularly welcomed Germany's interest in collaborating with France to resolve South-Eastern Europe's agricultural crisis. He identified a series of other measures—standardization of passport procedures, standardization of postal services (for example, through the issue of uniform postage stamps), and, eventually, the creation of a monetary union. He also wondered whether it might be possible to administer and regulate credit issues across Europe.[117]

Hoesch went on to hold meetings with French economic experts to flesh out these radical proposals.[118] On 6 January he discussed matters at some length with the French Economics Minister, Louis Loucheur, a long-standing partisan for a European tariff union, who admitted that his government had yet to arrive at a definitive European strategy. However, he and Hoesch agreed in principle that their governments should coordinate efforts to assist the struggling grain producers of South-Eastern Europe before the Committee of Enquiry met. European coal mining, Loucheur added, was another sector ripe for discussion. 'As always', Hoesch reported, 'Loucheur was completely committed to the notion of economic cooperation with Germany, which he also regarded as particularly important in a European context.'[119] The French Cabinet finally came to discuss the Committee on 13 January, and embraced the substance of Franco-German diplomacy to date. Thereafter, Germany and France continued to disagree on the desirability or otherwise of admitting the Soviet Union (and Turkey) to the Committee, but Hoesch repeated that Germany remained keen to resolve the South-East European

[114] Ibid.

[115] AA R28631 D702984–89, here 985, Abschrift. Vbd. 3679 II. Signed Curtius, Berlin, 20 Dec. 1930.

[116] AA R28631 D702997, Telegramm Nr. 1191 v. 31/12. Signed Hoesch, Paris, 31 Dec. 1930.

[117] Ibid., D702997–8.

[118] Ibid., D702998.

[119] AA R28631 D703011–13, quote on 013, Telegramm Nr. 19 v. 6.1. Signed Hoesch, Paris, 6 Jan. 1931.

grain crisis 'and would value a confidential exchange of views with the French delegation on this subject. Briand declared himself here in absolute agreement.'[120]

COMPLICATIONS AND UPSETS

The Committee of Enquiry convened on 16 January 1931 without a set agenda. This served to complicate and prolong discussions, which continued for five days rather than the scheduled two. Particular attention was paid to Europe's grave economic and agricultural crisis,[121] while shifting coalitions of Committee members managed to override French objections and admit three non-League members—Iceland, the Soviet Union, and Turkey—to future discussions on economic matters. A business committee was created to draw up a constitution and procedural guidelines and a further session was agreed for May. However, this marked the high-water mark of Briand's European plan. Germany was not unconditionally supportive of France and could seem more focused on remaining in sync with Austrian interests, however discreetly, and in siding with Italy to see the Soviet Union included in future economic deliberations.[122] Nonetheless, Briand assured Hoesch that he was happy enough after the January session, although he remained unclear over how, exactly, the Committee would go about its work.[123]

It helped little that French domestic politics were particularly febrile at the time. The Radical parliamentarian, Théodore Steeg, had replaced Tardieu as Prime Minister on 12 December 1930 and allowed his Economics Minister, Louis Loucheur, free rein at the January meeting of the Committee of Enquiry. Given Loucheur's commitment to a continental customs union, his enunciation of radical plans for European economic integration came as little surprise. However, in the confusion of French domestic politics, Steeg resigned on 27 January 1931 to be replaced as Prime Minister by Pierre Laval. The latter would himself come to press for a European union built around a Franco-German partnership,[124] but his Cabinet's immediate response to Loucheur's efforts was less positive as it turned its attention to domestic affairs.[125] As the French diplomat, Pierre Arnal, remarked during discussions with Hoesch on 11 February: 'He believed that the new French government regarded the resolutions framed by Loucheur in Geneva as a rather uncomfortable inheritance, and that people like Flandin would doubtless have preferred a more thoughtful and circumspect approach.'[126] Arnal went on to

[120] AA R28631 D703051–2, quote on 052, Telegramm Nr. 52 vom 13. Signed Hoesch, Paris, 13 Jan. 1931.

[121] See, for example, AA R28631 D703128–32, Anlage zu Vbd. 318, Résolutions adoptés à la 2ème session de la Commission, le 16–21 janvier 1931. Unsigned.

[122] AA R28631 D703119–27, here 125, Auswärtiges Amt, Vbd. 318, Januartagung 1931 des Studienausschusses für die Europäische Union. Signed Weizsäcker, Berlin, 31 Jan. 1931.

[123] AA R28631 D703146, Telegramm Nr. 171 vom 11/2. Signed Hoesch, Paris, 11 Feb. 1931.

[124] See especially Ch. 4 under 'Preparations for the Berlin Ministerial Conference', 110–12, 121; Ch. 5 under 'A Successful Conference', 126 and 'Creating the Commission', 132–5.

[125] See Oudin, *Aristide Briand*, 526, 537.

[126] AA R28631 D703147, Telegramm Nr. 171 vom 11/2. Signed Hoesch, Paris, 11 Feb. 1931.

admit that the French authorities had as yet failed to agree a strategy for discussions on the European economy, scheduled for 23 February. 'French delegates', he continued, 'would likely ask their German counterparts what proposals Germany had in mind to resolve the [South-East European] grain surplus.'[127] Hoesch betrayed a touch of unease when reporting these discussions to Berlin. 'It appears to me', he observed, 'that the outcome of the Committee's work depends in essence on the attitude of Germany and of France. Accordingly, I must recommend that we agree on guidelines for our attitude on the Committee and perhaps contact the French government in advance regarding the parameters of the Committee's deliberations.'[128] However, the remaining two Committee meetings were to achieve little.[129]

Unease of a different sort took hold in London, for Britain had come to regard Franco-German rapprochement as integral to European federalism. British officials, Ralph White observed, 'tumbled to the possibility of a united Europe emerging at France's behest and under Franco-German hegemony', something they regarded as 'profoundly inimical' to British interests.[130] The British Ambassador at Paris, Lord William Tyrell, had already warned in January 1930 of the French government's 'willingness to do everything possible to bring Germany into the Europe which France is organising',[131] and continued: 'The Germans here [Paris] seem to be hand in glove with the French at the moment, and the intimacy of their relations constantly surprises me and would very probably very considerably startle people in London.'[132] Tyrell's concerns were strengthened after talks on trade policy with the French (Belgian-born) economist and President of the League of Nations Economic Committee, Daniel Serruys, who enjoyed close links with the Quai d'Orsay. Serruys complained to Tyrell that: 'It was so difficult to talk with British officials: many of them did not seem able to understand the continental theory or talk the continental language',[133] whereas Germany presumably did.

However, some of the Ambassador's colleagues were less convinced, with E. H. Carr, then a Second Secretary in the Central Section of the Foreign Office, dismissing his warnings as 'hot air'.[134] The British Ambassador at Berlin, Sir Horace Rumbold, also doubted Germany's commitment to the French-inspired scheme, but nonetheless sensed that the economic dimension of the French plan might attract the Germans.[135] The Foreign Office itself was, therefore, reduced to speculating on France's ultimate aims, on whether France was ultimately trying to shore up the 1919 political status quo or prioritizing the notion of a Franco-German economic bloc, as favoured by Loucheur in particular.[136] The answer, possibly, was both. Similarly, Germany was prepared to balance sincere economic collaboration with

[127] Ibid. [128] Ibid. [129] Vogt, 'Deutsche Haltung', 327.

[130] Ralph White, '"Through a Glass, Darkly": The Foreign Office Investigation of French Federalism, January–May 1930', in David Dutton (ed.), *Statecraft and Diplomacy in the Twentieth Century* (Liverpool, 1995), 75.

[131] Ibid., 77. [132] Ibid., 79. [133] Ibid., 80. [134] Ibid., 77.

[135] Ibid., 86–8. [136] Ibid., 85.

France against its wider revisionist agenda. Economics continued to offer Paris and Berlin a way to circumvent geopolitical differences which did not brook easy resolution, but these same deep-seated differences always threatened to undermine economic collaboration in turn. British diplomats appreciated this as well as anyone and Carr's scepticism regarding any Franco-German axis was doubtless nourished by German reactions to the Allied military evacuation of the Rhineland in June 1930.

THE RHINELAND EVACUATION AND ADDED TENSIONS

France stuck to the agreement brokered by Briand and Stresemann at the first Hague summit and withdrew its army of occupation from the southern Rhineland during June 1930, five years ahead of the schedule laid down by the Versailles Treaty. However, the German response, characterized by Rumbold as one of 'ingratitude and tactlessness', appeared crass at best.[137] As Hoesch remarked: 'While we regard the evacuation of the Rhineland as a long overdue act of justice obtained through great sacrifice . . . the abandonment of the left bank of the Rhine represents in French eyes an enormous, almost inconceivable act of magnanimity.'[138] To make things worse, Hoesch continued, rather than any obvious improvement in Franco-German relations, the evacuation appeared to have triggered precisely the opposite reaction:

> The French public have seen a chaotic mess unfold before their eyes, seemingly as a by-product or a consequence of the Rhineland evacuation: the hounding of [former] separatists, by the increasingly powerful National Socialist Party among others, the readmission of the Stahlhelm [war veterans association] into the Rhineland and Westphalia, the Reich-President's triumphal progress through the liberated territories, the invocation of Article 48 Emergency Powers by the national Government, the dissolution of the Reichstag, to name but some.[139]

Thus in French eyes a revival of German nationalism seemed to be the one and only consequence of the Rhineland evacuation.[140] Briand came under attack from his habitual enemies on the right for surrendering too much of France's peace dividend and erstwhile supporters of Franco-German rapprochement also openly harboured doubts. It helped little when much of the French press passed over relatively conciliatory German official speeches and focused instead on more colourful outbursts, including a pronouncement by President von Hindenburg during a tour of the newly evacuated territories. He openly questioned the legitimacy of the statutes (confirmed at Locarno in 1925) that provided for the permanent

[137] Vogt, 'Deutsche Haltung', 319.

[138] AA R70502, Abschrift II Fr. 2024, Deutsche Botschaft Paris A2649, Inhalt: Frankreich im Sommer 1930. Signed Hoesch, Paris, 25 Jul. 1930, 19pp., quote from 8–9.

[139] Ibid., 9–10. [140] Ibid., 10.

demilitarization of the Rhineland. Had the President let slip a secret revanchist agenda, French conservative statesmen asked?[141] Raymond Poincaré took space in the illustrated newspaper *Excelsior* to extend the attack from Hindenburg's politics to the 'German mentality' which, he claimed, 'had not changed significantly since the days of Treitschke and Bernhardi; German military training and the education of German youth in the universities continues in the old spirit'.[142]

In the midst of this uproar, the elderly French Foreign Minister appeared ready to throw in the towel, confiding to Hoesch that 'it was absurd at his advanced age utterly to exhaust himself, given that a peaceful life in the countryside would be much more congenial', adding that 'a minister should never completely exhaust his reserves of prestige, a principle he had always adhered to'.[143] Tardieu, Hoesch warned Berlin, was growing impatient with the slim pickings Briand's foreign policy now seemed to be offering and had begun to intervene personally in foreign affairs, egged on by elements of the nationalist right that formed a part of his parliamentary majority.[144] Meanwhile, outside parliament a group of French war veterans associations took space in the conservative newspaper *Figaro* to denounce the essentials of Briand's German policy, declaring that:

> No one stands as a stronger advocate of peace than the combatants who suffered during the war and even, if circumstances allow, as stronger advocates of an entente with the Germans, for this offers the best prospects of a lasting peace. Up until now the combatants' watch on the Rhine, a fruit of the victory, has guaranteed the peace. On the initiative of a Foreign Minister, a speculative policy which stakes everything on German goodwill has replaced guarantees that rested on good sense and experience.[145]

The German reaction to the evacuation of the Rhineland, the veterans continued, spoke volumes in this regard.[146] For its part, the Association of French Reserve Officers appealed publicly to Tardieu to recalibrate French foreign policy and in particular uphold France's rights in the Saarland.[147] It helped little when Germany's Minister for the Occupied Territories, Gottfried Treviranus, publicly demanded revision of the German–Polish frontier, despite Curtius' public adherence to the modalities of the peace settlement. The striking of a medal to commemorate the Allied departure from the Rhineland, with the inscription: 'The Rhine. Germany's river, not Germany's border' also became the subject of a tense exchange between Briand and Hoesch.[148]

141 AA 70502 K240356–7, Deutsche Botschaft Paris, A2737. Signed Hoesch, Paris 1 Aug. 1930. See also R70502, Telegramm Nr. 798 vom 12/8. Signed Hoesch, Paris, 12 Aug. 1930.

142 AA R70502 K240366–7, quote on 366, Deutsche Botschaft Paris, A2907. Signed Thiesser, Paris, 15 Aug. 1930.

143 AA R70502, Abschrift II Fr. 2024, Deutsche Botschaft Paris A2649, Inhalt: Frankreich im Sommer 1930. Signed Hoesch, Paris, 25 Jul. 1930, 19pp., quote from 11.

144 Ibid., 11–14.

145 AA R70502, Telegramm Nr. 746. Signed Hoesch, Paris, 26 Jul. 1930.

146 Ibid.

147 AA R70502, Deutsche Botschaft Paris, A 2802. Signed Hoesch, Paris, 6 Aug. 1930.

148 AA R70502 K240370–4, here 370–2, Telegramm Nr. ?64 v. 4/9. Signed Hoesch, Paris, 4 Sept. 1930.

Hoesch counselled a balanced response to these upsets which, after all, coincided with particularly intensive and constructive Franco-German diplomacy over the Briand Plan.[149] On 8 August, during a visit to Cologne, Brüning declared that the Allied powers had delivered on their promise to evacuate the Rhineland early and that history had already moved on with the framing of the Briand Plan: 'Amidst the economic and social challenges confronting Germany and the world, it is highly significant that the French statesman has responded with well-conceived plans for the creation of a European order.' Economic collaboration and political accord, Brüning continued, would need to progress hand in hand,[150] a stance that Briand in turn found very reassuring.[151] Hoesch was not alone in arguing that Germany should neither set its face against detente with France, nor pursue such detente to the exclusion of other international contacts, but he adjudged the Franco-German relationship as unique:

> What does Germany mean to London, Rome, or Washington? A great power among several great powers, alongside many other important issues and interests. What does Germany mean to France? The focal point of French policy, against which all other issues play second fiddle. It does not appear very different from a German point of view when it comes to ranking the French problem.[152]

A great deal of patience was called for and hard work remained to be completed, but Hoesch was struck by the extent and significance of Franco-German collaboration, ranging from a process of fruitful cross-fertilization in the scientific and cultural worlds, to the continued growth and extension of Franco-German business cartels.[153]

Thereafter, the dust settled slowly during a series of uneasy meetings between senior French and German figures.[154] Briand returned briefly to Paris in early August from his summer rural retreat, evidently in better spirits and convinced that whatever might appear in the press, wider public opinion was emphatically on his side.[155] He appeared more concerned over the forthcoming September Reichstag elections, and the prospect, in his eyes, of a devil's pact between the Communists and Nazis. Hoesch was reassuring, insisting that while the next German parliament might contain around 100 'purely negatively inclined deputies', any fundamental change in the direction of German foreign policy remained beyond the bounds of possibility.[156] Berlin's

[149] See, for example, AA R70502 K240351–5, here 353–5, Telegramm Nr. 769 vom 4/8. Signed Hoesch, Paris, 4 Aug. 1930.

[150] AA R70502, 'Eine programmatische Rede des Reichskanzlers Dr. Brüning', *Wolffs Telegraphisches Büro*, 81—Nr. 1590, Berlin, 9 Aug. 1930.

[151] AA R70502 K240370–4, here 372, Telegramm Nr. ?64 v. 4/9. Signed Hoesch, Paris, 4 Sept. 1930.

[152] AA R70502, Abschrift II Fr. 2024, Deutsche Botschaft Paris A2649, Inhalt: Frankreich im Sommer 1930. Signed Hoesch, Paris, 25 Jul. 1930, 19pp., quote on 17.

[153] Ibid., 18.

[154] See AA R70502 K240342–6, Herrn v. Friedberg, stamped II. Fr 2082. Unsigned, Berlin, 31 Jul. 1930.

[155] AA R70502 K240351–5, here 351–3, Telegramm, Nr. 769 vom 4/8. Signed Hoesch, Paris, 4 Aug. 1930.

[156] Ibid., here 352.

immediate priorities, the Ambassador insisted, involved political, financial, and economic consolidation at home, rather than any revisionist extraterritorial adventures. Germany's commitment to the Briand Plan remained intact and economic cooperation offered, 'with active German participation, to set in train all sorts of interesting possibilities'.[157] 'Beyond this,' Hoesch declared, 'German delegates would also be ready to discuss the specifics of German–French economic relations; influential German bodies are convinced that Germany's political and economic relations with France are of the utmost significance.'[158] He conceded that recent international agreements had not always fulfilled the hopes invested in them. The Young Plan, for example, had failed to deliver a widely anticipated German tax cut; instead deteriorating public finances had resulted in a tax increase of a billion marks, meaning that: 'France needs to commit if it wants to repair the situation; providing Germany with cheap long-term credit on the one hand and supporting the jobs market on the other.' The latter could include offering German companies contracts relating to major French infrastructural projects, something Briand promised to promote in Cabinet.[159]

All in all, the French Foreign Minister appeared reassured, concluding that the overall international situation demanded cooperation between Germany and France more than ever. 'Some china had been flung around the room, but the fundamentals of the rapprochement policy remained intact.' More generally, and particularly with regard to Poland, he advised Germany to play a long game, 'further consolidating its important and influential position in the world'. German bluster, Briand remarked, only served to play into Polish hands, warning that the Poles might even deliberately provoke a confrontation to serve their own ends. This, he insisted, 'was so obvious to him that he failed to understand how anyone in Germany could view things differently'.[160]

THE 1930 REICHSTAG ELECTION: CHALLENGES AND REASSURANCE

However, the outcome of the German Reichstag elections of 14 September 1930 created obvious difficulties for Franco-German relations. The tally of 'negatively inclined' deputies (presumably the NSDAP and the Communists) surged from 66 to 184, not forgetting the 41 deputies from the German National People's Party (DNVP) whose leader, Alfred Hugenberg, had bitterly opposed the Young Plan and had refused to participate in Weimar coalitions on any terms. This bloc of 225 malcontents was supported by individual deputies from various splinter parties, but fell short of the 289 seats needed to form the majority in the 577-strong parliament. Chancellor Brüning could continue to govern, but by constitutionally tenuous means. Any formal coalition based around the Social Democrats (SPD), the liberal

157 AA R70502 K240370–4, here 372, Telegramm Nr. ?64 v. 4/9. Signed Hoesch, Paris, 4 Sept. 1930.

158 Ibid., here 373.

159 Ibid.

160 Ibid., here 374.

parties, and Brüning's Centre Party, although mathematically possible, was ruled out on all sides. However, none of these moderate parties wished to allow Hitler a sniff of power. Short of a working majority, Brüning fell back, as noted,[161] on Article 48 of the constitution, which provided for government by decree during any national emergency, at the behest of the President, but subject to approval from a majority of Reichstag deputies. The SPD provided the necessary votes, tolerating Brüning's administration as a 'lesser evil' (to Hugenberg or Hitler), yet avoiding immediate responsibility for the conduct of government in the midst of an unprecedented domestic and international economic crisis.

Brüning's government may have stood by the existing fundamentals of German foreign policy, but the immediate impact of the September elections on French public opinion was devastating. Hoesch's deputy, Kurt Rieth, warned on 23 September that reassurances to Paris by leading figures in Berlin were of limited value 'as long as people here cannot conceive of any viable way for Germany to escape its current difficulties'.[162] Rieth continued that even the republican press in Germany had served to inflame French opinion with its panicky coverage of the elections and their aftermath: 'For example the alarmist report in the *Berliner Zeitung am Mittag* featuring an anticipated coup by Hitler and a calculation by the *Vossische Zeitung* that opponents of the Young Plan enjoyed a majority in the Reichstag. These articles have been reproduced and commented upon by the entire [French] press.'[163] Doubts over the sustainability of the German Republic and thus of its accommodating foreign policy, had combined with widespread public fear that a war with Germany threatened,[164] so fuelling demands from the French political right for rearmament rather than disarmament. At the end of the day, Rieth warned, Berlin had to get its house in order, by reaffirming its commitment to a constructive foreign policy and providing the French pro-rapprochement camp with the necessary ammunition.[165] On 10 October he reported that French media anxiety regarding Germany's future had only intensified further: 'While a section of the press, probably under official pressure, tried to calm the mood in the immediate aftermath of the elections, now, with the exception of the socialist press and a few far-left bourgeois editions, there is hardly a paper that does not speak . . . of the German menace.'[166] Right-wing French papers accused even the SPD of joining a conspiracy to overthrow the Versailles Treaty and concluded that the entire thrust of French policy towards Germany was profoundly misconceived. It was, they declared, time for Briand to step down and for France to rearm without delay. If the left-wing press was understandably reluctant to disown Briand, it nonetheless

[161] See Ch. 1 under 'Contrasting Perspectives', 3–4.

[162] AA R70502, Telegramm Nr. 913 v. 23/9. Signed Rieth, Paris, 23 Sept. 1930, 1.

[163] Ibid.

[164] See, for example, AA R70502 K240393, Telegramm Nr. 84 vom 11/10. Signed Adolf Müller, Bern, 11 Oct. 1930.

[165] AA R70502, Telegramm Nr. 913 v. 23/9. Signed Rieth, Paris, 23 Sept. 1930, 2–3.

[166] AA R70502 K240381–2, Deutsche Botschaft Paris, A 3393, Inhalt: Rückwirkungen der politischen Ereignisse in Deutschland auf die Stimmung in Frankreich. Signed Rieth, Paris, 10 Oct. 1930.

reported, more in sorrow than anger, on the changed and worrying situation in Germany.[167] A chauvinistic Stahlhelm parade, held in Koblenz on Sunday 5 October 1930, added to the mood of imminent crisis, as French journalists of all political persuasions reported on the presence of Nazis at the rally and noted that the Stahlhelm leader, Theodor Düsterberg, had raised the issue of Alsace-Lorraine's future status.[168]

French political leaders either shared these fears, or at the very least felt obliged to bend to public opinion. As Rieth warned:

> During the last few weeks a large number of prominent French politicians have publicly given expression to the belief that French foreign policy requires fundamental revision, and that it must in future be conducted with greater firmness, particularly with regard to Germany. The fact that even people like Herriot or for that matter Painlevé have publicly expressed doubts over whether existing policy can be sustained demonstrates that such thinking has penetrated deep into the political left, with a major shift in [the left's] attitude to the disarmament question and the strengthening of the French armed forces.

He conceded that French policy had been volatile throughout the post-war period and that 'it would be mistaken to exaggerate the significance of the current wave of mistrust towards Germany for the future development of German–French relations and of French policy more generally'.[169] He also noted that a crisis in Franco-Italian relations had served to intensify the nervous mood west of the Rhine. However, he concluded, the whole business had done German interests precious few favours. Briand had sustained his personal authority by using a speech in Geneva to take a tough line on disarmament, but he remained politically vulnerable when it came to the German question.[170]

In the event Brüning's ability to rebuild his centrist Reichstag coalition calmed the mood in France relatively quickly. Briand and the Quai d'Orsay had never wished to disown Franco-German rapprochement and asked the press to tone down coverage of German affairs. Perhaps expectations in France had slumped so dramatically in the immediate aftermath of the Reichstag elections that even the right-wing newspapers were now prepared to give Brüning the benefit of the doubt.[171] Ill-timed German efforts to reopen negotiations on the Saarland fell on deaf ears,[172] but French leaders were more receptive to the argument that Germany's devastating economic crisis had, directly or indirectly, triggered the series of political upsets that had destabilized Franco-German relations.[173] On returning from discussions in Berlin, Hoesch insisted during a meeting with Berthelot that there was no anti-French agenda in Germany and that 'developments

[167] Ibid., K240381–6, here 382–3. [168] Ibid., K240381–6, here 383.

[169] Ibid., K240381–6, quotes on 384.

[170] Ibid., K240381–6, here 384–6; regarding France–Italy see also: R70503 K40490–1, Deutsche Botschaft Paris. Signed Riesser, Paris, 14 Nov. 1930.

[171] AA R70502, Telegramm Nr. ??4 v. 18.10. Signed Rieth, Paris, 18 Oct. 1930.

[172] AA R70502 K240405–8, here 406–7, Telegramm Nr. 990 vom 23/10. Signed Hoesch, Paris, 23 Oct. 1930.

[173] See MAE Z761 7–17, 'La crise économique et financière . . . '. Unsigned, 1 Feb. 1930.

can principally be attributed to economic misery, which had engendered widespread and profound discontent regarding current conditions, this extending to all aspects of policy'.[174] The Ambassador went on to express regret that France had neither offered Germany bridging loans, accepted the payment of reparations in kind (which at least served to boost German business activity, whereas cash payments were a straightforward loss to the country's economy), nor provided long-term credits.[175] Berthelot replied that he and Briand were not unsympathetic on all these counts, but that domestic political considerations had prevented France from offering bridging finance on terms acceptable to Germany. As for payment in kind of reparations and long-term recapitalization of the German economy, it transpired that he was thinking on exactly the same lines as Hoesch and even produced and read from correspondence in which he had recently requested feedback from his economic advisers on an aid package for Germany. Discussions, he promised, would continue, adding that the successful relaunch of Brüning's government had reassured French politicians.[176] A subsequent meeting between Hoesch and Briand revisited the same issues (the Saarland excepted!) and brought the same French reassurances.[177] Nazism, Briand observed, was comparable to the populist Boulangist movement that had swept France during the late 1880s,[178] briefly threatening to topple the Third Republic, before proving to be an ephemeral force.

A catastrophic mining disaster, claiming 271 lives, in the town of Alsdorf on 21 October, provided the occasion for further talks, this time between Pierre de Margerie and President Hindenburg. The French Ambassador passed on condolences from the French President, Gaston Doumergue, while Hindenburg expressed particular gratitude for the assistance France had provided during mine rescue operations.[179] De Margerie went on to praise Brüning's efforts to rebalance German public finances, efforts Hindenburg supported unreservedly, but with the proviso that: 'If it nonetheless proves impossible to maintain the existing rate of reparations repayments, then [Germany] will have to petition the creditor powers for amelioration or alteration of our obligations.'[180] Just as Berthelot had responded positively to Hoesch's appeals for economic assistance, so de Margerie proved supportive, assuring Hindenburg that: 'In that case, if in spite of the budgetary savings and cuts, it transpires that fulfilment of the reparations obligations is impossible, then no one would question Germany's right to reopen negotiations, and [France] would participate in these talks with goodwill.'[181] During a trip to

[174] AA R70502 K240405–8, quote on 405–6, Telegramm Nr. 990 vom 23/10. Signed Hoesch, Paris, 23 Oct. 1930.

[175] Ibid. [176] Ibid.

[177] AA R70503 K240438–40, Telegramm Nr. 1034 vom 10/11. Signed Hoesch, Paris, 10 Nov. 1930.

[178] Ibid.

[179] AA R70502 K240410–12, Aufzeichnung, stamped II Fr 2975. Signed Büro des Reichpräsidenten, Berlin, 28 Oct. 1930.

[180] Ibid., here 411. [181] Ibid.

Switzerland Tardieu's Permanent Secretary, Henry Moysset, also went out of his way to reassure German listeners that he appreciated the scale of the economic and social catastrophe that had gripped the country, and understood that the Reichstag election result was primarily attributable to this domestic crisis. But as long as Brüning remained in office, Moysset insisted, he could count on Tardieu's support, subject to German politicians and public opinion displaying the necessary moderation and realism. Yet again, French financial support for an 'impoverished Germany' was perceived as central to any long-term resolution of outstanding issues in Franco-German relations. This extended to invoking the name of a former Prime Minister, Joseph Caillaux. Caillaux's administration had pursued a conciliatory policy towards Germany during the 1911 second Moroccan Crisis, which focused on collaborative business and financial relations,[182] while during the First World War Caillaux came to advocate a compromise peace with Germany. Accused of defeatism and subsequently tried for high treason, he was convicted, imprisoned, and thereafter exiled from France for five years. Yet, Moysset insisted, he was now a changed man, working hand-in-glove with Tardieu:

> No one is better suited than Caillaux to understand correctly the economic and financial tasks that fall to Germany and France. As a prosperous, indeed wealthy country, a country with a huge empire, France will be well placed to assist a Germany that acts in good faith. True, we did not participate in the last bridging credit for Germany, but in the near future will still have the opportunity to offer support and assistance.[183]

In the event, Caillaux remained outside government, but was an active contributor to debates in the press.[184] And his name and bona fides were again to be invoked during the summer of 1931 as efforts to forge an economic entente between Germany and France seemed finally to be bearing fruit.[185]

None of this, however, was palatable to the French right. Stormy debates followed during mid-November in the French Chamber of Deputies,[186] but Briand successfully defended his commitment to rapprochement with Germany. He convinced many when arguing that German domestic politics had been soured by unprecedented economic misery and that Berlin had every right under the circumstances to request a more moderate reparations payment schedule. 'The Minister', Hoesch reported, 'met with applause from almost the entire Chamber,

[182] On collaboration, see Ch. 1 under 'The Opening Gambits', 10; see also Wilsberg, *Terrible ami*, chs. 3 and 4.

[183] AA R70502 K240418–21, quote on 421, Abschrift. Abtlg II Fr. Aufzeichnung durch H. Ges. Müller—Bern, undated, filed among late October 1930 documentation. Unsigned.

[184] See, for example, AA R70503 K240547–8, Deutsche Botschaft Paris, A 3884. Signed Hoesch, Paris, 22 Nov. 1930.

[185] See Ch. 4 under 'Hopeful Signs: The Prussian Plebiscite and Economic Detente', 107.

[186] AA R70503 K240482–7, Deutsche Botschaft Paris, A 3787, Inhalt: Aussenpolitische Debatte in der Kammer. Signed Hoesch, Paris, 14 Nov. 1930; R70503, Deutsch-Franzoesisches Studienkomitee, Berliner Bureau, Rundschreiben an die Herren Mitglieder der deutschen Gruppe Nr. 1. Betrifft: Die aussenpolitische Debatte in der franzoesischen Kammer im November 1930. Signed Dr Max Clauss, 21 Nov. 1930, and appended annex.

with the exception of the Communists and extreme right',[187] although an ensuing vote of confidence delivered a narrower government majority of 323 to 270.[188] For one thing, even deputies who favoured rapprochement with Germany often rejected any revision of the peace treaties in Germany's favour, at least in the short term; for another, Briand's foreign policy continued to be supported most strongly on the political left, whereas Tardieu depended on considerable support from the (anti-rapprochement) right to remain in office.[189]

Tardieu's own contribution to the Chamber debate therefore consisted largely of an attack on treaty revision, with less said on rapprochement.[190] French concerns were reinforced when Curtius subsequently, and possibly in response to Tardieu,[191] used a Reichstag debate to placate the nationalist gallery. He placed revisionism, however cautious and measured his language, at the centre of Germany's foreign policy agenda,[192] which divided even pro-rapprochement French commentators. Caillaux took space in the Catholic newspaper, *L'Ere nouvelle*, to argue that while Germany's desire for treaty revision was perfectly understandable, overt revisionism was a dangerous force best avoided. 'Europe's salvation', he continued, 'should be sought by effecting economic cooperation.' The Radical deputy, Pierre Cot, was more critical of Tardieu's rejection of treaty revision through the use of Article 19, continuing in the Belgian liberal newspaper, *Le Soir*, that: 'We should not deprive nations who are struggling for peaceful revision of any prospect of a peaceful realization of frontier amendment.'[193] Similarly the senior Socialist politician and future Prime Minister, Leon Blum, wrote in *Populaire* that: 'We can only insist on Germany upholding the disarmament provisions if France also meets the obligation to disarm, adopted *de facto* at least in the Treaty of Versailles.'[194]

Tardieu, however, was altogether less happy with Curtius, for he had hoped 'to calm a very agitated Chamber by deploying facts and certainly had no wish to open any discussion with Germany'.[195] But now he felt obliged to refute Curtius' speech in a forthcoming Senate debate.[196] This all transpired during a meeting with Kurt, Baron von Lersner, who had played a leading role in the Paris peace

[187] AA R70503 K240447–8, quote on 448, Telegramm Nr. 1043 v. 13/11. Signed Hoesch, Paris, 13 Nov. 1930; see also R70503 K240482–7, here 486, Deutsche Botschaft Paris, A 3787, Inhalt: Aussenpolitische Debatte in der Kammer. Signed Hoesch, Paris, 14 Nov. 1930.

[188] AA R70503 K240482, Deutsche Botschaft Paris, A 3787, Inhalt: Aussenpolitische debate in der Kammer. Signed Hoesch, Paris, 14 Nov. 1930.

[189] See also AA R70503, Deutsch-Franzoesisches Studienkomitee, Berliner Bureau, Rundschreiben an die Herren Mitglieder der deutschen Gruppe. Signed Dr Max Clauss, Berlin, 21 Nov. 1930.

[190] Ibid., annex Tardieu, 1–9.

[191] AA R70504 K240555–6, Telegramm Nr. 1074 v. 23.11. Signed Hoesch, Paris, 23 Nov. 1930.

[192] See, for example, AA R70503, Telegramm Nr. 1076. Auswärtig Berlin. Im Anschluβ an Nr. 1072. Signed Hoesch, Paris, 22 Nov. 1930; R70503 K240541–5, Telegramm Nr. 1075 v. 22.11. Signed Hoesch, Paris, 22 Nov. 1930.

[193] AA R70503 K240547–8, Deutsche Botschaft Paris, A 3884. Signed Hoesch, Paris, 22 Nov. 1930.

[194] AA R70504 K240557, Deutsche Botschaft Paris, A 3895. Signed Rieth, Paris, 24 Nov. 1930.

[195] AA R70504 K240555–6, Telegramm Nr. 1074 v. 23.11. Signed Hoesch, Paris, 23 Nov. 1930.

[196] Ibid.

negotiations and now, during 'particularly amicable' discussions, persuaded the French Prime Minister to avoid prejudicing relations further. Instead, Lersner suggested, he might use the same Senate debate to flag up prospects for economic collaboration and so reset the process of Franco-German rapprochement. Tardieu hesitated, for despite a personal commitment to rapprochement, Lersner believed that he felt politically exposed in his own parliament. Eventually, however, Tardieu promised to accord economic cooperation 'serious consideration' when drafting his Senate speech.[197]

Parliamentary politics aside, Hoesch hoped that a planned joint meeting in Paris of the French and German sections of the Mayrisch Committee might improve the general diplomatic climate. Equally a forthcoming visit to Berlin by Yves Le Trocquer, in his capacity as convener of the French Parliamentary Committee for the Study of Franco-German Relations, to meet with his German counterpart, Joseph Wirth, offered to smooth over recent troubles.[198] And meanwhile de Margerie reassured Bülow that Brüning's government enjoyed 'the full confidence not only of all influential circles in France, but of Tardieu himself'. Even if Brüning's administration made heavy-handed use of its emergency powers, this 'was strongly preferable', de Margerie continued, 'to anything one might label as a Hitler dictatorship'.[199] Thus when all was said and done, both France and Germany remained committed at the highest level to the pursuit of rapprochement, but each country's domestic political circumstances, compounded in Germany by a devastating economic crisis and an unfortunate election result, repeatedly and seriously compromised these efforts. There was broad agreement that economic cooperation, founded on the complementary strengths of the two economies, offered a practical route to rapprochement, which skirted around the more intractable legacies of the recent war. Both countries envisaged this process advancing within the context of European integration, even union, and as we shall see, political Catholicism in particular provided this integration, organized around a Franco-German axis, with a significant measure of ideological legitimization. And for a few brief months in late 1931, it would appear that the hour of reconciliation had, indeed, come.[200]

Furthermore, despite the potholes of domestic crisis that peppered this challenging road to an enduring European settlement, the Wilhelmstraße, not for the first or last time, could seek solace in the striking range and volume of grassroots fraternization between citizens of these former enemies. A survey of developments during 1929 and 1930 revealed a mutual fascination in the life and culture of France and Germany respectively, with Germans displaying a particular interest in the French visual arts, and German artistic organizations seeking to forge links with their French counterparts. In France former prejudice against German cultural

197 Ibid.

198 AA R70503 K240541–5, here 545, Telegramm, Nr. 1075 v. 22.11. Signed Hoesch, Paris, 22 Nov. 1930.

199 AA R70504 K240563, 'Zum Schluß seines heutigen Besuches . . .'. Signed Bülow, Berlin, 1 Dec. 1930.

200 See Ch. 5 under 'A Successful Conference', 125–9 and 'Creating the Commission', 131.

achievement was evaporating, even if French artists continued to regard themselves as the bearers of an exceptional cultural mission and were slower to cultivate cross-border links. This, however, could not obscure growing mutual respect and recognition in France of German artistic and literary achievement. Academic exchanges at all levels exceeded pre-war volumes and if more German students and schoolchildren visited France than vice versa, the Germans almost always met with a hospitable, warm reception, while senior French and German academics were increasingly likely to collaborate at international congresses. Institutional frameworks had been established to promote exchanges, for example between the Akademischer Austauschdienst and the Office national des universités et écoles françaises, and were working well. Among the more prominent cultural exchanges had been the mounting of an exhibition in Paris by the Deutsche Werkbund (Bauhaus) on the invitation of its French counterpart, the Société des artistes décorateurs, with a summary of French press coverage reading that:

> The lightness, indeed elegance of the German work contrasted with the hitherto received wisdom of 'German heaviness'... This event allows the German nation's spiritual disposition to appear in a completely new light, one that the French nation can only find attractive.[201]

The same held for classical music, with German conductors, orchestras, and soloists being warmly received in France, whilst German audiences sought out French opera, and Bizet's *Carmen*, in particular. French plays had already enjoyed years of success in Germany, but the coming winter season also saw a dozen German plays scheduled by Parisian theatres. The experiences of the film and sporting world told a similar story.[202] For all the challenges domestic politics might have created for Franco-German rapprochement, there was this other story to tell, of high culture, schools, and sport adding to the political constituency (generally on the centre and centre-left) that sought finally to bury the hatchet between the two neighbours.

[201] AA R70502 K240398–402, quote on 401, Po 2 Frankr. Unsigned, undated, filed with mid-October 1930 documentation.

[202] Ibid.

4

From Paris to Berlin

Official Visits and the Origins of the Franco-German Commission

ENDURING TENSIONS AND THE AUSTRO-GERMAN CUSTOMS UNION

Franco-German relations continued their roller-coaster ride into 1931. If positive German engagement with the Briand Plan had served to mend fences during the latter half of 1930, the scars left on French opinion by the Rhineland evacuation had not entirely healed. In France the nationalist press was not alone in fearing that the activities of the Stahlhelm war veterans and other German paramilitary leagues represented serious preparations for war, leading Kurt Rieth, First Secretary in the German Embassy in Paris, to warn that: 'Fears of an imminent war are not confined to the general population; for some months now the same concern has been aired in sections of the press and in political circles.'[1] Weeks later Hoesch reported that he detected in Briand's tone 'for the first time somewhat less warmth and somewhat less trust'.[2] To a degree he was preaching to the converted. His colleagues in Berlin were well briefed on the stormy debates in the French National Assembly, where right-wing and some centrist deputies dismissed Briand's rapprochement policy as illusory, if not deluded.[3] Again and again, the Radical Socialist deputy, Henry Franklin-Bouillon, pressed Briand on the most sensitive aspects of interwar diplomacy, notably the disarmament question,[4] and if France's Foreign Minister 'dared to work with determination for disarmament and peace',

[1] AA R70504, Abschrift II Fr. 3520, Deutsche Botschaft Paris A. 4140. Signed Rieth, Paris, 23 Dec. 1930, 1; see R70502 K240393, Telegramm, Nr. 84 vom 11/10. Signed Adolf Müller, Bern, 11 Oct. 1930, for discussion of related Swiss fears.

[2] AA R70504 K240571–3, quote on 572, Telegramm, Nr. 53 v. 13.1.31. Signed Hoesch, Paris, 13 Jan. 1931.

[3] See, for example, AA R70503 K240482 7, Deutsche Botschaft Paris, A 3787, Inhalt: Aussenpolitische Debatte in der Kammer. Signed Hoesch, Paris, 14 Nov. 1930; R70503, Deutsch-Franzoesisches Studienkomitee, Berliner Bureau, Rundschreiben an die Herren Mitglieder der deutschen Gruppe. Signed Dr Max Clauss, Berlin, 21 Nov. 1930, here appendix, Aussenpolitische Debatte in der franzoesischen Kammer.

[4] AA R70503, Deutsch-Franzoesiches Studienkomitee Berliner Bureau, Rundschreiben an die Herren Mitglieder der deutschen Gruppe. Signed Dr Max Clauss, Berlin, 21 Nov. 1930, appendix, Die Abgeordneten, 1, 10; R70504, Telegramm Nr. 230. Signed Hoesch, Paris, 3 Mar. 1931.

he was doing so, Berlin understood, even 'as Stahlhelm and Hitler fanfares were increasingly in evidence on the German side'.[5]

The Head of Section II (the Western Desk) at the Wilhelmstraβe, Gerhard Köpke, was particularly sensitive to the impact of the Stahlhelm's bombastic rallies on French opinion. He struggled to curtail distribution of a film celebrating the notorious 1930 Cologne rally, held to mark the final Allied evacuation of the Rhineland, 'which will certainly further damage our currently strained relations with France'.[6] However, with nationalist politicians breathing down their necks, Köpke's superiors were inclined to bend to domestic pressure and clear the film for general release. It took a robust discussion with the Foreign Minister, Julius Curtius, before Köpke finally succeeded in having viewings restricted to private (Stahlhelm) audiences. Appealing for balance in public policy, he reminded the Minister that any toleration of the film would sit uneasily with the recent banning of the pacifist feature film, *All Quiet on the Western Front*,[7] following Nazi protests.[8]

Curtius, however, was struggling to build on Stresemann's legacy at a time when the German Nationalists (DNVP) and a greatly strengthened NSDAP continued to denounce the Republic and the new Foreign Minister personally for operating within the parameters of the 1919 peace settlement. Whatever his own political preferences he had to juggle the pursuit of constructive diplomacy with the appeasement in parliament of this vociferous right-wing gallery. Even under Stresemann, Weimar's foreign policy had been consistently revisionist, but had successfully balanced measured accommodation with the West against ambitions for peaceful border revision and eventual unification (*Anschluβ*) with Austria in the East. However, the cooling of Franco-German relations from late 1930 coincided with increasingly strident complaints by Berlin to the League of Nations over treatment of the (shrinking) German minority in western Poland. The Permanent Secretary at the Foreign Office, Bernhard von Bülow, and other senior officials also elaborated plans to increase German influence in South-Eastern Europe.[9] Although these schemes remained on the back burner,[10] it did not escape the notice of French politicians and diplomats that Berlin hoped to achieve an eventual revision of the peace settlement through the League, whereas they perceived the latter as a guarantor of the status quo.[11] The hostile French reaction to a major foreign policy speech by Curtius during February, in which he again played to the nationalist gallery, was typical in this regard, leading Hoesch to warn that 'reaction to the speech provides additional proof, if this were even needed, that our policy goals, as expressed, are completely unpalatable to the [French] public'. He conceded that

[5] AA R70504, Frankreich und England. Unsigned, Berlin, March 1931, 3.

[6] AA R70504, Aufzeichnung. Signed Köpke, Berlin, 13 Dec. 1930, 2. [7] Ibid.

[8] Elke Fröhlich, 'Joseph Goebbels: The Propagandist', in Ronald Smelser and Rainer Zitelmann (eds.), *The Nazi Elite*, trans. Mary Fischer (Basingstoke & London, 1993), 54.

[9] Kaiser, *Economic Diplomacy*, 27.

[10] Herbert Hömig, *Brüning. Kanzler in der Krise der Republik. Eine Weimarer Biographie* (Paderborn, 2000), 305.

[11] See, for example, Jeannesson, 'Jacques Seydoux', 141.

left-wing and centrist newspapers understood and regretted that Curtius had had 'to pander to German nationalist forces', but the resulting torrent of demands had obscured the Foreign Minister's simultaneous 'commitment to European cooperation and the need for Franco-German rapprochement'.[12]

Briand reminded French parliamentarians that Curtius, like any politician, had always to operate within the bounds of domestic political opinion: 'When in Geneva, M. Curtius, is, like me, obliged to bear in mind the reception awaiting him when he returns home.'[13] None of that, however, made the French Minister's own task any easier, leading him to implore Hoesch that 'when it came to eastern affairs, he would advise against constantly tabling demands that cannot currently be met'. Bargains, he continued, could surely be struck on Upper Silesia and the Polish Corridor if only 'Germany were to display skill and patience', adding that he had already urged the Polish Foreign Minister, August Zaleski, to seek an understanding with Germany.[14]

However, on 19 March 1931 Curtius announced that agreement had been reached between Berlin and Vienna for an Austro-German customs union. His démarche, which posed an obvious strategic threat to France's allies in East-Central Europe, played badly in Paris. Briand was beside himself with fury, while the Economics Minister, André François-Poncet, drew up a counter-strategy (the Plan constructif), presented at the League of Nations in May, which, in essence, offered conditional French financial support to Central and South-East European countries 'based on a universal desire for peace . . . linking economic imperatives definitively to political imperatives'.[15] In other words beneficiaries would need to accept unconditionally the provisions of the post-war peace settlement. Curtius, it is argued, had focused on the 'legality' of his initiative at the cost of its political impact, in a superfluous and ultimately futile test of Germany's room for manoeuvre.[16] His move was all the more curious given that he had envisaged establishing a system of agricultural customs preferences in South-Eastern Europe 'hand in hand' with France, a tactic that recognized French interest in developing a joint Franco-German strategy in the region and which did resurface in François-Poncet's Plan constructif.[17]

The deeper reasons for his Austrian initiative therefore remain a matter for debate. Stresemann had earlier mooted such a union before adjudging it inopportune,[18] yet serious discussions did begin in February 1930, when a Social Democrat, Hermann Müller, was still German Chancellor. Although Hoesch warned the Wilhelmstraβe on 17 March 1931 that 'there is no prospect of successful

[12] AA R70504, Telegramm Nr. 176 v. 12/2. Signed Hoesch, Paris, 12 Feb. 1931, 2. See also Arnold Wolfers, *Britain and France between Two Wars: Conflicting Strategies of Peace since Versailles* (New York, 1940), 64–5, 66.

[13] AA R70504, Telegramm Nr. 230, Kzl. Nr. 307. Signed Hoesch, Paris, 4 Mar. 1931, 4.

[14] AA R70504 K240631–3, quotes on 632–3, Telegramm Nr. 257 v. 12/3. Signed Hoesch, Paris, 12 Mar. 1931.

[15] Quoted in Knipping, *Deutschland, Frankreich*, 217.

[16] Rödder, *Stresemanns Erbe*, 222.

[17] Ibid., 222–6; Schirmann, *Crise*, 152–3.

[18] Kaiser, *Economic Diplomacy*, 27.

negotiations with France [regarding the *Anschluß*]',[19] Curtius persevered in the belief that a customs union, at least, would not violate existing international agreements.[20] But at the end of the day it seems that his foreign policy coup was intended primarily to address the deteriorating domestic political climate. He had always lacked Stresemann's charisma and presentational surefootedness, leading Sir Horace Rumbold, the British Ambassador at Berlin, to observe even before the September 1930 Reichstag elections that: 'Dr Curtius has, indeed, not for a moment lost his poise, and he is also possessed of the "courage of patience", but the trouble is that he cannot make himself interesting enough, and at the moment he is being overlooked.'[21] The Austrian adventure, his biographer Andreas Rödder concludes, amounted to an ill-judged effort to 'make himself interesting', only to do so in a manner he had not bargained for.[22] Heinrich Brüning disowned both the scheme and his Foreign Minister, while Bülow and his colleagues at the Wilhelmstraβe sought to repair fences with France. Badly wounded and censured in parliament, Curtius eventually resigned in early October shortly after the International Court at The Hague had ruled the customs union in breach of the peace settlement and subsequent accords—admittedly by the wafer-thin majority of seven votes to six.

However, by this time relations between Paris and Berlin had improved dramatically, culminating in the creation of a Franco-German Commission whose purpose was to bury the hatchet once and for all.[23] Jointly chaired by the Foreign Ministers of the two countries, its primary remit was to forge a customs and wider social and economic union between Germany and France. This projected union rested on the affirmation that, despite the traumatic experience and residual scars of recent conflict, deeper and essentially positive synergies either informed, or should henceforward inform, relations between the two countries.[24] Ambitions went further, for this Franco-German axis was envisaged as the first, indispensible, step on the road to a European union which would enable its founders finally to circumvent the more intractable dimensions of their complex bilateral relationship. This largely forgotten episode represented a tipping point in interwar European history, where success would have offered so much, but where ultimate failure served to reinforce the slide towards renewed war. However, the convoluted trail of events and initiatives that created this Commission demonstrates that this failure was tenaciously contested, even in the particularly inauspicious circumstances of the Great Depression. It is to the origins and course of this final battle for interwar Franco-German, and European, rapprochement that we shall now turn.

In March 1931, drawing on a lengthy report from Hoesch, Brüning observed that: 'Every German-French discussion concerning economic and financial issues concludes with the realization that, first of all, outstanding political issues need to be resolved. Every German-French discussion concerning political issues ends with

[19] AA R70504 K240628–9, quote on 629, zu II Fr. 786. Signed Brüning, 17 Mar. 1931.
[20] Hömig, *Brüning*, 292–6.
[21] Quoted in Rödder, *Stresemanns Erbe*, 84.
[22] Ibid., 84, 93.
[23] But cf. Wolfers, *Britain and France*, 66.
[24] For example Frank, 'Paradoxe', 180.

the realization that they are insoluble.' Nonetheless, after evaluating the key political flashpoints—reparations, the eastern frontier, disarmament, the Saarland question, the Anschluβ, and colonies—Hoesch had concluded that: 'If we maintain our established policy towards France, solutions will be found for all our demands. Although these will not satisfy our wishes in full, they will, even so, restore Germany as a free, emancipated, and powerful force in world affairs.'[25] In other words Franco-German rapprochement and the advancement of German national interests were seen as inherently complementary.

The Quai d'Orsay's reaction to the Austro-German customs union in the wake of Briand's initial fury also indicated that a more constructive Franco-German relationship was not beyond reach. In February Philippe Berthelot, Permanent Secretary at the French Foreign Office, had complained to Hoesch that agreement with London on economic matters was rendered next to impossible by British pride. 'Britain', Berthelot continued, 'was badly placed. The Empire was collapsing and domestically any confidence in future recovery was evaporating.' He gave Hoesch to understand that: 'Possible negotiations with Germany would in his view be much more significant', explaining that despite its current weakness, Germany would soon enough be a flourishing country with a population of 80 million [*sic*] whereas Britain would continue to decline.[26] Thereafter, in early March, Coudenhove-Kalergi suggested to a reasonably receptive Briand that the Austro-German customs plan might serve 'as a tactical device . . . to accomplish a regional customs union without Great Britain'.[27] French thoughts of harnessing German strength to the best advantage were of course nothing new, but during 1931 contributed decisively to efforts to reach a lasting accommodation.[28]

On 14 April Curtius proposed outlining the objectives of the Austro-German customs union to the League of Nations in Geneva, alongside workaday German proposals concerning the harmonization of petrol duty on international traffic.[29] The French response was low-key and essentially non-confrontational and as François-Poncet later observed, Austria's central European neighbours and Italy, rather than Paris, had been most strongly opposed.[30] French leaders were as irritated by Germany's modus operandi as by the substance of the customs union.[31] Briand still wished to face down the scheme and France continued to pressurize Austria into abandoning the proposed union, in part by exacerbating a

[25] AA R70504 K240628–9, zu II Fr. 786. Signed Brüning, Berlin, 17 Mar. 1931.

[26] AA R70504 K240603–5, here 603–4, Telegramm Nr. 205 vom 23/2. Signed Hoesch, Paris, 23 Feb. 1931; see also Schirmann, *Crise,* 131–3.

[27] Quoted in Bosco, 'British Foreign Office', 358.

[28] Cf. Wright, *Stresemann*, 518, who sees the customs union affair as 'abruptly ending French interest in assisting Germany'.

[29] MAE Y643 115–16, Société des Nations, Commission d'Étude pour l'Union Européenne. Note du Secrétaire Général, Geneva, 15 Apr. 1931. Traduction. Signed Curtius, Berlin, 14 Apr. 1931.

[30] AA Gegenseitige Besuche führender Staatsmänner (R70567–9), here R70568 H026184–91, Deutsche Botschaft Paris, Nr. 3420 A, Abschrift. Dr Kurt Ihlefeld. Pariser und Genfer Vertreter der Zeitungen des Verlages W. Girardet und des *Hannoverschen Kuriers*. Vertraulich. 2. Unterredung mit François-Poncet, Paris, 18 Sept. 1931. Here H026187.

[31] Ibid., H026186–7.

run during mid-1931 on the Austrian Schilling.[32] However, he simultaneously made a series of speeches advocating a European union built around Franco-German rapprochement.[33] Meanwhile, French diplomats in Geneva observed that the legality of the Austro-German accord had already been referred to The Hague by the British Foreign Secretary, Arthur Henderson, leaving further discussion on this score at the League redundant. Nonetheless, they advised: 'This [British] response, negative in character, demands quite logically a positive counterpart in the form of efforts to improve the economic organization of Europe.' Such a tactic would manoeuvre Germany into 'recasting its project on a larger and more European scale'.[34] Briand rehearsed comparable ideas in May in a memorandum to the Secretary General of the League, Sir Eric Drummond,[35] but so ambitious a scheme was for another day. In the meantime it was agreed to give Curtius the floor at an imminent meeting of the League subcommittee examining the Briand Plan, but only on day two and after the conclusion of formal business. Briand endorsed this strategy, which effectively sidelined the customs union crisis and minimized any prospect of open confrontation.[36]

BRÜNING IN PARIS

Furthermore, this disruption to Franco-German relations was a storm in a teacup when compared with Germany's wider economic and financial crisis.[37] On 5 June Brüning and Curtius arrived in Britain for talks in London and at Chequers on the budgetary and financial maelstrom that threatened to engulf Germany. British ministers heard Brüning out with a sympathetic ear and appreciated that he constituted the last line of defence against the radical right[38] but, with the Bank of England struggling to shore up the pound, were not in a position to offer decisive help. London looked to the United States for any such initiative[39] and the United States President, Herbert Hoover, with British encouragement,[40] announced on 20 June proposals for a year's moratorium for capital and interest payments on war

[32] For a wider discussion of the 1931 Austrian banking crisis, see Iago Gil Aguado, 'The Creditanstalt Crisis of 1931 and the Failure of the Austro-German Customs Union Project', *The Historical Journal*, 44, 1 (2001), 199–221.

[33] Gérard Unger, *Aristide Briand, le ferme conciliateur* (Paris, 2005), 576–85.

[34] MAE Y643 117–20, quotes on 117–18, Service Français, Société des nations, Note pour le Ministre, L'Union douanière austro-allemande devant la Commission européenne, 17 Apr. 1931.

[35] Elisha, *Aristide Briand*, 36–7.

[36] MAE Y643 159–60, Affaires Étrangères, Télégramme à l'Arrivée, No 2. Signed Massigli, Geneva, 11 May 1931; see also AA R70506 K240770, Deutsche Gesandtschaft, A. 25. Signed Dehn-Schmidt, Dublin, 12 Aug. 1931.

[37] MAE Z771 362–3, Ambassade de France à Berlin. L'Attaché Financier. Revue de Presse du 27 mai 1931, Berlin, 27 May 1931, 4–5, b) L'entrevue de Chequers et l'allègement des charges de reparations.

[38] Rödder, *Stresemanns Erbe*, 241–4.

[39] Schirmann, *Crise*, 132.

[40] MAE Z772 129–32, Ambassade de France à Berlin. L'Attaché Financier. Revue de Presse du 23 juin 1931, 1a, Berlin, 23 Jun. 1931.

debt, including German reparations. A conference was to be held in London in late July to flesh out the details.

Hoover's proposals, however, left Paris feeling isolated and particularly vulnerable, for 'what interested France', Sylvain Schirmann observes, perhaps rather harshly, 'was not the elimination of the crisis, but French hegemony'.[41] In addition, French sensitivities had been injured when, on 6 June, a German government decree echoed the vocabulary of the conservative newspaper, the *Deutsche Allgemeine Zeitung*, in describing reparations as 'tribute' payments. Heated diplomatic exchanges followed and soon enough degenerated into a pedantic row over whether reparations really had anything to do with 'repairs', whether the term was translatable into German, and whether French protests rested on the negative description of 'tribute' in the compact Larousse dictionary rather than the more neutral definition in the larger edition.[42] However, Hoover's initiative created more mundane budgetary problems for the French government, as the principal beneficiary of German reparations payments, and even the German nationalist press appreciated that the American President had touched on a raw nerve in Paris.[43] The French politician Pierre Viénot, who was particularly active in the cause of Franco-German reconciliation and European integration, nonetheless felt his countrymen were missing a trick. He regretted that France had not spontaneously accepted the moratorium for, he continued in a letter to the editor of *Europe nouvelle*, Louise Weiss: 'A fresh wave of optimism regarding a Franco-German entente has for some days been sweeping the Second Reich which, unfocused and desperate, is seeking to dedicate itself to a great cause.'[44] However, as the liberal *Frankfurter Zeitung* commented: 'At the end of the day no one can force France to cooperate if it does not wish to. It is to be hoped that German diplomacy does everything possible to establish contact with the French. Current negotiations between the Americans and French do not absolve Germany of its responsibility.'[45]

Equally, Paris needed to regain the initiative. The German press was already speculating that Franco-German negotiations would now follow on the Chequers meeting[46] and immediately before Hoover's announcement, the French diplomat, Oswald Hesnard, sounded out Berlin over the Chequers visit, adding 'that he had

[41] Schirmann, *Crise*, 133.

[42] AA R70505 K240675–7. Signed Bülow, Berlin, 9 Jun. 1931; R70505 K240681–2, Bemerkungen zum Schritt des französischen Botschafters betreffend die Bezeichnung der Reparationen als Tribute. Signed B, Berlin, 12 Jun. 1931; R70505 K240683–4, Sinn des Wortes Tribut. Unsigned, undated; R70505, Abschrift RM 708. Signed Curtius, Berlin, 20 Jun. 1931, 1–7.

[43] MAE Z772 116–22, here 119, Ambassade de France à Berlin. L'Attaché Financier. Revue de Presse du 24 juin 1931, II—Les reparations et la liquidation financière de la guerre, Berlin, 24 Jun. 1931.

[44] Quoted in Louise Weiss, *Mémoires d'une Européenne*, vol. II: *1919–1934*, 2nd edn (Paris, 1970), 306.

[45] MAE Z772 129–32, here 132, Ambassade de France à Berlin. L'Attaché Financier. Revue de Presse du 23 juin 1931, I—Les reparations et la liquidation financière de la guerre, Berlin, 23 Jun. 1931; see also Z772 53–6, here 55, Ambassade de France à Berlin. L'Attaché Financier. Revue de Presse du 11 juin 1931, IIb) La presse allemande et le discours de M. Briand, Berlin, 11 Jun. 1931.

[46] MAE Z772 53–6, Ambassade de France à Berlin. L'Attaché Financier. Revue de Presse du 11 juin 1931, IIb) La presse allemande et le discours de M. Briand, Berlin, 11 Jun. 1931.

heard it asked whether the two [German] gentlemen would now pay a visit to Paris'.[47] A delicate exchange followed over the etiquette of such an arrangement: 'We Germans only go where we are invited', but that 'the Chancellor and Foreign Minister would accept an invitation to Paris as enthusiastically as they had the extremely kind invitation to Chequers'.[48] Some colourful amateur diplomacy followed, involving French- and German-Jewish diamond merchants and the Convener of the Zionist Association in France, Senator Godard, before Hoesch took a grip on the situation and began to prepare the ground for an official German visit.[49]

On 23 June Brüning broadcast to the German nation, in terms that echoed his public response in August 1930 to the Briand Plan. At that time he had praised Stresemann and Briand in equal measure and declared that a form of European union founded on economic integration was indispensable to the future of Germany and the wider continent.[50] Now he went further, dedicating a good part of his broadcast to Franco-German relations, and insisting that despite 'certain difficulties and obstacles . . . with mutual goodwill ways and means could be found to emphasize areas of agreement and common interest'. In order to secure Europe's future and cement positive economic relations with the United States it was necessary that: 'Our two great peoples . . . overcome the moral burden of the past and turn to face the spiritual, economic, and political future together.'[51]

Much of the resulting comment in the German press was favourable. It was widely reported that: 'Franco-German entente would address in full the wishes of the American and British governments, which have not neglected to make their views known to their German counterparts.'[52] Only extreme right-wing commentators condemned Brüning's initiative as 'entirely inopportune'; the consensus within the mainstream press was that they 'were witnessing an "historic gesture" destined to restore vital contact with French politics, provided [Paris] took up this opportunity to improve relations between the two countries'.[53] French press reaction varied. *Le Journal*, a conservative newspaper, welcomed the broadcast 'as the most important announcement by a German statesman since the day on which Stresemann moved to end the "Battle of the Ruhr"', and over the following days left-wing papers, such as *République*, *Populaire*, and *La Victoire*, heaped praise on

[47] AA R70567 H025863, V. L. R. Reinebeck, G.A., 'Heute suchte mich . . .'. Signed Reinebeck, Berlin, 19 Jun. 1931.

[48] Ibid.

[49] AA R70567 H025864–7, R.M., St.S., Reichskanzlei, Aufzeichnung, stamped Auswärtiges Amt II Fr. 1927. Unsigned, Berlin, 23 Jun. 1931.

[50] AA R70502, zu II Fr 2169, 'Eine programmatische Rede des Reichskanzlers Dr Brüning', *Wolff's Telegraphisches Büro*, 81—Nr. 1590, Berlin, 9 Aug. 1930.

[51] AA R70567, 'Reichskanzler Dr. Brüning über die allgemeine politische Lage', *Wolff's Telegraphisches Büro*, 82—Nr. 1307, Berlin, 24 Jun. 1930.

[52] MAE Z772 116–20, here 118–20, Ambassade de France à Berlin. L'Attaché Financier. Revue de Presse du 24 juin 1931, II—Les reparations et la liquidation financière de la guerre, Berlin, 24 Jun. 1931.

[53] MAE Z772 123–6, here 124–6, Ambassade de France à Berlin. L'Attaché Financier. Revue de Presse du 25 juin 1931, II—Les reparations et la liquidation financière de la guerre, Berlin, 25 Jun. 1931.

Brüning. *Volonté* demanded that his 'highly conciliatory and sincere proposals be reciprocated without hestitation', but the right-wing *Echo de Paris* demanded to know 'what Germany wanted', warning that 'it was dangerous to let a man like Briand, who was so lacking in diplomatic culture and caution, sit at a table with Brüning'.[54]

The French government, led by Pierre Laval, did seek further reassurance from Berlin and on 6 July Brüning undertook not to exploit any suspension of reparations to raise expenditure on armaments.[55] Some members of the French Cabinet demanded more, but Hoesch and Laval agreed that preconditions for the visit itself were best avoided.[56] Brüning and Curtius arrived in the French capital on 18 July to a carefully staged welcome which saw hand-picked gendarmes inserted into a smallish crowd,[57] creating an atmosphere described by Hoesch as 'not unfriendly'.[58] There were a few whistles and counter-demonstrators from the right-wing Action française were in evidence,[59] but more insistent shouts of 'long live peace, long live Laval, long live France!' predominated before negotiations opened on conditions for a long-term French loan to Germany.[60] The German delegates had arrived in the immediate aftermath of a German budgetary crisis and banking collapse. Brüning had announced tax increases and cuts in welfare spending on 6 June and thereafter a run on the Darmstädter und Nationalbank (triggered by an Austrian banking crisis and a botched effort by the Darmstädter to speculate in wholesale wool prices) had spread through the commercial banking system. As lender of last resort, the National Bank (Reichsbank), which itself was desperately short of funds, became dangerously exposed. This triggered an international run on the currency (Reichsmark), forcing the National Bank to sell off its gold reserves to meet its obligations, but in vain. On 13 July, Germany's financial institutions were forced to close their doors, leaving French negotiators, with the ink barely dry on François-Poncet's Plan constructif, well placed to demand a high political and financial price for any loan.[61]

In fact it proved impossible to reach any agreement. Shortly before Brüning's visit French officials had offered the President of the German National Bank, Hans Luther, a ten-year loan of US$1 billion, but only on condition that Germany honour $4.8 billion of reparations over the same period and desist even from the limited naval shipbuilding programme permitted by the Versailles peace settlement. Laval now reiterated these terms and added fresh demands: that Germany forego for a decade any further revisionist efforts in Eastern Europe and exclude all paramilitary associations from the demilitarized Rhineland. Allied control of

[54] AA R70567 H025885–90, Ref. LS Graf Saurma, Betrifft: Das Echo der Reichskanzler—Rede vom 23.VI.31 in Frankreich. Aufzeichnung. Unsigned, undated, filed early July.

[55] Rödder, *Stresemanns Erbe*, 252.

[56] AA R70567 H025905–8, Telegramm Nr. 737 vom 8.7. Signed Hoesch, Paris, 8 Jul. 1931.

[57] Heinrich Brüning, *Memoiren 1918–1934* (Stuttgart, 1970), 327.

[58] AA R70567 H025922, Telegramm Kzl. Nr. 1132. Signed Fessler, Hoesch, Paris, 18 Jul. 1931.

[59] Brüning, *Memoiren*, 327–8.

[60] AA R70567 H025922, Telegramm Kzl. Nr. 1132. Signed Fessler, Hoesch, Paris, 18 Jul. 1931.

[61] See earlier comments in AA R70538 H020038–45, Aktennotiz über Eindrücke der Pariser Reise v. 12.–15. Febr. 31, undated. Sig. illeg., 7.

German customs and excise and a Franco-German non-aggression and arbitration pact were added to the list because, Laval explained, 'of events across the Rhine which France found profoundly disturbing'.[62]

Brüning had sought something very different, utilizing French credits to foster 'productive' Franco-German economic collaboration, for example in the French colonies. He had even dared hope that a shelving of reparations would underpin a lasting Franco-German entente. Laval countered that while he was personally disposed to deal generously with Germany, his Cabinet remained deeply divided and often sceptical, with the influential former Premier, André Tardieu, prominent among these sceptics.[63] The onerous conditions attached to any French loan, he continued, were the best deal available.[64] The former and future Prime Minister, Édouard Herriot, himself reasonably amenable to detente, added that the French government could not afford to repeal the reparations schedule before the elections due for spring 1932, since French public opinion would never endorse such a sacrifice.[65] Brüning felt he had little choice but to 'decline [the offer] politely, because he knew that were he to accept such a scheme it would be overturned by the Reichstag upon his return to Berlin',[66] adding that in any case: 'It has been precisely the surfeit of loans that has created our current difficulties.'[67]

Little if anything followed from talks that same evening in the United States' Paris Embassy between Brüning and a powerful American delegation consisting of Walter Evans Edge, US Ambassador at Paris; the Secretary of State, Henry L. Stimson; and the Secretary of the US Treasury, Andrew W. Mellon. Having persuaded the French to agree to the Hoover moratorium with some difficulty,[68] the Americans showed little sympathy for Germany's budgetary and financial crisis, instead insisting that Berlin fall in with French conditions regarding the moratorium without further ado.[69] The chill did however begin to dissipate on the second day of the visit, when during multilateral talks Mellon conceded that Germany's situation was far more serious than he had realized and Briand insisted that whatever the fate of any international loan to Berlin, Franco-German relations remained salvageable.[70] The resulting official communiqué of the visit, which was only agreed after some terse discussion between German and French officials, recorded that 'both sides recognized the importance of this meeting and emphasized that it marked the beginning of cooperation based on trust', economic and political, but without elaborating further.[71] However, if the general atmosphere had improved,[72] little of substance had been agreed and there was no agreed roadmap towards the rapprochement that both sides claimed to desire.

[62] Quoted in Schirmann, *Crise*, 166–7; see also Unger, *Aristide Briand*, 587–8.

[63] See, for example, AA R70506 K240792–4, Telegramm Nr. 46 vom 28.8. Signed Adolf Müller, Bern, 26 Aug. 1931.

[64] Brüning, *Memoiren*, 328–31.

[65] Ibid., 335–6.

[66] Quoted in Unger, *Aristide Briand*, 587–8.

[67] Quoted in Hömig, *Brüning*, 348.

[68] Rödder, *Stresemanns Erbe*, 252.

[69] Brüning, *Memoiren*, 332.

[70] Ibid., 334.

[71] Quoted in AA R70567 H025933–4, Anlage. Das Communique über die deutsch-französischen Verhandlungen. Unsigned, undated.

[72] AA R70506 K240770–2, Deutsche Gesandtschaft, A. 25. Signed Dehn-Schmidt, Dublin, 12 Aug. 1931.

Under the circumstances it might appear surprising that as the German and French delegations prepared to leave Paris for the scheduled London conference, relations warmed perceptibly. Laval insisted that Brüning and Curtius travel in the French ministerial carriage on the train from Paris to the Channel. During the journey Brüning engaged in discussions first with Laval and Briand and then with the French Minister for the Budget François Piétri, and Finance Minister Pierre-Étienne Flandin. Piétri at least came to appreciate the profound and intractable budgetary challenges confronting Germany. As the train passed through the Eure Valley the French and German leaders were moved by its beauty to ponder the importance of Europe's intimate landscapes for the survival of its peoples, despite all the catastrophes of the past millennium. But Briand appeared haunted by more immediate threats: 'I am afraid', he mused, 'of the peoples of the steppes and prairies, and I fear seeing them crush our poor, ancient Europe between themselves.'[73] Cultural fear and material awe of America,[74] alongside fear of Bolshevism, were indeed relatively widespread in France at the time. Whatever the hindrances, rapprochement with Germany seemed to Briand to offer France and Europe a degree of longer-term security.[75]

THE CATHOLIC CONNECTION

Briand was a member of the secular political majority in the Third Republic's parliament, but appreciated the increasingly intimate relations between the Roman Catholic communities on either side of the Rhine and Brüning's part in this.[76] As we saw earlier, these had begun to improve in the wake of the Ruhr Crisis and the Catholic intellectual and politician, Marc Sangnier, continued during the early 1930s to promote reconciliation between French and German youth in particular.[77] He did so with official blessing as well as support from the Church and it was no secret that during the early 1930s the French Ambassador at the Vatican perceived the values common to European Catholics as a potential bridge between France and Germany. The Archbishop of Paris also promoted Franco-German detente,[78] and a meeting with Brüning in 1931 convinced the Pope that the German Chancellor was a partisan of international reconciliation and a bulwark against Nazism.[79] It was appreciated that Brüning's ethical brand of internationalism went back to his student days, which had seen him undertake a study visit to Paris before the Great War, and exchange views with Robert Schuman.[80] And his

[73] Quoted in Brüning, *Memoiren*, 336.
[74] For example, Georges Duhamel, *America the Menace: Scenes from the Life of the Future*, trans. Charles Miner Thompson (London, 1931), esp. 216–17.
[75] For example, AA R70506 K240770–2, Deutsche Gesandtschaft, A. 25. Signed Dehn-Schmidt, Dublin, 12 Aug. 1931.
[76] Brüning, *Frankreich und Heinrich Brüning*, 363; see also Barry, *Disarmament of Hatred*, *passim*.
[77] Barry, *Disarmament of Hatred*, 153–74.
[78] Brüning, *Frankreich und Heinrich Brüning*, 372–3.
[79] Ibid., 375. [80] Ibid., 361–2.

trade union background, in the Catholic wing of Germany's labour movement, served as a further token of his anti-Nazi credentials.[81] All of this reassured leading French politicians, including Édouard Daladier, Raymond Poincaré, and Éduourd Herriot, that Catholicism could help to secure reconciliation with Germany,[82] and for those on the centre-right of the political spectrum it was easier to identify with Brüning and the Centre Party than with 'Prussian and Protestant Germany',[83] of which Stresemann had been a part. In addition, whilst the various German Protestant-focused parties, from the DNVP, through the liberals to the SPD, had all suffered losses to extremist parties in the 1930 elections, support for the Catholic Centre and the BVP had held firm.

Upon arriving in Paris, Brüning's first meeting was with the leader of the French Popular Democratic Party, Auguste Champetier de Ribes, who served as Pensions Minister in Laval's government. The Popular Democrats were a young and relatively small party, speaking for the more forward-looking elements of French political Catholicism whose ideology anticipated that of post-1945 Christian Democracy. They sought to reconcile Catholicism and republicanism, transcend the left–right political divide in domestic politics, and also advocated Franco-German rapprochement as the continental cornerstone of a democratic and Christian counter to Bolshevism and Fascism. This stance marked an obvious break with wartime Catholicism in France which had sought reintegration within the nation. Placing loyalty to France above that to Rome, the Church had at that time promoted a peace delivered through a God-given French victory.[84] A minority, however, had held true to the principle of Christian universalism[85] and now, during a parliamentary debate on foreign policy, the Popular Democratic deputy, Ernest Pezet, argued that French security required a moral dimension founded on a patient and intelligent search for detente with Germany. 'The Franco-German question', he continued, 'is, whether one likes it or not, at the heart of any peaceful European order, economic or political.'[86] Their ideology therefore left the Popular Democrats well placed to serve as a lightning rod between the French political community and the German Centre Party with its pivotal role in Weimar government. Brüning's attendance the next day at Sunday mass alongside Champetier de Ribes and Popular Democratic members of parliament in Notre Dame des Victoires was, therefore, a highly significant political and moral gesture. 'My participation in this mass', Brüning later recounted, 'gave rise to unspeakable defamation from within German nationalist circles',[87] but on balance the visit was well received by public opinion.[88] Optimism was reinforced by the concurrent success of a major

[81] Ibid., 364–6, 376. [82] Ibid., 373. [83] Ibid., 366–7.

[84] Claudia Schlager, *Kult und Krieg. Herz Jesu—Sacré Coeur—Christus Rex im deutsch-französischen Vergleich 1914–1925* (Tübingen, 2011), 44, 139–201.

[85] Ibid., 44; Barry, *Disarmament of Hatred*, chs. 2–4.

[86] AA R7050, Deutsch-Franzoesisches Studienkomitee, Berliner Bureau, Rundschreiben . . . Nr. 1. Betrifft: Die aussenpolitische Debatte in der franzoesischen Kammer im November 1930. Signed Dr Max Clauss, Berlin, 21 Nov. 1930; Die Abgeordneten, 3) Ernest Pezet, 2–8, quote on 2.

[87] Brüning, *Memoiren*, 333. [88] Hömig, *Brüning*, 346–9.

Franco-German youth congress in Rethel in the Ardennes, a scene of major battles during the Great War.[89]

The Quai d'Orsay was particularly interested in the Catholic dimension of Franco-German relations. Despite tentative contacts between Brüning's government and the NSDAP, the French Ambassador at Berlin, Pierre de Margerie, spoke for many of his colleagues when asserting that, 'German Catholicism and the National Socialist movement are completely incompatible.'[90] And if doubts were sometimes expressed in France over certain details of Brüning's policies, his moral integrity was seldom in question.[91] Brüning aside, an increasingly dense network of exchanges between French and German Catholics accompanied and reinforced the wider improvement in Franco-German relations from the mid-1920s. Of Centre Party grandees, the mayor of Cologne, Konrad Adenauer, was highly regarded in French diplomatic circles. He had welcomed Édouard Herriot to the Rhenish city in 1928 and in early 1929, during an International Press Exhibition hosted in Cologne to mark the tenth anniversary of the League of Nations, he had made the French Deputy Convener of the Exhibition particularly welcome. Together with the local French Consul, Adenauer also elaborated plans to promote tourism within cities of the wider Rhine–Rhône region: Lyon, Geneva, Strasbourg, Cologne, and Antwerp. A visit by the mayor to Paris and to Herriot's political base in Lyon was proposed to seal the deal, with the Consul advising Briand that Cologne deserved its place in this putative transnational network: 'Its history, monuments, geographical position and rail links, the Rhine, its industry and the drive of a mayor who is arguably the best in Germany, all would contribute in an era of rapprochement to Cologne becoming one of the largest and most beautiful cities of Europe.'[92]

Adenauer's stance on Franco-German rapprochement did however differ from that of the Centre Party's new chairman, Ludwig Kaas. A noted academic and theologian, Kaas had joined the Centre Party in 1919 and sat in the Reichstag throughout the Weimar era, becoming party chairman in 1928. He was a staunch Rhinelander, but also a German patriot who had opposed the post-war Rhenish separatist movement. Backed by France, these separatists had launched an armed but unsuccessful insurrection during the autumn of 1923.[93] Nonetheless, Kaas spoke out for Franco-German reconciliation shortly after the failed rising and thereafter was a consistent supporter of Stresemann's and then Brüning's policy of rapprochement with France. However, when it came to particular points of contention, notably the terms of the 1929 reparations settlement and the resolution of the Saarland's status, he took a harder line than most of his Centre Party colleagues. He also shared a more general sympathy within the Centre Party for the powerful Alsatian autonomist movement. The French press reacted negatively to speeches 'whose tone was regarded as somewhat too strident and in the current

89 Unger, *Aristide Briand*, 588.
90 Brüning, *Frankreich und Heinrich Brüning*, 374.
91 Ibid., 374–5.
92 MAE Z603 2–3, quote on 3, Consulat de France à Cologne & Mayence, Direction des Affaires Politiques et Commerciales. Signed A. Laffon, Cologne, 18 Feb. 1929.
93 See Ch. 1 under 'The Opening Gambits', 20.

circumstances [January 1931] perhaps not especially opportune'.[94] The French Foreign Office therefore already tended to view him as a threat to detente and to the Centre Party's bona fides when it came to foreign relations.[95]

This judgement was overly harsh, for Kaas did nothing to undermine the increasingly positive relationship between French and German Catholics. In July 1928 an exchange of political views in Paris was deemed successful, and was followed by reciprocal discussions in Berlin, organized by the Centre Party, during December 1929.[96] Prominent among the French delegates were Auguste Champetier de Ribes and Adéodat Boissard, the former Convener of a Catholic think tank, the Semaines Sociales de France, which had initiated the 1928 Paris meeting.[97] The Semaines Sociales dedicated a good part of their interwar agenda to the issues of democracy and peace (and thus Franco-German relations), whilst Champetier de Ribes was no stranger to Germany. He had visited Bavaria and also Austria in 1928, securing an audience with the Bavarian Minister President, Heinrich Held, through the resident French Ambassador. 'The tone of the meeting', the Ambassador reported, 'was more than courteous, and the Minister President displayed a warmth towards the French Deputy... befitting [a member] of a [French] party which undoubtedly displays close affinities with the Centre Party and the Social Christians of Germany and Austria.'[98] During August and September 1929 the French University Catholic Mission spent over a month touring Germany, holding a series of successful conferences that covered subjects ranging from French cultural and social life to Franco-German economic collaboration.[99] French delegates were also warmly welcomed in September at the annual gathering of the German Catholic Congress (Katholikentag) in Freiburg-im-Breisgau, a success which encouraged the Quai d'Orsay to underwrite French participation in ensuing German Catholic events.[100]

Although French diplomats continued to fret over Kaas,[101] there is nothing to suggest that the large contingent of French Catholics bound for Berlin in December 1929 anticipated difficulties on the eve of their journey. The banker and former Prime Minister, Frédéric François-Marsal, stressed in an interview with the

[94] AA R70538 H019869–70, Deutsche Botschaft A 40?. Signed Hoesch, Paris, 31 Jan. 1931; see also R70504, 'Pariser Nervosität. Phantasien über das Kaas-Vorwort', *Berliner Börsen-Courier*, 604, 29 Dec. 1930.

[95] MAE Z602 20, République Française, Ministère des Affaires Étrangères. Direction des Affaires politiques et commerciales. Note pour le Cabinet du Ministre, Paris, 14 Oct. 1929.

[96] Ibid.; AA R70534 H019246–8, Auswärtiges Amt, II Fr. 2961, Aufzeichnung. Tagung deutscher und französischer Katholiken. Signed Ow-Wachendorf, Berlin, 13 Sept. 1929.

[97] AA R70534 H019246, Auswärtiges Amt, II Fr. 2961, Aufzeichnung. Tagung deutscher und französischer Katholiken. Signed Ow-Wachendorf, Berlin, 13 Sept. 1929.

[98] MAE Z 602 18, Légation de la République Française en Bavière, Direction des Affaires Politiques et Commerciales, Europe, No 31. Passage à Munich de M. Champetier de Ribes, Deputé. Signed André d'Ormesson, Munich, 28 Feb. 1928. Bavaria, though an integral part of the German Federation, received an ambassador from France, this anomaly being tolerated by Berlin.

[99] MAE Z602 7 and preceding page, Voyage en Allemagne de la Mission Catholique Universitaire (Août–Septembre 29)... Unsigned, Paris, 27 May 1929.

[100] MAE Z602 20, République Française, Ministère des Affaires Étrangères. Direction des Affaires politiques et commerciales. Note pour le Cabinet du Ministre, Paris, 14 Oct. 1929.

[101] Ibid.

newspaper *Paris-Midi* that both governments were happy to support an initiative which sought 'to bring together forces that shared a similar domestic political agenda', and which, alongside complementary economic interests, constituted 'powerful elements [working towards] understanding and cooperation'.[102] Hoesch agreed, adding that 'the Berlin meeting is particularly significant given that among the French representatives are people who, hitherto, were very cool, if not hostile, towards Germany', and urged his colleagues to liaise with the Centre Party to arrange some sort of official welcome, perhaps involving the Foreign Minister himself.[103]

Delegates from either side of the Rhine included figures from the Church, cultural life, academics, the business world, trade unionists, agriculture, and serving politicians,[104] who freely conceded that a host of problems bedevilled Franco-German relations. However, there was near-unanimous agreement to do everything possible 'to excise the reciprocal hereditary mistrust' between the two peoples. The French and Germans needed to develop a deeper understanding of each other, to which end the conference welcomed the establishment of closer relations between the Catholic press and journalists of the two countries, the promotion of academic and student exchanges, and the creation of a Commission for International Intellectual Cooperation by the Union of Catholic Universities, '[o]ne of whose goals will be Franco-German rapprochement, considered an essential element on the road to peace'.[105]

The Centre Party's newspaper, *Germania*, reported on the conference in glowing terms,[106] although the *Echo de Paris* was more measured. Despite the positives, including the two 'dazzling' official receptions hosted in turn by the French Ambassador and the German Foreign and Justice Ministers, the newspaper regretted that Germany still appeared to link improved relations with France to revision of its eastern frontier.[107] Nonetheless, Briand's reaction to the conference was essentially upbeat, and Hoesch reported that in France: 'the impression is growing that the meeting of German and French Catholics in Berlin has been useful and it has undoubtedly encouraged circles previously opposed to a German–French dialogue to reconsider.'[108] If this positive French response to the Catholic

[102] AA R70535 H019282–5, here 282–3, Telegramm Nr. 1274. Signed Hoesch, Paris, 19 Dec. 1929.

[103] AA R70535, doppel zu II Fr. 3847, Telegramm Nr. 1229. Signed Hoesch, Paris, 12 Dec. 1929.

[104] Lists: AA R70535 H019271–3, Programme des rencontres catholiques franco-allemandes des 20 et 21 décembre 1929 à Berlin. Entretiens franco-allemands. Liste provisoire des adhérents aux reunions de Berlin. Unsigned, undated; R70535 H019315–20, Liste der deutschen Teilnehmer. Unsigned, undated.

[105] AA R70535, Telegramm Nr. 1292, Kzl. –Nr. 3740. Signed Hoesch, Paris, 22 Dec. 1929.

[106] MAE Z618 7 10, here 10, HM. 19, Presse allemande décembre 1929, 3 Jan. 1930, 2. Politique Extérieure.

[107] AA R70535, Telegramm Nr. 1292, Kzl. –Nr. 3740. Signed Hoesch, Paris, 22 Dec. 1929, 4.

[108] AA R70535 H019364–6, quote on 366, Deutsche Botschaft Paris. B 3700/29. Betr. Zusammenkunft deutscher und französischer katholischer Persönlichkeiten in Berlin am 20. und 21.d.M. Signed Hoesch, Paris, 27 Dec. 1929; R70535 H019382–5, Deutsche Botschaft Paris, B 140. Signed Hoesch, Paris, 14 Jan. 1930; R70536 H019423, II Fr 508, 'Hochverehrter Herr Reichskanzler!' Signed B, Berlin, 8 Mar. 1930.

conference initially passed the Centre Party's leaders by, Hoesch made it his business to forward summaries of French press opinion to the Centre Party politician and former Chancellor, Wilhelm Marx, and indirectly to Heinrich Brüning at the time of his own appointment as Chancellor.[109]

A further meeting was agreed for the spring[110] and chaired in Paris on 18 March 1930 by the Russian-born Count Wladimir d'Ormesson, a retired French army officer turned journalist. The French Foreign Office and German Embassy were represented as d'Ormesson welcomed the success of the Berlin conference and continued: 'To get to know one another, to be convinced that nothing human divides the Germans and French, that the members of these equally civilized societies share the same interests, same fears, and same needs, that is fundamental to German–French rapprochement becoming reality.'[111] Similar events continued through the summer,[112] before, in October, senior Centre Party politicians sounded out the prospects for a visit to Paris. These seemed particularly favourable. Parallel efforts by French and German diplomats to find common ground on the Briand Plan were making progress, whilst the French Prime Minister, André Tardieu, made known that he particularly welcomed the proposed visit and wished to meet the Centre Party grandees personally.[113] The visit was agreed for late November.

However, the underlying complexities of Franco-German relations delayed the visit for several months. Whatever Tardieu's feelings on the Centre Party's bona fides, France's immediate priority remained the promotion of the Briand Plan at the League of Nations and, as we saw earlier,[114] that touched on sensitive dimensions of Franco-German relations. On 13 November 1930, in a speech to parliament, Tardieu confirmed that the initial thrust of the Briand Plan would now be towards international economic integration, rather than the political confederation that Briand had mooted just months earlier. This accorded with German wishes, but also served to sideline a process of political integration which, Briand had postulated, would seal the territorial arrangements of the Paris Peace Settlement. For many deputies in the French governing coalition this was a concession too far and Tardieu himself harboured doubts. Thus, he continued, its economic focus notwithstanding, the Briand Plan would also underpin the territorial verdict of the peace treaties.[115] Although these words must have reassured many French deputies

[109] AA R70536 H019421–2, Deutsche Botschaft Paris, 'Sehr geehrter Graf Bassenheim'. Signed Gerth, Paris, 13 Feb. 1930; R70536 H019423, II Fr 508. Signed B, Berlin, 8 Mar. 1930; for Brüning's involvement: R70536 H019424, Der Reichskanzler, Rk. 2507. Signed Brüning, Berlin, 10 Apr. 1930.

[110] AA R70535, zu II Fr 3971, 'Allemagne. Le Congrès catholique franco-allemand', *Le Temps*, 24 Dec. 1929.

[111] AA R70536, 'Eine Kundgebung deutscher und französischer Katholiken in Paris', *Wolff's Telegraphisches Büro*, 81—Nr. 569, Berlin, 19 Mar. 1930.

[112] For example, AA R70536 H019595, Deutsche Botschaft Paris, B. 2111. Signed Gerth, Paris, 27 Jun. 1930.

[113] AA R70537 H019716, Telegramm Nr. 991 vom 23/10. Signed Hoesch, Paris, 23 Oct. 1930.

[114] See Ch. 3 under 'The (Problematic) Launch of the Briand Plan', 58 and 'Franco-German Exchanges', 60–7.

[115] AA R28631 D702984–9, esp. 985–6, Abschrift. Vbd. 3679 II. Signed Curtius, Berlin, 20 Dec. 1930.

on the political centre-right, senior members of Chancellor Brüning's party felt unable to visit Paris under the circumstances and the two sides agreed to postpone, but not cancel, the visit.[116]

The delay was relatively brief. The row failed to dampen parallel efforts at rapprochement, whether through the Franco-German Study Committee which continued to promote economic cooperation,[117] or the Pen Club which sought rapprochement on a moral plane.[118] Furthermore, Tardieu demitted office in December 1930, eventually to be replaced in late January by the rapprochement-minded Laval, while the Alsatian-born Deputy Chairman of the Centre Party, Joseph Joos, visited Paris to sound out counterparts in the Popular Democratic Party. Hoesch hosted one of several such meetings which saw agreement that a powerful German delegation, comprising the parliamentarians Heinrich Brauns, Andreas Hermes, Franz von Papen, Erwin Respondek, Heinrich Brüning, and Joos himself, would visit France between 12 and 14 February 1931. Receptions were mooted, hosted by prominent members of the Popular Democrats, and, as the meat of the visit, discussions proposed with leading French financiers. Hoesch stressed the importance of the initiative, 'which will see official participation on a social level at the very least'. He counselled avoiding the well-worked flashpoints of Franco-German relations, and proposed discussions with the Foreign Office to prepare an agenda focused on financial and economic collaboration, where the prospects of success had always been strongest.[119]

The German representatives among the 120 participants included Brauns, Joos, Respondek, von Papen, and another Centre Party parliamentarian, Heinrich Vockel, all of whom were well qualified to speak for the German government, and two representatives from Cologne: Julius Stocky, publisher of the Catholic newspaper *Kölnische Volkszeitung*, and Konrad Adenauer's brother-in-law, Councillor Willi Suth. Their French counterparts included a number of grandees from the French financial and business world: Louis, Marquis de Vogüé, a director of the Bank of France and President of the Suez Canal Company; Ernest Picard, Director General of the Bank of Algeria; Henri de Peyerimhoff, President of the Mining Association; and Alfred Lambert-Ribot, Secretary General of the Ironmasters Association. Delegates discussed the significance of personal contacts in international relations, before turning to the German financial crisis. French delegates certainly supported Franco-German economic and financial cooperation in principle, but, as Hoesch observed, for all the warm words: 'The various speakers confined themselves in essence to generalities, desisting from any practical proposals.'[120]

[116] AA R70537 H019756–8, Deutsche Botschaft Paris, A 3967, Betr. Reise von Zentrumsvertretern nach Paris. Signed Kühn, Paris, 28 Nov. 1930; R70537 H019757, Nr./V./B1. Abschrift, Herrn Professor Boissard. Signed Vockel, Berlin, 15 Nov. 1930; R70537 H019758, Abschrift, 'Mon Cher et très Honoré Secrétaire Général'. Signed Boissard, Paris, 27 Nov. 1930.

[117] AA R70538 H019871–2, Aufzeichnung zu W 508. Signed Wiehl, Berlin, 31 Jan. 1931.

[118] AA R70538 H019892, Aufzeichnung, II Fr 427, Berlin, 10 Feb. 1931.

[119] AA R70538 H019877–9, quote on 878, Telegramm Nr. 130 v. 2/2. Signed Hoesch, Paris, 2 Feb. 1931.

[120] AA R70538 H020003–10, quote on 006, Deutsche Botschaft Paris, B 597, Inhalt: Pariser Besprechungen zwischen deutschen und französischen Katholiken. Signed Hoesch, Paris, 18 Feb. 1931.

Briand insisted that 'German-French collaboration and rapprochement on their own would save the world and heal its wounds', welcomed the French take-up of Reichsbahn (German Railways) preference shares which had just received parliamentary approval,[121] and looked forward to further cooperation,[122] but he too was short on specifics. The old conundrum, that economic rapprochement would have to await political detente, which itself remained unattainable,[123] surfaced emphatically during exchanges between von Papen and the French Finance Minister, Pierre-Étienne Flandin. '*C'est l'incertitude partout*' [there is so much uncertainty], Flandin concluded, as he recited back German demands on reparations, the Polish border, and disarmament.[124]

Hoesch also regretted that French parliamentary engagement in this Franco-German Catholic exchange remained largely confined to the Popular Democrats, who in size and influence were hardly the equivalent of the Centre Party. Indeed, the fact that half of the Popular Democrats' parliamentarians were Alsatian, and as such needed to be treated by German officialdom with kid gloves, complicated things still further. He concluded that the meeting did bear witness to a trend within the French Catholic community from (anti-German) chauvinism towards rapprochement, but observed that for now the 'chauvinists' remained in the majority, with the *Echo de Paris* providing a virulent mouthpiece for these sceptics.[125] Franz von Papen, better known as the architect of Hitler's appointment as German Chancellor, but also a partisan of Franco-German rapprochement and a founding member of the Franco-German Study Committee, set out his thoughts on the Paris meeting in a private report to the Permanent Secretary at the Wilhelmstraße, Bernhard von Bülow. His discussions with Flandin had confirmed the political obstacles to further economic and financial cooperation, but he also felt able to accentuate the positive:

> The big difference in the [French] attitude towards Germany since my last visit in November 1930 is notable. Whereas any public discussion concerning German-French collaboration was then unthinkable, attention is being devoted to this issue today in the widest of circles. The general impression made by the [German] Chancellor is particularly striking; his focused and energetic conduct of government is regarded here with undisguised admiration.[126]

[121] On railway shares, AA R70538 H020038–45, here 039, Aktennotiz über Eindrücke der Pariser Reise v. 12.–15. Febr. 31. Signed Papen.

[122] AA R70538 H020003–10, here 005, Deutsche Botschaft Paris, B 597, Inhalt: Pariser Besprechungen zwischen deutschen und französischen Katholiken. Signed Hoesch, Paris, 18 Feb. 1931.

[123] Ibid., here 007.

[124] AA R70538 H020038–45, here 042, Aktennotiz über Eindrücke der Pariser Reise v. 12.–15. Febr. 31. Signed Papen.

[125] AA R70538 H020003–10, here 009–10, Deutsche Botschaft Paris, B 597, Inhalt: Pariser Besprechungen zwischen deutschen und französischen Katholiken. Signed Hoesch, Paris, 18 Feb. 1931.

[126] AA R70538 H020038–45, here 038, Aktennotiz über Eindrücke der Pariser Reise v. 12.–15. Febr. 31. Signed Papen.

Events appeared to bear out Papen's optimism. Delegates agreed that the next session of the French Comité national d'études sociales et politiques, scheduled for 9 March, should discuss relations between French and German Catholics and invited Joos to address the meeting, alongside the Reichstag Deputy Helene Weber,[127] a specialist on welfare and youth policy whose familiarity with France extended to a period of study in Grenoble before the war. The Comité National had been founded in 1916 by the philanthropist and pacifist Albert Kahn, with a view to promoting international reconciliation. Its membership was drawn largely from the French elite, including the politician Édouard Herriot, the industrialist André Michelin, and the army commander Marshal Ferdinand Foch, and its meetings, Hoesch reported, 'were always held in the presence of a carefully selected and individually invited audience which consisted of prominent right-oriented figures from academic life, politics, journalism, and the military'. Twenty-seven French generals were present to hear out Joos.[128]

Days before the meeting, Wladimir d'Ormesson took space in the liberal German daily, the *Berliner Tageblatt*, to argue that while practical economic collaboration offered a way forward, this needed to be underpinned by a 'mutual reconciliation', which he maintained was not beyond reach.[129] This theme of Franco-German reconciliation also underpinned Joos's address. He lamented the tragedy of past relations as the two neighbours 'sought, found, split apart, fought, and then tried again to seek each other'. He freely conceded that: 'Scarcely any two nations differ so markedly in character as France and Germany', but appealed for a revival of erstwhile spiritual links and sense of common destiny, maintaining that: 'The medieval era witnessed an extraordinarily diverse range of spiritual connections between France and Germany, founded on the values of occidental universalism.' 'The Catholics of today', he concluded, 'must once again consciously adopt and promote this Christian-occidental concept.'[130] Such thinking continues to inform the Franco-German relationship,[131] and Joos's vision was not confined to an evocation of past friendship, for he saw a practical expression of Catholic universalism in the European social Catholic movement of the pre-war era. Interrupted by the war itself, this transnational movement had been given new life by the Papal encyclical of 1922: 'The peace of Christ in Christ's Kingdom'. Weber spoke largely on women's affairs and the moral impact of the economic crisis on

127 AA R70539 H020077–82, here 077, Deutsche Botschaft Paris, B 820, Betr. Aussprache über die Beziehungen zwischen deutschen und französischen Katholiken im Comité National d'Études Sociales et Politiques ... Signed Hoesch, Paris, 13 Mar. 1931.

128 Ibid.

129 AA R70539, Graf Wladimir D'Ormesson, 'Für deutsch-französische Verständigung', *Berliner Tageblatt*, 102, 1 Mar. 1931.

130 AA R70539 H020077–82, quotes on 078–9, Deutsche Botschaft Paris, B 820, Betr. Aussprache über die Beziehungen zwischen deutschen und französischen Katholiken im Comité National d'Études Sociales et Politiques ... Signed Hoesch, Paris, 13 Mar. 1931.

131 For example, Claudia Kunde et al., *Der Naumburger Meister. Bildhauer und Architekt im Europa der Kathedralen* (Petersberg, 2011).

German society,[132] whilst among the French speakers Adéodat Boissard looked forward to the next Franco-German meeting which would address the challenge posed to the Christian world by left- and right-wing extremism.[133]

Yet again, Hoesch observed that meetings such as these could not be expected to produce concrete results, but he appeared encouraged by the growing support for rapprochement in French right-wing circles. The Archbishop of Paris, Cardinal Jean Verdier, was a convinced supporter of the Pope's campaign for Franco-German rapprochement, which included the outlawing of the ultra-nationalist Action française, and had played a significant part in this process.[134] French press comment varied, but was largely positive. The Lorraine newspaper, the *Lothringer Volkszeitung*, pilloried French right-wing nationalists for their denunciation of the Alsace-born Joos as a traitor to France,[135] as did the leading Catholic journal *Politique* and the newspaper *La Croix*.[136] The *Journal des débats* poked fun at the same hardliners, when reporting that 'M. Joos spoke in excellent French—with an Alsatian accent', whilst Mme Weber, 'an interesting example of the female parliamentarian to be found today in quite a few countries, also spoke very good French, albeit without an Alsatian accent'. The newspaper counselled progress through a realistic policy of modest steps,[137] as did *Le Temps* which advised tempering hope with the 'corrective' of patience as Catholicism worked, in Joos's words, to 'transform Europe into a place of work rather than a battlefield'.[138] The right-wing *Echo de Paris*, which had lambasted French delegates to the December 1929 Berlin meeting, this time preferred to remain silent.[139]

Days later Curtius announced the Austro-German customs union, but without derailing the dialogue between French and German Catholics. In April, fourteen Catholic organizations, representing a particularly broad spectrum of French society, launched a poster campaign which appealed for international reconciliation and looked to success in the forthcoming 1932 Disarmament Conference in Geneva. This manifesto, distributed by mail shots and posted on placard boards, evoked the

[132] AA R70539, Pierre de Quirielle, 'Le rapprochement franco-allemand. Les contacts entre Catholiques', *Journal des Débats*, 11 Mar. 1931.

[133] AA R70539 H020077–82, here 080–1, Deutsche Botschaft Paris, B 820, Betr. Aussprache über die Beziehungen zwischen deutschen und französischen Katholiken im Comité National d'Études Sociales et Politiques... Signed Hoesch, Paris, 13 Mar. 1931.

[134] Ibid., H020081.

[135] AA R70539, 'Politik des Hasses? Nein! Europa verlangt nach Entspannung und Frieden', *Lothringer Volkszeitung*, 27 Mar. 1931.

[136] AA R70540 H020241, Deutsche Botschaft Paris. B 1630, Betr. Verteidigung des Reichstagabgeordneten Joos (gegen Angriffe in der französischen Presse) durch französische Katholiken. Signed Kühn, Paris, 15 May 1931.

[137] AA R70539, Pierre de Quirielle, 'Le rapprochement franco-allemand. Les contacts entre Catholiques', *Journal des Débats*, 11 Mar. 1931. However, for a different reception in the same newspaper, see R70540 H020241, Deutsche Botschaft Paris. B 1630, Betr. Verteidigung des Reichstagabgeordneten Joos (gegen Angriffe in der französischen Presse) durch französische Katholiken. Signed Kühn, Paris, 15 May 1931.

[138] AA R70539, 'Au comité national d'études', *Le Temps*, 11 Mar. 1931.

[139] AA R70539 H020077–82, here 081–2, Deutsche Botschaft Paris, B 820, Betr. Aussprache über die Beziehungen zwischen deutschen und französischen Katholiken im Comité National d'Études Sociales et Politiques... Signed Hoesch, Paris, 13 Mar. 1931.

Papacy's repeated calls for peace during and since the war, concluding that: 'Although spread across different homelands which they serve completely loyally, Catholics form a great family answerable to a common Father, and more than anyone they can and must work for the cause of peace.'[140] Its domestic impact was considerable, and although the manifesto made no specific mention of Germany, its authors, among them Champetier de Ribes, lobbied the German Embassy for a reciprocal response east of the Rhine. Hoesch was initially non-committal, but on 30 April Father Jean-Marie Desgranges, who sat as an Independent in the French National Assembly, and Christian Schreiber, the Catholic Bishop of Berlin, addressed the Deutsch-Französische Gesellschaft in Berlin on the subject of 'the common religious and moral principles which will serve to facilitate and nourish rapprochement between French and German Catholics'.[141] This German-French Society had been founded in December 1926 to promote Franco-German friendship within a framework of European collaboration and, as seen, its executive included prominent and eminent personalities from either side of the Rhine.[142] During these discussions Bishop Schreiber 'warmly welcomed the French peace manifesto and offered support for the French Catholics' commitment to peace'.[143]

In early May the Papal newspaper, the *Observatore Romano*, published the text of Desgranges and Schreiber's talks and made plain the importance it attached to this exchange, concluding that 'the crusade for reconciliation had made new friends'.[144] Hoesch now urged action:

> I feel the time is ripe to give the manifesto an airing in Germany through publication and review in the press and to consider, in conjunction with figures in the Centre Party, how the French wish for German participation [in this campaign] might be satisfied. Encouragement of French Catholics supportive of rapprochement lies in our interests.[145]

The response from the Wilhelmstraße was lukewarm. Officials noted that the manifesto was an unofficial venture, saw some value in affording it a welcome in the German press, but otherwise decided to let the matter lie.[146]

However, Brüning's advocacy of Franco-German rapprochement in his speech of 23 June had not come out of a clear blue sky. On the previous day, a well-attended and widely reported meeting of the Comité national d'études sociales et

140 AA R70540, 'Les Catholiques veulent la paix'; covering letter R70540 H020232–3, Deutsche Botschaft Paris. A 1542, Betr. Friedensmanifest französischer Katholiken. Signed Hoesch, Paris, 7 May 1931.

141 AA R70540 H020226, Deutsche Botschaft beim Papstlichen Stuhle No. 105. Signed Bergen, Rome, 7 May 1931.

142 See Ch. 2 under 'The Grautoff Initiative', 29–36.

143 AA R70540 H020232–3, Deutsche Botschaft Paris, A 1542, Betr. Friedensmanifest französischer Katholiken. Signed Hoesch, Paris, 7 May 1931.

144 AA R70540 H020226, Deutsche Botschaft beim Papstlichen Stuhle No. 105. Signed Bergen, Rome, 7 May 1931.

145 AA R70540 H020232–3, quote on 233, Deutsche Botschaft Paris. A 1542, Betr. Friedensmanifest französischer Katholiken. Signed Hoesch, Paris, 7 May 1931.

146 AA R70540 H020236, zu II Fr. 1516, Berlin, May 1931.

politiques, involving prominent figures from the French and German business, political, and cultural worlds, concluded after lively debate 'that it was high time to achieve Franco-German rapprochement',[147] further confirming that Brüning's initiative formed part of an ongoing (Catholic) dialogue. With time this was engaging a growing number of influential people in both countries and if it stood at one remove from formal diplomacy, it nonetheless served to reinforce and lend a degree of credibility and consistency to the various Franco-German efforts to secure rapprochement. Brüning's visit to Paris and his attendance at mass alongside Champetier de Ribes served as an important example of this process. The warmth shown by Laval to Brüning during the Paris meeting contrasted with the failure to seal any significant economic and financial accord, but Franco-German relations were built on more than money alone. Political Catholicism nourished a wider, genuine will to set aside the traumas of the recent past.

HOPEFUL SIGNS: THE PRUSSIAN PLEBISCITE AND ECONOMIC DETENTE

Beyond the Catholic community, the Ligue des droits de l'homme and its German counterpart, the Liga für Menschenrechte, spared no effort in promoting rapprochement through a series of reciprocal visits and meetings and public appeals to their governments.[148] And if the Austro-German customs union had compromised the process of detente, other developments exerted a decidedly positive influence. In March 1931 Prussia's nationalist right and communists joined forces to table a motion of no confidence in the state's ruling republican coalition. A plebiscite followed in August which most of the Prussian electorate simply boycotted, so confirming its support for the governing Social Democratic–Centre Party coalition and Prussia's commitment to democratic and constitutional government. Since these same democratic parties were the most strongly committed to detente, the failure of the nationalist plebiscite provided a significant boost to French advocates of rapprochement.[149] Commentators noted that the nationalist right and radical left between them had failed to maintain the support they had gained in the September 1930 election, with press reaction ranging from elation on the left, to qualified relief within the political centre. Only the nationalist right remained fundamentally reserved, declining to trust Germany on any terms.[150] Returning to the positive, the leading Radical politician and future Prime Minister Édouard Daladier took space in *La République* under the headline 'From the defeat

[147] AA R70540 H020292, Deutsche Botschaft Paris, A 2308, Betr. Vorträge des Reichsministers a. D. Dr Dernburg und des Redakteurs Dr Ernst Feder in Paris. Signed Kühn, Paris, 26 Jun. 1931.

[148] See, for example, AA R70540 H020355–6, Deutsches Konsulat Bordeaux, Nr. A 415, Betr. Gruppenreise der deutschen Liga für Menschenrechte. Signed Goes, Bordeaux, 21 Jul. 1931; R70540 H020400–1, Deutsche Liga fuer Menschenrechte EV, filed under II Fr. 2397. Signed Kurt Grossmann, Berlin, 7 Aug. 1931.

[149] AA R70541 H020430, Deutsche Botschaft Paris, A 2947. Signed Forster, Paris, 14 Aug. 1931.

[150] AA R70506 K240766–9, Telegramm Nr. 846 vom 10.8. Signed Hoesch, Paris, 10 Aug. 1931.

of the nationalists to a Franco-German accord' to dismiss Hitler, a would-be pocket Mussolini, as a spent force whose plans for a plebiscitary dictatorship were now in ruins. France, Daladier continued, needed to respond accordingly 'and persevere with renewed energy in the vital task of reconciliation and collaboration between our two peoples'.[151] Daladier looked back to the fateful period before war broke out in 1914, when from 1911 the French Prime Minister, Joseph Caillaux, had engaged energetically and controversially with German interests until forced from office in January 1912, to be replaced by the more abrasive Raymond Poincaré. Daladier warned his countrymen to avoid the dangers inherent in confronting Germany anew, continuing:

> If M. Caillaux's policy had been pursued vigorously, it would undoubtedly have prevented the conflict which devastated the world for four years. We are determined to adhere to this policy of sincere entente between two great peoples enjoying equal rights and to work for its success, whatever the outcry from the pedlars of hatred in both countries, who seek to block indispensable efforts to achieve understanding and accord.[152]

The wider French press went on to support Laval's efforts to secure Franco-German detente, although the conservative *Avenir* qualified its support when concluding that: 'We gladly wish Brüning luck, but not at our expense.'[153] Economic agreement continued to offer the most realistic and practical path to rapprochement and here too, despite the stalemate at the Paris talks, the portents were reasonably good. In August the London Conference acknowledged that Germany had only been able to pay reparations by raising loans, a situation that was hardly sustainable and pointed to a termination of payments once the Hoover moratorium had run its course.[154] In the meantime a $100 million international loan to Berlin was extended for a further three months, it was agreed that foreign credits in Germany would remain there (the Standstill Agreement), and efforts were initiated to transform short-term credits to Berlin into long-term loans.[155] The economics correspondent of the liberal *Vossische Zeitung* dared speculate that the adoption by Germany of the franc could be to both countries' advantage, the currency to be regulated by a Franco-German joint directorate.[156]

Meanwhile, if France had only agreed very reluctantly even to the suspension of reparations payments, certain other dimensions of Franco-German economic relations were essentially positive. The 1927 Franco-German trade treaty demonstrated that economic exchange could and did operate to their mutual advantage, not least through burgeoning Franco-German collaboration within a range of international

[151] AA R70541 H020430, Deutsche Botschaft Paris, A 2947. Signed Forster, Paris, 14 Aug. 1931: Édouard Daladier, 'De la défaite des nationalistes à l'accord franco-allemand', *La République*, 13 Aug. 1931.

[152] Ibid.

[153] AA R70575, 'Fragen und Warnungen an Laval. Pariser Presse fragt, was geschehen soll', *Berliner Börsen-Courier*, 370, 11 Aug. 1931.

[154] See Schirmann, *Crise*, 167–8.

[155] Rödder, *Stresemanns Erbe*, 259–62.

[156] MAE Z773 171–2, Ambassade de France à Berlin. L'Attaché Financier. Revue de Presse du 31 août 1931, Berlin, 31 Aug. 1931: IV a) Les relations franco-allemandes.

business cartels. These private organizations were often seen by their founders as a substitute for failed political efforts to rebuild a stable European economic environment after the Great War, but this had not prevented politicians, including Stresemann, from viewing the same Franco-German cartels as a cornerstone of European cooperation and integration. Or as the French Cabinet minister Louis Loucheur observed: 'Bonds are forged and strengthened and the two trade systems learn, every day, to work together.'[157] The prominent industrialist, politician, and academic Louis Marlio elaborated further in the *Revue de Paris* in February 1930:

> Industrial cartels are proliferating under the direct influence of the two countries that played the preponderant roles in the war—Germany and France. They bear witness to the close economic synergies between these countries, to a progressive calming of the atmosphere, to a reciprocal desire for agreement and collaboration.[158]

Cartels aside, the Union douanière européenne (UDE/European Customs Union), whose founders in 1925 included the German political journalist and editor, Edgar Stern-Rubarth, and the distinguished French economist Charles Gide, continued to promote the principles of pacifism and internationalism, to be realized through a common European trading system built on Franco-German rapprochement. As noted, the former Cabinet minister, Yves Le Trocquer, chaired the French bureau,[159] the serving Cabinet minister Georges Bonnet was a member, and Briand served as its Honorary President. Given these personal links to the French political establishment, it is not surprising that the UDE consulted regularly with the Quai d'Orsay and promoted official foreign policy initiatives which, as often as not, drew in analogous organizations, such as the Franco-German Study (Mayrisch) Committee. It was not uncommon for men of influence to belong to several of these rapprochement-minded bodies,[160] with the French politician Pierre Viénot a case in point: founder member of the Mayrisch Committee and son-in-law of Émile Mayrisch, commentator on German current affairs, and a close acquaintance of Gerhard Köpke at the Wilhelmstraβe.[161]

The Mayrisch Committee itself had met on 13 and 14 June 1931 in Paris when French and German delegations of industrialists, bankers, retired diplomats, and academics exchanged views.[162] The journalist, Max Clauss, had been fairly pessimistic before the meeting, observing that France's wartime generation continued to govern the country and sought security more in the maintenance of the Versailles settlement than in rapprochement.[163] His view was echoed at the meeting itself, where German delegates argued that 'French economic and political intransigence, in the form of a stubborn adherence to the status quo created by Versailles' had

[157] Quoted in Wurm, 'Internationale Kartelle', 100. [158] Ibid., 97–8.

[159] See Ch. 2 under 'The First Hague Conference', 44–5.

[160] Badel, 'Promoteurs français', 19–25.

[161] See Ch. 2 under 'Diplomatic Headwinds and Unofficial Initiatives', 27–8 and Ch. 6 under 'Impasse', 183–4.

[162] AA R70540 H020276, Anlage 1) Deutsches Communiqué des Deutsch-Französischen Studienkomitees. Unsigned, Paris, 15 Jun. 1931.

[163] AA R70540 H020279–91, esp. 291, Deutsch-Französisches Studienkomitee, die Deutschland-Politik der Französen. Eine Uebersicht. Signed Dr Max Clauss, Berlin, 1 Jun. 1931.

done much to nourish political extremism east of the Rhine.[164] However, the chairman of the German delegation, Alfred von Nostitz-Wallwitz, reported to Curtius that his French counterparts 'took on board the German presentation with far greater understanding and objectivity than, given current circumstances, one might have expected'.[165] And rather than dwelling on current difficulties, the independently drafted German and French communiqués agreed that Europe's future depended on Franco-German rapprochement which needed to be pursued vigorously by both governments.[166] In other words, a number of private organizations, who through their membership and close contacts with both governments had assumed quasi-official functions, continued to work throughout this difficult period for the betterment of Franco-German relations as the main prerequisite for the creation of a more closely integrated, economically sound, and peaceful Europe.

The events surrounding Brüning's Paris visit appear to have lent this process added steam. On 30 July Hoesch reported to Berlin on the formation of a new pressure group, the Comité d'entente international, otherwise known as the Comité Fougère after its founder, Étienne Fougère.[167] Comprising parliamentarians, largely from the political centre, and a particularly strong contingent from the business world,[168] its origins, Hoesch explained, lay in the activities of the UDE, the Franco-German Study Committee, and the Franco-German Catholic exchanges. These had brought together individuals from the business and political world who sought to promote European economic integration and, in particular, Franco-German collaboration. The announcement of the Austro-German customs union had briefly threatened to derail these exchanges. However, the French government's decision to complement a veto of the Austro-German plans with constructive proposals for European economic collaboration organized around a Paris–Berlin axis provided a way forward. François-Poncet's Plan constructif constituted the official response, while Étienne Fougère, a left-radical deputy in the National Assembly with a background in international trade and the textiles industry, worked in parallel to bind the French business world to government objectives. Fougère had bridled at the Austro-German customs union proposals, but even in May informed Hoesch at an embassy reception that he had now taken on the task, unencumbered by the formalities of government, to forge 'an economic rapprochement between [Germany and France] on a grand scale'. During this

164 AA R70540 H020274–5, here 274, Der Vorsitzende der deutschen Gruppe des Deutsch-Französischen Studien-Komitees. Signed Nostitz-Wallwitz, Berlin, 18 Jun. 1931.

165 Ibid., here 275.

166 AA R70540 H020276, Anlage 1) Deutsches Communiqué des Deutsch-Französischen Studienkomitees. Unsigned, Paris, 15 Jun. 1931; R70540 H020277, Anlage 2) Französisches Communiqué des Deutsch-Französischen Studienkomitees. Unsigned, Paris, 15 Jun. 1931.

167 AA R70567 H025971–8, Deutsche Botschaft, A 2771, Inhalt: Gründung eines französischen wirtschaftlich-parlamentarischen Komitees zur Herbeiführung einer deutsch-französischen Zusammenarbeit. Signed Hoesch, Paris, 30 Jul. 1931; R70576 H026937–8, Telegramm. Nr. 809, Kzl. Nr. 1206. Signed Hoesch, Paris, 30 Jul. 1931.

168 AA R70567 H025971–8, here 975–6, Deutsche Botschaft, A 2771, Inhalt: Gründung eines französischen wirtschaftlich-parlamentarischen Komitees zur Herbeiführung einer deutsch-französischen Zusammenarbeit. Signed Hoesch, Paris, 30 Jul. 1931; R70576 H026937–8, Telegramm. Nr. 809, Kzl. Nr. 1206. Signed Hoesch, Paris, 30 Jul. 1931.

conversation Hoesch and Fougère were joined by the convener of the French Mining Association, Henri de Peyerimhoff, who offered his unreserved support.[169]

Discussions had continued during the June meeting of the Franco-German Study Committee in Paris. Some sixty 'prominent German and French public figures' agreed to create reciprocal committees to negotiate a 'German-French economic accord, possibly to be complemented by parallel discussion of political issues'.[170] It was at this point that Fougère received the nod from the French government to found the Comité d'entente, which hoped to negotiate 'extensive German-French coordination of production and exchange, to be accompanied by political detente between the two countries'.[171] On 29 July the committee began its work and on the following day France's Commercial Attaché in Berlin, Lefeuvre, contacted the head of the Economics Section in the German Foreign Office, Karl Ritter, to brief him on Fougère's objectives. Lefeuvre alluded to Hoesch's involvement in this process, continuing that the French-based Committee now required a German counterpart, since it 'believed that the precondition for international entente was Franco-German entente'.[172]

PREPARATIONS FOR THE BERLIN MINISTERIAL CONFERENCE

A basic desire for Franco-German rapprochement apart, official French involvement in Fougère's initiative was driven by preparations for Laval and Briand to visit Berlin. In terms of diplomatic protocol the French statesmen were simply returning the German ministerial visit to Paris, but Laval was determined this time to achieve something tangible.[173] No sooner had Fougère founded his committee than Laval asked François-Poncet 'to try to draft a programme for Franco-German negotiations through the good offices of this committee, and simultaneously to examine whether this might serve to provide the ministerial visit with an effective outcome'.[174] Discussions followed between François-Poncet and Hoesch during which it was agreed to prioritize economic objectives. Politicians on the Committee (and on a German equivalent) would be excluded from these opening talks, all the better to avoid any unfortunate exchanges over Germany's eastern frontier or some other bone of contention.[175] And François-Poncet had already personally drawn up a provisional five-point agenda:

[169] AA R70567 H025971–8, here 973–4, Deutsche Botschaft, A 2771, Inhalt: Gründung eines französischen wirtschaftlich-parlamentarischen Komitees zur Herbeiführung einer deutsch-französischen Zusammenarbeit. Signed Hoesch, Paris, 30 Jul. 1931.

[170] Ibid., here 974. [171] Ibid., here 975.

[172] AA R70576 H02639–41, Ambassade de France. L'Attaché Commercial. Signed I. Lefeuvre, Berlin, 30 Jul. 1931.

[173] AA R70576 H026944–9, here 947, Telegramm Nr. 813 vom 31.7. Für Reichsminister und Staatssekretär. Signed Hoesch, Paris, 31 Jul. 1931.

[174] Ibid. [175] Ibid., here 948.

> Discussion regarding the extension of the Franco-German Trade Treaty; the advancement of private-sector economic accords with a view to rendering customs barriers superfluous, step by step, so working towards a customs union; industrial integration through share swaps; support for struggling but essentially sound German enterprises through an injection of capital by French companies operating in the same sectors; a similar process in the banking sector.[176]

Hoesch exhorted the Wilhelmstraβe to sound out possible German participants since events lent the affair some urgency.[177] Laval and Briand's visit to Berlin was imminent and the French had in the Fougère Committee a vehicle and in François-Poncet's five-point plan an agenda for this visit. Germany, Hoesch warned, had come up with nothing, 'which looks pretty bleak from a French perspective' even if Brüning (and Laval) had scarcely had time as yet, in the ongoing rush of international diplomacy, to give the matter any detailed thought.[178] Bülow was sympathetic, but Curtius and Brüning were away for several days on the third of their international visits, this time to Rome, and the Permanent Secretary felt unable to commit to anything in their absence.[179] Curtius had already invited Hermann Bücher, Director General of the electrics giant AEG, to serve as convener of a German equivalent of the Fougère Committee,[180] but the Foreign Minister was reluctant to combine the official diplomacy of the ministerial visit with the activities of this ad hoc body.[181] And in contrast to Laval (and Hoesch), he saw little need for a substantive agenda for the visit, instead maintaining that in itself it was 'of the greatest significance, for the very fact that the French statesmen are coming to Berlin will rightly be interpreted by international commentators as a positive symptom of an ongoing relaxation in German-French relations'.[182]

Whatever the case, the formation of a German committee quickly ran into the sand. Initial support dissipated as the members of other German societies dedicated to Franco-German reconciliation feared that the new body would merely duplicate their existing efforts and create unnecessary confusion. The German wing of the Franco-German Study Committee in particular dismissed Fougère's venture as 'superfluous' and continued that most of the latter's adherents were already members of the Study Committee in any case. Furthermore Laval's initial enthusiasm dimmed as Fougère demanded of him political control of the rapprochement process, thereby infringing on powers habitually reserved to the state, not to mention cutting across the French Premier's personal ambitions. At this point Berlin decided quietly to kick the Fougère initiative into the long grass[183] even if

[176] Ibid., here 948–9. [177] Ibid., here 949.

[178] AA R70567 H025982–4, here 983, Orig II Fr 2341. Signed Bülow, Berlin, 6 Aug. 1931.

[179] AA R70567 H025982–4, ibid.

[180] AA R70576 H026950–1, Conzept, zu II Fr 2300. Signed Köpke, Berlin, 4 Aug. 1931.

[181] AA R70567 H025979–81, here 979, Abschrift II Fr... diplo Paris Nr 419, R.M. Telegramm in Ziff. Signed Curtius, Berlin, 5 Aug. 1931.

[182] Ibid., here 980.

[183] AA R70576 H027005–9, Aufzeichnung. Signed Friedberg, Berlin, 26 Aug. 1931; R70567 H026014–16, here 015–16, Telegramm Nr. 874 v. 22.8. Signed Hoesch, Paris, 22 Aug. 1931; R70576 H027041–4, Deutsche Botschaft Paris. A 3189, Lieber Herr von Friedberg!. Signed Forster,

Hoesch and François-Poncet continued to lobby for the creation of a German counterpart to the French committee.[184] Some weeks later the Economics Ministry did draw up a provisional list of possible German participants, but without actually consulting the business figures concerned, or providing any timetable for further developments.[185]

Nonetheless, whatever specific problems the Fougère episode might have created, the German authorities remained enthusiastic about the French ministerial visit and Curtius pressed for an early date, in late August. This, he argued, would maintain the momentum of Franco-German detente within the existing sequence of international ministerial exchanges,[186] while any delay risked undermining confidence in the rapprochement process at a time when things were already difficult enough. He was particularly anxious to pre-empt the September meeting of the League of Nations, where ongoing discussion of the Austro-German customs union threatened to sour the atmosphere, added to which a judgement on the legality of this union was imminent at The Hague. And what fresh difficulties might flare up in German domestic politics by October was, he mused, anybody's guess.[187] Laval agreed and on 13 August accepted an invitation from Hoesch to visit Berlin on 26 and 27 August, noting that 'it would be completely unnecessary and undesirable to engender press speculation over the reasons for any delay'.[188]

However, the Quai d'Orsay was less happy about this schedule for a variety of reasons. Berthelot questioned the wisdom of rushing to return the Paris visit and, off the record, suggested to Hoesch that late September or early October might better serve their cause.[189] Furthermore, it was an open secret that Briand's health had suffered during the summer[190] and whilst his convalescence was going well, Berthelot felt it unwise to exhaust the Minister before the September meeting of the League of Nations. Briand's private secretary, Gilbert Antoine Peycelon, was even less happy, only agreeing to consult his boss against his own better judgement. Briand, he complained, 'would certainly be far from pleased to cut short his recuperation, but would probably agree [to the visit]'.[191] Even Laval, for all his impatience, felt obliged to warn his German hosts against staging any major evening events, because 'Briand was unable to stay up late',[192] and it must have

Paris, 5 Sept. 1931; R70567 H025992–8, here 996, Telegramm Nr. 852 vom 13.8. Signed Hoesch, Paris, 13 Aug. 1931.

[184] AA R70567 H026014–16, here 16, Telegramm Nr. 874 v. 22.8. Signed Hoesch, Paris, 22 Aug. 1931.

[185] AA R70576 H027062–3, Notiz W 4330. Signed Woermann, Berlin, 21 Sept. 1931.

[186] AA R70567 H025979–81, here 80, Abschrift II Fr., R.M., diplo Paris Nr. 419. Signed Curtius, Berlin, 5 Aug. 1931.

[187] Ibid.

[188] AA R70567 H025992–8, here 992, Telegramm Nr. 852 vom 13.8. Signed Hoesch, Paris, 13 Aug. 1931.

[189] AA R70567 H025964–5. Signed Kordt, Berlin, 3 Aug. 1931.

[190] AA R70503, 'Frankreich – Deutschland', *Der Überblick. Querschnitt durch Politik und Wirtschaft*, 2, Nr. 16, Berlin, 15 Aug. 1931. (Filed in R70503, a 1930 file).

[191] AA R70567 H025992–8, here 993, Telegramm Nr. 852 vom 13.8. Signed Hoesch, Paris, 13 Aug. 1931.

[192] Ibid., here 994.

surprised no one when the Foreign Minister's doctors declared that their patient was unfit to travel anywhere before the September session of the League.[193]

If Briand's illness had disrupted the diplomatic timetable, his withdrawal from active politics had provided something of an opening for André François-Poncet. The Economics Minister knew Germany well from his travels there before the First World War and his later presence as a press bureau chief in Düsseldorf during the 1923–4 Ruhr Crisis.[194] He had, as seen, later played a significant part during 1931 in formulating French proposals for economic detente with Germany and in early August Paris announced that he would replace the time-served French Ambassador at Berlin, Pierre de Margerie.[195] The German authorities suspected that the latter's professionalism and experience might serve the cause of rapprochement better,[196] a sentiment reflected in the moderate German press. The liberal-leaning *Königsberger Allgemeine Zeitung* praised de Margerie's 'efforts, executed with the discretion of a diplomat of the old school . . . to restore and strengthen Franco-German relations after the brutal caesura of the war and Versailles', but preferred to reserve judgement when it came to François-Poncet.[197] However, the French government insisted 'that the appointment of a Cabinet Minister to this key post served as a token of its desire to continue the negotiations initiated in Paris in an atmosphere of trust',[198] while François-Poncet himself stressed in an extended interview with the German journalist, Kurt Ihlefeld, that Berlin took priority over his domestic political ambitions.[199] Leaving aside the outrage François-Poncet's conciliatory words provoked in French nationalist circles,[200] it only remained to juggle the change of Ambassador with the ministerial visit to Berlin. If de Margerie was keen to seal his tenure in Berlin by presiding over the occasion, Laval and Briand decided that it made better sense to have their new man in place to initiate a fresh start in Franco-German relations.[201]

The Berlin visit was eventually agreed for 27 and 28 September, but French press coverage of the early September session of the League of Nations, where Germany and Austria formally abandoned their proposed customs union, and the reaction of the nationalists in the Reichstag to this were such that Brüning felt unable, on

[193] AA R70567 H026007–8, Telegramm Nr. 857, Auswärtig Berlin. Signed Hoesch, Paris, 14 Aug. 1931; but see also R70506 K240755–7, here 756, Société des Nations 2549, Dufour an Kamphoevener. Signed Albert Dufour, Geneva, 31 Jul. 1931.

[194] AA Akten der früheren Deutschen Botschaft in Paris 1817–1944 (563, Akten betreffend Beziehungen Frankreichs zu Deutschland, here c), Dr Kurt Ihlefeld, Unterredung mit François-Poncet. Unsigned, Paris, 20 Aug. 1931.

[195] AA R70567 H025964–5, Botschafter von Hoesch rief soeben . . . Signed Kordt, Berlin, 3 Aug. 1931.

[196] Brüning, *Memoiren*, 342.

[197] MAE Z619 42–3, here 42, Consulat de France à Koenigsberg. Direction des Affaires Politiques et Commerciales. Europe. No 121. Sig. illeg., Koenigsberg, 18 Sept. 1931.

[198] AA R70567 H025964–5, here 964, Botschafter von Hoesch rief soeben . . . Signed Kordt, Berlin, 3 Aug. 1931.

[199] AA Paris 563c, Dr Kurt Ihlefeld, Unterredung mit François-Poncet. Unsigned, Paris, 20 Aug. 1931.

[200] AA R70506, Deutsche Botschaft A 3173. Signed Forster, Paris, 1 Sept. 1931.

[201] AA R70567 H026014–6, Telegramm Nr. 874 v. 22.8. Signed Hoesch, Paris, 22 Aug. 1931.

4 September, to make any official announcement concerning the planned Franco-German summit.[202] As the German nationalists raged that the French ministerial visit 'was hypocritical and a provocation of the German people',[203] Bülow and his colleagues struggled to reassure the French Ambassador[204] and also avert a Franco-German media war.[205] As we shall see, the cumulative impact of the Austrian fiasco was soon enough to cost Curtius his ministry, forcing his resignation in early October,[206] but in the meantime he threatened to reignite media tensions by damning with faint praise the Berlin visit at the League of Nations: 'He treated France coldly, adding accusations that, allegedly, culminated in threats . . . All in all the speech is an inauspicious omen for the [Berlin] visit, an event now set in stone', an appalled senior German diplomat complained.[207] This was in stark contrast to Briand's measured but warm welcome at the League for the forthcoming Berlin conference.[208] Curtius did however manage to retrieve the situation two days later at a reception for the international press corps in Geneva, where he showed particular warmth towards Briand 'and so helped restore the atmosphere . . . particularly with regard to the Berlin visit'.[209]

However, right-wingers in Germany continued to denounce the visit on any terms. The wartime hero and military adventurer Rüdiger, Count von der Goltz, wrote to Brüning on behalf of the German 'patriotic leagues' to condemn the whole tenor of Franco-German relations. These, von der Goltz declaimed, consisted of French efforts to 'extort fresh concessions from Germany', making it astonishing that 'after everything that has happened, French Ministers have the nerve to come to Germany as "guests"'. German diplomacy, the Count concluded, had a duty to prevent the visit,[210] a view echoed by the patriotic league, the Jungdeutscher Orden.[211] The *Berliner Börsen Zeitung*, which spoke for conservative business opinion, accused French ministers of dishonourable bullying with regard to the Austro-German customs union and claimed that the majority of Germans had no wish to witness their triumphal entry into the German capital. The *Deutsche*

[202] AA R70567 H026038–9, Telegramm Nr. 920 vom 4/9. '(ohne Unterschrift)', Paris, 4 Sept. 1931.

[203] MAE Z773 198ff, here 203, Ambassade de France à Berlin. L'Attaché Financier. Revue de Presse du 5 septembre 1931, Berlin, 5 Sept. 1931: V a) Pays étrangers. Le voyage des Ministres français à Berlin.

[204] AA R70571 H026820, Abschrift, 'Der Französische Botschafter fragte mich heute sehr besorgt . . .'. Signed Bülow, Berlin, 5 Sept. 1931.

[205] AA R70506 K240799–800, e.o. II Fr. 2631, Germadiplo Paris. Signed Bülow, Berlin, 4 Sept. 1931; R70506, Telegramm Nr. 922 vom 4.9. Signed Forster, Paris, 4 Sept. 1931. See also MAE Z619 42–3, Consulat de France à Koenigsberg. Direction des Affaires Politiques et Commerciales. Europe. No 121. Sig. illeg., Koenigsberg, 18 Sept. 1931.

[206] See Ch. 5 under 'Creating the Commission', 132–3.

[207] AA R70506 K240820–1, quote on 821, Telegramm Nr. 948 vom 13/9. Signed Forster, Paris, 13 Sept. 1931.

[208] Elisha, *Aristide Briand*, 384.

[209] AA R70506, Telegramm Nr. 952 v. 15.9. Signed Forster, Paris, 15 Sept. 1931.

[210] AA R70567 H026041, Vereinigte Vaterländische Verbände Deutschlands. Präsidium. Signed v.d. Goltz, Berlin, 7 Sept. 1931.

[211] AA R70568 H026167, Jungdeutscher Orden. Der Groβkomtur für Hessen-Nassau. Sig. illeg., Giessen, 16 Sept. 1931.

Allgemeine Zeitung, which stood on the centre-right, condemned the visit as 'grotesque and intolerable', concluding that any Franco-German customs union would come of 'brutal political and financial pressure'.[212] Days later the leader of the DNVP, Alfred Hugenberg, used a party congress in Stettin to attack the whole tenor of Brüning's rapprochement policy, continuing that he would not be bound as a future Chancellor by any agreements reached with France.[213]

Liberal opinion in Germany was more supportive, but cautious. The *Berliner Tageblatt* was hazy on the details, but understood industrial and economic cooperation to be on the agenda, something that had been mooted in the past, but had come up against one problem or another.[214] The former liberal Finance Minister, Peter Reinhold, took space in the *Vossische Zeitung* to hope that with a customs union—he claimed—now effectively a done deal, 'France would desist from a policy of pinpricks and from stirring up German opinion to no good purpose.'[215] Days later, the *Vossische Zeitung* was rather more optimistic, seeing in François-Poncet's appointment as Ambassador the basis for substantive progress on detente. His background in coal mining and metallurgy and his notion of wedding German industrial power to French financial strength provided a basis for agreement during the forthcoming French ministerial visit to Berlin,[216] while the well-informed *Frankfurter Zeitung* believed that the Franco-German Committee would open the way to more fruitful Franco-German collaboration in South-Eastern Europe. German exports of manufactured goods to the region would be financed by German imports of wheat, all underpinned by the 'productive employment' of French capital.[217] Such notions, of course, formed part of François-Poncet's Plan constructif.

Across the Rhine, an essentially positive centrist and left-wing attitude contrasted with the scepticism or even hostility of many conservative newspapers. The longstanding French advocate of rapprochement, Jules Sauerwein, welcomed the initiative in *Le Matin*, but warned against 'according the visit too great a significance'. Any Franco-German special economic commission 'would be in itself an important

212 MAE Z773 198ff, here 203, Ambassade de France à Berlin. L'Attaché Financier. Revue de Presse du 5 septembre 1931, Berlin, 5 Sept. 1931. V a) Pays étrangers. Le voyage des Ministres français à Berlin. Further press coverage in Z773 230, Ambassade de France à Berlin. L'Attaché Financier. Revue de Presse du 15 septembre 1931, Berlin, 15 Sept. 1931. VII? a) La visite des ministres français à Berlin. Relations franco-allemandes.

213 MAE Z773 263, Ambassade de France à Berlin. L'Attaché Financier. Revue de Presse du 22 septembre 1931, Berlin, 22 Sept. 1931. IV Les relations franco-allemandes.

214 AA R70567, 'Das Programm für Berlin. 27. September Ankunft Lavals und Briands. – Kohle, Eisen und Elektrizität', *Berliner Tageblatt*, 423, 8 Sept. 1931.

215 MAE Z773 209–10, Ambassade de France à Berlin. L'Attaché Financier. Revue de Presse du 7 septembre 1931, Berlin, 7 Sept. 1931. V Pays Étrangers, a) La visite des Ministres français à Berlin.—La sentence de La Haye.

216 MAE Z773 238–9, Ambassade de France à Berlin. L'Attaché Financier. Revue de Presse du 16 septembre 1931, Berlin, 16 Sept. 1931. V Pays Étrangers, a) La visite des ministres français.—Commentaires sur la nomination de M. François-Poncet.

217 MAE Z773 245, Ambassade de France à Berlin. L'Attaché Financier. Revue de Presse du 19 septembre 1931, Berlin, 19 Sept. 1931. V Pays Étrangers, a) La collaboration franco-allemande dans les pays du Sud-est de l'Europe.

step [but] at the beginning of a long road'.[218] However, the conservative *Le Figaro* warned that the German press was predicting hostile demonstrations, that Brüning's Cabinet teetered on the brink of disintegration, and that the spectacle of policemen firing warning shots to restrain mobs pressing in on the French visitors was scarcely a happy one. Such thoughts, the left-leaning *L'Oeuvre* riposted, were self-serving and nothing would please French nationalists more than to see their German counterparts, or still better the Nazis, wreck the ministerial visit.[219]

Days later, on 17 September, Bülow drafted a comprehensive set of German proposals for the visit, which focused primarily on a range of economic and commercial issues.[220] The Wilhelmstraβe had at its disposal an extended situation report from Hoesch, dated 21 August,[221] which evaluated the shaping of Franco-German relations since his earlier March 1931 report which had weighed hope for the future against a degree of qualified pessimism.[222] Events, Hoesch now continued, had vindicated his earlier caution, and weeks later a supplementary report would remind Berlin of the damage wrought by the grudging German reaction to the Allied military evacuation of the southern Rhineland, by the September 1930 Reichstag elections, and by the Austro-German customs union plan.[223] However, Hoesch noted that the passage of time and events, and also Brüning's visit to Paris, had created a greater willingness in France to engage in cross-border economic initiatives, including a growing readiness to forge a comprehensive economic alliance with Germany. The positive personal chemistry between the current French and German leaders had also been helpful, by bringing each side to appreciate more fully the other's limited room for political manoeuvre and reducing the potential for accidental misunderstandings.

Hoesch still saw little or no prospect of successful Franco-German negotiations on outstanding political issues, such as the eastern frontier, the Saar, and disarmament, or on reparations, noting that little had changed in this respect since March.[224] Meaningful discussions would have to wait a year or two at least. Nor did he see any prospect of unconditional French financial assistance to Germany, adding that Laval had made it very clear that he had no wish to discuss the financial question during his forthcoming visit to Berlin. But, the Ambassador continued:

> If the political and financial dimensions cannot presently contribute positively to German-French negotiations, there remains the broad and important area represented

[218] AA R70567, Telegramm Nr. 934. Signed Forster, Paris, 10 Sept. 1931.

[219] AA Handakten Friedberg. Akten betreffend: Französischer Besuch (R70571–3, here 571), H026819, *Wolff's Telegraphisches Büro*, France vom 8.9.1931 morgens. Blatt vier/fünf, Paris 8 September.

[220] AA R70567, H026103–13, St.S. Telegramm i.Z. Germadiplo Paris Nr. 499. Signed Bülow, Berlin, 17 Sept. 1931.

[221] AA R70506 K240776–89, Deutsche Botschaft Paris, A. 3035. Inhalt: Ausblick für die weitere Gestaltung der deutsch-französischen Beziehungen. Signed Hoesch, Paris, 21 Aug. 1931.

[222] See Ch. 4 under 'Enduring Tensions and the Austro-German Customs Union', 88–9.

[223] AA R70506 K240851–5, here 851–2, Politische, wirtschaftliche und kulturelle Beziehungen zu Frankreich. Unsigned, stamped Auswärtiges Amt, II Fr. 2891, 21 Sept. 1931.

[224] For Foreign Office caution on the Saar question see AA R70573 H026866–71, Abschrift II S G 1350, Saarfrage (Aufzeichnung vom 17. Juli 1931). Signed von Friedberg.

> by the economy. Here things appear different, and it is in this field that I see the opportunity currently for making progress . . . The [French] government and in particular the Prime Minister Laval are now unmistakeably committed to serious engagement on economy-related problems.[225]

He envisaged Franco-German collaboration running in parallel with wider international initiatives, noting that François-Poncet's five-point agenda contained a number of particularly interesting ideas, not least for French investment in German companies and banks. 'Under certain circumstances,' he observed, 'private capital flows of this kind could serve as a substitute of sorts for a French official loan which, currently, is not practicable.'[226] Hoesch concluded that many, including Laval's Chef de Cabinet, Alexis Léger, regarded the emerging focus on economic detente as disappointingly limited, but he urged realism. Laval's proposal to create a Franco-German Commission to preside over the process of economic rapprochement, he maintained, demanded support.

It was no accident, therefore, that Bülow's own proposals focused on the economy. They served as a counterpoint rather than a direct response to François-Poncet's earlier five-point agenda, some parts of which were more attractive to Berlin than others. Bülow feared, for example, that renegotiation of the Franco-German trade treaty would compromise German interests, whereas a customs union was to be welcomed and was supported by influential figures in the European business world.[227] The Permanent Secretary regarded his agenda as a continuation of the earlier Franco-German dialogue on the Briand Plan, and thus as a means of breathing fresh life into Briand's ambitions: 'These must not remain on paper', he urged, 'but be made reality through active German-French collaboration.'[228]

German objectives, he continued, focused on three areas: the normalization and improvement of German-French relations generally; finding ways and means for joint Franco-German initiatives to tackle the increasingly threatening world economic crisis; and finally, harnessing German-French economic cooperation in the cause of broader rapprochement. This, he argued, would require discussions firstly on purely German-French matters, secondly on German-French collaboration in specific countries including Turkey and Persia [Iran], thirdly on German commerce in the French Empire, and, finally, on relatively informal cooperation between Paris and Berlin on European and global issues. He joined Hoesch in welcoming French proposals to create a Franco-German

225 AA R70506 K240776–89, quote on 785, Deutsche Botschaft Paris, A. 3035. Inhalt: Ausblick für die weitere Gestaltung der deutsch-französischen Beziehungen. Signed Hoesch, Paris, 21 Aug. 1931. See also R70506 K240851–5, here 852, Politische, wirtschaftliche und kulturelle Beziehungen zu Frankreich. Unsigned, stamped Auswärtiges Amt, II Fr. 2891, 21 Sept. 1931.

226 AA R70506 K240776–89, here 787, Deutsche Botschaft Paris, A. 3035. Inhalt: Ausblick für die weitere Gestaltung der deutsch-französischen Beziehungen. Signed Hoesch, Paris, 21 Aug. 1931.

227 For examples of business collaboration: AA R70505 K240749–52, Deutsche Gesandtschaft Brüssel. A 273 Betr.: Gespräch mit dem belgischen Staatsminister Francqui. Signed Graf Lerchenfeld; R70506 K240851–5, here 853, Politische, wirtschaftliche und kulturelle Beziehungen zu Frankreich. Unsigned, stamped Auswärtiges Amt, II Fr. 2891, 21 Sept. 1931.

228 AA R70567 H026103–13, quote on 111, St.S. Telegramm i.Z. Germadiplo Paris Nr. 499. Signed Bülow, Berlin, 17 Sept. 1931.

joint economic commission with a permanent executive, and suggested that a Franco-German customs union might emerge out of existing private cartel arrangements. He also echoed Hoesch in supporting François-Poncet's scheme for share swaps between French and German industry and financial institutions, seeing the iron and coal industries as ripe for such a deal, where Belgian and Luxembourg participation was also desirable. Free movement of labour between Germany and France, bringing with it the abolition of visa requirements and coordination of social security provision, formed further elements of Bülow's vision of the future. Finally, he looked to legal collaboration based on the cancellation of France's war crimes lists and *in absentia* verdicts, to be replaced by a new extradition treaty.[229] Major war-related scars, such as the Saar question and reparations, were, he agreed, for another day.[230] Rapprochement would thus focus on agreement and cooperation where the prospects were brightest rather than engaging in a dialogue of the deaf over issues whose relevance, one hoped, would fade with the passage of time.

Bülow knew that in some respects he was pushing at an open door. Berthelot had already assured Hoesch that he was working to lift visa requirements and to reach a final resolution of the war criminals issue as well as pressing the authorities in Morocco to permit German access to the French colony.[231] Discussions between Hoesch's deputy, Dirk Forster, and Berthelot on 21 September brought an elaboration of the French agenda. The French trade deficit with Germany, Berthelot suggested, would best be addressed through an overall increase in trade rather than through any restrictions on German exports to France; he went on to advocate the further development of international and Franco-German cartels in heavy industry, chemicals, textiles, and the electrical industry as a means to this end. The coordination of river and railway transport and the promotion of joint Franco-German projects in Central and Eastern Europe, as well as in the colonies, completed Berthelot's list. He preferred to leave details of the exact structure of the Franco-German Commission to the Berlin meeting, anticipating that agreement would easily be reached.[232] Senior diplomats fleshed out these ideas on 22 September during which one small, dark cloud appeared on the horizon. Pierre Arnal, French Chargé d'Affaires at Berlin,[233] explained 'that the French government would need to achieve rectification of the trade treaty to take into account the wishes of the French economy'.[234] French parliamentary elections were in the offing and although Berthelot remained sanguine, the latent tension generated

[229] Ibid.; see also R70571 H026806–7, Bülow, undated.

[230] AA R70567 H026103–13, here 108–9, St.S. Telegramm i.Z. Germadiplo Paris Nr. 499. Signed Bülow, Berlin, 17 Sept. 1931.

[231] AA R70506 K240758, Deutsche Botschaft Paris. A 2787. Signed Hoesch, Paris, 7 Aug. 1931.

[232] AA R70568 H026228–32, Telegramm Nr. 970 vom 21/9. Signed Forster, Paris, 21 Sept. 1931; but for a degree of French caution, R70568 H026296, Telegramm Nr. 978 vom 23/9. Signed Forster, Paris, 23 Sept. 1931.

[233] Arnal held this post between de Margerie's departure from, and François-Poncet's arrival in, Berlin.

[234] AA R70568 H026251–2, quote on 252, Telegramm Nr. 974 vom 22/9. Signed Forster, Paris, 22 Sept. 1931.

by the imbalance in Franco-German trade would soon enough undermine efforts by the diplomats of both countries to exploit closer economic relations to achieve wider rapprochement.

At this point François-Poncet fell prey to stage fright. During his earlier interview with the journalist Kurt Ihlefeld, aimed at a German readership, the French Minister had claimed never to have shot directly at Germans during his war service. Unremarkable perhaps, but the right-wing Action française reacted furiously and this in turn stirred up the French war veterans leagues against François-Poncet. He was unconcerned by Action française's outrage, dismissing its members as 'nutters',[235] but the influential veterans associations were another matter. Their hostility came at a high political price and also reinforced his growing unease over German reactions to the Austro-German customs union affair. During a second, off-the-record, interview with Ihlefeld he complained that:

> In Germany, you always lurch from one extreme to the other. You launched into the customs union with Austria with baseless and exaggerated enthusiasm. Your bitterness over the humiliation of failure is no less exaggerated... In fact we did everything possible in Geneva to avoid anything that might be construed as humiliation. On the eve of the French ministerial visit you overwhelm us with hatred and hostility. But it is not us making political demands.[236]

He dwelt briefly and more calmly on the agenda for Berlin before turning to the terms of the 1918 Armistice and the Peace Treaty, complaining that Germany had never appreciated how moderate the French position had been at the time. The scabs on wartime wounds were being picked raw, providing an unequivocal reminder of the enduring challenges faced by advocates of rapprochement.

Perhaps de Margerie, whose successful ambassadorship at Berlin had seen him weather the tempestuous events of the 1923–4 Ruhr Crisis,[237] might have displayed a cooler head. German diplomats believed as much. However, with François-Poncet's thoughts remaining off the record, open pessimism was for another day. Furthermore, alongside high-level exchanges, a positive, cultural 'soft' diplomacy continued to reinforce the wider post-war recovery in Franco-German relations. On 24 September Norbert Eckel, who had served as German Consul at Lyon since 1926, sketched out the state of Franco-German cultural relations in positive, almost glowing, terms.[238] Political tensions had been set aside as scientific exchanges and collaboration saw frequent cross-border events, including lectures to university audiences and learned societies. The celebrated French

[235] AA R70568 H026185–91, here 185, Abschrift. Dr Kurt Ihlefeld. Vertraulich. 2. Unterredung mit François-Poncet, undated. Covering letter: Deutsche Botschaft Paris A 3420. Signed Forster, Paris, 18 Sept. 1931.

[236] Ibid., quotes on 186 and 188.

[237] Fischer, *Ruhr Crisis*, 224–5, 228; Adamthwaite, *Grandeur and Misery*, 83.

[238] AA R70568 H026316–19, Aufzeichnung über kulturelle Beziehungen mit Frankreich. Signed Konsul Eckel, 24 Sept. 1931; see also R70576 H027126–31, Aktivierung der deutsch-französischen Zusammenarbeit auf dem Gebiet des Auswanderungswesen und der Kulturpolitik. Signed Freytag, Berlin, 5 Oct. 1931; R70576 H027132–6, Aufzeichnung. Signed Sievers, undated.

Germanist, Henry Lichtenberger of the Institut d'études germaniques, ranked among the more prominent sponsors of these exchanges.[239] In 1925, Eckel continued, France and Germany had reached a unique agreement to exchange all university-level doctoral dissertations and the wider exchange of scientific literature had regained pre-war levels.[240] French language instruction was blossoming in Germany, supported by 'numerous native French language tutors', although German instruction in France remained less well resourced. Thirty-three French language lectors had been appointed to German universities, as against ten meagrely paid Germans in France.[241] In 1930 the Academic-Pedagogical Exchange Bureau in Paris and the French Academics' House in Berlin were opened to administer exchanges, with more German students visiting France than before the war—well over 1,000 annually. Germans made up the largest contingent of foreign students in Paris and if only forty to fifty French students visited Germany, other forms of contact compensated for this.[242] Plans for organized Franco-German cross-border group student travel had been initiated by the French Senator André Honnorat, while large-scale Franco-German student conferences had been held since 1930.[243] School exchanges were also well established, and summer schools flourished at which French and German children were taught together.[244] Joint sporting events in France, 'at which German participants were always particularly warmly received', were generating further contact.[245] Finally, successful concerts in France by the Leipziger Gewandhaus and the Berlin Philharmonic Orchestra and a favourable reception for modern German art, design, and architecture gave Eckel added grounds for optimism.[246] The German Foreign Office continued to support cultural rapprochement, particularly through the efforts of Johannes Sievers, a political liberal and Head of its Cultural Section. Now, supported by the French Embassy, it was pressing the Berliner Staatsoper to include the French opera *Ariane* in its next programme, and was also encouraging efforts by the Deutsche Kunstgesellschaft and the Societé pour l'échange artistique to match the steady stream of German musical performances in France with concerts by French soloists in Germany. Comparable efforts were dedicated to the film

[239] AA R70568 H026316, Aufzeichnung über kulturelle Beziehungen mit Frankreich. Signed Konsul Eckel, 24 Sept. 1931; R70576 H027129, Aktivierung der deutsch-französischen Zusammenarbeit auf dem Gebiet des Auswanderungswesen und der Kulturpolitik. Signed Freytag, Berlin, 5 Oct. 1931.

[240] AA R70568 H026317, Aufzeichnung über kulturelle Beziehungen mit Frankreich. Signed Konsul Eckel, 24 Sept. 1931.

[241] AA R70568 H026316, ibid.; for figures R70576 H027126–31, here 127, Aktivierung der deutsch-französischen Zusammenarbeit auf dem Gebiet des Auswanderungswesen und der Kulturpolitik. Signed Freytag, Berlin, 5 Oct. 1931.

[242] AA R70568 H026316–17, Aufzeichnung über kulturelle Beziehungen mit Frankreich. Signed Konsul Eckel, 24 Sept. 1931; see also R70576 H027127–8, Aktivierung der deutsch-französischen Zusammenarbeit auf dem Gebiet des Auswanderungswesen und der Kulturpolitik. Signed Freytag, Berlin, 5 Oct. 1931.

[243] AA R70568 H026317–18, Aufzeichnung über kulturelle Beziehungen mit Frankreich. Signed Konsul Eckel, 24 Sept. 1931.

[244] AA R70568 H026318, ibid.

[245] AA R70568 H026319, ibid.

[246] Ibid.

industry, including the dubbing of 'really good films' and the joint production of feature films that promoted Franco-German rapprochement.[247]

None of this could wish away the painful legacies of two Franco-German wars, but demonstrated that alongside those on both sides who could 'never forget', there were powerful forces working for a new beginning. On the morning before Laval and Briand's visit to Berlin, the French press welcomed and attached great significance to the event. Most newspapers echoed official briefings which had stressed that while the talks would not seek to resolve major political problems they were more than a matter of courtesy. The right-wing press nonetheless advised the French ministers to deal cautiously with Germany, while those on the centre and left hoped for positive steps towards Franco-German economic collaboration. It remained however for Germany to provide France with the necessary reassurances.[248] During a press interview shortly before his departure Laval conceded that the task facing French and German negotiators 'is delicate, difficult, but cannot be beyond reach'. Previous meetings in Paris and London had laid the groundwork for agreement on economic issues, thus paving the way for 'the resolution of others in a spirit of mutual understanding'. Laval stressed the positive psychological impact this workmanlike approach would have on public opinion, creating 'an atmosphere of calm and confidence, without which we shall not be able to resolve the grave problems that confront the world'.[249]

The succession of conferences, the activities of various associations and pressure groups, the support of the Church, and of significant elements of the business world had therefore culminated at this point in a carefully considered and coherently articulated state-sponsored agenda. If the French and German political right remained essentially hostile to all of this, the responsible government ministers and the professional diplomats were not. It was striking that both sides agreed that the repeated rows and unresolved tensions that sometimes came to dominate their relationship could not be allowed to drag on unchecked. The devastating impact of the Great Depression demanded cooperation in some shape or form, but the Franco-German diplomatic agenda had progressed well beyond such utilitarianism. Rather than seeking simply to ameliorate the worst effects of the global economic crisis, France and Germany had come to agree that economic collaboration provided a vital first step on the road to wide-ranging

247 AA R70576 H027126–31, here 131, Aktivierung der deutsch-französischen Zusammenarbeit auf dem Gebiet des Auswanderungswesen und der Kulturpolitik. Signed Freytag, Berlin, 5 Oct. 1931; for Sievers' own assessment of cultural relations see R70576 H027132–6, Aufzeichnung. Signed Sievers, undated, with film discussed on H027133 and in Hand-Akten Samml. Akten betreffend: Frankreich (Ges. Eisenlohr), (R105386–8), here R105388, Telegramm Nr. 583. Signed Hoesch, Paris, 29 May 1931.

248 AA R70568 H026333–4, Telegramm Nr. 1007 vom 26/9. Signed Forster, Paris, 26 Sept. 1931.

249 AA R70568 H026355–6, Telegramm Nr. 1008. Signed Forster, Paris, 26 Sept. 1931; see also R70575, 'Le voyage à Berlin de MM. Laval et Briand. La phase économique du rapprochement franco-allemand', *Le Journal*, 14224, 27 Sept. 1931.

rapprochement, to a partnership that offered to turn on its head the tortured history of previous Franco-German relations. Put very simply, an effort would be made to rebuild Europe not at the point of a gun, but through the good offices of a comprehensive Franco-German alliance forged from the mutual respect and goodwill accorded by one equal to the other.[250]

[250] But see the more dismissive comment in Robert W. D. Boyce, 'Business as Usual: The Limits of French Economic Diplomacy, 1926–1933', in Robert W. D. Boyce (ed.), *French Foreign and Defence Policy, 1918–1940: The Decline and Fall of a Great Power* (London, 1998), 121–2.

5

Berlin and the Creation of the Franco-German Commission

A SUCCESSFUL CONFERENCE

Heinrich von Friedberg handled French affairs at the Wilhelmstraße, answering to the Head of Section II, Gerhard Köpke, who himself enjoyed close links with prominent figures in French public life.[1] Friedberg's earlier career included responsibility for economic relations with Western Europe and for Allied-occupied German territory, expertise complemented by a distinguished family history. The grandson of an illustrious ennobled Prussian jurist who had been one of the more prominent nineteenth-century converts from Judaism to Protestantism, he was now entrusted with the logistical details of the French ministerial visit. Brüning had already held his nose and struck a deal with the NSDAP's regional chief in Berlin, Joseph Goebbels, that the Nazis would steer clear of the visit if the criminal trial of an SA general was put on ice.[2] Friedberg's own concerns focused on security during the lengthy train journeys between Paris and Berlin and from 16 September he held a series of meetings with railway and police officials and representatives of the Prussian government to this end. Briand, Laval, and their colleagues were to travel to Berlin by scheduled train, leaving Paris at 16.25 on Saturday 26 September on the L11 Nordexpreß, arriving at Berlin Friedrichsstraße station at 08.37 the following morning. The French statesmen and other dignitaries were to travel in two standard international sleeper carriages, hooked immediately behind the locomotive and guard's van.[3] A special dining car and then two carriages reserved for registered French, and a few German, journalists completed the sealed section of the night train.[4]

On arrival at the last Belgian station, Herbesthal, a senior French-speaking Prussian police officer, was to join the train, followed in Aachen by a representative of the Foreign Office, a senior railways executive, and the first of a series of engineers

[1] AA R70575, 'Die deutsch-französischen Tage. Warmer Empfang der französischen Staatsmänner in Berlin', *Berliner Tageblatt* 457, 28 Sept. 1931; on Köpke, AA R70544 H021103, 'Sehr verehrter Herr Viénot!' Signed Köpke, Berlin, 5 Dec. 1932.

[2] Brüning, *Memoiren*, 411; Hömig, *Brüning*, 367. SA: Sturmabteilung—Storm Section/Storm Troopers.

[3] AA R70571 H026771–2, II Fr 2895. Ang. 3. An die Deutsche Reichsbahngesellschaft, Hauptverwaltung. Signed v. Friedberg, Berlin, 22 Sept. 1931.

[4] AA R70571 H026728–9, Telegramm Nr. 985 v. 24.9. Signed Forster, Paris, 24 Sept. 1931.

familiar with particular stretches of the track. The locomotive itself would see the driver and stoker joined by a further senior railways engineer. Thought was given to running a decoy locomotive ahead of the train, but this was deemed unnecessary given that another scheduled service used the same route just seven minutes ahead of the Nordexpreβ. All stations along the route were to be guarded and, with the exception of travel ticket holders, closed to the general public, regardless of whether the train was scheduled to stop or not. A chain of police officers standing along station platforms two metres from the official carriages was to serve as a security screen, and police with dogs would watch over the entire route.[5] These guards would complement personnel manning standard telephone points and signal boxes and be posted along the track at two-kilometre intervals, with more where visibility was restricted. Bridges and culverts were to be particularly carefully checked, each shortly before the passage of the express.[6] All of this was not lost on at least one of the accredited journalists on board the train, the French newspaper editor Louise Weiss. While crossing eastern France, she recounted: 'Men raised their hats, women held up their babies', whereas in Germany, 'Soldiers [*sic*] watched over the track. We had barely passed one by when the next appeared.'[7] Fearing that overzealous officiousness might sour the atmosphere, Friedberg instructed German customs officers at Aachen to desist from any passport or baggage inspection 'and refrain from disturbing the guests in any way whatsoever, particularly by boarding their carriage'.[8]

There then remained the tricky business of conveying the French visitors the relatively short distance from Friedrichstraβe station to the Hotel Adlon, a stone's throw from the Brandenburg Gate and also the French Embassy. The station was one of Berlin's busiest and the crowded night train from Paris would only add to the congestion. It was decided to stop the Nordexpreβ at Charlottenburg station, short of Friedrichstraβe, uncouple the French party's carriages, and leave the rest of the train to stand for ten minutes while the delegation continued to its destination. The official carriages would pull into the southernmost platform, above Georgenstraβe, where cars would be waiting to transfer the visitors to the Adlon. The platform would be sealed off, along with the two nearest tracks, and an empty train used to block any view from passing metro (Stadtbahn) trains which also used the station. The guests were to be whisked down steps and into a reception room to a welcome from French residents of Berlin, including the presentation of flowers by a girl in French folk costume, and a limited opportunity offered for press photographs. Customers using a restaurant next to the reception room would be locked in without warning during the ceremony and hotels outside the station placed under intensive police surveillance. Wider protocol reflected the German visit to Paris, something not lost on Briand: the welcoming crowd outside the station was

[5] AA R70571 H026791–5, here 794–5, e.o. II Fr 2841, Aufzeichnung. Signed von Friedberg, Berlin, 18 Sept. 1931.

[6] AA R70571 H026742–3, Abschrift II Fr 2933. Signed Deutsche Reichsbahn-Gesellschaft. Hauptverwaltung. Der Generaldirektor, Berlin, 22 Sept. 1931.

[7] Weiss, *Mémoires*, 309–10.

[8] AA R70571 H026787, II Fr 2861 I. Abschrift. Signed Im Auftrag (v. Fr.), Berlin, 21 Sept. 1931.

hand-picked by the Prussian Prime Minister's office, comprising policemen in civilian clothes, civil servants, and members of republican leagues. Thereafter, the motor convoy took a left, then a right turn to arrive in Unter den Linden, and so on to the heavily guarded Hotel Adlon where a sizeable crowd of some 2,000 cheered the French statesmen to cries of '*Vive la paix*!'[9]

Negotiations were to build on the diplomatic exchanges of the preceding weeks. Background briefing papers did review nagging problems such as the Saar question, but these contentious issues were to remain off the agenda. The Saar referendum, which was scheduled for 1935, had the potential to whip up unwelcome and unhelpful nationalist feeling and German diplomats doubtless remembered the damage wrought by the triumphal celebrations that followed France's early military evacuation of the southern Rhineland in June 1930. However, if a pre-emptive agreement might have had its attractions, German efforts at negotiation on the Saar during the 1929 Hague Conference were now seen as botched; and in any case the price France expected for an early return of the territory, to include long-term domination of its heavy industrial assets, was unacceptably high.[10]

A Franco-German customs union offered more in the longer term even if the two countries prioritized different routes to this common end: France through expanding existing private cartel agreements, Germany through tariff reductions supplemented by cartel agreements. Either way, this bilateral arrangement would go on to form the cornerstone of a wider European union, Berlin in particular favouring a multilateral approach.[11] Beyond this, the visa question, the war criminal issue, the development of comradely links between the two armies, German access to Tangier and Morocco, and the future payment of reparations through deliveries in kind (the means most favourable to Germany and least attractive to France) were either resolved or agreed in principle before the Berlin meeting. François-Poncet's earlier five-point agenda also remained on the table, for both sides could do business on wider trade relations, the reciprocal exchange of shares in private companies, the injection of French capital into struggling German companies and banks, and joint enterprises in third countries.[12]

Substantive issues apart, the German hosts planned at an appropriate moment to offer words of appreciation for the work of the former French Ambassador, Pierre de Margerie, enquire solicitously after Briand's health, and thank the French government for its punctilious care of the millions of German war graves on French soil. Germany, the French statesmen would be informed, planned to follow its neighbour's lead by dedicating a monument to the 'unknown soldier'. The German

[9] AA R70571 H026791–5, e.o. II Fr 2841, Aufzeichnung. Signed von Friedberg, Berlin, 18 Sept. 1931; R70571 H026728–9, Telegramm Nr. 985 v. 24.9. Signed Forster, Paris, 24 Sept. 1931; Brüning, *Memoiren*, 411; Hömig, *Brüning*, 366–7.

[10] AA R70573 H026866–71, Abschrift II S G 1350. Saarfrage (Aufzeichnung vom 17. Juli 1931). Signed von Friedberg.

[11] AA R70573 H026881–2, Verständigung in allgemeiner Richtung einer Zollunion. Unsigned, Berlin, 23 Sept. 1931.

[12] AA R70571 H026806–7, Bülow, I. Normalisierung der deutsch-französischen Beziehungen... Unsigned, undated; see also R70571 H026749. Unsigned, undated.

delegation would laud Briand's earlier cooperation with the late Gustav Stresemann, which would now find its fulfilment as the current talks served finally to normalize relations between the two countries.[13]

Much of this agenda was distilled into Brüning's welcoming speech. The French statesmen's visit, he began, was much appreciated on the German side: 'Its significance is best characterized by the fact that... no senior French statesman has visited Berlin in an official capacity since the Congress of Berlin [1878].'[14] He continued that world opinion regarded Franco-German rapprochement as central to overcoming the intensifying global economic crisis, which had scourged Germany in particular. But with statesmen of Laval and Briand's reputation and calibre in office detente was in safe hands. Echoing his own earlier speeches and the substance of Franco-German Catholic discourse, Brüning accepted that 'there was a huge amount that divided Germany and France if one looked back into history', but insisted that: 'European peace will only be secured when the two great neighbouring peoples of Germany and France have spiritually overcome their past and turned their gaze to a common future, cultural, economic, and political.'[15]

As German and French officials began work the same day on the technicalities of the proposed agreement, Laval and Brüning held private discussions in French. Their remit was to build on the personal trust established during the Paris meeting, but privacy also allowed them to dwell on less comfortable matters. Brüning let slip his unease regarding François-Poncet, with whom he would never hit it off, while Laval warned (as he had during the Paris meeting) that he was under considerable domestic pressure not to concede too much to Germany.[16] Brüning appreciated that Laval himself was committed to rapprochement, but understood that thanks to its financial strength France could also pursue other objectives. Laval's next port of call, after Berlin, was to be Washington, where he hoped on agreement to revive the German reparations schedule in some shape or form once the Hoover moratorium had run its course. Brüning, however, believed that when it came to reparations US opinion had shifted in Germany's favour and therefore saw no reason to cross swords with Laval on this particular score.[17] Events bore out Brüning's expectations. While Laval and Hoover reaffirmed their commitment to the international gold standard and seemed at one on the armaments question, agreeing that 'arms reduction had to follow on the establishment of political security', they remained divided on reparations. For a decade or more French diplomacy had struggled in vain to see reductions in Germany's reparations bill offset by commensurate cuts in France's external war debts (primarily to the USA), but Hoover would have none of it.[18]

Later that morning the French Premier was interviewed on German radio, while Briand, accompanied by François-Poncet, paid his respects at Stresemann's grave.

[13] AA R70571 H026733–4, Gesprächstoff. Unsigned, undated.

[14] AA R70569 H026371–4, quote on 371, Aussprache des RK. Unsigned, date stamped II Fr. 3016, 28 Sept. 1931.

[15] Ibid., quote on 373.

[16] AA R70575, 'Bilan Politique de la première journée d'entretiens franco-allemands', *Le Journal*, 14225, 28 Sept. 1931; Hömig, *Brüning*, 368–73.

[17] Brüning, *Memoiren*, 411–13.

[18] Schirmann, *Crise*, 185.

Laval's broadcast was predictable enough, underlining his hopes for Franco-German detente,[19] but Briand's pilgrimage was marked by a bizarre encounter. As his car drew up at the cemetery it happened upon a group of Nazi activists bearing the coffin of a comrade killed during a clash with communists. His police escort swept the Nazis aside, reducing them to offering, silently, a Hitler salute. Briand raised his hat in reply, any irony perhaps wasted on this particular audience.[20] The Foreign Minister then visited Curtius. They could agree that 'the current negotiations offered limited possibilities', but equally that 'the Commission and its remit would be of major significance in promoting rapprochement between our two countries'.[21] Briand was gloomy on France's economic prospects, repeating that collective action offered the only escape from the crisis. Curtius reassured him that Germany would not unilaterally resort to inflation even if his own position was (after the Austrian business) precarious: 'We are all subject to the vagaries of public opinion and foreign policy catastrophes.'[22]

The two ministers spoke again at the official reception, with Briand predicting that a left-wing victory at the forthcoming French parliamentary elections in March 1932 'would contribute decisively to the furtherance of German-French cooperation'.[23] Curtius then sounded out Berthelot on the modalities of normalizing relations. The French Permanent Secretary was reassuring on German access to Morocco and stressed his personal commitment to detente, adding that over the past year he 'had repeatedly told Briand that his rapprochement policy lacked any substantive linkages or conceptualization'.[24] Finally, Curtius turned to Laval, whose thoughts now seemed to be elsewhere. He warned of the danger posed to Europe by Bolshevism, observing that wars had grown in scale, from between countries, to between empires, and now to intercontinental conflict, predicting that: 'Sooner or later the Russians and Chinese will attack Europe.'[25] Curtius was sceptical, but during the ensuing formal negotiations thought was given to depositing a part of Germany's foreign currency earnings from its Russian trade in Paris rather than in London. Apart from this lending France a stake in German Soviet trade, German exporters had recently been stung by the unilateral devaluation of sterling, whereas the franc remained tied to gold.[26]

The practicalities of the Franco-German agreement were resolved that afternoon without difficulty and the visit also proved a public-relations triumph. If Louise Weiss (the daughter of an Alsatian Protestant pastor) dwelt in her memoirs of the visit on late Weimar Berlin's alleged moral decay and rampant sexual perversion,[27] the wider press response on both sides of the Rhine was positive. Among the liberal

[19] AA R70575, 'Die deutsch-franzosischen Tage', *Berliner Tageblatt*, 457, 28 Sept. 1931.
[20] AA R70575, 'Bilan Politique de la première journée d'entretiens franco-allemands', *Le Journal*, 14225, 28 Sept. 1931.
[21] AA R70506, Abschrift RM 1160. Doppel von II Fr. 3105. Signed Curtius, Berlin, 28 Sept. 1931, quote on 1.
[22] Ibid., quote on 2. [23] Ibid., quote on 3.
[24] Ibid., quote on 2–3. [25] Ibid., quote on 4.
[26] AA R70575, 'Die deutsch-französischen Tage', *Berliner Tageblatt*, 457, 28 Sept. 1931.
[27] Weiss, *Mémoires*, 311, 313–14.

German dailies, the *Berliner Tageblatt* looked forward to far-reaching detente founded on economic collaboration,[28] while the French press 'with the exception of a few on the extreme right' welcomed the improved atmosphere and the eventual prospect of resolving deeper-seated issues. As Forster reported: 'They feel in effect that if "it isn't a lot, it's more than a little," or in other words that this beginning is well measured, cautious, but robust and capable of further development.'[29] The former French Ambassador at Berlin, Charles Laurent, took space in the newspaper *L'Ordre* to recall his part in talks between the Ministers Louis Loucheur and Walther Rathenau during 1920 also designed to forge an economic alliance, continuing that: 'He believed that German-French rapprochement was not only desirable but essential... albeit confined for the moment to economic relations.'[30] French journalists were also pleasantly surprised by the cordiality of the reception in Berlin, and the respect and even warmth displayed by President Hindenburg when receiving the French visitors.[31] (His recent removal from the French war criminals list had made this meeting possible.) A columnist for *Le Journal* took time out to assess the public mood, remarking that:

> On this beautiful autumn Sunday the streets of Berlin were fairly quiet. But there were bigger crowds in the Tiergarten and around the Kurfürstendamm. In taking a stroll I could listen in on conversations. People were talking a lot about the French Ministers' visit. There was almost unanimous support for [the visit], even if I heard one or two ironic or hostile comments. In Unter den Linden a trader was selling postcards bearing Aristide Briand's portrait. He was doing a brisk trade and I asked if he didn't also have a card of Pierre Laval. He replied: '*Schade nicht noch*! [Not any more I'm afraid!]'[32]

And again mirroring the protocol of the Paris visit, the statesmen attended a packed Catholic service in the Dominican Maria-Viktoria-Kapelle,[33] before spending the Monday sightseeing, agreeing the final drafting of the official communiqué, and ending the day with a banquet in the French Embassy.[34] 'Early on Tuesday 29 September', Brüning recounted, 'the French gentlemen departed', by which time the German Chancellor had already turned his attention to the budgetary crisis besetting German local government and a politically delicate move to cut wages in the Ruhr mining industry by 7 per cent.[35]

The communiqué was released on the same day, reaffirming the commitment of both governments to a stable and trusting relationship founded initially on economic collaboration. To this end, a Joint Commission, chaired by government ministers and supported by a permanent secretariat, would draw its membership from the two civil services, figures from the business world, and employees'

[28] AA R70575, 'Die deutsch-französischen Tage', *Berliner Tageblatt*, 457, 28 Sept. 1931.
[29] AA R70506, Telegramm Nr. 1021 vom 29/9. Signed Forster, Paris, 29 Sept. 1931, quote on 2.
[30] AA R70577, 'Botschafter a.D. Laurent über eine deutsch-französische Verständigung', *Wolff's Telegraphisches Büro*, 82, 2128, Berlin, 9 Oct. 1931.
[31] AA R70506, Telegramm Nr. 1021 vom 29/9. Signed Forster, Paris, 29 Sept. 1931, quote on 2.
[32] AA R70575, 'Bilan Politique de la première journée d'entretiens franco-allemands', *Le Journal*, 14225, 28 Sept. 1931.
[33] Hömig, *Brüning*, 366–8. [34] Brüning, *Memoiren*, 414. [35] Ibid.

representatives. Meetings would be held in either country, as appropriate, and work was to begin without delay.[36]

LATOUR IN BERLIN

The positive impact left by the founding of the Joint Commission was reinforced in October when the Lord Mayor of Berlin, Heinrich Sahm, played host to his Parisian counterpart. Previously President of the Danzig Senate and politically unaffiliated, Sahm moved to Berlin in 1931 to tackle the city's crumbling finances and deal with a whiff of corruption that hung over the City Hall. Seen as a new broom, Sahm received some favourable press coverage in France[37] and in August learned from the German Embassy in Paris that the city's Lord Mayor, François Latour, wished to visit Berlin. This had first been mooted by Latour's predecessor, Jean Count de Castellane,[38] who had blood ties with German nobles active in the diplomatic service, including the von Pourtalès and von Welczeck families.[39] De Castellane was strongly committed to Franco-German rapprochement, but the furore surrounding the announcement of the Austro-German customs union in March 1931 saw the visit cancelled and then his period of office expire. However, in August he approached Hoesch on behalf of Latour, whose own interests extended well beyond municipal politics. The new Mayor was keen to enhance the ongoing thaw in Franco-German relations by visiting Berlin in the immediate wake of the ministerial conference,[40] an event, Hoesch observed, whose political significance far exceeded that of any ordinary municipal exchange. The office of Lord Mayor of Paris was held in the highest esteem within France itself and earlier visits by de Castellane to London and Madrid had witnessed a commensurate measure of pomp and ceremony. Hoesch added that François-Poncet had already shown a keen interest in Latour's plans and that protocol demanded a reception by political figures of appropriate rank.[41]

A more than cordial exchange of letters between Sahm and Latour saw the visit arranged for late October,[42] prompting the authorities in Berlin to study the etiquette and agendas of the visits by de Castellane to Madrid and London down

36 AA R70575, 'Die deutsch-französischen Tage', *Berliner Tageblatt*, 457, 28 Sept. 1931; R70575, 'Les Discours de Berlin', *Le Temps*, 29 Sept. 1931; R70575, 'Arbeitsbeginn schon Mitte Oktober', *Kölnische Zeitung*, 530, 29 Sept. 1931.

37 AA R70505, 'Le docteur Sahm, bourgmestre de Berlin, nous expose les charges de sa cite', *La Tribune Républicaine*, 188, 7 Jul. 1931.

38 AA R70506, II Fr. 2583, Sehr geehrter Herr Oberbürgermeister, Paris, 26 Aug. 1931, 1–2; see also covering letter, R70506, Deutsche Botschaft Paris, A 3111, Orig von II Fr. 2583. Signed Forster, Paris, 26 Aug. 1931.

39 AA Memoiren Stresemann (R70518) E684845–6, Deutsche Botschaft in Spanien, Madrid, 6 Jun. 1932.

40 AA R70506, II Fr. 2583, Sehr geehrter Herr Oberbürgermeister, Paris, 26 Aug. 1931, 2.

41 Ibid., 3–6.

42 AA R70506 K240838, Übersetzung. Gemeinderat Paris. Der Präsident. Signed François Latour, Paris, 11 Sept. 1931.

to the last detail.[43] A French press release made very clear the contribution of this second Berlin visit to the cause of Franco-German rapprochement:

> The programme has not as yet been finalized, but it is beyond doubt that the significance of this visit exceeds by far that of similar journeys. It can be regarded as a further stage in a new relationship that was initiated by Laval's and Briand's visit to Berlin.[44]

Or as Latour himself declared: 'A steadfast policy of collaboration between nations is currently more vital than ever and this rapprochement must extend from the economic realm to embrace the cause of civilization and peace.'[45] He arrived in the German capital on 19 October, alongside senior members of his administration, to an enthusiastic welcome characteristic of the heady, if short-lived, optimism that followed the successful ministerial summit. High politics aside, Latour stressed that the economic collaboration envisaged by their respective governments had already become reality at municipal level where 'technical advances and comparable problems demand that we work together ever more closely', before alluding to Brüning's appeal not to let the past poison future relations. Madame de Stael, he recalled, had once written that: 'Disunity between France and Germany meant a divided Europe',[46] while Sahm endorsed Latour's declaration as 'the leitmotiv' of his visit, adding that:

> The supreme goal that we advocate, without wishing away all the problems that divide us and which it would be futile to deny, is to forge rapprochement through a common effort, fulfilled for the well-being of our two nations and indeed for the well-being of the whole world.[47]

Sahm did not mince his words when alluding to the social misery that was plaguing Berlin and the financial crisis that had prevented the German capital from 'welcoming your arrival with a series of brilliant receptions', but hoped 'that you will take back to France and to your beautiful Paris the certain knowledge that your visit has given us enormous pleasure and genuine satisfaction. I am utterly convinced that this visit has served to guarantee friendship between Paris and Berlin.'[48]

[43] AA R70506 K240840–1, Abschrift! Der Oberbürgermeister. Signed Dr Sahm, Berlin, 17 Sept. 1931; R70506 K240836, zu Fr. 2814, Ref.: Kons. Eckel, sehr verehrter Herr Oberbürgermeister. Sig. illeg., Berlin, 21 Sept. 1931.

[44] AA R70506, 'Französischer Besuch für Berlin', *Berliner Tageblatt*, 476, 9 Oct. 1931.

[45] AA R70506 K240870, zu II Fr. 3305, Auswärtiges Amt. Sprachendienst Spr. i 3990. An das Referat II Fr. Herrn Konsul Eckel. Signed Der Leiter des Sprachendienstes, Berlin, 12 Oct. 1931; and attached translation, R70506 K240871–3, quote on 872. Unsigned, undated.

[46] AA R70507 K240897–9, quote on 898, Städtischer Nachrichtendienst, Rede des Präsidenten des Pariser Stadtrats François Latour beim Empfang in Berliner Rathaus. Unsigned, Berlin, 19 Oct. 1931.

[47] AA R70506 K240871–3, quote on 871, zu II Fr. 3305. Unsigned, undated. For covering letter, R70506 K240870, zu II Fr. 3305, Auswärtiges Amt. Sprachendienst Spr. i 3990. An das Referat II Fr. Herrn Konsul Eckel. Signed Der Leiter des Sprachendienstes, Berlin, 12 Oct. 1931. See also R70506, 'Besuch aus Paris. Die Oberhäupter der Pariser Stadtverwaltung in Berlin eingetroffen', *Berliner Tageblatt*, 493, 19 Oct. 1931.

[48] AA R70506 K240871–3, quote on 873, zu II Fr. 3305. Unsigned, undated.

Official niceties aside, Latour gave a series of press interviews on his return to Paris in which he stressed 'the warm reception he had received in Berlin, both from officials and from the public', adding that his visit had provided lessons valuable for his own stewardship of Paris.[49] Wider newspaper coverage was generally positive, albeit with the inevitable reservations in the right-wing press which criticized Latour for dwelling too much on foreign policy issues.[50]

CREATING THE COMMISSION

Returning now to the Ministerial visit, Curtius' immediate response was decidedly cool. He complained on 29 September in a circular to German diplomatic missions that the visit had achieved little of substance beyond the establishment of the Joint Commission and regretted that issues such as disarmament or reparations had remained off the agenda.[51] However, his professed disappointment was curious at best and inconsistent to boot. The Director of the United Press of America, Frederick Kuh, had forwarded to him questions regarding the Joint Commission which elicited virtually the opposite response. The Commission, Curtius explained to Kuh, sought detente in areas where 'political interference and accidents are least likely', with the economy offering the best prospects. This, he continued, 'opened the way to political détente' as well as addressing the immediate challenges of the world economic crisis. The accord was potentially advantageous to the USA, for European prosperity would, among other things, enhance its relations with France and Germany.[52] And when Curtius subsequently issued a general press release on 30 September his optimistic persona held sway as he pronounced that:

> This exchange of views... was not part of a mere courtesy visit but instead the continuation and broadening of talks opened in Paris. The particular significance of our current meeting was not simply that we examined various issues openly and in an atmosphere of trust, but equally that we found the means to achieve what can, we believe, be achieved. We have created a body which should promote economic relations between our two countries, and which, through collaboration between governments and the business world, promises to bring about a positive and practical outcome.[53]

This accorded with the clear understanding on both sides that the creation of the Joint Commission was the primary purpose of the visit, and, as noted, Curtius

[49] AA R70507 K240880–1, quote on 880, Deutsche Botschaft Paris A 3858. Signed Forster, Paris, 23 Oct. 1931; see also R70507 K240884, J. Chautard, 'M. François-Latour nous parle de son voyage en Allemagne', *La Liberté*, 23 Oct. 1931.

[50] AA R70507 K240880–1, Deutsche Botschaft Paris A 3858. Signed Forster, Paris, 23 Oct. 1931.

[51] AA R70569, e.o. II Fr. 3062, Telegramm in Ziffern. Zur persönlichen Information. Signed Curtius, Berlin, 29 Sept. 1931.

[52] AA R27998 396–8, quotes on 397–8, zur RM 1178, Sehr geehrter Herr Kuh. Unsigned, 29 Sept. 1931.

[53] AA R27998 393, Eigentum von *Wolffs Telegraphischem Büro*, France vom 30.9.1931 morgens. Blatt zwei.

himself had stressed to Hoesch in August that the wider significance of the planned meeting lay in the simple fact that it was taking place at all.[54]

Many others simply accentuated the positive. The habitually cautious Berthelot was particularly optimistic, speaking of 'an unmistakable and enormous change in the atmosphere', while an ailing Briand declared that 'in the light of his Berlin experience he would hang on as Foreign Minister for as long as his health allowed'.[55] As the French statesmen's train back to Paris reached the Franco-Belgian frontier at Jeumont where a large welcoming crowd awaited them, both Laval and Briand issued upbeat press releases stressing the importance of the Franco-German summit for the cause of world peace.[56]

Meanwhile, however self-contradictory his feelings, Curtius spent his final days in office working on the internal structure and modus operandi of the Joint Commission, in part because France's diplomatic timetable demanded quick decisions. The formal accord reached in Berlin had been relatively short on detail and Laval was keen to reach agreement on specifics before he left for the United States on 16 October.[57] As noted, reparations remained on the French Premier's agenda for Washington[58] and he was no doubt anxious to reassure his American hosts that, despite France's attachment to key tenets of the Versailles Treaty, he remained committed to rapprochement with Germany through the Commission. Curtius, though, had no wish to see Laval's US timetable leave Germany pre-empted by a unilateral French announcement on the workings of the Commission.[59] He therefore asked the German Embassy in Paris to float a few ideas of his own: that the Commission should be chaired by the two Foreign Ministers, or, more often, by their nominees, and that civil servants be co-opted onto the body, with economic experts and other specialists seconded to meetings as required from approved German and French lists. He also proposed a Press Office, or at least the formal involvement of senior newspaper correspondents, and supported Laval's intention of funding the Commission through the French and German national budgets.[60]

By the time the Embassy's reply reached Berlin, confirming that Laval was by and large happy with Curtius' proposals,[61] the German Foreign Minister had finally paid the price for his failed Austrian adventure. Pressure from President Hindenburg combined with right-wing fury in the Reichstag to force his resignation as part of a wider Cabinet reshuffle, which saw the complexion of the German government shift a notch to the right. Nonetheless, Hindenburg was happy enough

[54] AA R70567 H025979–81, R.M. diplo Paris Nr 419. Signed Curtius, Berlin, 5 Aug. 1931.

[55] AA R70569 H026503, Telegramm Nr 49 vom 2.10. Signed Adolf Müller, Bern, 2 Oct. 1931.

[56] AA R27998 393, Eigentum von *Wolffs Telegraphischem Büro*, France vom 30.9.1931 morgens. Blatt eins.

[57] AA R70576, Abschrift. Auswärtiges Amt Nr. II Fr 3088. Signed Curtius, Berlin, 2 Oct. 1931, 1–2; R70577 H027196–200, here 200, Telegramm No. 1079 vom 9.10. Signed Forster, Paris, 9 Oct. 1931.

[58] See Ch. 5 under 'A Successful Conference', 126.

[59] AA R70576, Abschrift. Auswärtiges Amt Nr. II Fr 3088. Signed Curtius, Berlin, 2 Oct. 1931, 1–2.

[60] Ibid., 1–6; see also R70577 H027148–50, e.o. RM 1201 vom 5.10.1931. Signed Curtius, Berlin, 5 Oct. 1931.

[61] AA R70577 H027196–200, Telegramm No. 1079 vom 9.10. Signed Forster, Paris, 9 Oct. 1931.

with the general tenor of foreign policy[62] and Brüning was able to add the Foreign Minister's portfolio to that of the Chancellorship, thus providing continuity in that regard. Even so, German diplomats were left scrambling to address the political upheaval in Berlin while keeping pace with events in Paris. On 8 October the French Undersecretary of State for the National Economy, Claude-Joseph Gignoux, was appointed de facto Chairman of the French section of the Commission, although it was left open for Briand as Foreign Minister and titular Chairman to preside over key meetings. The full membership of the French section was announced on the same day, with the high-ranking diplomat and trade expert Robert Coulandre named as Secretary General. He was supported by senior officials from the Trade, Agriculture, Finance, Public Works, and Labour Ministries, while grandees from the business world, including enthusiastic trade union officials,[63] were nominated for co-option as expert advisers whenever required.[64] Although the contrasting structures of the French and German economies complicated efforts to match up the membership of the French and German sections of the Commission and the Cabinet reshuffle in Berlin delayed the definitive announcement of German personnel still further, matters were resolved by the middle of the month.[65]

Laval inaugurated the French section of the Commission on 15 October,[66] with Brüning chairing the first meeting of the German section on 3 November. The German Chancellor reminded delegates that their ultimate task was to further cooperation and mutual understanding between the two countries, something to be achieved 'through permanent consultation and collaboration'. There were to be four 'Subcommissions'; the first dealing with overall economic relations (review of the 1927 Franco-German Trade Treaty and, in a further subdivision, private cartels), the second would work on the integration of national transport systems, the third the integration of particular economic sectors, and the fourth Franco-German collaboration elsewhere in the world.[67] Expert advisors were attached to one or

[62] Wolfram Pyta, *Hindenburg. Herrschaft zwischen Hohenzollern und Hitler* (Munich, 2007), 685–98, 862.

[63] AA R70577 H027253, Telegramm Nr. 1098, Auswärtig Berlin. Signed Hoesch, Paris, 14 Oct. 1931.

[64] AA R70577 H027161–5, zu II Fr. 3213. D. Signed I.A. (Köpke), Berlin, 8 Oct. 1931.

[65] AA R70577 H027196–200, Telegramm No. 1079 vom 9.10. Signed Forster, Paris, 9 Oct. 1931; R70577 H027238–42, Auswärtiges Amt, Die Zusammensetzung der deutsch-französischen Wirtschaftskommission, zu II Fr 3299. Signed Im Auftrag Köpke, undated but filed between 12 and 13 Oct. 1931; see also appendices H027243, Anlage 1 Deutsch-französische Wirtschaftskommission. Mitgliederliste; H027244, Anlage 2 Deutsche Sachverständigenliste; H027245, Anlage 3 Französische Sachverständigenliste; R70577 H027208, Durchdruck als Reinkonzept. Auswärtiges Amt II Fr. 3253. Signed Im Auftrag, Feine, 10 Oct. 1931; R70577 H027251–2, Telegramm Nr. 1094 vom 13.10. Signed Hoesch, Paris, 13 Oct. 1931; R70577 H027269–71, Telegramm Nr. 1104. Signed Hoesch, Paris, 15 Oct. 1931; R70577 H027299, Durchdruck für Herrn Min. Dir. Köpke, e.o. II Fr. 3364. I. Signed RF, Berlin, 19 Oct. 1931; R70577 H027297, Germadiplo Paris Nr. 581, zu II Fr 3354. Signed Ritter, Berlin, 20 Oct. 1931.

[66] AA R70577, 'Die ersten Beratungen der französischen Abteilung des deutsch-französischen Wirtschaftsausschusses', *W.T.B.* Nr. 2177, 16 Oct. 1931.

[67] AA R70578, 'Erste Sitzung der deutschen Mitglieder des deutsch-französischen Wirtschaftskomitees', *Wolff's Telegraphisches Büro*, 82, Nr 2311, Berlin, 3 Nov. 1931; see also R70577 H027283–4, Deutsch-Franzoesisches Studienkomitee Berliner Bureau. Bericht Nr. 2 unseres deutschen Sekretaers in Paris, 'Deutsch-Franzoesische Zusammenarbeit', Paris, 16 Oct. 1931.

more such Subcommissions,[68] all of which did something to lift French public opinion. The press there had been disturbed by the German Cabinet crisis and also by a rally held by Brüning's right-wing opponents in the DNVP, Stahlhelm, and NSDAP at Bad Harzburg on 11 October which only served to accentuate the febrile atmosphere. As the Franco-German Study Committee reported:

> What people were reading and hearing [in France] over the past few days regarding the progressive weakening of Brüning's position harked back to the bad old days of spite and malice—believed long past. On the day after the Harzburg rally even the moderate press did not hesitate to threaten Germany should a radical right-wing government come to power there.

However, the Committee continued, the renewed progress on the Joint Commission had reassured people 'that official activity has continued and that it seeks, at the very least, to create the practical preconditions for the collaboration announced in Berlin'.[69] Not that the ongoing economic crisis and each government's resulting preoccupation with national economic interests would make for plain sailing.[70]

None of this was lost on the diplomats and politicians. François-Poncet had already spoken with Bülow of Laval's wish for a spectacular inaugural meeting of the full Joint Commission to engage world opinion. Bülow felt Paris was the appropriate location for this, given that the founding treaty had been signed in Berlin, although he doubted the practicality of sending every last German expert adviser to an essentially ceremonial meeting. In any case, both agreed the substantive business of setting up subcommittees and drafting a concrete agenda was vital[71] and the prioritization of substantive achievement over ceremony gained ground over the coming days. During discussions with Berthelot on 13 October, Hoesch warned against overdoing any ceremony, which threatened to backfire by stirring up domestic and foreign opposition. Instead, he suggested that things begin with an informal private meeting between the Chairmen and Secretaries General.[72] On the following day Laval seemed to agree: 'Remarking [to Hoesch] that our Commission has a job to do and must as a priority prove itself in this regard. Nonetheless, [he] was confident that, however modest its beginnings, the Commission would chalk up substantial achievements within a relatively short space of time.'[73] However, just a week later Coulandre warned Hoesch that Laval still hankered after a ceremonial launch of the Joint Commission. The German Ambassador rehearsed his earlier misgivings and agreed with Coulandre that the practicalities of exactly how the

[68] See, for example, AA R70578 H027332–3, Telegramm Nr. 1220, Kzl. Nr. 1796. Signed Hoesch, Paris, 10 Nov. 1931.

[69] AA R70577 H027283, Deutsch-Franzoesisches Studienkomitee Berliner Bureau. Bericht Nr. 2 unseres deutschen Sekretaers in Paris, 'Deutsch-Franzoesische Zusammenarbeit', Paris, 16 Oct. 1931.

[70] Ibid., H027283–4.

[71] AA R70577 H027218–19, stamped Auswärtiges Amt II Fr 3290. Signed Bülow, Berlin, 12 Oct. 1931.

[72] AA R70577 H027251–2, Telegramm Nr. 1094 vom 13.10, Für Staatssekretär persönlich. Signed Hoesch, Paris, 13 Oct. 1931.

[73] AA R70577 H027266–8, quote on 267, Telegramm No. 1101 vom 14.10. x) II Fr. 3251. Signed Hoesch, Paris, 14 Oct. 1931.

Commission would begin work were anything but straightforward and demanded attention.[74] François-Poncet was equally anxious to see the Commission notch up some achievement or other, suggesting that recently successful talks between Germany, France, and Czechoslovakia on the porcelain trade be attributed to it. He added that the establishment in Paris or Berlin of a Franco-German Chamber of Trade might also fit the bill.[75]

There were some hopeful portents. Belgium had already expressed strong interest in the Joint Commission, saying 'it would particularly value being involved in the work of the planned Commission at the earliest possible moment, given Belgium's close ties with Germany and France'.[76] That was not to be, but discussions between Berthelot and Hoesch revealed that although the French Permanent Secretary bemoaned Gignoux's rigidity, 'leaving it doubtful whether he possessed the necessary enthusiasm and inventiveness',[77] he believed Coulandre well up to the demands of the moment, 'thus compensating in full for Gignoux's initial weakness'. He added that Coulandre was already busying himself with a wide range of ideas and initiatives:

> Among other things Berthelot showed me a memorandum concerning German-French collaboration in Turkey and Russia. This reinforced his conviction that really significant results could and must be forged from the Berlin agreements. As for a date for the commencement of negotiations, Berthelot observed that Laval desired an early start.[78]

Berthelot also reassured Hoesch that an agreement on German access to Morocco would be concluded very shortly, providing for a step-by-step relaxation of restrictions culminating in German 'equal rights' within a few years. Hoesch was able to announce off the record that the former Economics Minister and current Permanent Secretary in the Economics Ministry, Ernst Trendelenburg, a political liberal, would be nominated as de facto Chairman of the German section of the Commission. Karl Ritter, Head of the Economic Section of the Foreign Office, would serve as Secretary General. Days later German responsibility for the Joint Commission was indeed transferred from Köpke's desk in Section II (France) to Ritter's.[79] Berthelot welcomed these appointments[80] which, Hoesch stressed, provided the German section with leadership of the necessary calibre to engage with French

[74] AA R70577 H027312–15, Telegramm Nr. 1126 vom 20.10. Signed Hoesch, Paris, 20 Oct. 1931.

[75] AA R70578 H027324–6, Abschrift, stamped Auswärtiges Amt II Fr. 3513. Signed Bülow, Berlin, 29 Oct. 1931.

[76] AA R70577 H027211–12, Deutsche Gesandtschaft Brüssel. A 326 Betr.: Die deutsch-französische Wirtschaftskommission, signed Lerchenfeld, Brussels, 9 Oct. 1931.

[77] AA R70577 H027251–2, quote on 251, Telegramm Nr. 1094 vom 13.10. Signed Hoesch, Paris, 13 Oct. 1931.

[78] Ibid.

[79] AA R70577 H027316, Abschrift W 4831 V. Signed Ritter, Berlin, 21 Oct. 1931; this contrasts with Krüger, 'Abgebrochene Dialog', 299–301, where Ritter is seen as essentially excluded from European affairs by 1930.

[80] AA R70577 H027251–2, Telegramm Nr. 1094 vom 13.10. Signed Hoesch, Paris, 13 Oct. 1931.

personnel: 'who, one can say, are pre-eminent within French economic life and are thus always able to speak authoritatively and act decisively'.[81]

When, on 13 November, Laval opened the first full session of the Commission in Paris, practicalities did take precedence over ceremony. The Subcommissions worked through the afternoon and into the next morning to define their various remits. The signs were positive. Gignoux, Briand, and Hoesch held receptions at which existing personal contacts were renewed and new ones forged, while the formal discussions 'proceeded in a friendly manner with both sides ready and willing to pursue collaboration based on mutual understanding'.[82] German delegates had set out remits for the Subcommissions before the Paris meeting and, since these were essentially uncontentious, they were accepted by the French representatives.[83] It was agreed that the French and German sections of each Subcommission would work separately to prepare the ground for detailed negotiations, which were scheduled for Berlin in mid-December (Subcommissions I and III) and Paris in late November (Subcommission II) and mid-December (Subcommission IV). Expert advisors were asked not to brief the press independently; Subcommission records would be kept by a French-speaking and a German-speaking secretary.[84]

Subcommission I's 'Subgroup Commerce' was to amend the 1927 Franco-German Trade Treaty to accord with 'current conditions' and provide for Franco-German collaboration in international economic affairs. Its 'Subgroup Cartels' was to enhance the existing network of private business cartels in order, eventually, to render traditional customs and tariff barriers obsolete. Subcommission II was to coordinate railways, maritime and inland shipping, and air travel in the interests of transport companies and their users. Subcommission III looked to the integration of the French and German economies through the creation of umbrella companies which would embrace compatible French and German firms in key sectors. Finally, Subcommission IV would coordinate French and German economic activity in the wider world, seeking to develop new markets and thereby boost consumption and combat unemployment.[85]

Much of this built on earlier plans. Subcommission I would, *inter alia*, coordinate French and German efforts to realize the League of Nations' economic initiatives. Among other things, the Subcommission hoped to breathe fresh life into the Briand Plan,[86] an area where Paris and Berlin had first mooted bilateral collaboration during the autumn of 1930.[87] Parts of François-Poncet's five-point

[81] AA R70577 H027266–8, quote on 267, Telegramm No. 1101 vom 14.10, x) II Fr. 3251. Signed Hoesch, Paris, 14 Oct. 1931.

[82] AA R70578 H027344–6, quote on 345, Deutsche Abteilung der Deutsch-Französischen Wirtschaftskommission. No. W.5592. Signed Ritter, Berlin, 23 Nov. 1931.

[83] Ibid. [84] Ibid.

[85] AA R70578 H027347–50, Programme des Travaux de la Commission Economique Franco-Allemande. Unsigned, undated, but attached to R70578 H027344–6, quote on 345, Deutsche Abteilung der Deutsch-Französischen Wirtschaftskommission. No. W.5592. Signed Ritter, Berlin, 23 Nov. 1931.

[86] AA R70578 H027347, Programme des Travaux de la Commission Economique Franco-Allemande, as above, Première Sous-Commission. Relations commerciales.

[87] See Ch. 3 under 'Franco-German Exchanges', 65, 67, 69, 71–2.

agenda and Bülow's essentially positive response to this are also discernible in the wider agenda of the four Subcommissions. Similarly, elements of François-Poncet's Plan constructif, which sought to address the economic misery of South-Eastern Europe,[88] looked set to occupy Subcommission IV. The Central European economies would trade manufactured goods for foodstuffs from the Balkans, the whole exchange financed and underwritten by French capital.[89] This would complement simultaneous efforts by the League of Nations to resolve the deep-seated economic crises of the Danube basin and South-Eastern Europe.[90]

However, reference to the 1927 Trade Treaty betrayed growing French concern over its mushrooming trade deficit with Germany.[91] The Franco-German Study Committee was alarmed by off-the-record comments from well-placed French sources which seemed to question whether the Joint Commission's efforts to forge a Franco-German customs union were reconcilable with an upsurge in protectionist sentiment within France itself: 'We are therefore confronted with highly regressive forces, which for sure relate to the exceptional economic situation, but which, for all that, remain no easier to resolve.'[92] And it was not long before this disjuncture began to prejudice the wider prospects of the Commission very seriously indeed.

AN IMMINENT TRADE WAR AND THE QUOTA ISSUE

Economic and trading links had, of course, been utilized to further Franco-German rapprochement even before the First World War.[93] Thereafter, post-war France remained attached to Britain as its principal military partner (the lack of a formal alliance notwithstanding), but repeatedly sounded out Berlin's views on some sort of Franco-German economic partnership. Paris believed that the 1925 Locarno Agreement offered an ideal opportunity to realize this strategy and with the ink barely dry on the treaty, Briand's Chef de cabinet, Alexis Léger, as noted, had proposed to German leaders that the two countries exploit the re-emerging network of private cartels to deepen bilateral collaboration within the context of an integrating Europe.[94] However, tariff relations between the two countries took precedence, for in 1925 Germany had regained customs sovereignty and thereafter

[88] For discussion of the situation in South-Eastern Europe, Derek H. Aldcroft, *Europe's Third World: The European Periphery in the Interwar Years* (Aldershot, 2006), esp. ch. 4.

[89] MAE Z773 245, Ambassade de France à Berlin. L'Attaché Financier. Revue de Presse du 19 septembre 1931, Berlin, 19 Sept. 1931: V) Pays étrangers. a) La collaboration franco-allemande dans les pays du Sud-est de l'Europe.

[90] See Schirmann, *Crise*, 174–80.

[91] See Ch. 4 under 'Preparations for the Berlin Ministerial Conference', 111, 117–19.

[92] AA R70577 H027283–4, Deutsch-Franzoesisches Studienkomitee Berliner Bureau. Bericht Nr. 2 unseres deutschen Sekretaers in Paris, 'Deutsch-Franzoesische Zusammenarbeit', Paris, 16 Oct. 1931.

[93] See Ch. 1 under 'The Opening Gambits', 8–10.

[94] Bariéty, 'France and the Politics of Steel', 43.

signed a series of trade treaties with its major commercial partners. Among these was the 1927 Franco-German treaty, agreed at a time when the French economy was booming and enjoyed an annual trade surplus of more than 2 billion francs with Germany alone.[95]

The details of this treaty were staggeringly intricate, classifying items as liable for the standard tariff, a reduced rate, and occasionally subject to quotas. If anything German exports to France encountered more restrictions than French exports to Germany, and the post-war reparations settlement required 26 per cent of the value of German exports to be surrendered to the French state. However, both countries were benefiting from a rapid and mutual expansion in trade and all in all the treaty favoured this process.[96] Soon enough this played to Germany's advantage. The country's formidable manufacturing and industrial base had been temporarily handicapped by the war and short-term restrictions built into the peace treaty. However, as anti-German feeling in France faded and German businessmen and diplomats worked hard to rebuild trade relations,[97] Germany came to replace Britain as France's second-largest source of imports by 1929, with the United States the largest. However, French exports to Germany plummeted, resulting in a French deficit in 1930 of more than 3.5 billion francs in trade between the two countries.[98] Despite an officially sponsored campaign west of the Rhine to 'buy French',[99] Germany's trade surplus with France continued to grow remorselessly into 1931.[100] The first signs of trouble concerned French producers' anger at the flood of German woollen socks, and then women's artificial silk stockings, that was crowding their market. The Wilhelmstraβe conceded that trade relations with France had evolved 'catastrophically in our favour', and urged a speedy resolution of the so-called stocking war (*Strumpfkrieg*) before other products entered the equation.[101] Peace was duly restored in March 1931.

However, it was not as if the wider German economy was flourishing. The country's domestic market had been deeply depressed for two years or more, resulting in 'buy German' campaigns that were every bit as strident as their

[95] AA R87062, Anl. zu W. 2783, 23 Aug. 1932. Aus 'Les Echos' vom 21. August 1932, 'Faut-il dénoncer le Traité de Commerce Franco-Allemand?'

[96] For full text of the draft agreement: MAE Z384 203–13, *Journal Officiel* du 12 Août 1926. Publication et mise en application à titre provisoire de l'accord commercial provisoire, entre la France et L'Allemagne. Signé à Paris, le 5 Août 1926; on reparations and other modalities: AA R87062, Zollblatt Nr. 10, Frankreich, Stand: 10.2.1928, esp. 5.

[97] AA R87062, Deutsche Botschaft Nr. 335, Inhalt: New York Times über die Besserung der deutsch-französischen Beziehungen. Signed Prittwitz, Washington, D.C, 27 Feb. 1929; file R87062 contains various further examples of this process.

[98] For 1929: MAE Z525 296, Ambassade de France à Berlin. Direction des Affaires Politiques et Commerciales. Europe. No 726, Échanges commerciaux franco-allemandes, Berlin, 18 Sept. 1929; for 1930: AA R87062, Anl. zu W. 2783, 23 Aug. 1932. Aus 'Les Echos' vom 21. August 1932, 'Faut-il dénoncer le Traité de Commerce franco-allemand?'

[99] AA R87062, Deutsche Botschaft Nr. 765, Betrifft: Propaganda-Feldzug gegen ausländlische Erzeugnisse. Signed Maltzan, Paris, 3 Apr. 1930.

[100] AA R87062, Anl. zu W. 2783, 23 Aug. 1932. Aus 'Les Echos' vom 21. August 1932, 'Faut-il dénoncer le Traité de Commerce Franco-Allemand?'

[101] AA R105387, Abschrift, Lieber Eisenlohr! Signed Posse, Geneva, 19 Sept. 1930.

counterparts in France.[102] The implosion of German demand for French primary and semi-finished products hit home particularly sharply,[103] a situation exacerbated by the 1931 German banking crisis. This had forced the German authorities to impose draconian foreign exchange controls which severely hampered the country's importers, while its exporters priced their goods so cheaply on the French market as to foster accusations of dumping, which surely breached the spirit of the Franco-German Trade Treaty if not its letter. In August officials from the Quai d'Orsay complained of as much during a tense meeting with Germany's Commercial Attaché in Paris, warning that a political storm threatened which would 'deal a fatal blow to the Trade Treaty'.[104] French officials reluctantly conceded that the German authorities had had little choice other than to impose currency controls[105] and the French business press accepted that the collapse of Germany's domestic economy had forced German companies to clear inventories by exporting at any price, but the mainstream press became increasingly hostile. Headlines screamed 'Germany gets rich' and 'Germany cleans up on foreign trade',[106] while the French Agriculture and Trade Ministries fretted over the likely impact of the French trade deficit on the centre-right coalition's electoral prospects when the country went to the polls in March 1932.[107] The swathe of small family businesses that constituted such an important part of the French economy and delivered up much of the centre-right's vote lived in a very different world from the large-scale enterprises, organized in international cartels, which favoured closer links with Germany.

The business newspaper, *Journée industrielle*, feared for the prospects for Franco-German economic relations and in particular the outlook for the Joint Commission,[108] all of which suggested that the Quai d'Orsay's strategy of using economic synergies to further Franco-German rapprochement was becoming dangerously detached from the realities of the domestic situation. In fact the French authorities had begun imposing quotas on imported goods some months before Laval signed the Berlin agreement. The 1927 Trade Treaty allowed either country to respond to any threat to 'vital national interests' and Paris did just that, citing rising unemployment to justify unilateral restrictions on the import of coal,[109] wine, and

102 MAE Z761 166, Légation de la République Française en Bavière. Direction des Affaires Politiques et Commerciales. Europe. No 128, Manifestation à Munich en faveur de l'echat exclusive des produits allemands. Signed André d'Ormesson, Munich, 27 Sept. 1931.

103 MAE Z761 209–13, Ambassade de France à Berlin. Relations Commerciales No 964, La situation économique en l'Allemagne à la fin d'octobre. Signed André François-Poncet, Berlin, 29 Oct. 1931.

104 AA R105388, Telegramm Nr. 833 vom 6/8. Signed Hoesch, Paris, 6 Aug. 1931, 1.

105 Ibid., 2–3.

106 AA R87062, Deutsche Botschaft W. 1966. Betrifft: Letzte deutsche Handelbilanz und französische Presse. Signed Schellhorn, Paris, 21 Aug. 1931, 1–2.

107 For background, AA R105388, Telegramm Nr. 833 vom 6/8. Signed Hoesch, Paris, 6 Aug. 1931.

108 AA R87062, Deutsche Botschaft W. 1966. Betrifft: Letzte deutsche Handelbilanz und französische Presse. Signed Schellhorn, Paris, 21 Aug. 1931, 1.

109 AA R105388, Telegramm Nr. 766 vom 16.7, Auswärtig Berlin auch für Zetefa. Signed Hoesch, 16 Jul. 1931.

timber,[110] and soon enough on cattle, meat, dairy products, and fish, again on coal, and also nitrogen.[111] These measures were not directed uniquely against Germany, but Berlin doubted the legality of the quotas, comparing the 'national emergency' of fewer than 100,000 jobless in France with the 4.6 million east of the Rhine.[112] Just weeks before the Berlin conference, the Reichstag's Trade Committee had complained that the succession of French quotas breached the Franco-German Trade Treaty[113] and during November the Wilhelmstraβe came to fear that tit-for-tat retaliation by France's trading partners would trigger a race to the bottom: 'The very opposite to the measures promoted in Geneva in recent years is occurring. We are reverting to the situation that existed between 1920 and 1923.'[114]

Opinions differed in Berlin over how to react. The 1925 Franco-German Trade Arbitration Agreement and 1927 Trade Treaty allowed Germany to retaliate in kind, but Bülow had no wish to inflame things just days before the first scheduled plenary meeting of the Franco-German Joint Commission. Instead he proposed formal arbitration,[115] and prepared to inform Paris accordingly.[116] Karl Ritter had been in Geneva as this storm brewed, but returned to Berlin in time to persuade a sceptical Bülow that even arbitration might compromise economic rapprochement from the outset. Instead, he suggested, the Commission itself could resolve the burgeoning trade dispute, but he had to agree to 'immediate negotiations on the French import restrictions as soon as the German-French Commission is convened'.[117]

Ritter and Coulandre had already agreed to hold talks in Berlin to discuss the Commission's wider agenda,[118] but when they did meet in early November their discussions were dominated by the import quota dispute. The mood turned gloomy as Ritter insisted that the Commission prioritize a speedy resolution of this dispute. He stressed that the Wilhelmstraβe had intended to take a tougher line and that he had struggled to dissuade his colleagues from resorting to formal arbitration. Coulandre and Max Hoschiller from the French Economics Ministry were 'anything but delighted' and 'concerned that the Commission would have to

[110] AA R105388, Nr. W.H.A. 376. Nr.30. Sitzung des Handelspolitischen Ausschusses vom 8. September 1931. Signed Wiehl, Berlin, 8 Sept. 1931; see also R105388, Anl.9. Statistische Unterlagen zur Frage der deutschen Holzausfuhr nach Frankreich. Unsigned, 8 Sept. 1931.

[111] AA R70578 H027334–7, Abschrift. Auswärtiges Amt. II Fr. 3582. Signed von Bülow, Berlin, 11 Nov. 1931; R70578 H027338–41, here 339, Abschrift zu Fr. 3582. Aufzeichnung, [11 Nov. 1931]. Unsigned.

[112] AA R70578 H027338–41, here 340, Abschrift zu Fr. 3582. Aufzeichnung, [11 Nov. 1931]. Unsigned.

[113] AA R105388, Nr. W.H.A. 376. Nr. 30. Sitzung des Handelspolitischen Ausschusses vom 8. September 1931. Signed Wiehl, Berlin, 8 Sept. 1931.

[114] AA R70578 H027338, Abschrift zu Fr. 3582. Aufzeichnung, [11 Nov. 1931]. Unsigned.

[115] AA R70578 H027334–7, here 334, Abschrift Auswärtiges Amt. II Fr. 3583. Signed von Bülow, Berlin, 11 Nov. 1931.

[116] AA R70578 H027342–3, here 342, Abschrift zu II Fr. 3582, Aktenvermerk. Signed Ritter, Berlin, 9 Nov. 1931.

[117] Ibid.

[118] AA R70577 H027297, Berlin Ausw Nr. 57, Germadiplo Paris Nr. 581, zu Fr 3354, Telegramm, offen. Auf Nr. 1114. Signed Ritter, Berlin, 20 Oct. 1931.

tackle so difficult an issue at the very outset'.[119] Speaking off the record, Coulandre conceded that Germany's concern at the legality of the French quotas 'was understandable', adding that:

> The Quai d'Orsay had fought against these quotas with all the power at its disposal and that we could rest assured that had it not, then the scale of quota restrictions would have been very much greater. The Foreign Ministry had to date at least been able to prevent the Trade Ministry from making additions to the quota list. However, the Agriculture Ministry had prevailed [with its own demand for quotas].[120]

Coulandre lamented that France's embassies and consulates had borne the brunt of furious complaints from France's major trading partners. Although Berlin had so far remained silent he 'could only advise', privately, that Germany protest energetically, so strengthening the Foreign Ministry vis-à-vis the domestic Ministries.[121]

However, German protests remained low-key. Rumours were circulating in Paris that the government planned to introduce a universal quota system and so repeal all existing trade treaties, but the French Commerce and Industry Minister, Louis Rollin, reassured Hoesch that the quotas would be very selective and designed only to protect the most vulnerable sectors of the French economy and certainly not to reverse the overall balance of trade. Nonetheless, the German Ambassador warned that the peremptory imposition of quotas, particularly by the Agriculture Minister André Tardieu, threatened seriously to compromise Franco-German relations, and had Rollin's sympathy on this score at least.[122]

GROWING DISCORD IN THE COMMISSION

On 16 December Subcommission I convened in Berlin and began by discussing the financial and economic crisis that was plaguing the Danube countries and the Balkans. It agreed that Paris and Berlin should adopt a common position at a forthcoming economic conference at the League of Nations, whose agenda included the creation of some form of Danube basin trading bloc. The Subcommission suggested that a series of bilateral trading agreements could serve to clear the region's chronic wheat surplus, but added that these particular accords should form part of a greater game: 'Every effort must be made to achieve progress along the road to a European customs union, even if various countries have very recently taken steps that complicate this strategy.'[123] In the event Paris and Berlin failed at Geneva to agree any common solution to the Danube crisis,[124] while Franco-German commercial relations proved a more immediate and serious irritant. As the

[119] AA R70578 H027342–3, here 342, Abschrift zu II Fr. 3582, Aktenvermerk. Signed Ritter, Berlin, 9 Nov. 1931.

[120] Ibid., here 343. [121] Ibid.

[122] AA R105388, Telegramm Nr. 1309 vom 30.11. Signed Hoesch, Paris, 30 Nov. 1931.

[123] AA R70578 H027536–43, here 537–8, Nr. 6, Sitzung der Präsidialkommission der deutsch-französischen Wirtschaftskommission am Donnerstag, den 17. Dezember 1931... in Berlin.

[124] Schirmann, *Crise*, 194–201.

Subcommission turned its attention to the 1927 Trade Treaty, German frustration began to bubble up. Although it was initially agreed that this whole vexed and 'insignificant issue' would not be discussed by the Subcommission but instead 'handed over to the two governments who should arrive at a common position before the Geneva [League of Nations] talks',[125] the dam finally burst when discussions turned to Franco-German trade in agricultural products. German delegates complained that French import quotas breached the terms of the Trade Treaty, while their French counterparts riposted that the emergency of rising unemployment legitimized the quotas.[126] With immediate agreement impossible it was left to the French and German Conveners of the Subcommission to resolve matters at an extraordinary meeting early on 17 December. They duly came up with proposals for a Franco-German common agricultural policy, recognizing:

> the necessity of regulating agricultural production in order to put an end to the anarchy that currently prevails in the marketplace and to control overproduction . . . which has very severe consequences. In order to regulate production we must in the first instance undertake a Franco-German audit—later to be extended to other countries—in order to establish what each country produces and, above all, can sell to market, and so set down specific output quotas for each country.[127]

A special Agricultural Committee was proposed to deliver on these proposals, serviced by its own expert advisers.[128]

Later that day the full Joint Commission held a plenary session at which French and German members of Subcommission I voiced warm support for their Presidents' agricultural proposals.[129] This positive news was no doubt welcome, but the Subcommission's primary remit had concerned the identification, strengthening, and creation of industrial cartels, characterized somewhat idealistically as the means 'to a reduction in high tariffs' on the road 'to an ever closer European economic union'.[130] However, nothing meaningful would be achieved here without resolving the more immediate and delicate issue of French import quotas.

Preparatory work was seconded to the General Confederation of French Industry and the National Confederation of German Industry and by 22 December the French body had consulted with its government and drawn up a near-exhaustive list of industrial sectors for discussion. Subdivided into 'cartels to be renewed or strengthened', 'cartels proposed by the Joint Commission', 'talks concerning further products as recommended by our governments', and 'further industries where we would welcome equivalent negotiations', the already extensive list left the way open for the addition of still more sectors.[131] The President of the French

[125] AA R70578 H027536–43, here 537, Nr. 6, Sitzung der Präsidialkommission der deutsch-französischen Wirtschaftskommission am Donnerstag, den 17. Dezember 1931... in Berlin.

[126] Ibid., here 540–1. [127] Ibid., here 542–3.

[128] Ibid., here 541. [129] Ibid., here 543.

[130] Ibid., here 538; see also Wurm, 'Internationale Kartelle', 98–103.

[131] AA R87144, Abschrift. Confédératon Générale de la Production Française. Monsieur le Président de la Reichsverband der Deutschen Industrie. Signed Le Président, 'Unterschrift', Paris, 22 Dec. 1931, 1–4.

Confederation, René Duchemin, assured his German counterpart that: 'I am anxious to inform you how happy I am regarding this collaboration which can only serve to strengthen the ties that unite us for the greater good of our two countries', adding that Berlin might care to add any sector that had slipped through the French net.[132] However, if this was innocuous enough, his general observations were less so as he continued:

> We had the opportunity during the Berlin discussions of 15, 16, and 17 December to explain to you the difficult situation confronting many of our industries; each and every day factories close their doors and the tally of unemployed is rising at a disturbing rate. All of the major economic sectors are at one in recognizing that the only possible remedy for this state of affairs lies in the imposition of import quotas.[133]

French industry understood full well that these French quotas had unleashed a storm of international protests, but, the President of the Confédération générale maintained, direct talks between French and German industrialists were a lesser evil than 'quotas imposed by governmental decree', and he urged 'that dates be set for meetings between French and German industrialists from every sector' with all possible speed.[134]

These meetings began within days and although a series of agreements were concluded and official quota documentation quickly drawn up,[135] the overall atmosphere deteriorated rapidly. A few examples must suffice. German exporters of metal agricultural tools—sickles, scythes, and pitchforks—were ready to accept quota restrictions, but midway through negotiations the French Trade Minister declared that his government would impose these quotas unilaterally.[136] It did the same for imported toys and triggered German protests that French governmental *force majeure* and 'blackmail was endangering the industry-based negotiations very seriously indeed'.[137] Matters failed to improve when, during renewed talks on agricultural tools, the French Senator and sickle manufacturer Martin Binachon shouted down his German counterparts and brushed aside efforts by the official interpreter to restore calm. German exasperation was compounded when it transpired that four French Ministries had unilaterally signed a quota order for the same agricultural tools five days before these abortive 'negotiations',[138] and at this point the talks collapsed entirely.[139]

132 Ibid., 1. 133 Ibid.

134 Ibid., 1–2; see also R105388, Telegramm. Nr. 1289, Auswärtig Berlin, Kzl. Nr. 1891. Signed Hoesch, Paris, 26 Nov. 1931.

135 AA R87144, Deutsches Reich. Certificat de Contingentement. Décret et arêté ministerial du 7 Janvier 1932. Année 1932.

136 AA R87144, Aktenvermerk. Betrifft: Deutsch-Französisches Wirtschaftskomitee. Sp./GM., 7 Jan. 1932.

137 AA R87144, Abschrift! Kommerzienrat Justin Schwarz... An den Reichsverband der Deutschen Industrie. Betr.: Ihr Telegramm vom 30. Dez. Deutsch-Franz. Wirtschaftsverhandlungen. Signed Schwarz, Nuremberg, 3 Jan. 1932, 1.

138 AA R87144, Bericht über deutsch-französische Wirtschaftsverhandlungen am Dienstag, den 12. Januar 1932,... in Paris in der Confédération de la production française.

139 AA R70578 H027619–22, Abschrift zu W. 459. Aufzeichnung des Reichswirtschaftsministeriums über deutsch-französische Industriellenverhandlungen, 22 Jan. 1932.

The German Economics Ministry took stock of the situation on 22 January in a report that made for depressing reading. It had gone along with Ritter's initiative to see quotas negotiated by individual private cartels, with a view to limiting their scale and numbers. It was also anxious to head off any official involvement in the quota regime and 'so allow the remainder of German exports to France free rein'.[140] However, things were turning out very differently indeed. French Ministries had imposed unilaterally a series of quotas which had combined with the privately negotiated deals to reduce German export volumes to between 30 and 40 per cent of their pre-crisis level. The Economics Ministry proposed that Germany should limit further damage whether by tabling counterproposals to any additional French quotas, exempting German goods from customs duties, or reducing overall tariff levels.[141] Thoughts turned to delivering an official protest in Paris after all, but Hoesch advised that this was unlikely to achieve anything useful. He described the general political atmosphere in Paris as unprecedentedly febrile, adding that Briand's final illness and resignation as Foreign Minister had compounded the difficulties. Laval had stepped in for Briand and also stood in as Chairman of the French section of the Joint Commission. However, as a Prime Minister embroiled in domestic political upheaval he had neither the necessary clout nor the focus to pursue a coherent foreign policy. 'An official protest', Hoesch concluded, 'therefore threatens to worsen the situation still further.'[142]

This may have been so, but, Foreign Office officials warned, the integrity of the Franco-German Trade Treaty and the work of the Joint Commission were so seriously compromised as to override Hoesch's doubts:

> We cannot accept France's tactic of imposing temporal and material ultimatums. They have led to threats of resignation by influential members of the German-French Economic Commission. We therefore asked Herr von Hoesch on 5 February to inform the French accordingly and to ensure that the announcement of further [quota] negotiations is limited in number and guarantee us the opportunity to table counterproposals.[143]

Hoesch met with Laval on 9 February. The French Prime Minister was sympathetic and 'agreed absolutely that it was undesirable and worrying if the existence of the

[140] Ibid., here 619; see also R70578 H027671–2, f. Konsul Eckel. Für die von Herrn Staatssekretär für 6. Februar 1932 eingeforderten Notizen zu Gesprächsthemen für Herrn Reichskanzler und Herrn Staatssekretär in Genf wird gebeten, folgendes in den von dort vorzulegenden Vermerk aufzunehmen.

[141] AA R70578 H027619–22, here 621–2, Abschrift zu W. 459. Aufzeichnung des Reichswirtschaftsministeriums über deutsch-französische Industriellenverhandlungen, 22 Jan. 1932; R70578 H027632–6, here 634, Ministerialrat Ruelberg hat heute die Ressorts mündlich über das Ergebnis seiner Pariser Besprechungen unterrichtet. Sig. illeg., Berlin, 29 Jan. 1932; R70578 H027671–2, f. Konsul Eckel. Für die von Herrn Staatssekretär für 6. Februar 1932 eingeforderten Notizen zu Gesprächsthemen für Herrn Reichskanzler und Herrn Staatssekretär in Genf wird gebeten, folgendes in den von dort vorzulegenden Vermerk aufzunehmen.

[142] AA R70578 H027632–6, here 634, Ministerialrat Ruelberg hat heute die Ressorts mündlich über das Ergebnis seiner Pariser Besprechungen unterrichtet. Sig. illeg., Berlin, 29 Jan. 1932.

[143] AA R70578 H027671–2, f. Konsul Eckel. Für die von Herrn Staatssekretär für 6. Februar 1932 eingeforderten Notizen zu Gesprächsthemen für Herrn Reichskanzler und Herrn Staatssekretär in Genf wird gebeten, folgendes in den von dort vorzulegenden Vermerk aufzunehmen.

German-French Economic Commission were to be threatened by the reckless imposition of French quotas'.[144] He promised that German complaints would be taken seriously, but offered nothing of substance, confessing that he was not up to speed on the details. It was left to Coulandre to discuss the crisis with Hoesch in greater depth. In certain respects the French diplomat was accommodating. He condemned the behaviour of particular French economic sectors, notably mechanical engineering, in imposing 'risible quota restrictions on German manufacturers, and reducing German parties to negotiating under blackmail'.[145] He went on to assure Hoesch that he intended to give the mechanical engineers' representative body an unalloyed carpeting, and stated that there would be no further official interference in the negotiations. He also appeared ready to see German exporters compensated by other means, but when it came to discussing the ultimate scope of the quota system Coulandre was much less forthcoming. He noted that French and German industry had agreed to set quota levels between themselves, and could have added that it was Ritter who had first suggested taking such an approach.[146]

Hoesch continued negotiations the following day with the Minister of Commerce, Louis Rollin, who maintained that the entire quota system was a temporary measure designed to tide over those sectors of the French economy that were confronted with total collapse. Rollin insisted that France's commitment to the Franco-German Joint Commission and its role in negotiating quotas in effect amounted to favoured treatment. He admitted that the approaching elections had undoubtedly strengthened the hand of the protectionist lobby, something 'he had done his utmost to resist to the very limits of what was possible',[147] but was as reluctant as his colleagues to offer Hoesch any substantive concessions. 'The Commerce Ministry,' the Ambassador reported, 'which is subjected to the full weight of France's [industrial] lobby, is less able to take an independent line than the Quai d'Orsay and consequently less willing to act against the interests of French producers.'[148]

Heinrich Ruelberg, a senior official in the Economics Ministry, had travelled to Paris in late January to find some way to address the deteriorating situation. His counterpart in the French Commerce Ministry, Paul Elbel, had also served on the Joint Commission and was trusted in Berlin, but was now drawn into France's domestic political turmoil. Seconded to the electoral campaign, he was relieved of other duties and played no further part in the Commission. His successor, Ruelberg reported, was Roger Fighiera, a legal expert in the Commerce Ministry, 'who has little time for Germany'.[149] Fighiera initially delegated talks to the former Commerce attaché at Prague, Leblanc, who proved accommodating up to a point. He

[144] AA R70578 H027675–6, quote on 675, Telegramm Nr. 202 vom 9/2. Signed Hoesch, Paris, 9 Feb. 1932.

[145] Ibid., quote on 676. [146] Ibid.

[147] AA R70578 H027677–81, quote on 678, Telegramm Nr. 210 v. 10.2.32. Signed Hoesch, Paris, 10 Feb. 1932.

[148] Ibid., quote on 680–1.

[149] AA R70578 H027632–6, here 632, Ministerialrat Ruelberg hat heute die Ressorts mündlich über das Ergebnis seiner Pariser Besprechungen unterrichtet. Sig. illeg., Berlin, 29 Jan. 1932.

reassured Ruelberg that France would desist from imposing future quotas unilaterally,[150] but with a number of caveats. New measures would be backdated to 1 January, leaving it irrelevant to Paris how quickly or otherwise agreements were struck. Contrary to Coulandre, he felt that government involvement would be necessary after all to bring negotiations to a successful conclusion, prompting Ruelberg to demand that this involvement be genuinely reciprocal and include French concessions to German exporters. This Leblanc would not, or perhaps could not, concede, explaining 'that the parliamentary situation precludes any reciprocal concessions'.[151] He added, presumably by way of comfort, that France: 'regarded the quotas as a temporary measure and that once normal conditions returned (mentioning this coming August!) it would lift all quotas and restore the *status quo ante*. Agreements would therefore provisionally be struck for a six months period.'[152]

Despite the quota storm, Paris remained sufficiently committed to the Joint Commission and its ultimate goals to seek a deal through its Berlin Embassy. A series of meetings during February saw agreement that Subcommission I would meet in Paris to review the situation, and also 'to demonstrate to the French public that despite a degree of political tension, economic collaboration continues'.[153] Subcommission II, at least, had made excellent progress on transport coordination and a further meeting was agreed for late March.[154] However, on 20 February Laval's government collapsed and André Tardieu returned as Prime Minister and also Foreign Minister. Laval remained within government and also continued as French Chairman of the Joint Commission, a body Tardieu went out of his way to praise when stressing 'the possibility, almost the necessity of rapprochement between the two nations'.[155] That said, both sides accepted that until Tardieu had familiarized himself with the Commission's work, there was little point in setting a timetable for Subcommission I or for the intergovernmental talks desired by Berlin.[156] Hoesch was reassured when Berthelot confirmed on 23 February that the new French government 'would continue to support the Commission and its economic and political objectives',[157] but the impact of Elbel's departure was compounded by the deployment of other key French personnel to League of Nations business in Geneva.[158] Meanwhile the German press protested that Tardieu's reassurances regarding the work of the Commission hardly corresponded

150 Ibid., here 632–3. 151 Ibid., here 634. 152 Ibid.

153 AA R70578 H027696, Aktenvermerk. Signed Ritter, Berlin, 20 Feb. 1932; for wider exchange: R70578 H027685–6, Aktenvermerk. Signed R, Berlin, 13 Feb. 1932; R70578 H027690–1, Aktenvermerk. Signed R, Berlin, 17 Feb. 1932; R70578 H027697–8, Aktenvermerk. Signed R, Berlin, 22 Feb. 1932.

154 AA R70578 H027690–1, Aktenvermerk. Signed R, Berlin, 17 Feb. 1932.

155 MAE Z619 145–6, quote on 146, Section d'Étude de la Presse Étrangère 32/153, Le Ministère Tardieu, Frankfurter Zeitung, 24 février 1932, matin.

156 AA R70578 H027697–8, Aktenvermerk. Signed R, Berlin, 22 Feb. 1932.

157 AA R70578 H027704–5, quote on 704, Telegramm Nr. 271 v. 23.2. Signed Hoesch, Paris, 23 Feb. 1932.

158 AA R70578 H027702–3, Telegramm Nr. 268 v. 23.2. Signed Hoesch, Paris, 23 Feb. 1932.

with the reality of French import quotas 'which rendered impossible a continuation of the Commission's work'.[159]

Leading diplomats did meet on 29 February when Hoesch presented Germany's counterproposals. He stressed 'that the list of demands was restricted to goods in which, it transpired, French exporters had little interest, so doing everything possible to avoid undermining the basis of the Trade Treaty'.[160] The French response was cool and Fighiera 'clarified the French government's view, asserting that the legality of the quotas was beyond question and that France therefore believed it impossible to offer [Germany] any concessions'.[161] Although Hoesch normally made it his business to extract the best from any situation, he saw little point in prolonging discussion over the legality or otherwise of the French quotas, 'because of fundamental and irreconcilable differences on this issue'.[162] But none of this, he continued, altered the fact that the 'quotas were prejudicial to German exporters' rights' as secured in the Trade Treaty and that French concessions were necessary, warning that any further French initiatives would trigger a German response.[163]

A further meeting set for 2 March seems to have been cancelled[164] and on 11 March Hoesch and Coulandre agreed to delay the next meeting of Subcommission I until April. The French diplomat insisted that Laval's personal commitment to the Joint Commission was beyond doubt and that he was now able to give it his full attention,[165] but this meeting, it seems, was also postponed. Laval did attend an open meeting of Subcommission II in Berlin on 14 April, but the newspaper *Le Temps* reported that any meeting of Subcommission I, the key body, had been postponed indefinitely: 'The members of this Subcommission, French and German, are as it happens engaged on other business.'[166]

POLITICAL INSTABILITY AND DIPLOMATIC STALEMATE

Parliamentary elections followed in France during early May resulting in a slender majority for the centre-left Cartel des Gauches. The Radical Party leader, Édouard Herriot, eventually formed a government on 3 June and on the face of it this should have boded well for Franco-German relations. Herriot had been Prime Minister in 1924 when the crisis surrounding the French occupation of the Ruhr District was resolved and a new, less severe reparations schedule (the Dawes Plan) agreed. He now relayed a personal offer through the French Embassy in Berlin to revive the

[159] MAE Z619 140, Affaires Étrangères. Telegramme à l'Arrivée. H No. 433, Berlin, 24 Feb. 1932.

[160] AA R70578 H027729–30, quote on 729, Telegramm. Del. Nr. 2, Auswärtig Berlin. Signed Weymann. Hoesch, Paris, 29 Feb. 1932.

[161] Ibid. [162] Ibid. [163] Ibid.

[164] There is no record of any such proceedings in the files.

[165] AA R70579 H027733, Telegramm Nr. 363 vom 11.3. Signed Hoesch, Paris, 11 Mar. 1932.

[166] AA R70579 H027737–8, quote on 738, Telegramm No. 545, Auswärtig Berlin. Signed Hoesch, Paris, 11 Apr. 1932.

Joint Commission and 'develop trading links' with Germany,[167] and invited the economist and former Convener of the League of Nations Economic Committee, Daniel Serruys, to lead the Commission's French section. However, the German response was not encouraging, with Ritter responding that:

> The words 'developer les échanges commerciaux' had assumed for us an unpleasant savour in the light of the German-French Commission's activity to date. When the Brüning–Laval communiqué was issued we did not interpret its commitment to German-French trade relations to mean that the Commission would confine its activity almost entirely to dealing with France's unilateral imposition of trade quotas. If the Commission's remit is to be defined anew, then the outcomes must be more even-handed than hitherto. The Third and Fourth Subcommissions have barely started their work and I cannot imagine that now is the appropriate moment for these two Subcommissions to achieve anything of substance. Subcommission I also collapsed immediately it came to discussing a quid pro quo for the [quota] concessions made by Germany.[168]

Concluding on a slightly more positive note, Ritter observed that the problems facing Europe 'were far more serious than the imposition of tariffs and quotas', and that since a joint Franco-German approach was indispensable to any resolution of the wider continental crisis, perhaps the Subcommission might eventually establish a common position on the economic and financial problems confronting Europe as a whole.[169]

The process of Franco-German rapprochement had always demanded a firm political guiding hand, as provided by Briand and later Laval or by Stresemann and later Brüning. However, Briand's illness then death (in April) and Laval's departure from government created a strategic vacuum and if Herriot might have picked up the pieces, his appointment as Prime Minister coincided with renewed political upheaval in Germany. Hindenburg and his entourage had for several years been seeking a way to recast the German constitution on more authoritarian lines, but through parliamentary legislation. Brüning was unwilling to go down this road and in any case would have been unable to muster the two-thirds majority in parliament that any constitutional amendment required. Support from the powerful, anti-Weimar NSDAP seemed to offer another means to this end, but Hitler's price included the dismissal of Brüning and fresh parliamentary elections. On 30 May Brüning was asked to resign, to be replaced two days later by Franz von Papen, a minor nobleman and also a member of the Centre Party. However, Papen was disowned by the Centre's Chairman, Ludwig Kaas, for betraying Brüning. The new Chancellor also failed to enlist Nazi support for his increasingly dysfunctional administration,[170] and struggled to assemble any sort of parliamentary coalition,

[167] AA R70579 H027739–41, quote on 739, Aktenvermerk. Signed R, Berlin, 2 Jun. 1932.

[168] Ibid., quote on 739–40. [169] Ibid., quote on 740.

[170] Hitler was offered the Vice Chancellorship, but as leader of the largest party, demanded the Chancellorship. The President refused to countenance this and the Nazis went into opposition, in effect forming a negative blocking majority in the Reichstag in tandem with the Communists.

still less to garner any respect. François-Poncet was among those who saw in Papen little more than a vainglorious buffoon.

The Ambassador at London, Konstantin Baron von Neurath, took on the Foreign Minister's portfolio, but without injecting any urgency into the faltering Franco-German relationship. He and Ritter welcomed Herriot's initiative, but felt that any substantive agenda for a revived Commission would best await inter-ministerial discussions at the Lausanne Conference on reparations,[171] which was to open on 16 June. This particular suggestion came to nothing, but on 20 July François-Poncet's deputy in Berlin, Pierre Arnal, offered to wind down the French quota system. The Quai d'Orsay had found a new ally in Herriot's Minister of Commerce, Jean Durand, who was notably more liberal than his predecessor and wished to scrap the quotas as soon as possible.[172] Arnal proposed that the two sides pick up where the springtime negotiations in Paris had left off, continuing that effective private cartels might replace the existing quota agreements and that there was scope to liberalize the 1927 Trade Treaty by eliminating limitations on trade. Here too the ultimate aim was to eradicate French import quotas and Arnal invited his German counterparts to add to the agenda for negotiations as they saw fit.[173]

This approximated to the accommodation sought vainly by Ritter and Coulandre during the previous November and offered a way to revive the fortunes of the Joint Commission. However, the German response was lukewarm. Ritter observed that while Germany also wished to revive the Commission, it would not be possible to arrange anything during the remainder of July:

> People here are at present on vacation and the officials and private members attached to Subcommission I's Sub-Group B [Cartels] are currently unavailable. I also added that I utterly failed to understand why there was suddenly such an air of urgency.[174]

Arnal regretted that French delegates in turn would be unavailable during August—holidays again—and that September would be taken up by League of Nations business in Geneva. 'One could therefore only look to October in the first instance and that was too late for the French Government.' In some desperation the Frenchman suggested an initial meeting involving anyone who happened to be available, perhaps to discuss less contentious aspects of his agenda. However, Berlin insisted that there was insufficient time available to arrange a July meeting on any terms, continuing that any changes to the Trade Treaty could not be one-sided and that Germany needed a good measure of time to formulate and communicate its own proposals in full.[175]

With that, Subcommission I departed the historical stage, although in the dying weeks of 1932 and of the Weimar Republic a meeting of Subcommission IV, which dealt with Franco-German collaboration abroad, offered a glimpse of what might have been. France proposed the meeting and used the occasion to sign off pre-existing deals on joint foreign business ventures, to include British participation

[171] AA R70579 H027743–4, Aktenvermerk. Signed R, Berlin, 10 Jun. 1932.
[172] AA R70579 H027752–4, here 752, Aktenvermerk. Signed R, Berlin, 20 Jul. 1932.
[173] Ibid., here 752–3. [174] Ibid., here 753. [175] Ibid., here 753–4.

and finance.[176] Delegates also agreed a limited future agenda, to examine indemnification procedures for these ventures, and also to examine the potential for collaboration in the electrical engineering sector.[177]

This was small beer given the hopes and ambitions that had accompanied the October 1931 Berlin summit. Any real momentum had evaporated, and the tone to be found in relevant German paperwork, once proactive and emphatically positive, was now passive at best, but as often guarded or even sceptical. And as we shall see, events in Germany served to nourish French doubts over the wisdom of bargaining with Berlin at all.[178] It should be remembered that the underlying purpose of the Franco-German Joint Commission had been to forge far-reaching agreement on economic integration, ultimately on a pan-European level, in order to circumvent the seemingly intractable differences between Paris and Berlin over key elements of the Versailles Treaty: on disarmament, (German) borders, reparations, and the current and future status of the Saar District. Paris could never countenance sacrificing its national 'security' as it was described, for which the Versailles Settlement served as a guarantee. Berlin however strove to attain 'equal rights' with the other great powers, France included, which implied the revision, if not dismantling, of the same Settlement. If economic integration had seemed to offer a relatively unproblematic way to secure the rapprochement that both governments desired by evading the impasse on 'equal rights' or 'security', the ensuing Franco-German trade crisis meant that this visionary strategy began to unravel with the ink barely dry on the September 1931 Berlin Agreement. Commercial relations became a bone of contention to add to the deeper-seated post-Versailles antagonisms that now began to crowd in on the dangerously vacant space. The dysfunctional atmosphere that often characterized political life in the French Third Republic and the increasingly destructive dynamic that undermined orderly policymaking in late Weimar Germany did nothing to help; elements of this wider process now demand our attention.

[176] AA R70579 H027755–6. Signed Bülow, 11 Oct. 1932; R70579 H027757, Auswärtiges Amt 7.9066. Signed Im Auftrag, Berlin, 28 Dec. 1932; R70579, H027758–64, Abschrift zu W. 9066, Vermerk über die Tagung der 4. Unterkommission der deutsch-französischen Wirtschaftskommission am 11. und 12. November 1932. Unsigned, Berlin, 30 Dec. 1932.

[177] AA R70579, H027758–64, here 764, Abschrift zu W. 9066, Vermerk über die Tagung der 4. Unterkommission der deutsch-französischen Wirtschaftskommission am 11. und 12. November 1932. Unsigned, Berlin, 30 Dec. 1932.

[178] See Ch. 6 under 'Impasse', 176–7, 179–83.

6

Breakdown

The Stresemann Memoirs Scandal and Wounds that Failed to Heal

A DIFFICULT CLIMATE

As the Franco-German Commission struggled to make real headway older tensions reignited. The public mood in both countries was volatile and from time to time each government felt the need to defend its tenuous parliamentary majority by appeasing nationalist backbenchers. At the turn of the year 1931/32 another 'war in sight' scare filled the pages of the French right-wing press, regardless of the fact that Germany's truncated armed forces were in no fit state to square off against France. The Alsatian newspapers *Elsässer Kurier* and the *Straßburger Neueste Nachrichten* suggested that the scare formed part of a concerted effort to discredit Laval's rapprochement policy,[1] but it was reinforced by developments east of the Rhine. It was an open secret that Berlin sought to replace the Hoover moratorium with a permanent annulment of the country's reparations liabilities, while the rise of Nazism had combined with the recent, if abortive, Austro-German customs union to increase unease over Germany's real intentions.[2] Beyond these issues, concern over Germany's likely stance at the forthcoming Disarmament Conference extended well beyond the pages of France's right-wing press.[3]

Pierre Laval remained committed to Franco-German rapprochement and his War Minister, André Tardieu, denounced rumours that France was on the point of mobilizing army reservists, briefing the pro-government newspaper *Le Matin* accordingly.[4] However, even before this war scare had erupted, the French Ambassador in Berlin, André François-Poncet, warned a senior German diplomat of the brittle popular mood in France. 'One would need to proceed very cautiously',

[1] For example, AA R70508, Deutsches Konsulat Lyon, J. Nr: 9. Betr: Kriegspsychose in Lyon. Signed Strohm, Lyon, 14 Jan. 1932; for Alsatian press reports and further war scare material, R70508 K241044–6, Auszug aus dem Halbmonatsbericht des Bezirksamts Germersheim vom 26.1.32. Unsigned.

[2] AA R70508 K241027–31, Deutsche Botschaft Paris. A 341. Inhalt: Krieg-in-Sicht-Stimmung in Frankreich? Signed Hoesch, Paris, 22 Jan. 1932.

[3] AA R70508 K241033–6, Deutsche Botschaft Paris. A. 467. Anschluβ an den Bericht A.341 vom 22. Januar. Signed Hoesch, Paris, 29 Jan. 1932.

[4] AA R70508 K241037, 'La liberation du premier contingent de la classe 1930', *Le Matin*, 27 Jan. 1932.

he remarked, 'in familiarizing the French public with the notion that the Young Plan cannot be fulfilled.'[5] And when the French Chamber of Deputies came to debate foreign policy on 26 November 1931, Laval played to the widespread unease over Germany among conservatives on the government benches. He had taken care to forewarn the Wilhelmstraβe and the German Embassy in Paris, but as the German Ambassador, Leopold von Hoesch, subsequently reported: 'The overall impression left by the debate was not exactly gratifying.'[6] 'Laval', he continued, 'adapted to the prevailing mood in his speech yesterday... [and] as feared, given the unmistakably chilly atmosphere in the Chamber, adopted a regrettably abrasive choice of words when criticizing Germany's financial policies and German nationalist demonstrations.'[7] The French Premier did also speak at length on Franco-German rapprochement, praising Heinrich Brüning as a man of integrity and judging the establishment of the Franco-German Joint Commission as profoundly significant.[8] However, he insisted that because France had acceded to a more general 'mutilation of its rights' since Versailles, reparations had become 'sacrosanct'.[9] The Hoover moratorium, he assured the Chamber, would run for a year only and the payments Germany had deferred were in the form of interest-bearing debt, to be honoured within ten years.[10] Weeks later, François-Poncet reprised these arguments during a confidential interview with the editor of the liberal *Königsberger Allgemeine Zeitung*, a newspaper that was broadly supportive of the Brüning government's foreign policy. To annul reparations, the ambassador repeated, was off the agenda, adding that if Laval conceded on this issue his government would not survive a single day. In any case, the imminence of French parliamentary elections was making the conduct of foreign policy even more difficult.[11]

The same applied to German parliamentary business, where any concessions on reparations were simply grist to the Nazis' mill.[12] It was increasingly difficult for any German politician to justify further reparations transfers to a patently wealthier neighbour, and François-Poncet was well aware of the devastating social and political price exacted by German unemployment. On 29 October 1931 he reported to Briand that joblessness stood 27.5 per cent higher than a year earlier, at some 4.5 million, while the German index of economic output (1928: 100)

[5] AA R70507, Abschrift. Signed Bülow, Berlin, 12 Nov. 1931, 2.

[6] AA R70507, Telegramm Nr. 1302 vom 27.11. Signed Hoesch, 27 Nov. 1931, 1.

[7] Ibid., 2; see also R70507, Abschrift W. Rep. 2794. *Journal Officiel* 27 Novembre 1931. Débats Parlementaires Nr. 101. Chambre des Députés. Séance du Jeudi 26 Novembre 1931. S. 4061, 4.

[8] AA R70507, Abschrift W. Rep. 2794. *Journal Officiel* 27 Novembre 1931. Débats Parlementaires Nr. 101. Chambre des Députés. Séance du Jeudi 26 Novembre 1931. S. 4061, 4–8.

[9] Ibid., 11. [10] Ibid., 2.

[11] AA R70508 K241122, Abschrift zu Rk. 13889, *Königsberger Allgemeine Zeitung* Die Hauptschriftleitung Dr Mü./Kr. Signed Dr Müller, Königsberg i. Pr., 21 Dec. 1931; R70508 K241123–7, here 124–5, Abschrift zu Rk. 13889/31. Unterredung mit dem französischen Botschafter François Poncet am 18.12.31. Signed Dr Müller.

[12] AA R70507 Telegramm Nr. 1401, Auswärtig Berlin. Signed Forster, Paris, 22 Dec. 1931.

continued to spiral downwards, plumbing new depths in August at 68.1.[13] Christmas, he noted, fostered 'a kind of civil truce' in the otherwise stormy political life of the impoverished German Republic, but the truce itself also laid bare the profound social polarization of the Depression era:[14]

> It does not appear as if the Germans are any less preoccupied than usual with illuminated Christmas trees, the centrepieces of family reunions. Nor have they stinted when exchanging numerous and lavish presents after they have finished singing Christmas carols. Travel agents report that railway sleeping cars are fully booked, that mountain resorts have notified that their hotels are full, and that fifty-two special trains were laid on today from Berlin. Nonetheless, all the newspapers have published the latest unemployment figures, which reveal that the number of jobless has increased again, to exceed 5.3 million. And so Germany represents a massive agglomeration of contrasts and contradictions, which remain to us inexplicable.[15]

Such levels of polarization, François-Poncet repeated, were the midwife of political turmoil, 'where changes in . . . opinion are as frequent as they are rapid; perspectives change from one day to the next'.[16] This, he continued, influenced the formulation of foreign policy, creating a far from reassuring situation as a beleaguered government sought to achieve the annulment (rather than mere suspension) of reparations payments. 'We are far from being able to believe', he concluded, 'that Germany will desist from playing for all or nothing, or that it will, any time soon, appreciate that its creditworthiness and economic recovery make it advisable to avoid appearing before the world as in acute conflict with us.'[17]

More generally, François-Poncet was no admirer of Heinrich Brüning, but did remain committed to the cause of Franco-German rapprochement, which he hoped would mark the defining achievement of his ambassadorship. Personally, he believed that 'the world had simply become too small for states on today's scale', and continued to anticipate that the Franco-German Commission, 'his child who would not disappoint him', marked the way to European union. An accord between the two neighbours required more time, 'perhaps six months, perhaps a year, perhaps longer', but he declared that he was patient and had no wish to become trapped within the short-term constraints of France's imminent parliamentary elections.[18]

Small steps might offer a way forward. Early in the New Year he discerned an opportunity to moderate hostile coverage of France in the conservative financial daily, the *Berliner Börsen Zeitung*, which was owned by the media magnate and leader of the arch-nationalist German National People's Party (DNVP), Alfred

[13] MAE Z761 209–13, here 209, Copie. Ambassade de France à Berlin, Relations Commerciales, No 964, La situation économique de l'Allemagne à la fin d'octobre. Signed André François-Poncet, Berlin, 29 Oct. 1931.

[14] MAE Z761 256–63, here 256, Copie No 1136, L'Allemagne pendant la trève de Noël. M. André François-Poncet, Ambassadeur de France à Berlin à M. Briand, Ministre des Affaires Étrangères, Berlin, 24 Dec. 1931.

[15] Ibid. [16] Ibid., quote on 260. [17] Ibid, quote on 263.

[18] AA R70508 K241123–7, here 125–6, Abschrift zu Rk. 13889/31. Unterredung mit dem französischen Botschafter François Poncet am 18.12.31. Signed Dr Müller.

Hugenberg. Recently the newspaper 'had adopted a violently anti-French attitude, sometimes bordering on the puerile', in stark contrast to its liberal counterpart, the *Berliner Börsen-Courier*. At least, the Ambassador reported, the *Börsen Zeitung* was poorly produced and its language was opaque, but its importance as a newspaper of record could not be overlooked and by chance a means had arisen to influence its tone and content.[19] A retired army general, Otto von Stülpnagel, who retained close links with the army command, took up a senior position with the newspaper. François-Poncet had himself cultivated links with the politically active Generals Kurt von Scheicher and Kurt von Hammerstein and, with a view to toning down the *Börsen Zeitung*'s reporting, planned:

> To suggest to them that they might wish to utilize their influence on General von Stülpnagel to modify this state of affairs. With the Disarmament Conference imminent, preparations for which have triggered particularly acute polemical outbursts [in Germany], we have every interest in seeing this widely read newspaper adopt a less hostile and more objective tone.[20]

Weeks later, however, Paris took a more robust approach when expelling the liberal *Stuttgarter Neues Tagblatt*'s Paris correspondent for allegedly inflammatory reporting, most recently on the war scare, but also on the Saarland question.[21]

As we saw, Laval's government fell on 20 February 1932, with Tardieu regaining the Premiership as leader of the same parliamentary coalition. Briand's health had by then declined to the point where he could no longer serve in government, leaving Tardieu to double up as Foreign Minister. These changes exacted their price on the dynamic of French foreign policy, but without significantly altering its tone or content. The conservative press in Germany complained that France would, as ever, remain fixated on upholding its legal rights, 'which it has recently come to defend in a narrow-minded and inflexible spirit'.[22] But most German newspapers agreed that Laval had been a disappointment, a man who had promised much, but ended up as the prisoner of France's prevailing intransigence.[23] The liberal *Berliner Tageblatt* predicted that Tardieu would prove a tough negotiating partner at the Disarmament Conference, but more generally compared favourably Tardieu's 'absolute clarity' in the conduct of policy with Laval's approach, which it judged well-meaning, but hesitant and ineffectual.[24] The liberal *Frankfurter Zeitung* echoed these sentiments, preferring Tardieu to the unstatesmanlike Laval and noting the new Premier's moderate tone on foreign policy issues, including relations with Germany.[25]

[19] MAE Z619 65–6, Ambassade de France à Berlin. Direction Politique et Commerciale. Sous Direction Europe No 7. Signed André F. Poncet, Berlin, 4 Jan. 1932.

[20] Ibid., quote on 66.

[21] MAE Z 619 98, BC/16, Direction Politique et Commerciale. Europe. Unsigned, 13 Feb. 1932.

[22] MAE Z618 108–9, quote on 109, Affaires Étrangères. Télégramme à L'Arrivée. No 381. Signed François-Poncet, Berlin, 17 Feb. 1932.

[23] Ibid., here 109.

[24] MAE Z619 133, Section d'Étude de la Presse Étrangère 32/145. 'Le Ministère Tardieu', *Berliner Tageblatt*. Signed Paul Badek, 22 Feb. 1932.

[25] MAE Z619 145–6, Section d'Étude de la Presse Étrangère 32/153. 'Le Ministère Tardieu', *Frankfurter Zeitung*, 22 Feb. 1932.

ALSATIAN SENSITIVITIES

The demise of economic partnership also served to enhance existing sensitivities in the Franco-German relationship, among them the status of Alsace. The Alsatian question fuelled repeated diplomatic exchanges between Berlin and Paris which extended back into Stresemann's lifetime. Germany had ceded Alsace and the Moselle (the northern, German-annexed part of Lorraine) to France in the Treaty of Versailles and Berlin confirmed this transfer at Locarno. There was nothing to suggest that interwar German irredentism, as it applied to the Polish border, to Austria, or even Bohemia-Moravia, extended to a desire to reclaim Alsace.[26] Nor should the interwar Alsatian (cultural) autonomist movement be confused with any great desire within the province to restore German rule.[27] However, the fact that Alsace was primarily German-speaking and retained certain pre-war social and religious privileges led to difficulties of one kind and another.[28] If the Alsatians were largely happy to be French, many were less happy to have imposed on them either French secularist values or the French language if this came at the cost of their distinctive culture.[29] Furthermore, many pre-war residents of Alsace and the Moselle who had been born elsewhere left for Germany after the war, to be joined by a number of native-born Alsace-Lorrainers including many who had intermarried with incomers, those who preferred to continue with German-based careers, or whose cultural affinities with Germany were strong.[30] These population transfers further compounded tensions as various German-based Alsatian émigré organizations lobbied the German government, the media, and wider German public opinion.[31]

Many French politicians and commentators, however, were convinced that the autonomist movement was directly fuelled by support and interference from the German authorities. In French eyes, therefore, Alsatian autonomism posed a significant security risk and Alsatian public servants who subscribed openly to the autonomist cause faced official sanctions.[32] In 1928 a group of autonomist leaders stood trial in Colmar, charged with plotting 'to change or overthrow the government',[33] although German involvement could not be adequately proved in court.[34] Berlin regarded this as 'proof that no official German agency nourishes the

26 See, for example, AA Elsass-Lothringen A: Die Stellung Elsass-Lothring. im französ. Staat sowie die elsass-lothring. Autonomiefrage (R30201a) E439510–17, here 510, Nr. II Fr 110. Signed Bülow, Berlin, 9 Jan. 1929.

27 François G. Dreyfus, *La Vie politique en Alsace 1919–1936* (Paris, 1969); Christopher Fischer, *Alsace to the Alsatians? Visions and Divisions of Alsatian Regionalism, 1870–1939* (New York and Oxford, 2010).

28 Dreyfus, *Vie politique*, 64–9, 97; Fischer, *Alsace*, 131ff.

29 For example, Politische Beziehungen Elsaß-Lothringens zu Deutschland (R71141) L442352–3, Aufzeichnung. Signed Sievers, Berlin, 6 Aug. 1930.

30 See, for example, Carolyn Grohmann, 'From Lothringen to Lorraine: Expulsion and Voluntary Repatriation', in Conan Fischer and Alan Sharp (eds.), *After the Versailles Treaty: Enforcement, Compliance, Contested Identities* (London, 2008), 153–69.

31 AA R30201a E439510–17, here 510–11, Nr. II Fr 110. Signed Bülow, Berlin, 9 Jan. 1929.

32 Fischer, *Alsace*, 186–7.

33 Dreyfus, *Vie politique*, 133.

34 Ibid., 134.

discontent in Alsace-Lorraine or supports the autonomist movement'[35] and while some of the accused were nonetheless found 'guilty', the verdicts rested on flimsy foundations and were annulled by a second court in Besançon.[36] However, this did nothing to soothe French fears. In January 1929, for example, the conservative daily, *Le Gaulois*, reported in alarmist terms on Germany's covert support for all manner of Alsatian separatism, adding that the conservative German war veterans' association, the Stahlhelm, had formed a 'Strasbourg Section', based in Frankfurt-am-Main.[37] Subsequent German enquiries confirmed the existence of such a group containing thirty or forty members, but beyond some individual personal links with Alsace, Foreign Office and Prussian officials believed the group to be politically passive.[38]

Similar fears surfaced in March 1932 when the French Senate debated the annual budget for Alsace-Lorraine and the Alsatian Senator, Frédéric Eccard, accused Germany of conducting a virulent propaganda campaign in Alsace and the Moselle, driven by 'certain circles in Germany who have still not come to terms with the loss of these two provinces'.[39] Eccard was a strongly Francophile founder member of the Ligue d'Alsace français, whose aim was to 'assure the complete and rapid assimilation of Alsace by France from a political as well as an economic point of view'.[40] As such, the Ligue, with limited exceptions, decried the concept of Alsatian autonomism, all of which left Eccard particularly sensitive to any hint of German involvement in his birthplace. This extended to the widespread presence of German-language entertainment, including the 'particularly dangerous' musical film (later operetta) *Two Hearts in Waltz Time* (*Zwei Herzen im dreiviertel Takt*), simply because of its (apolitical) attractiveness as a piece of light-hearted entertainment.[41] Eccard maintained that a significant part of Germany's propaganda budget was dedicated to Alsace alone, an assertion endorsed by his fellow Senator, Henry Chéron, even if their claims on the size of this budget differed wildly—at 100 million marks and 50 million marks respectively.[42]

All of this, Chéron maintained, was a central pillar of German foreign policy as, in the wake of defeat, Berlin worked 'to preserve the German language and customs in these [lost] provinces by every means possible'.[43] This propaganda, he continued,

[35] AA R30201a E439510–17, quote on 510, Nr. II Fr 110. Signed Bülow, Berlin, 9 Jan. 1929.

[36] Dreyfus, *Vie politique*, 136; Fischer, *Alsace*, 196.

[37] AA R71141 L442266–7, Telegramm Nr. 47. Auswärtig Berlin. Signed Hoesch, Paris, 17 Jan. 1929.

[38] AA R71141, Ref. LR. Grf. Bassenheim. Konzept Reinschr. 1b II Fr. 199, Berlin, 24 Jan. 1929; R71141 L442274, Der Preuβische Minister des Innern. II 1420 b 1/29. Signed Schönner, Berlin, 27 Feb. 1929.

[39] AA R30201b E439719–20, Deutsche Botschaft Paris. A. 1511. Signed Forster, Paris, date stamped 4 Apr. 1932.

[40] Quoted in Fischer, *Alsace*, 139.

[41] AA R30201b E439719–20, here 719, Deutsche Botschaft Paris. A. 1511. Signed Forster, Paris, date stamped 4 Apr. 1932.

[42] Ibid.

[43] AA R30201b, No 311 Sénat Année 1932, session ordinaire. Annexe au process-verbal de la 2e séance du 18 mars 1932. Henry Chéron, *Rapport fait au nom de la Commission des finances charge d'examiner le projet de loi, adopté par la Chambre des Députés, portant fixation du budget general de l'exercice 1932. Services d'Alsace et de Lorraine* (Paris, 1932), 56.

may have 'cloaked itself in a cultural guise, but its ulterior political motivation constantly and unmistakably reveals itself'.[44] The efforts of a number of autonomist organizations, some allegedly funded or subsidized by Berlin, were complemented, Chéron noted, by theatrical performances in Alsace by the Freiburg Theatre and the widespread circulation of German 'talkie' films, evoking memories of 'German life, the habits and customs of that country'.[45] And the Freiburg Theatre had previously become embroiled in an Alsatian political squabble between autonomists and Francophiles, following a performance in early 1930 by the Straβburger Theater in the neighbouring German city. The mayor of Strasbourg, Charles Hueber, had accompanied the Alsatian troupe to Freiburg and at the end of the performance, in an emotional outburst, thanked the 'free city' for playing host to the 'city on the street' before expressing hope that the latter would itself soon become a 'free city' again. Subsequently challenged on Strasbourg city council over the meaning of this, Hueber reiterated that:

> He, Hueber, had declared in Freiburg that Strasbourg was not a 'free city', alluding to the fact that when the Freiburg Theatre players came to perform in Strasbourg, they faced the greatest difficulties in obtaining entry visas. By way of contrast the Strasbourg players received German entry visas without delay, and indeed a special train had been provided for them from Kehl [immediately across the Rhine from Strasbourg].[46]

The matter had been complicated by efforts in the Francophile Alsatian press to attribute the controversial words to the mayor of Freiburg, an accusation that proved an unwelcome distraction to the business of the German Embassy in Paris.[47] However, there was no smoke without fire, and, special trains apart, German newspapers allegedly published more than 120 reports and features on Alsace during January 1932 alone, many of which appeared concurrently in the Alsatian autonomist press.[48] However 'insane' this propaganda may have been, Chéron concluded, it posed a long-term threat to the public mood, thus 'making it necessary that we defend ourselves and respond to it, in the interests, no less, of world peace'.[49]

If many Alsatian parliamentarians, including the Socialist deputy Salomon Grumbach, insisted that the autonomist movement was indigenous and posed no threat to France's territorial integrity, the residents of neighbouring German lands nonetheless retained an interest in the fate of the region.[50] This was not lost on Chéron and his colleagues and also featured strongly in French diplomatic correspondence from south-western Germany in particular. The French Consul in Karlsruhe, for example, reported in June 1929 on a speech by the leader of the

[44] Ibid. [45] Ibid., 60.

[46] AA R71141 L442333, Deutsche Botschaft Paris, A 499. Signed Hoesch, Paris, 6 Feb. 1930.

[47] AA R71141 L442319, Deutsche Botschaft Paris. A 324. Signed Hoesch, Paris, 24 Jan. 1930.

[48] AA R30201b, No 311 Sénat Année 1932, session ordinaire. Annexe au process-verbal de la 2e séance du 18 mars 1932. Henry Chéron, *Rapport fait au nom de la Commission des finances charge d'examiner le projet de loi, adopté par la Chambre des Députés, portant fixation du budget general de l'exercice 1932. Services d'Alsace et de Lorraine* (Paris, 1932), 60.

[49] Ibid.

[50] AA R30201a E439510–17, here 510–11, Nr. II Fr 110. Signed Bülow, Berlin, 9 Jan. 1929.

left-liberal German Democratic Party (DDP), Ludwig Haas, at the University of Heidelberg. Haas's main purpose was to promote Franco-German rapprochement, but he judged Alsace's role in this process as problematic. 'By race, culture and language', he declared, 'the Alsatians are Germans', but he accepted that German rule had lacked sensitivity and that the region now had no wish to rejoin Germany. However, he continued: 'Matters could become more complicated if France continues to misunderstand Alsace. Should France pursue a sensible policy in Alsace, then its people could come to serve as the link between France and Germany.'[51] These sentiments echoed Alsatian autonomist efforts to evoke the spirit of Locarno and make Alsace 'a meeting place between two cultures' that would help foster 'reconciliation between Germany and France',[52] but the Consul was alarmed, commenting that:

> Dr Haas gave his audience to understand that the status of Alsace was not definitively settled by the Locarno Accords. Moreover, this reflects the prevailing mood in the state of Baden. The shared language and religion and the numerous family ties established between Baden and Alsace between 1871 and 1918, as well as the memory of many business links formed during this period, links which are currently severed, result in most citizens of Baden following Alsatian affairs and the autonomist movement very closely. People here are convinced that the Locarno Accords have a provisional character and that, sooner or later, favourable circumstances will permit Germany to absorb German-speaking minorities which the peace treaties detached from the Reich, the Alsatians included.[53]

In the following year a correspondent from the *Leipziger Abendpost* reported on a trip through Alsace and the Moselle. The chicanery of French border officials, he claimed, was laced with paranoia, while in Strasbourg he asked a uniformed policeman for directions, in French, only to hit a wall of incomprehension. 'Do you perhaps speak German?' the correspondent continued. '[The policeman] blushed and replied, smiling, in his Alsatian dialect, "As well as you do."' There might have been no great desire to rejoin Germany, but Alsatians' loyalty to France appeared conditional. 'One could say', the correspondent concluded, 'that on the whole the greater part of the population does not wish to be French or German; their ideal is, and remains, to see Alsace become autonomous.'[54] This report was forwarded to Paris by the French Consul General at Dresden and Leipzig without comment, but on other occasions German press coverage was adjudged decidedly problematic. The French Consul in Stuttgart, for example, reported on

[51] MAE Z392 211–12, quote on 211 back, République Française, Consulat de France en Bade. Direction des Affaires Politiques. Sous Direction d'Europe, No 8. Sig. illeg., Karlsruhe, 22 Jun. 1929.

[52] Fischer, *Alsace*, 183; see also 191.

[53] MAE Z392 211–12, here 212, République française, Consulat de France en Bade. Direction des Affaires politiques. Sous Direction d'Europe, No 8. Sig. illeg., Karlsruhe, 22 Jun. 1929.

[54] MAE Z618 94, République Française, Consulat Général de France à Dresde et Leipzig. Direction des Affaires politiques et commerciales. Europe, No 108. Sig. illeg., Dresden, 20 Sept. 1930; see appendix: Z618 96–9, 'Un Voyage en Alsace-Lorraine', *Leipziger Abend-Post*, 17 Sept. 1930.

openly anti-French and pro-Alsatian autonomist reporting in Württemberg's right-wing press.[55]

However, political comment aside, the wider attractiveness of the German media in Alsace continued to worry French officialdom. This extended to German newspapers or magazines with an Alsatian readership and, echoing Chéron's concerns, the Quai d'Orsay fretted over the influence of lifestyle features, crime reporting, or even newspapers such as the pro-small business *Kleinkapitalist* whose political vitriol, such as it was, was directed at the Weimar authorities.[56] Finally, in February 1932, Paris contemplated banning the mass-circulation *Die Grüne Post* in the recovered provinces rather less because of its nationalist tone and more because: 'A measure directed specifically against the *Grüne Post* can, all things considered, be justified simply by the sole fact of its considerable circulation in Alsace-Lorraine, which guarantees the articles it publishes a substantial readership.'[57] The ban extended to sales at railway station kiosks in Alsace and the Moselle, as well as on the French-operated Luxembourg railways, and took in other magazines, including *Sonntag Morgen* and *Uhu*, the latter noted for its lavish illustrations and attractive lifestyle and entertainment features. The German Embassy in Paris eventually protested that such restrictions on the sale of German newspapers and magazines in France breached the terms of the 1927 Franco-German trade treaty,[58] but the Quai d'Orsay reacted by asking its legal section to provide 'arguments that would permit it to reject the request from the German Embassy'.[59] The lawyers obliged, concluding that the trade treaty applied to taxable merchandise rather than 'intellectual products such as magazines',[60] adding that any challenges to this interpretation could be blocked under Article 12 of the trade treaty, which permitted a ban on any imports 'on the grounds of public safety'.[61] The German Embassy's request was declined.[62]

These repeated incidents impressed on Berlin that French sensitivities regarding Alsace-Lorraine constantly threatened to complicate their wider relations. The Wilhelmstraße consistently distanced itself from any such thing that threatened to undermine efforts at Franco-German rapprochement, noting 'the sensitivity of the French government regarding anything relating to the maintenance of German culture in Alsace-Lorraine',[63] and it routinely censored or blocked potentially

55 MAE Z619 54–7, Consulat de France à Stuttgart, No 81, Direction des Affaires politiques et commerciales, Sous-Direction d'Europe. Sig. illeg., Stuttgart, 3 Nov. 1931.

56 MAE Z618 161, Le Ministre des Affaires Étrangères, No 1602, Europe, 19 Nov. 1930.

57 MAE Z619 147–8, Ambassade de France à Berlin. Direction des Affaires Politiques et Commerciales, Europe, No 175. Signed P. Arnal, Berlin, 2 Mar. 1932.

58 MAE Z620 86, Verbalnote W. 4066. An das Ministerium der Auswärtigen Angelegenheiten Paris, Paris, 7 Jan. 1933.

59 MAE Z620 87, Europe, Note pour Monsieur le Jurisconsulte du Département. Signed M. de Castellane, 11 Jan. 1933.

60 MAE Z620 92, ? Hubert, Jurisconsulte, Note pour la Sous-Direction d'Europe. Sig. illeg., 13 Jan. 1933.

61 Ibid.

62 MAE Z620 111, Direction Politique, Ambassade d'Allemagne à Paris. Signed de Castellane, 24 Jan. 1933.

63 AA R30201a E439510–17, here 513–14, Nr. II Fr 110. Signed Bülow, Berlin, 9 Jan. 1929.

disruptive material. This included a major project proposed by the Wissenschaftliches Institut der Elsass-Lothringer (Academic Institute of the Alsace-Lorrainers), which was established at the University of Frankfurt-am-Main in 1921 largely by former personnel of the Kaiser-Wilhelms-University in Strasbourg. The Institute completed and published projects pertaining to Alsace-Lorraine which had been initiated at the Kaiser-Wilhelms-University, although a number of new projects also featured among the 140 publications brought out before its closure in 1945. Whatever its role and record under Nazism, its academic output during the Weimar era was well regarded, but in 1929 the Wilhelmstraβe learned that the Institute planned to undertake a major work, in three volumes, dealing in turn with the economic development of Alsace-Lorraine between 1871 and 1918, the German administrative record in the region, and, finally, literature and art in the lost provinces. The Institute proposed scouring a series of German archives for suitable material, but the Foreign Ministry was deeply unhappy at this prospect. Bernhard von Bülow, then engaged within Section II (Western Europe), advised the Interior Ministry to proceed with extreme caution before sanctioning any such work, continuing:

> We are ignorant of the detailed content and political orientation of the project, but these are in any case irrelevant. Seen from the perspective of our foreign relations, the publication of such a work, irrespective of its content, is premature. The interval of time since the signing of the Treaty of Versailles remains too short, given the sensitivity of French public opinion when it comes to anything regarding Alsace-Lorraine, including Germany engaging with the affairs of Alsace-Lorraine in the manner envisaged by the Frankfurt Institute.[64]

The rise of Alsatian autonomism, Bülow continued, had heightened French sensitivities, leaving the appearance of the planned work 'thoroughly undesirable'.[65] Although any final decision rested with the Interior Ministry, Bülow insisted that were the project to proceed, the Foreign Office should have a veto over its publication, adding that: 'The Institute's request for access to the Foreign Office Political Archive has been rejected.'[66] Foreign Office sensitivities resurfaced when the Interior Ministry suggested that the diplomats' fears were exaggerated and that, in any case, the French had not desisted from publishing provocative material regarding Alsace after 1870.[67] A senior diplomat, Rudolf Count Waldbott von Bassenheim, retorted that Germany's 'political situation was immeasurably more difficult than France's after 1870, making invalid any comparison with [earlier] French behaviour'.[68] Friedberg accepted that a wide-ranging history of German-ruled Alsace-Lorraine was inherently desirable, and that the project needed to make progress while 'the men who served Alsace-Lorraine remain alive', but repeated

[64] AA R71141 L442290–2, quote on 290–1, stv. Dir., zu II Fr. 2626, An den Herrn Reichsminister des Innern. Signed v. Bülow, Berlin, 16 Aug. 1929.

[65] Ibid., here 291.

[66] Ibid., here 292.

[67] AA R71141 L442295–6, here 295, Aufzeichnung, zu II Fr. 2626. Signed Bassenheim, Berlin, 7 Nov. 1929.

[68] Ibid.

Bülow's demand that clearance by both the Interior and Foreign Offices remained a precondition for research and publication. In any case, he concluded, 'very few relevant records exist within the Foreign Office, given that such material was largely kept in Strasbourg'.[69]

The Foreign Office also balked at a proposed radio broadcast by a Dr Ernst on the Deutsche Welle in November 1929, purportedly on the uncontroversial subject of the Alsace-Lorrainer resident in the Reich. However, the waters were muddied since, 'unfortunately, Dr Ernst does not confine himself to this, but interlaces his factual remarks with very many political observations, particularly over the Alsace-Lorrainers' right to self-determination'.[70] A claim that German-resident Alsace-Lorrainers could never accept the region's current constitutional status was the final straw,[71] bringing the Wilhelmstraβe to remind the Interior Ministry that:

> The Foreign Office has informed the National Ministry of the Interior in a series of verbal and written presentations and memoranda that any critical German public engagement with events in Alsace-Lorraine is perceived in France as a politically hostile act against itself. Since, furthermore, it is common knowledge that, legally speaking, a radio broadcast requires official approval, Dr Ernst's remarks as a whole will be seen in France as semi-official or, as the next best thing, as officially sanctioned.[72]

The potential consequences for Germany's wider diplomatic interests, the Foreign Office continued, were serious and so: 'At the very moment when negotiations on the Saar and the second round of the Hague Conference are imminent, the pursuit of confrontation in affairs, such as the Alsace-Lorraine question, which do not directly concern us is completely inappropriate.'[73] Similar requests to permit broadcasts, particularly concerning the Alsatian autonomy movement, continued unabated through to the end of the Weimar era, but saw the Foreign Office 'always rule against the sanctioning of such presentations'.[74] Friedberg reiterated concerns that any such broadcast, requiring official permission, would be seen in France as direct German support for the autonomist movement, adding that: 'Furthermore, nothing damages the autonomy movement in Alsace-Lorraine more than the slightest suspicion of German support, particularly official German support.'[75] Yet again, therefore, reactions to the Alsatian question served simultaneously to confirm Berlin's desire to avoid fruitless, even futile, confrontation in an area far removed from its key foreign policy objectives, and to expose France's extreme sensitivity on the matter. Residual but powerful French fears of its German neighbour had by no means disappeared during the era of Stresemann, Brüning, and Briand.

69 Ibid., here 296; see also: R71141 L442326, Abschrift III 1403/3.1. Wissenschaftliches Institut der Elsaβ-Lothringer im Reich an der Universität Frankfurt a. Main. Betr.: Herausgabe eines Werkes über Elsaβ-Lothringen. Signed Prof. Dr Aurich, Prof. Dr Wolfram, Frankfurt a. M., 3 Jan. 1930; R71141 L442327, Der Reichsminister des Innern. III 1403/3/1. Signed Pellengahr, Berlin, 27 Jan. 1930.

70 AA R71141 L442304–5, quote on 304, zu II Fr 3573, St.S. i.R. Berlin, 14 Nov. 1929.

71 Ibid. 72 Ibid. 73 Ibid., quote on 305.

74 AA R71141 L442385, Konzept (R.l.b.) II Fr 3964. Signed v. Fr., Berlin, 5 Dec. 1932.

75 Ibid.

An equally sensitive case involved the activities of the Bishop of Strasbourg, Charles Joseph Eugène Ruch, who took office in August 1919. Ruch was of Alsatian origin, but had been educated and held earlier positions in France and spoke no German. He had served as a French military chaplain during the war and once installed in Strasbourg felt constrained to fend off any effort by Paris to secularize the province, but also denounced Alsatian autonomists (among them many of his clerical subordinates) with particular venom.[76] In as far as the Pope was determined to uphold the authority of the Church and was unenthusiastic about clerical involvement in politics,[77] he supported Ruch in the face of alleged insubordination by many Alsatian clerics.[78] However, although this assertion of authority was designed to support Ruch's position in the Catholic hierarchy, it also served to underpin his efforts to suppress regional autonomism.[79]

Berlin did its best to restrain German press reporting on events in Alsace,[80] but could not prevent Catholic, and other, newspapers detailing French efforts to lobby the Vatican in support of Ruch. German Catholic clergymen considered protesting directly to the Vatican, which the Wilhelmstraβe 'had managed with difficulty to prevent, for we appreciated that the consequences for us would be undesirable in every regard'.[81] Quite apart from the damage to Franco-German relations, the Alsatian issue—or rather German Catholics' reaction to it—threatened ongoing negotiations between Prussia and the Vatican to reach a Concordat designed to address a number of administrative and financial issues (eventually concluded in June 1929). This forced the German Ambassador at the Vatican, Diego von Bergen, to expend considerable energy in blocking direct protests which he feared would be interpreted in Rome as a direct attack on the Church's authority and even as a challenge to the peace settlement.[82] Bergen used personal contacts to emphasize that Germany stood by the peace settlement and Locarno, and had no wish 'to compromise German-French relations through particular issues, such as Alsace',[83] adding that he recognized that German press reporting on Alsace was doing the Concordat negotiations few favours.[84]

If the Catholic Church had, unwittingly, aroused French sensitivities regarding Alsace and threatened to compromise wider Franco-German relations, the activities of individual adventurers were also profoundly unhelpful. The existence of direct German funding for Alsatian autonomism and/or its extent remained a murky area, but the Foreign Office had provided financial support for a number of German-based exile organizations, particularly during the tense period between Versailles

[76] AA R30201a E439510–17, here 512, Nr. II Fr 110. Signed Bülow, Berlin, 9 Jan. 1929.

[77] AA R30201a E439520–4, here 523–4, Deutsche Botschaft beim Päpstlichen Stuhle. Nr. 11. Signed Bergen, Rome, 20 Jan. 1929.

[78] Ibid., E439521.

[79] AA R30201a E439510–17, here 511–16, Nr. II Fr 110. Signed Bülow, Berlin, 9 Jan. 1929; see also R30201a E439518–19, Nr. 222 v. 24. November 1928, zu II Fr. 110.

[80] AA R30201a E439510–17, here 514, Nr. II Fr 110. Signed Bülow, Berlin, 9 Jan. 1929.

[81] Ibid., here 516.

[82] AA R30201a E439520–4, here 520–1, Deutsche Botschaft beim Päpstlichen Stuhle. Nr. 11. Signed Bergen, Rome, 20 Jan. 1929.

[83] Ibid., 521. [84] Ibid., 522.

and the Locarno Accords. There was little to stop German-based autonomists siphoning this cash into Alsace itself, for example to adventurers and fantasists such as the group around René César Ley, Henri Muth, and Charles Rapp. Ley had already crossed swords with the German military administration during the war,[85] before falling out with the incoming French administration. Finally, the three were tried and convicted by the French authorities in May 1920 on a charge of trying to undermine the security of the French state.[86] After their release from custody in September 1925, Ley and his co-conspirators moved across the border to Baden-Baden, where they argued for Alsatian autonomy in the local press and Ley tried, unsuccessfully, to claim German citizenship and forge links with official circles.[87] Indeed, German officialdom regarded Ley's activities as 'a persistent impediment to our relations with France'[88] and the mayor of Freiburg was less than pleased when the local press began to speculate over what Ley was really up to. France had already protested formally over a sizeable military parade through Freiburg during May 1929 at which poems mourning Germany's lost territories were widely circulated. One included the lines: 'Foreign flags over Strasbourg mock Germany's suffering; oh Strasbourg, oh Strasbourg we will reclaim you.'[89] Months later, the *Freiburger Tagespost* reported on the activities of an alleged espionage and propaganda centre also based in Freiburg, leading the mayor to ask of the Wilhelmstraße whether such an operation really existed. If yes, he demanded its removal from the border zone, continuing: 'If we wish to secure the maximum freedom of movement between Baden and the neighbouring and ethnically related Alsace, for business reasons and in the national interest, then it is absolutely necessary that such activities cease in the border territories.'[90] The Foreign Office, however, 'knew nothing regarding an official or semi-official spy centre in Freiburg', and assumed that the mayor was referring to the thoroughly unhelpful activities of Ley, Rapp, and their confederates.[91] In the event Berlin reassured the mayor,[92] wrote off the whole unwelcome affair, and informed the French authorities that Germany had no truck with Ley's antics.[93]

Other random incidents further demonstrated French sensitivities and a determination in Berlin not to allow such incidents to disrupt the process of rapprochement which, after all, faced challenges of a much more substantial nature. These included an official French protest when a Bavarian schnapps distillery sent out a 1929 calendar as publicity, to all foreign diplomats among others. Its subject matter

[85] AA R30201b E439667–8, Aufzeichnung, II Fr. 735. Sig. illeg., Berlin, 12 Mar. 1930.
[86] Fischer, *Alsace*, 137–8.
[87] AA R30201b E439667–8, Aufzeichnung, II Fr. 735. Sig. illeg., Berlin, 12 Mar. 1930.
[88] Ibid., here 667.
[89] AA R71141, R.M., St.S., doppel zu II Fr 2096. Signed Köpke, Berlin, 25 Jun. 1929.
[90] AA R30201b E439584–5, quote on 585, Der Oberbürgermeister der Hauptstadt Freiburg im Breisgau. Signed Bender, Freiburg im Breisgau, 1 Oct. 1929; see also: R30201b, E439586–7, Abschrift, Die angebliche Spionagezentrale in Freiburg betr. Signed Dr Bender, Freiburg, 26 Jul. 1929.
[91] AA R30201b E439583, Herrn Grafen Bassenheim. e.o. II Fr 3197. Signed Bülow, Berlin, 10 Oct. 1929.
[92] AA R30201b E439590, zu II Fr 3197. Signed Terdenge, Berlin, 12 Oct. 1929.
[93] AA R30201b E439667–8, here 668, Aufzeichnung, II Fr. 735. Sig. illeg., Berlin, 12 Mar. 1930.

was 'Germany's lost cities and territories... including Strasbourg and Metz', something Bülow regarded as 'all the more regrettable since, in addition to the Foreign Minister, numerous other prominent figures have stressed unreservedly that as far as we are concerned there is no longer any Alsace-Lorraine issue'.[94] There was a rather more bizarre incident in June 1930 when Berlin hosted the World Energy Conference. The hosts took care to lay on a rich variety of entertainment, including folk dancing, choral singing, gymnastics displays, and also the modelling of German regional folk costumes.[95] Men and women from each area paraded behind placards identifying the Pomeranians, Prussians, Silesians, Alemannen, Bavarians, and so on, with the fifty or so Alemannen wearing folk costumes from the Black Forest and the upper Rhine basin, east and west of the river. The group, then, included up to eight women and girls wearing the distinctive Alsatian head-dress loop, prompting a protest from French conference delegates that 'Alsace was represented among the German costumes'.[96] Several French delegates were themselves Alsatian and one enquired of the women where they came from, to receive the answer 'Straßburg'. The enraged French delegates warned a hapless conference organizer that they would report the matter to their government in Paris and that they envisaged diplomatic consequences.[97]

German diplomats had understood that all the folk costume participants were residents of Berlin whose families originally hailed from whichever region and were given to believe that Alsace had not been specifically identified. However when, a day later, the French Chargé d'Affaires in Berlin raised the matter, informally, during talks with Köpke it transpired that the offending head-dress loops were in the red and white colours of Alsace and that the women alluded to this when declaring that they represented Alsace-Lorraine. Nor were they established residents of Berlin, for they spoke 'authentic Alsatian dialect'. The Chargé d'Affaires stressed that he did not wish to dwell on the matter but concluded that 'it was regrettable that a celebration which in other respects had passed so harmoniously and which had absolutely nothing to do with politics, particularly with the Alsatian problem, had been destroyed by such petty derailments'.[98] Köpke could only apologize and assure his French counterpart that 'had we got wind of the fact that a demonstration of this sort was planned we would certainly have taken the necessary steps to prevent it'.[99] On 30 June the conference organizers repeated that they had known nothing about the affair and believed that the Alsatian women had, quite simply, gate-crashed the event. They hoped that that marked the end of the matter.[100] However, the affair continued to haunt Franco-German relations for a few weeks more. When Pierre de Margerie, French Ambassador in Berlin, subsequently raised

[94] AA R71141 L442262, doppel zu II Fr. 94. Signed Bülow, Berlin, 28 Dec. 1928.

[95] AA R71141 L442345–6, Abschrift zu W 2681 I, Aufzeichnung. Signed Wiehl, Berlin, 23 Jun. 1930.

[96] Ibid. [97] Ibid., 346.

[98] AA R71141 L442347–8, quote on 348, St.S., Aufzeichnung. Signed Köpke, Berlin, 24 Jun. 1930.

[99] Ibid., 348.

[100] AA R71141 L442349, zu W 2681 II, Aufzeichnung. Signed Wiehl, Berlin, 30 Jun. 1930.

concerns with Bülow, by then the Foreign Office Permanent Secretary, over the status of the Stahlhelm in the demilitarized Rhineland, an increasingly heated conversation spilled over into events at the recent World Energy Conference. De Margerie reportedly complained that a souvenir brochure contained a map which included Alsace-Lorraine as part of Germany before protesting that:

> In addition during the World Energy Conference a [folk] costume parade was held in the Palace of Sport in which two women in Alsatian costumes filed past and, if I [Bülow] understood correctly, that they were bearing a red and white Alsatian flag. That was unacceptable to the French people.[101]

De Margerie hoped that this rise in tensions, primarily the result of German reactions to the recent Allied military evacuation of the Rhineland, would prove a passing difficulty. As the atmosphere in the room became calmer, the Ambassador reflected on 'the challenges of his office and on the eight years during which he had worked unremittingly for Franco-German rapprochement',[102] an objective Bülow was happy to endorse.[103]

The niggles continued. Bombastic outbursts at paramilitary events in south-western Germany, which often carried direct or indirect allusions to Alsace, continued to play very badly in France.[104] Further, often spurious, Alsace-based war scares[105] flared up periodically,[106] while French controls on its German frontier (effectively the Alsatian frontier) could be sufficiently stringent as to prompt German diplomats to ask whether they were reconcilable with the spirit of rapprochement.[107] And outside the German-built head post office in Strasbourg were statues of the three most recent German emperors, all decapitated after the resumption of French rule. Sightseeing tours of the Alsatian capital took in the mutilated statues, to the consternation of at least some German visitors, but repeated protests by Berlin were slow to effect their removal, despite assurances of prompt action by the Quai d'Orsay.[108] Suspicion and provocation, then, always constituted a counterweight to the rapprochement process and the Alsatian question served as a bellwether of wider uncertainties, which had, as seen, been significantly reinforced by the effective demise of the 1931 Berlin Agreement.

[101] AA R29449 381457–60, quote on 459. Signed Bülow, Berlin, 15 Jul. 1930.

[102] Ibid., quote on 460. [103] Ibid.

[104] AA R70509, Pressebericht. Signed Dewils, Brussels, 16 Aug. 1932; R70509 K241201, Telegramm No. 1162. Auswärtig Berlin. Signed Hoesch, Paris, 20 Aug. 1932; R70509 K241202, zu II Fr. 2857. Signed Friedberg, Berlin, 24 Aug. 1932.

[105] See, for example, Ch. 6 under 'A Difficult Climate', 151.

[106] For example: AA R70509, 'Französischer Aufmarsch an der Pfälzer Grenze?' *Berliner Börsen-Zeitung*, 267, 10 Jun. 1932; R70509 K241187–9, Abschrift. Nr. g 4474. Regierung der Pfalz, Kammer des Innern, Betreff: Französische Truppenzusammenziehungen an der pfälzischen Grenze im Juni 1932. Signed Staehler, Speyer, 24 Jun. 1932.

[107] AA R70509, Abschrift zu II Fr. 3198. Der Regierungspräsident. Betr: Vorgänge an der deutsch-französischen Grenze. Signed Dr Saassen, Trier, 10 Sept. 1932.

[108] AA R71141 L442355, Deutsche Botschaft Paris. A 1394. Signed Rieth, Paris, 17 Oct. 1930; R70507 K240888–9, Deutsche Botschaft Paris. A 3857. Inhalt: Behandlung verschiedener schwebender Fragen mit der französischen Regierung. Signed Hoesch, Paris, 23 Oct. 1931; R71141 L442367. Signed Dr P. Koenig, Forchheim, 2 Sept. 1932.

This had done much to undermine German goodwill by the spring of 1932, but no one could have anticipated the impact on French opinion of a publishing scandal that raged during mid-1932 and left confidence in the prospects for rapprochement with Germany very badly shaken indeed.

THE STRESEMANN MEMOIRS SCANDAL

Despite the repeated squalls that battered Franco-German relations, the close and constructive working relationship forged between Gustav Stresemann and Aristide Briand had always served as the guarantor, even totem, of Franco-German rapprochement. After Stresemann's death in October 1929 his legacy continued to be invoked in both capitals as the benchmark against which successors were measured and the benchmark against which they measured themselves. Briand continued to dominate French foreign policy until during 1931 his failing health saw the Prime Minister, Pierre Laval, take on an increasingly prominent role. However, the latter never questioned the established fundamentals of France's rapprochement policy; quite the reverse was the case and senior French diplomats continued to pursue this agenda with commitment and dispatch. Poincaré and Tardieu were prominent among the French conservatives who also came to agree that Briand's strategy of accommodation with, rather than confrontation and containment of, Germany best served their own country's interests. However, this all rested on the conviction that Stresemann had always acted in good faith and that he spoke for Germany, even from beyond the grave.

During 1932 all of this was unexpectedly laid open to doubt. A year after the great statesman's death, his family turned its thoughts to publishing his personal papers as a form of memoir and a commercial deal was struck with the Berlin-based Ullstein Press to issue the papers in three volumes. This influential Jewish-led publisher, whose activities extended from books to magazines and newspapers, served as a progressive and liberal counterpart to Alfred Hugenberg's media empire. Its recent titles included Erich Maria Remarque's pacifist novel, *Im Westen nichts Neues* (*All Quiet on the Western Front*); a new edition of Heinrich Mann's caricature of the Wilhelmine education system, *Professor Unrat* (*Small Town Tyrant*), which served as the basis for the 1930 Marlene Dietrich film, *Der Blaue Engel* (*The Blue Angel*); and then in 1931 Carl Zuckmayer's lampooning of Prussian militarist values in his play, *Der Hauptmann von Köpenick* (*The Captain of Köpenick*). Nonetheless, in 1931 the French Ambassador at Munich painted a very different figure when claiming that Ullstein had dismissed thirty of its editorial staff known for their 'progressive' ideas, including support for a Franco-German entente.[109] Whatever the case, Ullstein sold translation rights to a French publisher and various newspapers in France and Germany took up its offer of prepublication rights.[110]

[109] MAE Z619 58, Affaires Étrangères, Telegramme à l'Arrivée, J No 20. Signed Ormesson, Munich, 10 Nov. 1931.

[110] AA R70518 E684817–19, St.S. zu II Fr 1812. Signed St.S., Berlin, 4 Jun. 1932.

Therein lay the seeds of disaster, for many were owned or controlled by serving politicians who could be deeply involved in editorial policy and by no means all these politicians and newspapers were friends of Franco-German rapprochement.

Stresemann's former Private Secretary, Henry Bernhard, was assigned the task of selecting and editing the papers. Still a serving diplomat, he was granted formal leave for the duration of this editorship, but the Foreign Minister, Julius Curtius, at first anticipated that the Wilhelmstraβe would, through Bernhard, be able to avert any diplomatically damaging indiscretions.[111] However, the whole enterprise remained fraught with risk. Curtius prevailed on Bernhard to return any official or semi-official papers to the Foreign Office[112] and obtained agreement from Stresemann's widow that a suitably qualified senior academic should have oversight of the proofs before publication.[113] Yet doubts remained, for the Foreign Minister suspected from the outset that Ullstein would restrict Bernhard's role to the selection of documents,[114] while prepublication extracts would be distributed by the publisher and be further edited by the newspapers concerned. The translation of texts from German into French also offered ample opportunity for conscious or unconscious distortion of the original sense and content.

The storm broke in late April 1932 on the eve of French parliamentary elections, scheduled for 1 May (first round) and 8 May (second round), as the beleaguered political right exploited the Stresemann papers in a last-gasp effort to stave off defeat at the hands of the Left Alliance (Cartel des Gauches). With publication of the second volume of memoirs imminent, several nationalist newspapers printed a letter from Stresemann to the former Prussian Crown Prince, written in September 1925, in which the German statesman wrote of 'finessing' Briand. This, France's nationalist press asserted, revealed an aggressively revisionist foreign policy which had duplicitously exploited the language of detente, the Locarno Agreements, and subsequently German membership of the League of Nations. Stresemann's '"internationalist and pacifist language" had', it was claimed, 'merely served as a means to [these] ends'.[115] Ullstein attempted to dismiss the revelations as sensationalist nonsense, claiming that any dispassionate reading of the letter served as remarkable confirmation of Stresemann's publicly expressed aims and ambitions,[116] but this failed to calm the prevailing mood in France. Shortly before the second round of the French elections, German diplomats across Europe urged Berlin to arrange for Brüning to give a reassuring interview on the subject of Franco-German relations, but this proved too little too late.[117]

111 AA R70518 E684799–800, Abschrift. Signed Curtius, Mannheim, 22 Mar. 1930; R70518, Abschrift. zu RM 854. Germadiplo Paris. Nr. 389. Signed Curtius, Berlin, 13 Jun. 1930.

112 AA R70518, V. zu RM 842, Niederschrift betreffend Verlagsvertrag zwischen Konsul Bernhard und der Firma Ullstein über Herausgabe des Nachlasses von Stresemann. Signed Curtius, Berlin, 3 Jun. 1930.

113 AA R70518 E684799–800, here 799, Abschrift. Signed Curtius, Mannheim, 22 Mar. 1930.

114 Ibid., here 800.

115 AA R70518, 'Stresemanns Nachlaβ im französischen Wahlkampf. Ist Briand "hintergangen" worden?' *Vossische Zeitung*, No 209, 1 May 1932.

116 Ibid.

117 AA R70508, 'Herr von Moellendorf rief aus Genf an . . . '. Signed Bülow, Berlin, 6 May 1932.

Hoesch had been less sanguine than Curtius from the outset and wrote to Bernhard on 6 May, recalling that he had warned him personally in no uncertain terms that the whole memoirs project was fraught with unavoidable dangers. Now, he concluded: 'The reception accorded to *Stresemann's Legacy* in France to date demonstrates that my warnings were all too prescient.'[118] Hoesch went on to quote from extracts that had provided the French nationalist press with priceless ammunition in the electoral battle against Édouard Herriot, the leader of the Cartel des Gauches. Herriot had been Prime Minister at the time of the 1924 London Conference, which brokered the Dawes Plan for reparations and called time on France's legally tenuous occupation of Germany's Ruhr District. During the Conference, the memoirs claimed: 'Stresemann spoke of Poincaré's breach of faith when [Germany] abandoned passive resistance [against the occupation in September 1923], with Herriot agreeing emphatically.' For the Frenchman to disown his predecessor in this manner would have been extraordinary at best and, Hoesch reported, 'newspapers such as *Intransigeant*, the *Journal des débats*, *L'Ordre*, and *Ami du peuple* have not wanted for the opportunity to exploit this in their attacks on Herriot'.[119] The conservative *Echo de Paris* concurred, arguing that the Stresemann memoirs had discredited Briand (and by extension Herriot) from beyond the grave.[120]

It got worse when, amid the storm of French indignation, Herriot was informed that Stresemann had described him in the memoirs as a fat jellyfish. The Head of French Affairs at the Wilhelmstraße, Heinrich von Friedberg, demanded a response from the publisher and editor, but 'despite searching for hours, neither Bernhard nor the Ullstein Verlag managed to unearth the term "fat jellyfish" (*dicke Qualle*)'.[121] Friedberg suggested to Hoesch that a mistranslation from German into French might be to blame,[122] leading Hoesch's staff to comb the German and French texts for the offending phrase, but again they hit a blank. As the Ambassador concluded: 'If the term [fat jellyfish] is actually not to be found in the memoirs, then someone here must have tendentiously exploited the prevailing atmosphere to pass this [rumour] on to Herriot.'[123] He decided to broach the matter with Herriot once the dust had settled,[124] but quite apart from this personal slight, the publication of the memoirs left the French Prime Minister wondering whether he had ever been wise in seeking accommodation with Germany. He had already been deeply troubled by a Nazi breakthrough in the Prussian state elections in April 1932 and, as he now concluded in the Lyon newspaper *Démocrate*: 'The publication of the Stresemann papers reveals to us this minister's true intentions.'[125]

[118] AA R70518 E684804–6, quote on 804, Sehr geehrter Herr Bernhard! Signed Hoesch, Paris, 6 May 1932.

[119] Ibid., quotes on 804–5.

[120] AA Paris 564a, Pertinax, 'Une voix d'outre-tombe: Stresemann dénonce Briand', *L'Echo de Paris*, 13 May 1932.

[121] AA R70518, Fernschreibernotiz für Botschafter von Hoesch, stamped II Fr. 1919. Signed Friedberg, Berlin, 4 Jun. 1932.

[122] Ibid.

[123] AA R70518, Deutsche Botschaft Paris, A.2398. Signed Hoesch, Paris, 10 Jun. 1932.

[124] Ibid.

[125] AA R70508 K241171–3, quote on 172, Telegramm Nr. 763. Signed Hoesch, Paris, 29 May 1932.

François-Poncet had warned Bülow on 26 May that relations had been delicate enough before the memoirs scandal prejudiced French perceptions of German foreign policy,[126] and on 1 June Herriot's personal anger surfaced during wide-ranging discussions with Hoesch. Brüning had resigned as Chancellor on 30 May to be replaced by Franz von Papen and the main purpose of the meeting was to take stock of relations as new governments took office in Berlin and Paris respectively. Herriot, however, regarded the Stresemann memoirs as central to the conduct of Franco-German relations past and future, remarking that while he proposed dealing 'honestly and frankly',[127] this demanded a reciprocal approach on Germany's part:

> In this respect the reading of the Stresemann memoirs had been for him personally a particularly painful and embarrassing experience. He had engaged completely openly in 1924 with the German ministers, only to discern from the memoirs that Stresemann had taken some pride in duping him. Elsewhere Stresemann had alleged that he, Herriot, had betrayed the French Parliament, something which, alongside other pronouncements in the memoirs, had served to embarrass him and continued to do so. Finally, Stresemann had spoken disparagingly of him personally and described him as a 'fat jellyfish'. His reading of the memoirs had reinforced his conviction that frankness and candour are the primary preconditions for any successful liaison.[128]

This was not a passing storm, but a deep and personal wound to which Herriot returned repeatedly as each French concession to Germany failed 'to bring about the slightest thaw in Franco-German relations'.[129] Indeed, quite the reverse appeared the case. Papen's Army Minister, General Kurt von Schleicher, accused the French government of hypocrisy on the disarmament question, which Herriot remonstrated was particularly wounding and insulting in the light of the Stresemann scandal.[130]

Hoesch was 'no less' (and arguably considerably more) displeased to find that extracts from his own confidential, even coded, briefings to Berlin at the time of the 1924 London Conference had somehow found their way into the French press. These portrayed Herriot as 'well intentioned', but 'very weak and vulnerable', as a leader who 'appears completely to have lost his nerve', as being 'deeply depressed', and so on.[131] The whole business, Hoesch remonstrated, left the diplomatic process deeply compromised: 'It renders impossible frank, reliable reporting by any representative abroad to the Foreign Office, if he must reckon with strictly confidential statements being unreservedly surrendered to the public gaze and at a

126 AA R70508 K241174–6, esp. 175, stamped II Fr 1855. Signed Bülow, Berlin, 26 May 1932.
127 AA R70509, Telegramm Nr. 784 vom 1.6. Signed Hoesch, Paris, 1 Jun. 1932.
128 Ibid., 2.
129 AA R70509, Telegramm Nr. 1084 vom 28.7. Signed Hoesch, Paris, 29 Jul. 1932, reference to Stresemann, 1; quote, 5.
130 Ibid., 1.
131 AA R70518 E684804–7, quote on 805, Sehr geehrter Herr Bernhard! Signed Hoesch, Paris, 6 May 1932.

time when the people concerned are still alive and remain professionally active.'[132] Soon enough, French diplomats and politicians were just as unhappy to have 'a host of confidential statements' exposed to the public gaze[133] and to have a number of potentially damaging but purely fictitious Franco-German diplomatic exchanges presented in the press as fact.[134]

If these leaks had compromised his own bona fides, Hoesch was equally enraged by the undeserved damage to Stresemann's reputation wrought by the publication, out of context, of his letter to the former Crown Prince. And other extracts from Stresemann's writings left French readers to ponder whether Germany had really abandoned all hope of recovering Alsace and the Moselle, despite assurances to this effect forming an integral part of the 1925 Locarno Agreements.[135] Remonstrations against Bernhard aside, Hoesch offered the Foreign Office a despairing assessment of the memoirs' impact on French opinion. He repeated that events had confirmed his own initial misgivings in full, and that the letter to the former Crown Prince with its talk of 'finessing' French interests:

> has had an utterly devastating impact here on public opinion. Well-intentioned persons, who regarded Stresemann's period in office and in particular the Locarno Treaties as the keystone of post-war Franco-German relations, and based their future hopes on this, have had their convictions and expectations severely shaken. Again and again, we are hearing even the most convinced supporters of a German-French rapprochement policy express anxiety and doubt over whether, in the light of this dreadful revelation, it remains in any way possible seriously to discuss the notion of rapprochement between the two countries. Some have even finally lost hope.[136]

Hoesch continued that the Mayor of Laon had resigned from the Social Radical Party (which would form part of the victorious Cartel des Gauches coalition), declaring that 'the exposure of Stresemann's deception prevented him from remaining in a party that, together with the Socialists, wished to sacrifice France to German deceitfulness'.[137] Gustav Stresemann's son, Wolfgang, was given space in *Paris-Midi* to defend his father's memory[138] and found support from Joseph Caillaux in the Toulouse-published Radical Socialist newspaper, *La Dépêche*.[139] A further handful of figures on the French political left, such as the Republican

[132] Ibid.; see also AA Paris 564a, Telegramm in Ziff. geheim. Auswärtig Berlin Nr. 741. Signed Hoesch, Paris, 23 May 1932.

[133] AA R70518 684879, Telegramm Nr. 40 vom 19.1. Signed Koester, Paris, 19 Jan. 1933.

[134] AA Paris 564a, Telegramm in Ziff. geheim. Auswärtig Berlin Nr. 741. Signed Hoesch, Paris, 23 May 1932.

[135] AA R70518 E684804–7, here 807, Sehr geehrter Herr Bernhard! Signed Hoesch, Paris, 6 May 1932; see also R70518 E684801–3, here 802, Deutsche Botschaft Paris, A 2028. Signed Hoesch, Paris, 13 May 1932.

[136] AA R70518 E684801–3, here 801, Deutsche Botschaft Paris, A 2028. Signed Hoesch, Paris, 13 May 1932.

[137] Ibid., here 801–2.

[138] AA R70518, Wolfgang Stresemann, 'M. Wolfgang Stresemann defend la mémoire de son père. Il tente de répondre aux reproches qui ont été addresses à ce dernier à propos de sa lettre à l'ex-kronprinz', *Paris-Midi*, 2256, 4 Jun. 1932.

[139] AA R70518, Deutsche Botschaft Paris. A 2701. Signed Forster, Paris, 24 Jun. 1932; R70518, J. Caullaux, 'Il est plus grand mort que vivant', *La Dépêche*, 17 Jun. 1932.

Socialist, Paul Painlevé, were also relatively sanguine, but this could not offset the 'widespread' conviction that: 'Briand had been duped and betrayed by Stresemann.'[140]

There was confirmation aplenty in Paris of a fundamental shift in the wind regarding relations with Germany. In early May and before the 'fat jellyfish' scandal drew in Herriot personally, his predecessor, André Tardieu, undoubtedly spoke for many when, in an election broadcast, he argued that: 'Even international agreements, including Locarno, celebrated as honestly negotiated and freely concluded, now seem to have been burdened with mental reservations which must force us to reflect.'[141] A fortnight later, on 20 May, the distinguished elder statesman, Raymond Poincaré, was given space in *Le Matin* to declare: 'Stresemann now appears in his true colours. He was not a statesman, dedicated to the unification of Germany and France. He was brought up on the ideas of Bismarck and had not repudiated them.'[142] Hans Riesser, a Senior Councillor at the German Embassy, sought an explanation from *Le Matin*'s foreign editor for this unexpectedly hostile commentary, for the newspaper had hitherto fostered close relations with the Quai d'Orsay as a convinced supporter of Briand's rapprochement-minded foreign policy. When Riesser finally met the editor on 23 May he learned that the damage extended far beyond the publication of a critical article. The owner of *Le Matin*, Maurice Bunau-Varilla, formerly 'a great admirer of Stresemann' whose policies, he believed, formed the fixed point in German-French relations, had now joined the anti-German camp, 'seeing Briand and himself as the credulous victims of a sophisticated deception, which left him unable henceforth to lend German [policy] any credibility'.[143]

The interventions by Tardieu and Poincaré were also symptomatic of a deeper problem. Both statesmen had in 1919 pressed for a tough peace settlement with Germany and both, initially, had insisted on enforcing the Versailles Treaty as rigorously as possible. Only gradually were they convinced by Briand that rapprochement with Germany potentially offered France a greater measure of security, but once persuaded they retained him as their Foreign Minister in a succession of Cabinets. This brought both Prime Ministers into conflict with many of their nationalist backbenchers who in turn felt let down by the leaders they had trusted to take a firm line against Germany. Both Premiers did occasionally play to the nationalist gallery in parliament, a faction which had set limits on just how far or fast rapprochement with Germany could go. However, Poincaré and Tardieu had both contributed to a relatively consistent French policy towards Germany from

140 AA R70518 E684812–13, here 813, Telegramm Nr. 736 v. 21.5. Signed Hoesch, Paris, 21 May 1932; see also: R70518, 'Gerechtigkeit für Stresemann. Georges Bonnet widerlegt die französischen Angriffe', *Vossische Zeitung*, report from Paris, 9 Aug. 1932, where Bonnet defends Stresemann's memory in *Information*.

141 AA R70518 E684804–7, quote on 806, Sehr geehrter Herr Bernhard! Signed Hoesch, Paris, 6 May 1932.

142 AA R70518, II Fr. 1761, 'Stresemann et Briand. Un commentaire de M. Raymond Poincaré', *Le Matin*, 20 May 1932.

143 AA R70518 E684835–6, quote on 836, Telegramm, Nr. 741 vom 23/5. Signed Hoesch, Paris, 23 May 1932.

the time of Locarno through to the 1931 Berlin Agreement and beyond, even if much of the parliamentary support for this policy had come from the political centre-left. Now this cross-party collaboration of sorts had been destroyed and although the centre-left had prevailed in the May 1932 elections, the hopes and assumptions of the late Briand's allies on the centre-right were very badly scarred indeed.

With the memoirs scandal threatening to destabilize Franco-German relations for years to come, Hoesch urged the Foreign Office to prevent the publication of the third volume of papers, if at all possible.[144] Meanwhile the Belgian press picked over the records of Franco-German discussions at the time of Locarno regarding the return of Eupen-Malmédy from Belgium to Germany, demanding to know whether Belgium had even been informed by France of a proposal that certainly violated the letter and spirit of the Locarno Agreements.[145]

All of this hardly served to lighten the mood in Berlin where Chancellor Brüning, appalled at the damage to Franco-German relations, demanded an explanation and guarantees that no further harm would be done.[146] The Wilhelmstraβe promised a full enquiry and moved to prevent staff making personal copies of official papers in the future.[147] Meanwhile Köpke arranged for immediate dispatch of Hoesch's letter to Bernhard's private address, before summoning the latter to the Wilhelmstraβe, where he demanded that nothing potentially damaging to German interests appear in the forthcoming third volume.[148] Friedberg subsequently briefed Bernhard in graphic terms on the damage wrought by his efforts to date and instructed him to submit the draft to the Foreign Office for aggressive redaction of sensitive material which related to critical moments in German foreign relations, 'leaving the extent and scope of the third volume greatly reduced'.[149] Furthermore Bernhard, and not the publishers, was to select prepublication extracts from the surviving material for release to the media. This, the Wilhelmstraβe hoped, would 'safeguard us from any further surprises upon publication of the third volume of Stresemann memoirs'.[150]

Liberal German newspapers, such as the *Vossische Zeitung* (itself part of the Ullstein stable), initially viewed the controversy as part of the rough and tumble of a French election campaign;[151] or, as the *Frankfurter Zeitung* argued, as the product of an unbridgeable gulf between France's perception of its own foreign policy as universalist and pursued in the interests of humanity and its perception of

[144] AA R70518 E684801–3, here 802–3, Deutsche Botschaft Paris, A 2028. Signed Hoesch, Paris, 13 May 1932.

[145] AA R70518, Deutsche Gesandtschaft, A.177, Inhalt: Die belgische Presse zu Stresemann's nachgelassenen Aufzeichnungen über Eupen-Malmedy. Signed Bräuer, Brussels, 23 May 1932.

[146] AA R70518 E684816, Der Staatssekretär in der Reichskanzlei. Rk. 4948. Signed Pünder, Berlin, 25 May 1932.

[147] AA R70518 E684817–19, Sofort! zu II Fr 1812, St.S., Berlin, 4 Jun. 1932.

[148] AA R70518 E684809, St.S., Sofort! Signed Köpke, Berlin, 18 May 1932.

[149] AA R70518 E684841, St.S. zu II Fr 1743. Signed Bülow, Berlin, 3 Jun. 1932.

[150] AA R70518 E684810–11, quote on 811, St. S., zu II Fr 1706, Berlin, 4 Jun. 1932.

[151] AA R70518, 'Stresemanns Nachlaβ im französischen Wahlkampf. Ist Briand "hintergangen" worden?' *Vossische Zeitung*, 209, 1 May 1932.

Germany's as an egotistical challenge to these same values.[152] But nothing could contain the growing fury in France and deepening sense of mortification in Germany. As the Nuremberg-based and nationalist *Fränkischer Kurier* declared: 'The publication of the Stresemann memoirs constitutes a shocking addition to the downfall [of Weimar]. We might at the very least have spared ourselves this dose of elemental stupidity.'[153] Or as the venerable *Journal des débats* concluded in a withering attack on Briand's weakness and credulity when confronted by a domineering Stresemann: 'M. Briand—and there is no reason to cease repeating this because the truth has inalienable rights—has sacrificed the interests of France and weakened the peace.'[154]

Bernhard assured Köpke that he had recognized from the outset that: 'The release out of context of the so-called "Crown Prince Letter" in prepublication extracts . . . might elicit an unfavourable reaction and accordingly I excluded this letter from the index of material intended for publication.'[155] However, it appears that the French translation of the memoirs retained the letter, which found its way into the French press and subsequently into German newspapers.[156] Bernhard also responded in writing and at length to Hoesch's strictures, before concluding with the un-reassuring 'reassurance that further [editorial] work and subsequent publication will proceed in the same manner and spirit that have guided me to date'.[157] This was as untactful as it was unwise, but the Ambassador confined himself to reporting to Berlin in the briefest of brief communications that: 'I do not intend further to sustain the correspondence.'[158]

And still the ripples continued to spread. The German Ambassador at Madrid, Johannes Count von Welczeck, had in June spent a couple of days in Paris, where he was invited to an 'intimate family supper' by his French cousin, Stanislas Count de Castellane.[159] The noble Castellane family remained at the heart of political life in republican France. Stanislas served as Vice-President of the Chamber of Deputies and chaired its Foreign Affairs Committee, while his elder brother, Jean, had recently served a term as the President of the Municipal Council of Paris. Both had been consistent and long-standing advocates of Franco-German detente and Jean had, as noted earlier, during 1931 helped to organize the successful official visit to Berlin by his successor, François Latour.[160]

152 AA R70518, 'Frankreich kämpft mit dem Schatten Stresemanns. Ministerrat und Außenpolitik—Mahnungen an die künftige Regierung', *Frankfurter Zeitung*, 372/74, 21 May 1932.

153 AA R70518, Dr Erich Schlie, 'Bloßstellung der deutschen Außenpolitik: Unzeitgemäße Veröffentlichung der Stresemann-Erinnerungen', *Fränkischer Kurier*, 144, 26 May 1932.

154 AA R70518, Pierre Bernus, 'Un aveuglement sans precedent', *Journal des Débats*, 21 May 1932.

155 AA R70518 E684832–3, quote on 833, Konsul z.D. Henry Bernhard. Signed Bernhard, Berlin-Grunewald, 23 May 1932.

156 Ibid.

157 AA R70518, Abschrift zu A 2267, Konsul z.D. Henry Bernhard. Signed Bernhard, Berlin-Grunewald, 23 May 1932, 9.

158 AA R70518 E684834, Deutsche Botschaft Paris. A 2267. Signed Hoesch, Paris, 27 May 1932.

159 AA R70518 E684845–6, Abschrift, Deutsche Botschaft in Spanien. Signed Welczeck, Madrid, 6 Jun. 1932.

160 See Ch. 5 under 'Latour in Berlin', 129.

However, to use a carefully chosen word, the Castellane brothers were scunnered by the appearance and contents of the Stresemann memoirs. Bewildered over how their publication could have been allowed at all, they reportedly continued that:

> The impact in France was almost catastrophic and would poison the atmosphere for a long time to come. If it transpires that the memoirs were shown to a German government agency (substantial sections were presented to Briand by [Professor Oswald] Hesnard), and that this agency did nothing to prevent publication, then one is confronted by a mystery. By way of analogy, the guilty party in France would have been hanged and the [editor] or publisher charged with treason.[161]

'Our worst enemies', Welczeck maintained, 'could not have matched the damage done to Germany by the publication of these memoirs. The appearance of further volumes must be prevented by hook or by crook, if we don't wish to alienate our best friends abroad.' Stanislas Castellane, he continued, was a peaceful man of sound judgement, not wont to waste words, but as the evening progressed the Frenchman 'worked himself into a fury the likes of which I have never previously experienced on his part'.[162] With the memoirs also the gossip of the diplomatic community in Madrid, Welczeck demanded that 'not only should the appearance of further volumes be prevented, but we should find legal means to put an end to this memoirs plague'.[163]

Lessons, it seems, had been learned and although publication of the memoirs continued, Bernhard now found himself summoned repeatedly to meetings with senior diplomats as he worked on the third volume.[164] The Wilhelmstraβe proposed a series of amendments and deletions which Bernhard, after further discussion, by and large incorporated in the draft text.[165] The Director of the Ullstein Verlag, Hans Schäffer, also collaborated closely with the Wilhelmstraβe in an effort, as far as possible, to sanitize prepublication extracts that were destined for the same newspapers that had wrought such havoc during mid-1932.[166] The 1926 Thoiry discussions between Stresemann and Briand, which no one in Berlin wished to see presented out of context, were omitted,[167] but the Paris journal *L'Illustration* was already in possession of the full draft and had previously acquired the legal right to publish what it saw fit. Its editors saw no reason to impose any kind of voluntary censorship, instead 'insisting on the necessity of our being able to select [material]

[161] AA R70518 E684845–6, quote on 845, Abschrift, Deutsche Botschaft in Spanien. Signed Welczeck, Madrid, 6 Jun. 1932.

[162] Ibid. [163] Ibid., quote on 846.

[164] AA R70518 E684849–50, Konsul z.D. Henry Bernhard. Signed Bernhard, Berlin-Grunewald, 16 Jul. 1932.

[165] AA R70518 E684851–3, Konsul z.D. Henry Bernhard. Signed Bernhard, Berlin-Grunewald, 26 Jul. 1932.

[166] AA R70518 E684860–1, Dr Hans Schäffer. Signed Hans Schäffer, Berlin, 17 Dec. 1932; R70518 E684866–8, Rein-Konzept, stv.St.S., zu II Fr. 4201. Signed Köpke, Berlin, 20 Dec. 1932; R70518 E684869–70, Dr Hans Schäffer. Signed Hans Schäffer, Berlin, 9 Jan. 1933.

[167] AA R70518 E684873–6, here 873, St.S. zu II Fr 87. Signed St.S., Berlin, 15 Jan. 1933.

from the unadulterated memoirs'.[168] An eleventh-hour appeal was sent via the German Embassy in Paris to the Quai d'Orsay, asking French colleagues to prevail on *L'Illustration* to desist from publication. Berlin also hoped that this intervention would at least demonstrate to French diplomats that Germany had learned lessons from the earlier prepublication fiasco,[169] but by the time the note reached Paris *L'Illustration* had already published the offending Thoiry extracts.[170]

This time it was the late Briand who came off worst. The *Journal des débats* quoted at length from *L'Illustration*, commenting that: 'A reading of the "papers" gives the impression that during this meeting Stresemann pushed forward step by step without ever encountering any resistance . . . M. Briand's words were those of a man who had no sense of [being] the victor and who lacked any confidence in his own country.'[171] Among other things Briand reportedly complained to Stresemann that other ministries were doing their best to hinder an early Allied military evacuation of the Rhineland:

> I gave precise instructions to set things in train, but you cannot do anything with these technicians. When I first turned my attention to the ending of military control [in the Rhineland] our War Ministry sent me kilos of documents relating to German breaches [of the Treaty terms]. I threw them into a corner, demanded that they identify any major outstanding issues, while refusing to get caught up in these trifles.[172]

However, beyond the predictable outrage in the French nationalist press, the steam had largely gone out of the memoirs scandal, with most newspapers 'evidently awaiting the appearance of the final volume of Stresemann papers in book form in order to permit a balanced view of its contents'.[173] Hesnard spoke reluctantly with *Le Matin*, suggesting that Stresemann's records focused on the dimensions of his diplomacy that had played well for Germany, while ignoring the gains of his negotiating partners. 'Stresemann's writings', Hesnard concluded, 'do not constitute a historical record, providing an incomplete picture of his methods and character.'[174] Antonina Vallentin-Luchaire, whose own biography of Stresemann had appeared in 1930, agreed. Writing in *Volonté* she argued that Stresemann's impatience during the pursuit of his goals 'stemmed not from any wish to exploit Briand, but because he felt that domestic political developments in Germany left the speedy success of his foreign policy desirable in the interests of peace'.[175]

[168] AA R70518 E684872, Abschrift. *L'Illustration*. Signed E. Sorbets, Paris, 6 Jan. 1933; see also: R70518 E684871, Abschrift. Dr Kurt Fiedler, Stresemann. Signed M.S., 6 Jan. 1933; R70518 E684873–6, zu II Fr 87. Signed St.S., Berlin, 15 Jan. 1933.

[169] AA R70518 E684875–6, Lieber Herr Schäffer, [15 Jan. 1933].

[170] AA R70518 E684879, Telegramm Nr. 40 vom 19.1. Signed Koester, Paris, 19 Jan. 1933.

[171] AA R70518, 'Nouvelles revelations de Stresemann. L'entrevue de Thoiry', *Journal des Débats*, 14, 15 Jan. 1933.

[172] Ibid.

[173] AA R70518, Deutsche Botschaft Paris, A 368, Betr. Stresemann-Papiere. Signed Kühn, Paris, 27 Jan. 1933.

[174] AA R70518, Deutsche Botschaft Paris, A 536, Betr. Hesnard zu den Stresemann-Veröffentlichungen. Signed Kühn, Paris, 10 Feb. 1933.

[175] AA R70518, Deutsche Botschaft Paris, A. 610, Betr. Frau Vallentin-Luchaire zu Stresemanns 'Vermächtnis'. Signed Kühn, Paris, 17 Feb. 1933.

Yet by the time Joachim Kühn, German Cultural Attaché in Paris, dispatched this report to Berlin the very political implosion Stresemann had feared, and even anticipated, had become reality. Hitler's government was wasting little time in consolidating its grip on Germany, French commentators had bigger fish to fry than the memoirs of the late Weimar statesman, and the Wilhelmstraβe closed its file on the scandal. However, the real damage had been done well before Hitler had any direct role in foreign affairs. The Stresemann–Briand partnership constituted a powerful and largely convincing personification of Franco-German rapprochement, sufficiently strong to engage statesmen on both sides of the Rhine who had previously sought security at the expense of their neighbour. The memoirs scandal did enormous damage to this mobilizing narrative in France, damage compounded on both sides of the Rhine by the wave of economic protectionism that swept France and Germany during 1931 and 1932.[176] The undermining of the September 1931 Berlin Agreement through France's arbitrary and unilateral imposition of tariffs on imported foreign goods served, as we have seen,[177] to complement the damage wrought by the memoirs scandal by decapitating the practical route, through economic collaboration, to the realization of Briand's and of Stresemann's vision.

IMPASSE

Franco-German relations did not collapse during the latter half of 1932, but the drive to forge rapprochement within a European context was replaced by a messier relationship. André François-Poncet had predicted in May that 'unfortunately, agreement between [the new] left-wing government in France and a right-wing administration in Germany would be particularly difficult',[178] while days before the fall of the Brüning government on 30 May, the French authorities reportedly briefed their domestic press that: 'There was no point concluding agreements with a government . . . resisted by a strong opposition which, if it subsequently manages to take power, then disowns them.'[179] Briand's foreign policy, by contrast, had enjoyed support on both the government and opposition benches.[180] On 22 December 1932 François-Poncet remarked on this fundamental difference when observing that the previous year had indeed witnessed a sea change in German domestic politics, for:

[176] See also Robert J. Young, *France and the Origins of the Second World War* (Basingstoke, 1996), 16, 21.

[177] See Ch. 5 under 'An Imminent Trade War and the Quota Issue', 139–41.

[178] AA R29452 E189081–3, quote on 083. Signed Bülow, Berlin, 2 May 1932.

[179] AA R29452 E189098, Ref.: GR Braun v. Stumm. Aufzeichnung. Signed Braun v. Stumm, Berlin, 25 May 1932. See also Hagen Schulze, *Weimar. Deutschland 1917–1933*, rev. edn (Berlin, 1994), 357.

[180] Ibid.

> With the collapse of the Brüning Cabinet, the year 1932 has, to all intents and purposes, witnessed the end of governments resting on a combination of the Catholic and Socialist parties, and seen the elimination of Social Democracy from positions of power, not just nationally, but also in Prussia. [There, it has] not simply been eliminated from government, but above all from a Prussian administration which it had managed to master, step by step, and thereby make accessible to its own supporters. Twelve years of effort accompanied by a developing democratic tradition has now been completely eliminated in a matter of weeks, or at the very least called seriously into question.[181]

Nationalist sentiment, he continued, had intensified to the point where, in foreign relations, 'the face of Germany is no longer that of 1930', a change which found expression in each and every context.[182] If François-Poncet had been no admirer of Brüning, he conceded that in matters of foreign policy the former Chancellor 'had been obliged by domestic pressure to speak a language which accorded neither with his personal inclinations nor his habitual reserve'.[183] Thus while Brüning sought to address constructively French security interests right up to the end of his Chancellorship,[184] his successors espoused a more radical and uncompromising policy of their own volition, which saw the long-standing maxim of German 'equal rights' in international relations pressed increasingly vigorously and with considerable success. 'It dominates the country's entire [foreign] policy', François-Poncet continued, a country 'refusing to be treated as a second-rank nation, regaining the position in world affairs it had previously enjoyed'. Berlin's hard-line stance at the International Disarmament Conference was just one example among many and wider German policy, he warned, had secured the support, open or implicit, of certain victor powers,[185] and in the event Britain, the United States, and Italy were indeed prepared to make concessions.

Thus, as the Lausanne Conference of June/July 1932 debated yet another resolution of the reparations problem, British negotiators brokered a deal, replacing the Young Plan annuities with a final bill of 2.7 billion gold marks (or 3 billion paper marks) as and when Germany was capable of making such a payment. French negotiators struggled in vain to sweeten this imminent loss of regular reparations income with an immediate payment of the final sum, without which, the French Finance Minister insisted, it was hardly worth France turning up in Lausanne at all.[186] This, Paris suggested, could be underwritten by remortgaging the German state railways and other publicly owned assets, but Berlin refused and upped the stakes by insisting that any final payment should be linked to German rearmament

181 MAE Z762 144–53, quote on 144, No 1168, L'Ambassadeur de France à Berlin à Monsieur le President du Conseil, Ministre des Affaires Étrangères. Coup d'oeil rétrospectif sur l'année 1932. Unsigned, Berlin, 22 Dec. 1932.

182 Ibid., here 149. 183 Ibid.

184 For example, AA R29452 E189085–7, Aktennotiz. Signed Bülow, Berlin, 13 May 1932.

185 MAE Z762 144–53, quotes on 149–50, No 1168, L'Ambassadeur de France à Berlin à Monsieur le President du Conseil, Ministre des Affaires Étrangères. Coup d'oeil rétrospectif sur l'année 1932. Unsigned, Berlin, 22 Dec. 1932.

186 Schirmann, *Crise*, 217–18.

based on 'equal rights' and even a Franco-German military partnership directed against the Soviet Union, a proposal completely unacceptable to Herriot.[187]

The claim, therefore, that the eventual agreement reflected 'the development of confidence between nations in a mutual spirit of reconciliation, collaboration and justice'[188] was far removed from reality. The main beneficiaries of German reparations (France, Britain, Belgium, and Italy) sought to offset their losses by way of a 'gentleman's agreement', which, to Washington's undisguised fury, linked the termination of reparations to a reduction in European war debts to America. Ratification of the Lausanne Agreement, it was unilaterally declared, would be contingent on such a deal.[189] Herriot imagined that this gentleman's agreement had, finally, fulfilled a long-standing French objective, to establish a formal link between German reparations and inter-Allied war debts, but the United States rejected this thesis out of hand. Eventually, in December, Paris defaulted on its repayment schedule to the USA, but, after some prevarication, Britain honoured its obligation, leaving France isolated among the great powers and precipitating the fall of Herriot's government. Nonetheless, almost all the remaining European debtors followed France's lead, 'so bringing an end to a financial system established in the early 1920s'.[190]

French and German diplomats had suspected from the outset that the Lausanne Conference would mark but the first stage in resolving the web of economic challenges confronting the global economy[191] and it was left to a World Economic Conference, sponsored by the League of Nations and held during mid-1933, to try, unsuccessfully, to square the circle.[192] But even before the conference opened, the United States had unilaterally left the gold standard and devalued the dollar, in order to prioritize domestic economic recovery over its international obligations, while Britain and France were determined to resist any measures prejudicial to their particular interests. 'These differences between the three powers', Schirmann observes, 'readmitted the other European nations to the game',[193] and offered Berlin additional room for manoeuvre. French diplomats had during late 1932 observed a German financial recovery and strengthening currency[194] and now, in mid-1933, Paris was a bystander as London and Berlin concluded a bilateral debt agreement. An enraged President Roosevelt despaired of this outbreak of national egotism in the Old World, complaining that 'I am in an awful mess with Europe . . . European statesmen are a bunch of bastards',[195] but Europeans felt similarly about each other. The earlier collaborative vision of a European recovery based around a supranational Franco-German axis was displaced by national self-interest and a series of bilateral and regional agreements. A gold bloc continued

[187] Ibid., 215–20. [188] Quoted in Clavin, *Securing*, 82. [189] Ibid., 82–3.

[190] Schirmann, *Crise*, 276–8, quote on 278; see also: Clavin, *Depression*, 154–7.

[191] AA R29452 E189088–9. Signed Bülow, Berlin, 13 May 1932.

[192] Clavin, *Securing*, 116–23. [193] Schirmann, *Crise*, 353.

[194] MAE Z762 144–53, here 150–1, No 1168, L'Ambassadeur de France à Berlin à Monsieur le President du Conseil, Ministre des Affaires Étrangères. Coup d'oeil rétrospectif sur l'année 1932. Unsigned, Berlin, 22 Dec. 1932.

[195] Quoted in Clavin, *Depression*, 164.

to function under French direction; Germany, its economy now visibly on the mend, came to preside over the economies of the Danube basin; while Britain fell back on the resources of its empire.[196]

Leaving aside the traumas of global finance, François-Poncet warned Bülow in August that German-French relations had deteriorated alarmingly in the wake of the Lausanne Conference, not least thanks to the succession of bombastic Stahlhelm rallies and provocative ministerial pronouncements which had brought French opinion, and Herriot, to fear that the face of Germany had changed fundamentally and for the worse. He accepted that exaggerated French press reporting had exacerbated matters, but he had complaints of his own regarding the German press. When all was said and done, he added, Herriot felt entitled to expect meaningful German concessions on disarmament in return for France's concessions on reparations, which had left Paris with a 'trivial three billion final payment'.[197] And relations suffered an additional symbolic and material setback with the transfer in November 1932 of Leopold von Hoesch from Paris to Germany's London Embassy. His successor, Roland Köster, was a distinguished diplomat, born in 1883 into a bourgeois banking family in Baden, of a German father and Dutch mother. A close associate of Wilhelm II, and of Paul von Hindenburg after the latter became President in 1925, he cultivated a moderate conservatism which saw him work constructively within the Weimar Republic. He was a withering critic of Nazism and came close to resigning from the diplomatic service in early 1933, before struggling on for a couple of years under constant pressure from Joachim von Ribbentrop, the later Nazi Foreign Minister, who already advised Hitler on French affairs. Politically isolated and suffering from increasingly poor health, he announced his resignation in late 1935, but died in February 1936 shortly before this took effect. However, if Köster's political and ethical principles set him well apart from Nazism, he had previously been a measured critic of Stresemann's rapprochement policy and a robust supporter of German revisionism. This set him far apart from Hoesch, a partisan advocate of rapprochement, who had enjoyed the confidence of successive French administrations, as he steered Germany's diplomatic relations with France from the 1923 Ruhr crisis through the Locarno years and on to the 1931 Berlin Agreement.

Thus when Herriot held a farewell diplomatic breakfast to bid Hoesch farewell, his Under Secretary of State at the Quai d'Orsay, Joseph Paganon, was in gloomy mood as he bemoaned the (lack of) progress at the international disarmament talks. During a lengthy exchange with the German diplomatic councillor, Dr Dumont, he insisted that as a friend of Germany, with happy memories of visits to the country, 'he regretted all the more the current deterioration in Franco-German relations'.[198] The earlier spirit of reconciliation had given way in Germany to a 'revanchist and

[196] See, for example, Schirmann, *Crise*, 354.

[197] AA R29452 E189104–9, quote on 107, Durchdruck. Signed Bülow, Berlin, 23 Aug. 1932.

[198] AA R70509 K241233–6, quote on 234, Deutsche Botschaft Paris. Aufzeichnung. Signed Dumont, Paris, 21 Oct. 1932.

warlike mood' which had in turn nurtured French mistrust of its eastern neighbour. Now things had deteriorated further, for:

> The actions of the current German government had completely transformed sentiment here, something he regretted deeply but which remained undeniable. One could sum up the mood as: 'If Germany does not want peace with France, then *tant pis*.'[199]

Such sentiments, Paganon continued, extended well beyond the political milieu to encompass much of public opinion. Dumont retorted that anti-German hysteria in large sections of the French press was to blame for the poor state of relations, rather than anything German governments had said or done. If German public opinion was disappointed by recent French actions that appeared to cut across the country's rightful ambitions, he insisted that this had never translated into hatred of France. (Yet an unnamed official in the Wilhelmstraβe saw fit to pencil in a question mark after the word 'never.')[200] Paganon remained unconvinced, hoping things would take a turn for the better, but insisting that he would be failing in his duty were he not to emphasize the seriousness of the prevailing French mood.[201]

This exchange was more than a passing squall, as Köster discovered during his first meeting with Herriot. The French Prime Minister considered Franco-German relations 'currently to be poor' and was particularly exercised by a string of personal attacks against him in the German press. He insisted that he had worked tirelessly for improved German-French relations only to suffer a degree of abuse 'which Herr von Papen would never encounter in the French press'. Personalities apart, he deplored the repeated efforts by German newspapers to damage France's reputation as a peaceful nation, declaring that 'he would fight against this poisoning of the atmosphere with every means available'.[202] Herriot continued that in the light of France's wartime experiences, 'it was his highest duty to give absolute priority to France's uncontested security' at the disarmament talks. France, he warned, was perfectly aware that Germany was already engaging in covert rearmament and military training, 'meaning that equal rights would not be conceded prior to the conclusion of an international agreement'.[203]

It is striking that whilst Hoesch had almost invariably adopted a mediatory and reassuring tone at the most delicate of moments (and therefore quickly made his mark in his new London posting), Köster chose directly to confront Herriot. If France had suffered during the war, he replied, then so had Germany, compounded by the trauma and humiliation of the post-war occupation, particularly of the Ruhr. The Poles, he continued, engaged 'more or less daily' in provocative anti-German acts whilst hiding behind France's coat-tails, and it was this which had fuelled German demands for equal rights, particularly with regard to disarmament. Germany

[199] Ibid. [200] Ibid., 234–5, Dumont quoted on 235, the question mark is also on 235.
[201] Ibid., here 236.
[202] AA R70509 K241239–43, quotes on 239, Abschrift II F Abr. 4081, Deutsche Botschaft A 4330. Signed Köster, Paris, 18 Nov. 1932; see also R24952 E189137–9. Signed Bülow, Berlin, 17 Nov. 1932.
[203] AA R70509 K241239–43, quotes on 240, Abschrift II F Abr. 4081, Deutsche Botschaft A 4330. Signed Köster, Paris, 18 Nov. 1932.

was a League of Nations member, yet was denied a level of esteem accorded to other European powers, a situation, he claimed, that the German people found intolerable. As for the press attacks, the new Ambassador regarded French newspaper treatment of German affairs, for example in *Figaro*, *Ami du peuple*, and *L'Illustration*, as unashamedly bellicose, adding that powerful interests in France stood behind this onslaught. The atmosphere only belatedly thawed when Herriot closed the meeting by asking Köster to forward his warmest regards to President Hindenburg.[204] Yet just hours later the French Premier chose to recall Köster to make an offer of bilateral arms talks between senior members of the French and German military, but in some despair and palpably against his better judgement. As the Ambassador reported:

> In other regards this conversation gave me the impression that M. Herriot's thoughts are hedged by extreme caution, to avoid leaving him responsible in the eyes of French public opinion for a situation where the recognition of German equal rights triggers far-reaching rearmament which genuinely puts France's security at risk.[205]

The dispute rumbled on, leaving French foreign correspondents in Berlin alarmed at Germany's growing reluctance to accept the Versailles settlement.[206] Matters were further complicated by tortuous Franco-German negotiations concerning the revision and renewal of their 1927 Trade Agreement[207] and by a bomb attack by Breton nationalists, protesting against the four-hundredth anniversary of the Franco-Breton union. Herriot was scheduled to join celebrations in the Breton city of Vannes, but on 20 November the bombers targeted his train, which narrowly escaped derailment.

François-Poncet and Bülow attempted on 28 November to repair the damage with neither diplomat wishing to prolong the uproar triggered by the German press attacks on Herriot. Bülow observed that Hindenburg personally deplored any such defamation, conceded that, personally, he found the work of German cartoonists tasteless, but regretted that the German authorities were powerless to censor them. In any case, he continued, the French press caricatures of Herriot appeared to him far more devastating than their German counterparts. The Ambassador was conciliatory, observing that in reality the frequent lampooning of a statesman served to demonstrate his popularity, but continued that 'unfortunately Herriot finds the German caricatures offensive, but not the French'.[208] No doubt the legacy of the Stresemann memoirs scandal had increased his personal sensitivity. The two diplomats also agreed that exaggerated press coverage of the rearmament question

[204] Ibid., here 241–3.

[205] AA R70509 K241239–43, Abschrift II F Abr. 4081, Deutsche Botschaft A 4330. Signed Köster, Paris, 18 Nov. 1932, here K241244, Nachtrag. Signed Köster.

[206] See, for example, AA R70509, Telegramm, Nr. 1520, Auswärtig Berlin. Signed Botschaft, Paris, 24 Nov. 1932.

[207] Sylvain Schirmann, *Les Relations économiques et financières franco-allemandes 1932–1939* (Paris, 1995), 20–6.

[208] AA R70509 K241245–9, quote on 245–6. Signed Bülow, Berlin, 28 Nov. 1932; see also R29452 E189137–9. Signed Bülow, Berlin, 17 Nov. 1932.

in both countries served no useful purpose,[209] but happenstance in the form of the Breton nationalist incident created new challenges for Franco-German relations. Herriot was (understandably) beside himself, erroneously declaring on radio that German agents were behind the outrage and generating French newspaper headlines such as 'German assassination attempt on Herriot'.[210]

Bülow feared that the episode would leave an indelible mark on wider Franco-German relations,[211] but during the trade negotiations at least, Berlin was sufficiently receptive to French concerns as to allow an eventual agreement.[212] During discussions with Köpke on 3 December François-Poncet alluded to a recent thaw in the French public's attitude towards Germany, not least thanks to 'the excellent impression created by the conclusion of the Franco-German Trade Agreement in Paris'.[213] Days later, during talks with the new Chancellor, Kurt von Schleicher, who had replaced Papen, he went further, even suggesting that economic accord might yet provide the basis for 'Germany and France together to create step by step the basis for a European economic settlement'.[214]

However, tensions surrounding Germany's eastern frontier and the rearmament question proved far more significant during the twilight weeks of the Weimar Republic. In January 1933 the French politician and former Colonial Minister, Paul Reynaud, sounded out Germany's Foreign Minister, Konstantin von Neurath, over what, exactly, Berlin sought on its eastern frontier. Would a 'corridor through the corridor [*Korridor durch den couloir*]' serve German needs? Neurath rejected the idea out of hand, continuing that 'this would constitute no kind of solution, instead simply creating fresh tension and the perpetuation of what he [Reynaud] also described as intolerable circumstances'.[215] And it might be remembered that even in Stresemann's time the Wilhelmstraße had hoped, one day, to recover the northern and extreme western parts of the corridor, so reuniting East Prussia with the rest of Germany and leaving Danzig's land frontiers with Germany alone.[216] Reynaud's subsequent plea for Franco-German rapprochement (buttressed days later by a parallel offer to return to Germany some of its former colonies)[217] was deemed absolutely fine in principle by Neurath, but he continued that: 'I must unfortunately observe that all attempts on our part to initiate direct German-French negotiations have to date been rejected by our French counterparts',[218]

[209] AA R70509 K241245–9, here 246–7. Signed Bülow, Berlin, 28 Nov. 1932.

[210] Ibid., here 247.

[211] AA R70509 K241251–4, here 253–4, zu II Fr 3956 I. Signed St.S., Berlin, 29 Nov. 1932.

[212] AA R70509 K241245–9, quote on 247–9. Signed Bülow, Berlin, 28 Nov. 1932; see also: R29452 E189137–9. Signed Bülow, Berlin, 17 Nov. 1932; R70509 K241250, e.o.II Fr 3956, St.S. Signed Bülow, Berlin, 30 Nov. 1932; R70510 H013895–9, here 895, Abschrift. II F abr. 218. Signed Bülow, Berlin, 18 Jan. 1933.

[213] AA R70510 H013884–90, here 889–90, Ausw. Amt II Fr. 91, Aufzeichnung. Signed Köpke, Berlin, 3 Jan. 1933; for further detail, Schirmann, *Relations*, 20–32.

[214] AA R70510 E583986–8, here 988, Aufzeichnung über ein Gespräch des Herrn Reichskanzlers mit dem Herrn Französischen Botschafter am Freitag, den 6. Januar nachmittags, Berlin, 7 Jan. 1933.

[215] AA R70510 H013878, Doppel R.M. 21. Signed Freiherr von Neurath, Berlin, 5 Jan. 1933.

[216] Wright, *Stresemann*, 527, Map 2.

[217] AA R70510 H013894, stamped II Fr. 101. Signed Brückner, Berlin, 10 Jan. 1933.

[218] AA R70510 H013878, Doppel R.M. 21. Signed Freiherr von Neurath, Berlin, 5 Jan. 1933.

perhaps forgetting that some months earlier Germany had rebutted last-gasp French efforts to revive the 1931 Berlin Agreement.[219]

The German Foreign Office was aware that the Polish frontier question threatened to muddy the waters at a time when it was prioritizing the disarmament talks and diplomats emphasized in a series of interviews with French journalists that the Wilhelmstraβe 'would have quite enough on its plate dealing with the disarmament question' without actively bringing the eastern border question into play. Yet sensational reports to the contrary appeared in *Le Temps* and *Le Journal*,[220] suggesting that Berlin would seek to tie border revision to a future arms agreement. An alarmed François-Poncet raised the issue with Köpke, 'regretting anything on both sides of the border that was likely to inflame and unsettle the [prevailing] mood still further',[221] and while the German diplomat was able to reassure him, the Ambassador still felt the need to appeal for a 'degree of empathy and forgiveness during the Geneva disarmament talks'.[222] However, while French diplomats struggled to reconcile their determination to confine overall German military strength more or less at Versailles levels with the recognition that concessions of some sort would need to be offered, Berlin was determined to achieve greater military strength, purportedly of a defensive kind. France was willing to see the Reichswehr (German Army) replaced by a 'militia' with a wider recruitment base, but very short period of service, but Germany's thinking focused on a British-style Territorial Army to stand alongside the Reichswehr.[223] François-Poncet again proposed that direct military negotiations between the two countries parallel to the League of Nations disarmament conference might prove a way forward, but without eliciting a German response.[224] This impasse persisted, more or less, until, in October 1933, Hitler walked out of the disarmament conference and the League of Nations.

In December 1932 Gerhard Köpke wrote to his friend, the Republican Socialist politician and long-standing advocate of Franco-German rapprochement, Pierre Viénot, to congratulate him on a 'courageous speech at the Republican Socialist Congress'. 'In memory of our common effort to achieve German-French rapprochement', he continued, 'I wish you further luck and success in promoting the cause that is dear to all our hearts.'[225] However, the tone of Köpke's letter smacks of ill-disguised desperation, or perhaps resignation, given the repeated and multifarious blows to rapprochement, which were soon to be compounded by the consequences of the Nazi takeover. It is, perhaps, symptomatic that neither of the

[219] See Ch. 5, under 'Political Instability and Diplomatic Stalemate', 147–9.

[220] AA R70510 H013884–90, here 887–8, Ausw. Amt II Fr. 91, Aufzeichnung. Signed Köpke, Berlin, 3 Jan. 1933.

[221] Ibid., here 886; see also R70510 H013895–9, here 895, Abschrift. II F abr. 218. Signed Bülow, Berlin, 18 Jan. 1933.

[222] AA R70510 H013884–90, quote on 890, Ausw. Amt II Fr. 91, Aufzeichnung. Signed Köpke, Berlin, 3 Jan. 1933.

[223] See also Schulze, *Weimar*, 357.

[224] R70510 H013895–9, Abschrift. II F abr. 218. Signed Bülow, Berlin, 18 Jan. 1933; see also R29452 E189104–9, Durchdruck, 23 Aug. 1932.

[225] AA R70544 H021103, Sehr verehrter Herr Viénot! Signed Köpke, 5 Dec. 1932.

two fared well in the new world unfolding around them. Köpke had some Jewish antecedents and although his career survived the Nazi takeover, he resigned his post in 1935 as the Nuremberg Laws ushered in the segregation of Germany's Jewish community.[226] Viénot was later arrested by the Vichy authorities before escaping to join de Gaulle and the anti-German resistance in London, where he died on 20 July 1944.

[226] Conze, *Auswärtige Amt*, 81.

Conclusion

Confrontation and reconciliation may appear mutually exclusive, but interwar Franco-German diplomacy came to perceive them as interrelated parts of a complex whole. Neither country was prepared to surrender its vital national interests, which included French security from its latently powerful neighbour and Germany's rehabilitation within the international order. As long as this dichotomy was expressed in terms of military power, reparations, or territorial claims, each country's ambitions directly threatened the vital interests of its neighbour. Ultimately this demanded one of two basic solutions. Confrontation offered a means of simply overwhelming opposition if needs be by force of arms, while conciliatory diplomacy could enable the two powers to circumvent and ultimately defuse major, seemingly intractable disputes.

The years from 1919 to 1923 were characterized by mutual confrontation which culminated in France's military occupation of the Ruhr District. However, even during these years of latent hostility there were sporadic attempts at mediation, most of which largely focused on proposals for economic cooperation. The contentious reparations question aside, this form of collaboration appeared to offer the best prospects for defusing the post-war stalemate in Franco-German relations and even of engaging the two erstwhile enemies in a common effort to restore the well-being of a war-torn European continent. Collaboration of this kind came to predominate during 1924 and 1925 as French diplomacy prioritized economic rapprochement with Germany, essentially as a means of accommodating German ambitions on terms acceptable to Paris. This strategy met with a positive German response as Berlin came to appreciate that national rehabilitation required French goodwill. Furthermore, German diplomacy identified economic cooperation as the most promising means to secure rapprochement with Paris. This strategy was underpinned by Stresemann's diplomatic astuteness and personal touch, so offering the prospect of an enhanced German role in European and even global affairs. A curious symbiotic relationship ensued where well-rehearsed disputes proved intractable, whether over territorial revision or reparations, yet these same impasses lent added urgency to economic collaboration as the latter circumvented the otherwise damaging fallout from deep-seated grievances and allowed Paris and Berlin to sustain the process of rapprochement.

Conventional wisdom has it that the days of Franco-German detente were numbered after Gustav Stresemann's death in October 1929. However, this is to identify reconciliation too closely with him personally and so underestimate the degree of institutional commitment and strategic conviction which underpinned this process on both the French and the German sides. Nor did the advent of the Great Depression, which coincided with Stresemann's death, initially disrupt Franco-German reconciliation. France rode the economic tide well into 1931 thanks to its legacy from the boom years of massive gold reserves and a strong domestic economy. This created potential synergies between Germany's superior industrial and manufacturing potential and France's superior financial strength, a combination that offered the prospect of a long-term strategic partnership at least until France, too, slid into recession at the turn of 1931/32. The Berlin Agreement of September 1931 envisaged this putative partnership taking the form of an ever-deeper Franco-German bilateral economic union which would be complemented by a common response to the wider European economic crisis. This was to include joint efforts by Paris and Berlin to resolve the agricultural crisis that was devastating the economies of South-Eastern Europe and also involve a step-by-step expansion of their planned customs union as compatible European economies joined this Franco-German axis. This offered to revive the economic dimension of Briand's vision of European union in an age when the traditional and fragmented European state structure appeared unequal to the challenges posed by emergent continental or transcontinental economic superpowers.

Beyond the pursuit of national self-interest by means of international reconciliation, Franco-German rapprochement was steered by senior French and German diplomats, politicians, and figures from the business and cultural worlds who shared a personal commitment to the cause of reconciliation and peace. Many of the key players from both sides of the Rhine had previously lived in the other country and during the interwar era close bonds were formed between men who worked closely together sometimes for a decade or more. All invested considerable personal moral capital in the cause of Franco-German rapprochement, something they would not and did not abandon on a whim. Among them were adherents of political Catholicism, who played a significant role in the promotion of reconciliation on either side of the Rhine. Without this broadly based and multifaceted body of support it is hard to envisage circumstances where economic detente could have gained such traction in the face of fierce political opposition from the powerful nationalist right, and also radical left, in both countries' parliaments. For these were strange times when rapprochement was sponsored particularly energetically by the mainstream democratic parties yet the democratic process, particularly in Germany, was devouring itself as the Nazis rose to prominence.

However, beyond the inevitable *Realpolitik* that informed rapprochement, there is another tale to be told: of enormous energy expended by diplomats and politicians, by businessmen and prominent cultural figures who sought to create a European commonwealth in the place of traditional great power rivalry. Many of these key players were quite simply good men, who despite living in difficult times were determined to leave Europe a better place than they had found it and regarded Franco-German rapprochement as an indispensable part of this process. Not all have been kindly treated in the literature, while others have, more or less, disappeared from view. On one level this appears surprising, for the parallels between interwar Franco-German reconciliation and the process of (West-) European unification that followed the Second World War are striking. Even current British coolness towards European integration, it transpires, has deep historical roots. But many of the key interwar figures had died or were in retirement by the time Paris and Bonn resolved to pick up the pieces for a second time. Others had been too badly compromised by their part in the Third Reich or the Vichy State or were at least found guilty by association, and with a good dash of hindsight, of such culpability.

Whatever the case, most of the post-1945 advocates of European union and of Franco-German rapprochement, such as Robert Schuman,[1] had not been significantly engaged in the equivalent interwar events. However, Schuman had served as a member of the French delegation to the League of Nations during the Briand era and had been sufficiently influenced by the great statesman to conceive of a universal French mission in favour of the European cause, including a union accommodating the diversities of Europe's nations.[2] Such thinking, of course, became central to the process of European integration after 1945. There were other notable exceptions, including André François-Poncet and Konrad Adenauer,[3] but neither they, nor France's signatory to the 1963 Franco-German Friendship Treaty, Charles de Gaulle, cared to dwell on the interwar past where too many uncomfortable ghosts prowled. Other good men, among them Leopold von Hoesch and Pierre Viénot, did not live long enough to witness the defeat of Hitler's regime. In 1933 the liberal man of letters, Harry Count Kessler, recalled Hoesch's measured but devastating condemnation of the Third Reich: 'Abandon all hope ye who enter here. This is the most gruesome suicide ever committed by a great people.'[4] Hoesch's close colleagues in Berlin were of the same mind. Gerhard Köpke and Heinrich von Friedberg shared a degree of Jewish ancestry and were never going to prosper under Nazism. Friedberg died in mid-1933 while, as noted, an already deeply unhappy Köpke resigned his post in 1935 in response to the introduction of the Nuremberg Laws.[5] Others in France, perhaps most notably Pierre Laval, came to make grotesquely compromised choices when France's 1940 military defeat at the hands of Nazi Germany initiated collaboration of an entirely different kind.

After 1945, institutional memory of interwar rapprochement must have informed events to a degree, but beyond that the underlying rationality and logic of what had been attempted before and during the Great Depression remained equally applicable. Franco-German economic rapprochement had in itself been a rational, even optimal, choice from the beginning of the twentieth century and the intention of breaking out from this economic bridgehead to circumvent or engage

[1] Angeles Muñoz, 'L'Engagement européen de Robert Schuman', in Sylvain Schirmann (ed.), *Robert Schuman et les pères de l'Europe. Cultures politiques et années de formation* (Brussels, 2008), 39–48.

[2] Elisha, *Aristide Briand*, 79–80.

[3] See, for example, Marie-Luise Recker, 'Europa im Denken und Handeln Konrad Adenauers (1917–1949)', in Sylvain Schirmann (ed.), *Robert Schuman et les pères de l'Europe. Cultures politiques et années de formation* (Brussels, 2008), 133–41.

[4] Kessler's paraphrasing quoted in Michael Jonas, *NS-Diplomatie und Bündnispolitik 1935–1944. Wipert von Blücher, das Dritte Reich und Finnland* (Paderborn, 2011), 372.

[5] See Ch. 6 under 'Impasse', 183–4.

with the difficult, often traumatic legacies of past events remained perhaps the only realistic choice on offer. The warmth of the current Franco-German relationship provides a measure of retrospective confirmation of this and helps explain why it has been possible for some French historians to posit a *longue durée* characterized by faithful Franco-German partnership rather than by grievance and war. Current circumstances cannot serve to airbrush the dark years of the Third Reich or the Vichy State from the picture, but the story of interwar Franco-German relations does contribute to an understanding of how Europe has managed to emerge from the abyss of Nazism. For whatever else, it is hard to envisage a functioning European polity, whatever challenges it might face, bereft of a robust Franco-German axis at its heart.

Bibliography

ARCHIVAL SOURCES

AA: Politisches Archiv des Auswärtigen Amts

R105386–8 : (Ges. Eisenlohr) Frankreich

R105491 : Ges. Seeliger: Briand Memorandum

R27994–8 : Reden, Interviews und Aufsätze des Herrn Reichministers

R28263k : Deutsch-französische Verständigung

R28630–1 : Bund der Vereinigten Staaten von Europa. Antwort der deutschen Regierung auf das Briand Memorandum 11.7.1930

R29449 + 452 : Aufzeichnungen St.S. von Bülow über Diplomatenbesuche

R30181b + 182a : Polit. Beziehungen Frankreich-Deutschland

R30201a–b : Die Stellung Elsass-Lothring. im französ. Staat sowie die elsass-lothring. Autonomiefrage

R70501–10 : Politische Beziehungen zwischen Deutschland und Frankreich

R70518 : Memoiren Stresemann

R70534–44 : Bestrebungen zur Herbeiführung einer deutsch-französischen Verständigung

R70550–4 : Die deutsch-französische Gesellschaft (Grautoff) und deren Veröffentlichungen

R70562–3 : Die Bemühungen des Arnold Rechberg u.a. zur deutsch-französischen Verständigung

R70567–9 : Gegenseitige Besuche führender Staatsmänner

R70571 + 573 : Handakten Friedberg betreffend französischer Besuch

R70575 : Pressestimmen zum französischen Gegenbesuch in Berlin

R70576–9 : Die deutsch-französische Studienkommission sowie Gründung eines französischen wirtschaftlichen und politischen 'Comité d'Entente internationale' (Comité Fougère) und eines deutschen Gegenkomitees

R70941 : Deutschtum in Frankreich

R71141 : Politische Beziehungen Elsaβ-Lothringens zu Deutschland

R87019 : Finanzielle Beziehungen Frankreich zu Deutschland

R87062 : Frankreich. Handelsbeziehungen zu Deutschland

R87144 : Deutsch-französ. Wirtschaftsverhandlungen—Schreiben des Reichsverbandes der deutschen Industrie

R87343 : Deutsche Handelskammern in Frankreich

AA: Akten der früheren Deutschen Botschaft in Paris 1817–1944

563b : Beziehungen Frankreichs zu Deutschland

563c : Frankreich 3) Auswärtige Beziehungen. Beziehungen zu Deutschland

564a : Frankreich 3) Auswärtige Beziehungen. Beziehungen zu Deutschland

MAE: Archives du Ministère des affaires étrangères
Correspondence Politique et Commerciale 1914 à 1940 Tome 1

Série Z. Europe: Allemagne
Affaires administratives diverses
Économie. Finances
Instruction publique. Beaux-Arts
Politique étrangère
Presse

Série Y. Internationale
Conférences politiques et militaires et Conseil suprême
Société des nations
Union fédérale européenne
  Dossier général
  Presse et documentation
  Reponses au memorandum du gouvernement français: Allemagne

PUBLISHED DOCUMENTARY SOURCES

Akten der Reichskanzlei. Weimarer Republik. Die Kabinette Marx I und II, 30. November 1923 bis 3. Juni 1924. 3. Juni 1924 bis 15. Januar 1925, ed. Karl Dietrich Erdmann, Hans Booms, and Günter Abramowski (Boppard am Rhein, 1973).

Akten zur deutschen auswärtigen Politik 1918–1945. Serie A: 1918–1925, ed. Hans-Georg Fleck et al. (Göttingen, 1982–93).

Akten zur deutschen auswärtigen Politik 1918–1945. Serie B: 1925–1933, ed. Hans Rothfels et al. (Göttingen, 1966–83).

HMSO, *The Treaty of Peace between the Allied and Associated Powers and Germany* (London, 1928).

The Sydney Morning Herald, 'Reparations. Wiesbaden Agreement. British Objections' (10 November 1921), 7. http//nla.gov.au/nla.news-article%2015979751.

SECONDARY WORKS CITED

Adamthwaite, Anthony, *Grandeur and Misery: France's Bid for Power in Europe 1914–1940* (London, 1995).

Aguado, Iago Gil, 'The Creditanstalt Crisis of 1931 and the Failure of the Austro-German Customs Union Project', *The Historical Journal*, 44, 1 (2001), 199–221.

Aldcroft, Derek H., *Europe's Third World: The European Periphery in the Interwar Years* (Aldershot, 2006).

Badel, Laurance, 'Les Promoteurs français d'une union économique et douanière de l'Europe dans l'entre-deux-guerres', in Antoine Fleury (ed.), *Le Plan Briand d'Union fédérale européenne. Perspectives nationales et transnationales, avec documents. Actes du colloque international tenu à Genève du 19 au 21 septembre 1991* (Bern, 1998), 17–29.

Baechler, Christian, *Gustave Stresemann (1878–1929). De l'impérialisme à la sécurité collective* (Strasbourg, 1996).

Bariéty, Jacques, *Les Relations franco-allemandes après la Première Guerre Mondiale. 10 novembre 1918–10 janvier 1925. De l'exécution à la negotiation* (Paris, 1977).

Bariéty, Jacques, 'Aristide Briand. Les raisons d'un oubli', in Antoine Fleury (ed.), *Le Plan Briand d'Union fédérale européenne. Perspectives nationales et transnationales, avec documents. Actes du colloque international tenu à Genève du 19 au 21 septembre 1991* (Bern, 1998), 1–13.

Bariéty, Jacques, 'France and the politics of steel, from the Treaty of Versailles to the International Steel Entente, 1919–1926', in Robert W. D. Boyce (ed.), *French Foreign and Defence Policy, 1918–1940: The Decline and Fall of a Great Power* (London, 1998), 30–48.

Bariéty, Jacques, 'Aristide Briand et la sécurité de la France en Europe, 1919-1932', in Stephen A. Schuker and Elizabeth Müller-Luckner (eds.), *Deutschland und Frankreich. Vom Konflikt zur Aussöhnung. Die Gestaltung der westeuropäischen Sicherheit, 1914–1963* (Munich, 2000), 117–34.

Barry, Gearóid, *The Disarmament of Hatred: Marc Sangnier, French Catholicism and the Legacy of the First World War, 1914–1945* (Basingstoke, 2012).

Barthel, Charles, 'Émile Mayrisch et le pacte international de l'acier des années 1920', *Journal of European Integration History*, 1 (2006), 43–65.

Becker, Rolf and Joachim Scholtyseck, *Robert Bosch und die deutsch-französische Verständigung. Politisches Denken und Handeln im Spiegel der Briefwechsel* (Stuttgart, 1957).

Berghahn, Volker, *Quest for Economic Empire: European Strategies of German Big Business in the Twentieth Century* (Providence, RI, 1996).

Bergmann, Carl, *The History of Reparations* (Boston and New York, 1927).

Bernhardi, Friedrich von, *Germany and the Next War*, trans. Allen H. Powles (London, 1914).

Bock, Hans Manfred, 'Weimarer Intellektuelle und das Projekt deutsch-französischer Gesellschaftsverflechtung', *Themenportal Europäische Geschichte*, http://www.europa.clio-online.de/site/lang_de/ItemID_107mid_12198/40208769/, 4pp.

Boemeke, Manfred F., Roger Chickering, and Stig Förster (eds.), *Anticipating Total War: The German and American Experiences 1871–1914* (Cambridge, 1999).

Boemeke, Manfred F., Gerald D. Feldman, and Elizabeth Glaser (eds.), *The Treaty of Versailles: A Reassessment after 75 Years* (Cambridge, 1998).

Bosco, Andrea, 'The British Foreign Office and the Briand Plan', in Antoine Fleury (ed.), *Le Plan Briand d'Union fédérale européenne. Perspectives nationales et transnationales, avec documents. Actes du colloque international tenu à Genève du 19 au 21 septembre 1991* (Bern, 1998), 347–58.

Boyce, Robert W. D., 'The Briand Plan and the Crisis of British Liberalism', in Antoine Fleury (ed.), *Le Plan Briand d'Union fédérale européenne. Perspectives nationales et transnationales, avec documents. Actes du colloque international tenu à Genève du 19 au 21 septembre 1991* (Bern, 1998), 121–44.

Boyce, Robert W. D., 'Business as Usual. The Limits of French Economic Diplomacy, 1926–1933', in Robert W. D. Boyce (ed.), *French Foreign and Defence Policy, 1918–1940: The Decline and Fall of a Great Power* (London, 1998), 107–31.

Boyce, Robert W. D. (ed.), *French Foreign and Defence Policy, 1918–1940: The Decline and Fall of a Great Power* (London, 1998).

Brüning, Franziska, *Frankreich und Heinrich Brüning. Ein deutscher Kanzler in der französischen Wahrnehmung* (Stuttgart, 2012).

Brüning, Heinrich, *Memoiren 1918–1934* (Stuttgart, 1970).

Bussière, Eric, 'Les Aspects économiques du projet Briand. Essai de mise en perspective. De l'Europe des producteurs aux tentatives régionales', in Antoine Fleury (ed.), *Le Plan Briand d'Union fédérale européenne. Perspectives nationales et transnationales, avec documents. Actes du colloque international tenu à Genève du 19 au 21 septembre 1991* (Bern, 1998), 75–92.

Chancellor, Edward, *Devil Take the Hindmost: A History of Financial Speculation* (London, 1999).

Clavin, Patricia, *The Great Depression in Europe, 1929–1939* (Basingstoke, 2000).

Clavin, Patricia, 'Europe and the League of Nations', in Robert Gerwarth (ed.), *Twisted Paths: Europe 1914–1945* (Oxford, 2007), 325–54.

Clavin, Patricia, *Securing the World Economy: The Reinvention of the League of Nations, 1920–1946* (Oxford, 2013).

Cohrs, Patrick O., *The Unfinished Peace after World War I: America, Britain and the Stabilisation of Europe, 1919–1932* (Cambridge and New York, 2006).

Conze, Eckart, *Das Auswärtige Amt. Vom Kaiserreich bis zum Gegenwart* (Munich, 2013).

Dreyfus, François G., *La Vie politique en Alsace 1919–1936* (Paris, 1969).

Duhamel, Georges, *America the Menace: Scenes from the Life of the Future*, trans. Charles Miner Thompson (London, 1931).

Dutton, David (ed.), *Statecraft and Diplomacy in the Twentieth Century* (Liverpool, 1995).

Elisha, Achille, *Aristide Briand. La paix mondiale et l'union européenne* (Groslay, 2003).

Feldman, Gerald D., *The Great Disorder: Politics, Economics and Society in the German Inflation, 1914–1924* (Oxford, 1993).

Feldman, Gerald D., 'Hugo Stinnes and the Prospect of War before 1914', in Manfred F. Boemeke, Roger Chickering, and Stig Förster (eds.), *Anticipating Total War: The German and American Experiences 1871–1914* (Cambridge, 1999), 77–95.

Fischer, Christopher, *Alsace to the Alsatians? Visions and Divisions of Alsatian Regionalism, 1870–1939* (New York and Oxford, 2010).

Fischer, Conan, *The Ruhr Crisis, 1923–1924* (Oxford, 2003).

Fischer, Conan, 'Soziale Verwerfungen im Ruhrkampf durch Hunger und Evakuierung', in Gerd Krumeich and Joachim Schröder (eds.), *Der Schatten des Weltkriegs. Die Ruhrbesetzung 1923* (Essen, 2004), 149–67.

Fischer, Conan, 'Scoundrels without a Fatherland? Heavy Industry and Transnationalism in Post-First World War Germany', *Contemporary European History*, 14, 4 (2005), 441–64.

Fischer, Conan, 'The Human Price of Reparations', in Conan Fischer and Alan Sharp (eds.), *After the Versailles Treaty: Enforcement, Compliance, Contested Identities* (London, 2008), 81–95.

Fischer, Conan, *Europe between Democracy and Dictatorship 1900–1945* (Oxford, 2011).

Fischer, Conan and Alan Sharp (eds.), *After the Versailles Treaty: Enforcement, Compliance, Contested Identities* (London, 2008).

Fischer, Fritz, *Germany's Aims in the First World War* (London, 1967).

Fischer, Fritz, *War of Illusions: German Policies from 1911–1914* (London, 1975).

Fischer, Fritz, *From Kaiserreich to Third Reich: Elements of Continuity in German History* (London, 1986).

Fiss, Karen, *Grand Illusion: The Third Reich, the Paris Exposition, and the Cultural Seduction of France* (Chicago, IL, 2009).

Fleury, Antoine (ed.), *Le Plan Briand d'Union fédérale européenne. Perspectives nationales et transnationales, avec documents. Actes du colloque international tenu à Genève du 19 au 21 septembre 1991* (Bern, 1998).

Frank, Robert, 'Le Paradoxe Franco-Allemand du siècle', in Robert Frank, Laurent Gervereau, and Hans Joachim Neyer (eds.), *Course au modern. France et Allemagne dans l'Europe des années vingt. 1919–1933* (Nanterre, 1992), 180.

Frank, Robert, Laurent Gervereau, and Hans Joachim Neyer (eds.), *Course au modern. France et Allemagne dans l'Europe des années vingt. 1919–1933* (Nanterre, 1992).

Friedrich, Otto, *Before the Deluge: A Portrait of Berlin in the 1920s* (London, 1974).

Fröhlich, Elke, 'Joseph Goebbels: The Propagandist', in Ronald Smelser and Rainer Zitelmann (eds.), *The Nazi Elite*, trans. Mary Fischer (Basingstoke and London, 1993), 48–61.

Gerwarth, Robert (ed.), *Twisted Paths: Europe 1914–1945* (Oxford, 2007).

Grohmann, Carolyn, 'From Lothringen to Lorraine: Expulsion and Voluntary Repatriation', in Conan Fischer and Alan Sharp (eds.), *After the Versailles Treaty: Enforcement, Compliance, Contested Identities* (London, 2008), 153–69.

Hömig, Herbert, *Brüning. Kanzler in der Krise der Republik. Eine Weimarer Biographie* (Paderborn, 2000).

Horne, John, 'Demobilising the Mind: France and the Legacy of the Great War, 1919–1939', *French History and Civilisation. Papers from the George Rudé Seminar*, 2 (2006), 101–19.

Jeannesson, Stanislas, 'L'Europe de Jacques Seydoux', *Revue historique*, 299, 1 (1998), 123–44.

Jeannesson, Stanislas, *Poincaré, la France et la Ruhr (1922–1924). Histoire d'une occupation* (Strasbourg, 1998).

Jonas, Michael, *NS-Diplomatie und Bündnispolitik 1935–1944. Wipert von Blücher, das Dritte Reich und Finnland* (Paderborn, 2011).

Kaiser, David E., *Economic Diplomacy and the Origins of the Second World War: Germany, Britain, France, and Eastern Europe 1930–1939* (Princeton, NJ, 1980).

Keiger, John F. V., *Raymond Poincaré* (Cambridge, 1997).

Keynes, John Maynard, *The Economic Consequences of the Peace* (London, 1920).

Knipping, Franz, *Deutschland, Frankreich und das Ende der Locarno-Ära 1928–1931. Studien zur internationalen Politik in der Anfangsphase der Weltwirtschaftskrise* (Munich, 1987).

Krüger, Peter, *Deutschland und die Reparationen 1918/19. Die Genesis des Reparationsproblems in Deutschland zwischen Waffenstillstand und Versailler Friedensschluß* (Stuttgart, 1973).

Krüger, Peter, *Die Außenpolitik der Republik von Weimar* (Darmstadt, 1985).

Krüger, Peter, *Versailles. Deutsche Außenpolitik zwischen Revisionismus und Friedenssicherung*, 2nd edn (Munich, 1993).

Krüger, Peter, 'Der abgebrochene Dialog: die deutschen Reaktionen auf die Europavorstellungen Briands in 1929', in Antoine Fleury (ed.), *Le Plan Briand d'Union fédérale européenne. Perspectives nationales et transnationales, avec documents. Actes du colloque international tenu à Genève du 19 au 21 septembre 1991* (Bern, 1998), 289–306.

Krüger, Peter, 'Carl von Schubert und die deutsch-französischen Beziehungen', in Stephen A. Schuker and Elizabeth Müller-Luckner (eds.), *Deutschland und Frankreich. Vom Konflikt zur Aussöhnung. Die Gestaltung der westeuropäischen Sicherheit, 1914–1963* (Munich, 2000), 73–96.

Krumeich, Gerd and Joachim Schröder (eds.), *Der Schatten des Weltkriegs. Die Ruhrbesetzung 1923* (Essen, 2004).

Kunde, Claudia, Holger Kunde, Hartmut Krohm, and Guido Siebert, *Der Naumburger Meister. Bildhauer und Architekt im Europa der Kathedralen* (Petersberg, 2011).

Lauter, Anna-Monika, *Sicherheit und Reparationen. Die französische Öffentlichkeit, der Rhein und die Ruhr 1918–1933* (Essen, 2006).

Ministère des relations extérieures, *Les Archives du Ministère des relations extérieures depuis les origines. Histoire et guide suivis d'une étude des sources de l'histoire des affaires étrangères dans les dépôts parisiens et départmentaux* (Paris, 1984).

Mommsen, Hans, *Die verspielte Freiheit. Der Weg der Republik von Weimar in den Untergang 1918 bis 1933* (Frankfurt-am-Main, 1990).

Müller, Barbara, *Passiver Widerstand im Ruhrkampf. Eine Fallstudie zur gewaltlosen zwischenstaatlichen Konfliktaustragung und ihren Erfolgsbedingungen* (Münster, 1996).

Muñoz, Angeles, 'L'Engagement européen de Robert Schuman', in Sylvain Schirmann (ed.), *Robert Schuman et les pères de l'Europe. Cultures politiques et années de formation* (Brussels, 2008), 39–55.

O'Riordan, Elspeth Y., *Britain and the Ruhr Crisis* (Basingstoke, 2001).

Oudin, Bernard, *Aristide Briand. La paix. Une idée neuve en Europe* (Paris, 1987).

Overy, Richard, *The Morbid Age: Britain between the Wars* (London, 2009).

Pogge von Strandmann, Hartmut (ed.), *Walther Rathenau: Industrialist, Banker, Intellectual, and Politician. Notes and Diaries 1907–1922*, trans. Caroline Pinter-Lacraft (Oxford, 1985).

Pohl, Karl Heinrich, *Gustav Stresemann. Biographie eines Grenzgängers* (Göttingen, 2015).

Poidevin, Raymond, *Les Relations économiques et financiers entre la France et l'Allemagne de 1898 à 1914* (Paris, 1969).

Poidevin, Raymond, 'Le Nationalisme économique et financier dans les relations franco-allemandes avant 1914', *Revue d'Allemagne et des pays de langue allemande*, 28, 1 (1996), 63–70.

Posselt, Martin, 'Die deutsch-französischen Beziehungen und der Briand-Plan im Spiegel der Zeitschrift *Paneuropa*, 1927–30', in Antoine Fleury (ed.), *Le Plan Briand d'Union fédérale européenne. Perspectives nationales et transnationales, avec documents. Actes du colloque international tenu à Genève du 19 au 21 septembre 1991* (Bern, 1998), 31–51.

Pyta, Wolfram, *Hindenburg. Herrschaft zwischen Hohenzollern und Hitler* (Munich, 2007).

Réau, Élisabeth du, *L'Idée d'Europe au XXe siècle. Des myths aux réalités* (Paris, 2008).

Recker, Marie-Luise, 'Europa im Denken und Handeln Konrad Adenauers (1917–1949)', in Sylvain Schirmann (ed.), *Robert Schuman et les pères de l'Europe. Cultures politiques et années de formation* (Brussels, 2008), 133–47.

Reibel, Charles, 'Une grand occasion manqué, le premier drame de la Ruhr', *Écrits de Paris*, 55 (1949), 24–31.

Rödder, Andreas, *Stresemanns Erbe. Julius Curtius und die deutsche Außenpolitik 1929–1931* (Paderborn, 1996).

Rollo, Paul J. V., 'Britain and the Briand Plan: The Common Market that Never Was', Inaugural Lecture, University of Keele, 6 Dec. 1972.

Ruck, Michael, *Die Freien Gewerkschaften im Ruhrkampf 1923* (Frankfurt-am-Main, 1986).

Schirmann, Sylvain, *Les Relations économiques et financières franco-allemandes 1932–1939* (Paris, 1995).

Schirmann, Sylvain, *Crise, coopération économique et financière entre États européens 1929–1933* (Paris, 2000).

Schirmann, Sylvain (ed.), *Robert Schuman et les pères de l'Europe. Cultures politiques et années de formation* (Brussels, 2008).

Schlager, Claudia, *Kult und Krieg. Herz Jesu—Sacré Cœur—Christus Rex im deutsch-französischen Vergleich 1914–1925* (Tübingen, 2011).

Schmitt, Carl, *The Crisis of Parliamentary Democracy*, trans. Ellen Kennedy (Cambridge, MA, 1988).

Schuker, Stephen A. and Elizabeth Müller-Luckner (eds.), *Deutschland und Frankreich. Vom Konflikt zur Aussöhnung. Die Gestaltung der westeuropäischen Sicherheit, 1914–1963* (Munich, 2000).

Schulze, Hagen, *Weimar. Deutschland 1917–1933*, rev. edn (Berlin, 1994).

Selbach, Hans-Ludwig, *Katholische Kirche und französische Rheinlandpolitik nach dem Ersten Weltkrieg. Nationale, regionale und kirchliche Interessen zwischen Rhein, Saar und Ruhr (1918–1924)* (Cologne, 2013).

Sharp, Alan, *Consequences of the Peace: The Versailles Settlement: Aftermath and Legacy 1919–2010*, 2nd edn (London, 2015).

Smelser, Ronald and Rainer Zitelmann, *The Nazi Elite*, trans. Mary Fischer (Basingstoke and London, 1993).

Sonnabend, Gaby, *Pierre Viénot (1897–1944). Ein Intellektueller in der Politik* (Munich, 2005).

Soutou, Georges-Henri, 'La France et les marches de l'est, 1914–1919', *Revue historique*, 578 (1978), 341–88.

Soutou, Georges-Henri, 'Vom Rhein zur Ruhr: Absichten und Planungen der französischen Regierung', in Gerd Krumeich and Joachim Schröder (eds.), *Der Schatten des Weltkriegs. Die Ruhrbesetzung 1923* (Essen, 2004), 63–84.

Spethmann, Hans, *Zwölf Jahre Ruhrbergbau. Aus seiner Geschichte von Kriegsanfang bis zum Franzosenabmarsch 1914 bis 1925, iii. Der Ruhrkampf 1923 bis 1925 in seinen Leitlinien* (Berlin, 1929).

Spethmann, Hans, *Zwölf Jahre Ruhrbergbau. Aus seiner Geschichte von Kriegsanfang bis zum Franzosenabmarsch 1914 bis 1925, iv. Der Ruhrkampf 1923 bis 1925. Das Ringen um die Kohle* (Berlin, 1930).

Steiner, Zara, *The Lights that Failed: European International History 1919–1933* (Oxford, 2005).

Stevenson, David, 'French War Aims and Peace Planning', in Manfred F. Boemeke, Gerald D. Feldman, and Elizabeth Glaser (eds.), *The Treaty of Versailles: A Reassessment after 75 Years* (Cambridge, 1998), 87–101.

Strachan, Hew, *The First World War*, vol. I: *To Arms* (Oxford, 2003).

Tooze, Adam, *The Deluge: The Great War and the Remaking of the Global Order* (London, 2015).

Trachtenberg, Marc, *Reparation in World Politics: France and European Diplomacy 1916–1923* (New York, 1980).

Trebitsch, Michel and Hans Manfred Bock, 'L'Image du voisin. Opinions et rencontres', in Robert Frank, Laurent Gervereau, and Hans Joachim Neyer (eds.), *Course au modern. France et Allemagne dans l'Europe des années vingt. 1919–1933* (Nanterre, 1992), 28–31.

Unger, Gérard, *Aristide Briand, le ferme conciliateur* (Paris, 2005).

Vallentin, Antonina, *Stresemann vom Werden einer Staatsidee* (Munich and Leipzig, 1930).

Vogt, Martin, 'Die deutsche Haltung zum Briand-Plan im Sommer 1930. Hintergründe und politisches Umfeld der Europapolitik des Kabinetts Brüning', in Antoine Fleury (ed.), *Le Plan Briand d'Union fédérale européenne. Perspectives nationales et transnationales, avec documents. Actes du colloque international tenu à Genève du 19 au 21 septembre 1991* (Bern, 1998), 307–29.

Weiss, Louise, *Mémoires d'une européenne*, vol. II: *1919–1934*, 2nd edn (Paris, 1970).

White, Ralph, '"Through a Glass, Darkly": The Foreign Office Investigation of French Federalism, January–May 1930', in David Dutton (ed.), *Statecraft and Diplomacy in the Twentieth Century* (Liverpool, 1995), 75–97.

Wilsberg, Klaus, *'Terrible ami—aimable ennemi'. Kooperation und Konflikt in den deutsch-französischen Beziehungen 1911–1914* (Bonn, 1998).

Winkler, Heinrich August, *Weimar 1918–1933. Die Geschichte der ersten deutschen Demokratie*, 2nd edn (Munich, 1994).

Winkler, Heinrich August, *Der lange Weg nach Westen, I. Deutsche Geschichte vom Ende des Alten Reiches bis zum Untergang der Weimarer Republik* (Munich, 2002).
Wolfers, Arnold, *Britain and France between Two Wars: Conflicting Strategies of Peace since Versailles* (New York, 1940).
Wright, Jonathan, *Gustav Stresemann: Weimar's Greatest Statesman* (Oxford, 2002).
Wurm, Clemens August, 'Internationale Kartelle und die deutsch-französischen Beziehungen 1924–1930. Politik, Wirtschaft, Sicherheit', in Stephen A. Schuker and Elizabeth Müller-Luckner (eds.), *Deutschland und Frankreich. Vom Konflikt zur Aussöhnung. Die Gestaltung der westeuropäischen Sicherheit, 1914–1963* (Munich, 2000), 97–115.
Young, Robert J., *France and the Origins of the Second World War* (Basingstoke, 1996).

Index

Aachen 123, 124
Action française 41, 93, 119
Adenauer, Konrad 5, 34, 97, 101, 187
AEG 111
Akademischer Austauschdienst 84
Alsace(-Lorraine) 11, 12, 13, 23, 79, 101, 102, 104, 127, 151, 155–65
  autonomism 97, 155–8, 160–4
  Church in 155, 158, 162
  Colmar treason trial 155–6
  emigration to Germany from 155, 161, 162
  France and 155–61
  German culture/media in 156–7, 159
  German language in 155–9, 163
  Germany and 155, 156, 158, 160–4, 170
  Kaiser-Wilhelms-University 160
  Ligue d'Alsace français 156
  Wissenschaftliches Institut der Elsass-Lothringer 160
Alsdorf mining disaster 80
Amitiés internationales 33–4
Antwerp 97
Arnal, Pierre 72–3, 118, 149
Austria 12, 72, 86, 87–90, 98, 155
  banking crisis 93
Austro-German Customs Union 87–90, 104, 106, 109, 112–14, 116, 119, 127, 129, 132, 151
  International Court at The Hague and 88, 90, 112

Baden 158, 179
Baden Baden 163
Bank for International Settlements 47, 53
Bank of England 19–20, 90
Bank of France 101
Bariéty, Jacques 24
Basel 47
Bassenheim, Count Waldbott von 31, 160
Bauhaus (Deutsche Werkbund) 84
Bavaria 39, 41, 98, 163
Becker, Carl Heinrich 44
Belgium 14, 23, 27, 45–7, 57, 63, 65, 69, 82, 118, 123, 178
  and Eupen-Malmédy 26, 172
  and Franco-German Joint Commission 135
  and Ruhr occupation 17
  Herbesthal 123
  Jeumont 132
Bergen, Diego von 162
Berlin 6, 13, 14, 16, 28, 30, 31, 39, 83, 98, 99, 105, 127, 135, 136
  Berliner Staatsoper 120
  Congress of Berlin (1878) 126
  finances 129–31
  French Ministerial visit to 6, 110–17, 119, 121, 123–9, 131, 150
    protocol of 124–5
    security during 123–5
  Maria-Viktoria-Kapelle 128
  Philharmonic Orchestra 120
  visit by Latour, Lord Mayor of Paris 129–31
  World Energy Conference in 164–5
Berlin Agreement (1931) 25, 123–9, 150, 165, 172, 176, 179, 183, 186
Berlin–Baghdad Railway 9
Bern 12–13
Bernhard, Henry 167–8, 170, 172–4
Bernhardi, Friedrich von 75
Berthelot, Philippe 21, 24, 45–6, 52, 53, 67, 79–80, 89, 112, 118, 127, 132, 134, 135, 146
Binachon, Martin 143
Bismarck, Otto von 171
Blum, Leon 82
Boissard, Adéodat 98, 104
Bolshevism vi, 71, 95, 96, 127
Bonnet, Georges 108
Bosch, Robert 35
Boulangists 80
Bournemouth 45–6
Bradbury, Sir John 15, 17
Brauns, Heinrich 101
Breitscheid, Rudolf 45
Brexit referendum (2016) vi–vii
Briand, Aristide v, 11, 14–15, 32, 44, 48, 93, 94–5, 97, 99, 108, 137, 161, 174, 187
  and Pan-Europa 28
  appeasement and 5
  as Foreign Minister 22–5, 26–9, 36–8, 42–5, 48, 56–8, 64–8, 85–7, 89–90, 132, 136, 166, 168, 171
    resignation 144
  death of 148
  health of 112–13, 125, 132, 144, 148, 166
  in Berlin 6, 110–15, 121, 124–8, 130, 132
  Laval and 5, 127
  Nobel Peace Prize and 4
  partnership with Stresemann v, 3, 5, 11, 13, 24–5, 26, 29, 31, 36, 49, 50, 57, 74, 92, 125, 126–7, 148, 166, 168, 173, 175, 176
Briand Plan v, 3, 6, 27, 55, 56–74, 76, 85, 90, 92, 100, 117, 136, 186
  British reaction to 57–60, 62

Britain 19–20, 21, 23, 28, 45, 149–50
  Ambassador at Berlin 42
  and Entente Cordiale 10, 22, 46, 48–9
  and Europe vi, vii, 22, 36, 56–60, 68, 73–4, 187
  and France 45–9, 73–4, 92, 178
  and Germany 22, 73–4, 92, 127, 177, 178
  and USA 49, 58, 178
  Conservative Party 20
  empire 58, 59–60, 89, 179
  Foreign Office 73
  free trade and 56, 69
  gold standard and 54, 127
  media 46
  peace treaty enforcement 21–2
  reparations and 12, 14, 15, 16, 47–8, 178
  war aims 12
  war debt 15, 16, 178
Brittany 181
  terrorist attack in 181–2
Bruneau, Louis 9
Brüning, Heinrich 4, 51, 54–5, 76, 77, 78, 88, 90, 95, 97, 100, 111, 113–14, 116, 128, 130, 134, 161
  and Catholicism 7, 95, 100
  and detente 5, 7, 92–5, 97, 115, 130, 148
  and Franco-German Joint Commission 133, 148
  and French Ministerial visit to Berlin 114, 123, 126, 128
  and Stresemann memoirs scandal 167, 169, 172
  as Foreign Minister 133
  French view of 7, 79, 80, 81, 83, 92–3, 96, 97, 102, 107, 152, 153, 177
  in Paris 6, 92–5, 106, 109, 116, 126
    and broadcast to German nation 92, 105
  resignation of 169, 176–7
Brussels 46
Bücher, Hermann 111
Bülow, Bernhard von 33, 51, 63–4, 83, 86, 88, 102, 111, 114, 116, 117, 134, 137, 140, 160, 161, 164, 165, 169, 179, 181
Bunau-Varilla, Maurice 171
business cartels 22, 24, 26–7, 56–7, 63, 76, 107–8, 118, 125, 133, 136–7, 139, 142, 144, 149
  International Steel Cartel 26–7
BVP 96

Caillaux, Joseph 10, 11, 81, 82, 107, 170
Cambon, Jules 10
Cambon, Paul 19
Carr, Edward Hallet 73–4
Cartel des Gauches 20, 167, 168, 170
Castellane, Jean Count de 129, 173–4
  links with German nobility 129, 173
  Lord Mayor of Paris 129, 173
Castellane, Stanislas Count de 173–4
Catholicism 4, 19, 68, 82, 95–106
  and Franco-German rapprochement 95–106, 109, 121, 126, 128, 186
  and transnationalism vi
  Church 95, 162
    Papacy 95, 103, 104, 105, 162
  French University Catholic Mission 98
  German Catholic Congress (Katholikentag) 98
  political ideology and 7, 83, 95–9, 103, 106
    Christian Democracy 96
    Social Catholicism 103
Centre Party 4, 43, 44, 51, 78, 96–100, 102, 103, 105, 106, 148, 177
Chamberlain, Austen 4
Champetier de Ribes, August 96, 98, 105, 106
Chequers 90, 91, 92
Chéron, Henri 47, 156–7, 159
China 127
Churchill, Winston 59
Clauss, Max 108
Clemenceau, Georges 11, 12, 14, 38
Clémentel, Étienne 12
Cologne 76, 86, 97, 101
Comité d'entente international, *see* Comité Fougère
Comité des Forges 19
Comité Fougère 109–12
Comité national d'études sociales et politiques 103, 105–6
Cot, Pierre 82
Coudenhove-Kalergi 27–8, 89
Coulandre, Robert 133–5, 140–1, 145, 146, 147, 149
Cuno, Wilhelm 17–18
  fall of government 18
Curtius, Julius 82, 88, 89, 104, 109, 111
  and Briand Plan 60–1, 63–5, 66, 69–71
  and French Ministerial visit to Berlin 111, 112, 114, 127, 131–2
  and Stresemann memoirs scandal 167, 168
  as Economics Minister 41, 51–2
  as Foreign Minister 50–5, 60–1, 75, 85–90
  French view of 7, 51–2
  in Paris 93, 95
  resignation of 114, 132
Czechoslovakia 135
  Bohemia-Moravia 155

Dachau concentration camp 28
Daladier, Édouard 96, 106–7
Danzig 129, 182
Darmstädter und Nationalbank 93
Dawes, Charles 20–1
DDP 158
de Gaulle, Charles 5, 184, 187
  and Free French 184

Desgranges, Jean-Marie 105
Deutsch-französische Gesellschaft 31, 33–4, 105
  children's exchanges 34
  funding of journals 30–6
Deutsche Kunstgesellschaft 120
Deutsche Welle 161
de Wendel combine 9
Dietrich, Marlene 166
  Der Blaue Engel 166
disarmament 6, 65, 82, 85, 89, 102, 116, 126, 131, 150, 169, 179, 183
  Geneva Conference (1932–3) 104, 151, 154, 177, 180, 183
  rearmament 78, 79, 93, 177–8, 180, 181–2
Dix, Otto 34
DNVP 37, 39, 42, 77, 86, 96, 115, 134, 153–4
  Stettin Congress (1931) 115
d'Ormesson, Wladimir 100, 103
Douaumont 37
Doumergue, Gaston 80
Drummond, Sir Eric 70, 90
Dubarry, Albert 45
Duchemin, René 143
Duisburg 14
Durand, Jean 149
Düsseldorf 14, 113
Düsterberg, Theodor 79
DVP 16, 51, 96

East Prussia 43, 65, 182
Ebert, Friedrich 23
Eccard, Frédéric 156
Eckel, Norbert 119, 120
Edge, Walter Evans 94
Einstein, Albert 34
Elbel, Paul 145, 146
electrics industry 14
Entente Cordiale 10, 22, 46, 48–9, 55
Eure Valley 95
European Customs Union, *see* UDE
European union, integration vi, 3, 5, 6, 13, 22, 23–4, 27–8, 30, 34, 36–7, 40, 44–5, 55, 69–74, 76, 83, 88–92, 96, 103–5, 108, 109, 121–2, 125, 127, 137, 142, 153, 176, 178, 182, 185, 186
  customs union 56–7, 61, 63, 65, 68–9, 71–2, 88–9, 115, 117, 125, 141, 142, 186
  economic union 57–74, 76, 82, 90, 92, 96, 100, 108, 109, 150, 182
  Pan-European March 69
  political union 57–74, 76, 96, 100
European Union (current) vi, 2, 32, 186–7, 188

Fascism vi, 96
Federation of Chambers of Commerce (German) 58
Fehrenbach, Konstantin 14
Fighiera, Roger 145, 147
First World War v, 1, 22, 27, 81, 83, 95–7, 103, 105, 113, 119, 137, 163
  aftermath of 1, 2, 14, 54, 88, 105, 108, 119, 125
  armistice 11, 119
  French war veterans 75, 119
    Gueules Cassées 34
  outbreak of 10–11, 107
  propaganda during 12
  reactions to 1, 2, 96
  war graves 125
Flandin, Pierre-Étienne 63, 72, 95, 102
Fleuriau, Aimé de 46
Foch, Ferdinand v, 19, 103
Foreign Press Association (Berlin) 41
Forster, Dirk 118, 128
Fougère, Étienne 109–12
France:
  agriculture (Ministry) 99, 139, 141, 142
  army 75, 100, 103, 125, 175, 181
    Association of French Reserve Officers 75
  banking/finance in 8, 9, 101, 111, 127, 137
    and war debt 11–12, 15, 16, 36–7, 126, 178
  business/industry in 8–9, 12, 14–19, 24, 26–7, 28, 47, 60, 76, 77, 99, 101, 106, 109–10, 111, 115, 118, 121, 125, 128, 131, 136, 142–3, 145, 186
  Commerce Ministry 141, 145, 149
  cultural relations with Germany 6, 27–8, 29–36, 44, 76, 83–4, 97, 98, 99, 105, 106, 119–22, 186
  economic relations with Germany vi, 5, 7–10, 13–19, 22–5, 37, 42, 44–5, 47, 57, 60, 61, 67–9, 71, 73, 76, 77, 80, 81, 83, 88, 93–4, 98, 99, 101–3, 106–8, 110, 111, 113, 115, 116–17, 119, 121, 125, 127, 128, 130, 131, 133, 135, 136, 137–41, 141–7, 147–8, 150, 155, 176, 182, 185–7
    customs barriers/union 111, 117, 118, 125, 137–41, 141–7, 149, 176
    German investment in France 8–10
  Economics Ministry 140
  elections (1932) 94, 118, 127, 139, 145, 147, 152, 153, 167, 172
  empire 81, 94, 117, 118
    Congo and 10
    Morocco and 9–10, 81, 118, 125, 127, 135
  foreign policy of vi, 2–5, 9–25, 26–9, 36–9, 40–55, 56–72, 85–95, 172–3
  Franco-German Friendship Treaty (1963) 5
  liberation (1944) of 5
  media 9, 34, 40–6, 59, 65, 68, 69, 74, 78–9, 81, 82, 84, 85, 87, 92–3, 97–8, 99, 100, 103, 104, 106–7, 112–16, 121, 123–4, 127–8, 129, 130–1, 132, 134, 139, 147, 151, 156, 157, 166–70, 172–5, 179, 180, 181–2, 183

France: (*cont.*)
propaganda 30–1, 104–5
rapprochement with Germany v, vi, 1–3, 5–8, 10, 13, 17, 21, 22, 24–5, 26, 27, 32, 35, 37–8, 42, 44–5, 47, 50, 51–2, 55, 57, 61, 65, 67, 71–4, 76, 77, 79, 81–5, 87–9, 91, 92, 94–7, 99–112, 117, 118, 119–22, 125–34, 136, 137, 139, 140, 148, 150, 151, 153, 159, 165–7, 170, 171, 176, 182, 183, 185–6, 187, 188
relations with Britain 10, 22, 45–9, 55, 56, 57–8, 65, 89, 137, 178
relations (general) with Germany 2–25, 26–9, 36–40, 47, 49, 55, 74–6, 78, 79, 81, 85–6, 93–4, 98, 99, 102, 107, 115, 116, 121, 131, 133, 149, 154, 160, 162, 169, 170, 171–2, 176–83, 185
Russia, alliance with 10
security of 21, 23–4, 27, 57, 75, 78, 96, 150, 171, 176, 177, 180, 181, 185
Third Republic 5, 22, 80, 150
Chamber of Deputies 81–2, 85–6, 105, 109, 152, 156, 173
Senate 82–3
Trade Ministry 139, 141, 143
trade unions 99, 128–9, 133
unemployment in 140, 142, 143
Vichy state 5, 184, 187, 188
war with Germany v, 10–11, 78, 85, 103, 121, 151, 154, 165, 180
war aims 10–13
war criminals list 23, 118, 125, 128
Franco-German axis, *see* Paris–Berlin axis
Franco-German Chamber of Trade 135
Franco-German Joint Commission 87, 88, 115–18, 123–9, 131–7, 139, 141–7, 147–50, 152
French section 133, 136, 148
German section 133, 135, 136
inaugural meeting 134–6
modus operandi 132–7
quota dispute and 140, 144, 147–9
Franco-German Parliamentary Liaison Committee 44, 83
Franco-German Study Committee, *see* Mayrisch Committee
Franco-German Trade Treaty (1927) 24, 107, 111, 117, 118, 133, 136–40, 142, 144, 149, 159, 181, 182
and French trade quotas 118, 142, 144, 147, 149
and Trade Arbitration Agreement 140
Franco-Prussian War 9
François-Marsal, Frédéric 98–9
François-Poncet, André 87, 89, 110–12, 119, 129, 134, 149, 151, 152, 153, 154, 169, 176, 179, 181, 182, 183, 187
Ambassador at Berlin 113, 115, 126
and Franco-German Joint Commission 134, 135, 136–7, 153
and French Ministerial visit to Berlin 110–11, 113, 117, 119, 125
Plan constructif 87, 93, 109, 115, 137
Frank, Robert, historian 5
Frankfurt-am-Main 69, 156
University of 160
Franklin-Bouillon, Henry 85
Freiburg-im-Breisgau 98, 163
Freiburg Theatre 157
mayor of 157, 163
French Communist Party 82
French Foreign Office 21, 24, 28, 30–1, 33–4, 49, 57, 65, 68, 79, 89, 97, 98, 100, 108, 112, 139, 141, 145, 149
French Consul at Cologne 97
French Consul at Karlsruhe 157–8
French Consul at Stuttgart 158–9
French Consul General at Dresden and Leipzig 158
French Embassy at Berlin 30–1, 33, 124, 128, 146, 147
French Legation at Munich 166
Intelligence Bureau 12–13
Legal Section 159
records of vi, 5–7, 69
French Ironmasters Association 101
French Mining Association 101, 110
French nationalists 23, 37, 38, 69, 71, 75, 81, 82, 85, 104, 113, 116, 121, 150, 167, 168, 171, 175, 186
French Socialist Party 42, 44, 82, 170
Friedberg, Heinrich von 123–4, 160–1, 168, 172, 187

General Confederation of French Industry 142–3
Geneva 26, 97, 104
Genoa Conference (1922) 15
German Communist Party 76, 77, 106, 127
German Foreign Office 3, 5, 18, 28–9, 30–6, 38, 50, 83, 86–8, 99, 101, 102, 105, 108, 110, 111, 116, 123, 135, 138, 140, 156, 160–2, 167–70, 172, 174, 176, 180, 182, 183
Cultural Section 120–1
Economics Section 110, 135
finances of 34–6
German Embassy at London 179
German Embassy at Paris 34, 44, 100, 105, 109, 129, 132, 139, 157, 159, 168, 171, 175
Press Section 31, 65
records of vi, 6–7, 160–1
German-French Society, *see* Deutsch-französische Gesellschaft
German Interior Ministry 160, 161
German National Bank 41, 53–4, 64, 93

German nationalists 7, 21–3, 37, 40, 42, 49, 51, 53, 54, 65, 74–6, 86, 90–2, 96, 106–7, 113–15, 116, 121, 150, 173, 177, 186
Bad Harzburg rally (1931) 134
patriotic leagues 114
Germany, *see also* Weimar Republic:
agriculture 41, 65, 99, 142
and Briand Plan v, 6, 56–74, 77, 92
formal response to 66–7
Ministerial discussions on 61–2, 63–4, 66
army 9, 125, 151, 169, 181, 183
business/industry 8–11, 12, 14, 16–20, 24, 26–7, 28, 30, 31, 33–5, 47, 60, 65, 76, 77, 80, 99, 106, 111, 112, 114, 115, 117, 118, 121, 125, 128, 131, 136, 138, 142–3, 145, 186
colonies of 41, 89, 182
confrontation with France 4, 7, 9–11, 23, 39, 74–7, 86
cultural relations with France 6, 27–8, 29–36, 44, 76, 83–4, 97, 99, 105, 106, 119–22, 186
economic relations with France vi, 8–14, 16–17, 18–20, 22–5, 37, 44–5, 47, 57, 60, 61, 67–9, 71, 73, 76, 77, 80, 81, 83, 88, 93–4, 98, 99, 102, 103, 106, 107, 110, 111, 113, 115, 116–17, 119, 121, 125, 127, 128, 130, 131, 133, 135, 136, 137–41, 141–7, 147–8, 150, 155, 176, 182, 185–6, 187
customs barriers/union 111, 117, 118, 125, 137–41, 141–7, 176
'stocking war' and 138
Economics Ministry 112, 144–5
equal rights 21, 27, 57, 66, 89, 107, 135, 150, 177, 178, 180, 185
foreign policy of vi, 2–5, 7, 9–10, 11, 13, 19–25, 26–36, 36–40, 40–55, 56–84, 85–122, 123–50, 151–4, 171–3
Franco-German Friendship Treaty (1963) 5
Gleichberechtigung, *see* Germany, equal rights
liberalism in 7, 44, 115, 120, 127–8, 154, 158, 172
media 34, 41, 43, 44–5, 49–50, 54, 65, 68, 69, 78, 91, 92, 99, 101, 103, 105, 107, 112–16, 123, 126–7, 128, 131, 146–7, 152, 153–4, 155, 157–9, 162, 163, 166, 167, 172–4, 179, 180, 181–2
propaganda 32–3, 35, 156–7, 163
rapprochement with France v, vi, 1–3, 5–8, 10, 13, 17, 21, 22, 24–7, 30, 32, 33, 35, 37–8, 39, 42, 44–5, 47, 50–2, 55, 57, 61, 65, 67, 71, 72–4, 76, 77, 79, 81–4, 87–9, 91, 92, 94–7, 99–112, 115, 117–22, 125–31, 132, 133, 134, 136, 137, 139, 140, 148, 150, 158, 159, 165–7, 170, 171, 176, 179, 182, 183, 185–6, 187, 188
relations (general) with France 6, 8–9, 32, 36–40, 47, 49, 55, 76–8, 81, 86, 92–4, 98, 99, 116, 121, 149, 161–3, 176–83, 185
trade unions 18, 47, 96, 99, 128–9
war with France v, 10–11, 85, 103, 121, 154, 165, 169, 170, 172, 180
Gide, André 28, 34
Gide, Charles 108
Gignoux, Claude-Joseph 133, 135, 136
Gilbert, Seymour Parker 40–1
Godard, Senator 92
Goebbels, Joseph 123
gold standard 1, 54, 126, 127, 178
Goltz, Rüdiger Count von der 114
Grautoff, Otto 29–36
Great Depression v, vi, 2, 4, 6, 54–5, 56, 78, 88, 134, 187
and collapse of Weimar vi, 50, 51, 54, 152
economic nationalism and 7, 178
Franco-German joint responses to 24–5, 71–2, 88, 117, 121, 126, 127, 131, 136, 148, 186
national reactions to v, vi, 7, 50, 56–60, 134
protectionism and 2, 7, 63, 69, 136, 176, 178
Wall Street Crash 4, 7, 54
Grenoble 103
Grumbach, Salomon 157

Haas, Ludwig 158
Haguenin, François-Émile 13
in Berlin 13
Hamburg 39
Hammerstein-Equord, Kurt von 62, 154
Harding, Warren G. 1
and 'return to normalcy' 1
Heidelberg, University of 158
Held, Heinrich 41, 98
Henderson, Arthur 45–6, 48, 58, 90
Henry, Jules 70
Hermes, Andreas 101
Herriot, Édouard 20–1, 44, 79, 94, 96, 97, 103, 147, 148, 149, 168, 169, 171, 178, 179, 180–2
Hesnard, Oswald 65, 91–2, 174, 175
Hessen 39
Hindenburg, Paul von 4, 52, 74–5, 80, 132, 179, 181
and Brüning's foreign policy 132–3
and dismissal of Brüning 148
and French Ministerial visit to Berlin 128
boycott of nationalist rally 39
elected German President 23
Hitler, Adolf 5, 7, 78, 83, 86, 107, 148, 176, 179, 183, 187
appeasement of 5
appointed Chancellor 36, 50, 176

Hitler, Adolf (*cont.*)
  foreign policy of 4
  Munich Putsch 20
Hoesch, Leopold von 28, 37–8, 43, 45, 51, 58, 62–3, 64, 67, 68, 71–81, 83, 85–9, 93, 99, 101, 104, 105, 109, 110, 111, 112, 116, 117–18, 129, 132, 134–6, 141, 144–7, 180, 187
  and Stresemann memoirs scandal 168, 169, 170, 172, 173
  transfer to London 179, 180
Honnorat, André 120
Hoover, Herbert 55, 91
  London Conference (1931) 94
Horne, John, historian 27
Hoschiller, Max 140
Hueber, Charles 157
Hugenberg, Alfred 37, 68, 78, 115, 153–4, 166

Ihlefeld, Kurt 113, 119
Iran 117
Italy 23, 56, 58, 60, 67, 69, 72, 79, 89, 177, 178

jazz age 1
Jeannesson, Stanislas, historian 18
Joos, Joseph 101, 103, 104
Judaism 69, 92, 123, 166, 184, 187
  French Zionist Association 92
Jungdeutscher Orden 114

Kaas, Ludwig 43, 97, 148
Kahn, Albert 103
Karlsruhe 157
Kastl, Ludwig 30
Kellogg, Frank 20
Kessler, Harry Count 187
Keynes, John Maynard 12
Kiderlen-Wächter, Alfred von 10
Kiep, Otto 31
Klotz, Louis 12
Koblenz 39, 79
Köpke, Gerhard 29, 33–5, 39–40, 63, 64, 70, 86, 108, 123, 135, 164, 172, 173, 182–4, 187
Köster, Roland 179–81
Krüger, Peter, historian 3, 4, 51
Krukenberg, Gustav 30
Kühn, Joachim 34, 176

Labour Party (British) 20, 45–9
Lambert-Ribot, Alfred 101
Laon 170
Latour, François:
  and French Ministerial visit to Berlin 129
  Mayoral visit to Berlin 129–31, 173
    protocol of 129–30
Laurent, Charles 128
Laval, Pierre 72, 93–5, 96, 101, 106, 107, 132, 144, 148, 151, 154, 166
  and Briand 5, 144, 148
  and Vichy 5, 187
    execution of 5
  collapse of government 146, 154
  German view of 154
  in Berlin 110–17, 121, 126–8, 130, 132
League of Nations v, 2, 3, 11, 21, 31, 42, 45, 55, 57, 58, 62–4, 67, 68, 86, 87, 89, 90, 100, 112–14, 136, 137, 141, 142, 146, 149, 180, 183, 187
  and peace treaty enforcement 21, 23, 86, 87
  and Saarland 12, 42
  Committee of Enquiry into the European Union 68–73
  Economic Bureau 57, 58, 73, 148
  German entry to 23–4, 26, 167
  Health Organisation 2
  International Labour Organization 2, 62
  International Press Exhibition (1929) 97
  reparations and 36
  Tariff Truce Conference 61
  World Economic Conference (1927) 56, 61
  World Economic Conference (1933) 178
Le Chatelier, Louis 8
  and Societé des Hauts Forneaux de Caen 8
Léger, Alexis 24, 117, 137
Leipziger Gewandhaus 120
Lersner, Kurt Baron von 82–3
Lesezirkel Höttingen 44
Le Trocquer, Yves 44, 83, 108
Ley, René César 163
Lichtenberger, Henri 34, 119–20
  and Institut d'études germaniques 120
Liga für Menschenrechte 106
Ligue des droits de l'homme 106
Lloyd George, David 15
Locarno, Treaty of (1925) 3, 4, 23–4, 26, 42, 74, 137, 155, 158, 162–3, 167, 170–2, 179
London 45, 46, 90, 91, 129, 179, 180, 184
Loucheur, Louis 14, 16, 57, 71, 72, 73, 108, 128
Lubersac, Louis de 16
Lucerne 45
Luther, Hans 64, 93
Luxembourg 27, 118
  railways 159
Lyon 97, 119, 168

MacDonald, Ramsey 20, 46, 49
McKenna, Reginald 20
Madrid 42, 129, 173, 174
Mann, Heinrich 166
  Professor Unrat 166
Mann, Thomas 27, 34
Margerie, Pierre de 18, 39–40, 41, 43, 47, 49, 51, 52, 54, 66, 68, 80, 83, 97, 119, 164–5
  retirement of 113, 125

Marlio, Louis 108
Marx, Wilhelm 19, 21, 32, 44, 100
Masse, Edwin 49
Massigli, René 48
Mayrisch Committee 6, 28, 30–3, 43–4, 83, 101, 102, 108–9, 111, 134, 137
Mayrisch, Émile 27–8, 108
Mellon, Andrews W. 94
Metz 164
Millerand, Alexandre 19
mining, metallurgy 12, 14, 19, 26–7, 71, 80, 101, 110, 115, 118, 128
Mommsen, Hans, historian 3
Moroccan crises (1907, 1911) 9–10, 81
Moselle, *see* Alsace(-Lorraine)
Moysset, Henry 81
Müller, Hermann 40, 50, 87
  resignation of 53
Mussolini, Benito 107
Muth, Henri 163

nationalists, *see* French nationalists, German nationalists
Netherlands 22, 36, 46, 57, 65
Neurath, Konstantin Baron von 149, 182
newspapers/magazines:
  Ami du peuple 168, 181
  Avenir 107
  Berliner Börsen-Courier 59, 154
  Berliner Börsen Zeitung 114, 153–4
  Berliner Tageblatt 31–2, 34, 50, 68, 103, 115, 128, 154
  Berliner Zeitung am Mittag 78
  Christian Science Monitor 70
  Daily Telegraph 59
  Démocrate 168
  Deutsch-französische Rundschau 29–36
  Deutsche Allgemeine Zeitung 69, 91, 115
  Deutsche Diplomatisch-Politische Korrespondenz 65
  Deutsche Wirtschafts-Zeitung 58
  Die Grüne Post 159
  Echo de Paris 93, 99, 102, 104, 168
  Elsässer Kurier 151
  Europe nouvelle 91
  Excelsior 75
  Figaro 69, 75, 181
  Frankfurter Zeitung 91, 115, 154, 172
  Fränkischer Kurier 173
  Freiburger Tagespost 163
  Germania 99
  Intransigeant 168
  Journal des débats 42, 168, 173, 175
  Journée industrielle 139
  Kleinkapitalist 159
  Kölnische Volkszeitung 101
  Königsberger Allgemeine Zeitung 113, 152
  La Croix 104
  La Dépêche 170
  La République 92–3, 106
  La Victoire 92–3
  La Volonté 44–5, 93, 175
  Le Figaro 116
  Le Gaulois 156
  Leipziger Abendpost 158
  Le Journal 92, 128, 183
  Le Matin 43, 65, 68, 69, 115, 151, 171, 175
    break with rapprochement 171
  L'Ere nouvelle 59, 82
  Le Soir 82
  Le Temps 104, 147, 183
  L'Illustration 174, 175, 181
  L'Oeuvre 116
  L'Ordre 128, 168
  Lothringer Volkszeitung 104
  New York American 70
  Observatore Romano 105
  Paris Midi 99, 170
  Petit Parisien 43, 44
  Politique 104
  Populaire 82, 92–3
  Revue d'Allemagne et des pays de langue allemande 29–36
  Revue de Paris 108
  Sonntag Morgen 159
  Straßburger Neueste Nachrichten 151
  Stuttgarter Neues Tagblatt 154
  Uhu 159
  Vorwärts 68
  Vossische Zeitung 78, 107, 115, 172
  Washington Post 47
Nostitz-Wallwitz, Alfred von 109
NSDAP 76, 77, 79, 80, 86, 95–7, 116, 123, 127, 134, 152, 160, 179, 188
  drive to power vi, 74, 148, 151, 176, 183–4, 186
  electoral breakthrough v, 4, 51, 53, 168
  Nuremberg Laws (1935) 184, 187
  SA 123
  Third Reich 187, 188
Nuremberg 173

Office national des universités et écoles françaises 84
Oudin, Bernard, historian 47

Paganon, Joseph 179–80
Painlevé, Paul 22, 79, 171
Palatinate 39
Pan Europa Movement 27–8
Papen, Franz von 101, 102, 103, 148, 169, 180, 182
Paris 6, 7, 18, 28, 30, 31, 33–4, 84, 92, 95, 97, 98, 100, 135, 136, 146, 173, 174
  Archbishop of 95, 104
  collaboration with city of Berlin 130–1

Paris (*cont.*)
  German Ministerial visit to 92–5, 106, 121, 131
    welcome for Germans 93
  inauguration of Franco-German Joint Commission in 134–6
  Notre Dame des Victoires 96
  office of Lord Mayor 129, 173
Paris–Berlin axis v, 55, 57, 60, 73, 88, 109, 171, 178, 186, 188
Paris Peace Conference/Settlement 2, 11, 13, 38, 57, 73, 82–3, 86, *see also* Versailles Settlement
  League of Nations and 23
  ratification of 2
  revision of 6, 17, 55, 66, 67, 70, 71, 74, 75, 82, 86, 93, 99, 100
  Vatican and 162
Pawlowski, Auguste 9
Pen Club 27, 101
Peycelon, Gilbert Antoine 112
Peyerimhoff, Henri de 101, 110
Pezet, Ernest 96
Picard, Ernest 101
  and Bank of Algeria 101
Pichon, Stéphen 9
Picot, Yves 34
Piétri, François 95
Pohl, Karl Heinrich, historian v
Poincaré, Raymond 10, 15, 28, 32, 37–8, 45, 75, 96, 107, 166, 171
  and Ruhr occupation (1923) 15–20, 168
  and Stinnes–Lubersac Agreement 17
  relations with political right 37, 171
Poland 13, 75, 77, 86, 102, 180
  East Prussia and 43, 182
  Polish Corridor/German eastern frontier 41, 56, 65, 87, 89, 102, 116, 150, 155, 182, 183
  Upper Silesia and 87
Popular Democratic Party (French) 96, 101, 102
Protestantism 7, 96
  and political liberalism 7
Prussia 69, 96, 106–7, 123, 125, 156
  government of and Versailles 39, 177
  plebiscite (1931) 106–7
  state elections (1932) 168
  Vatican and 162

Quai d'Orsay, *see* French Foreign Office

Radical Party (French) 18–19, 20, 22, 72, 82, 85, 106, 147, 170
Rapallo (1922 Treaty of) 15, 16
Rapp, Charles 161
Rathenau, Walther 11, 14, 16, 28, 128
  death of 16
RDI 30, 142–3
Rechberg, Arnold 28–9
Reichsbahn (German Railways) 102, 177
Reichsbank, *see* German National Bank
Reinhold, Peter 115
Remarque, Erich-Maria 166
  Im Westen nichts Neues/All Quiet on the Western Front 86, 166
reparations 6, 7, 11–13, 14, 20–1, 80, 89, 116, 131, 137, 185
  Britain and 12, 14–15, 47–8, 177–8
  commercialization of 19, 40
  Dawes Plan 20–1, 36, 40, 147, 168
  enforcement 15–22, 53, 93
  France and 12, 14, 16, 26, 39, 40, 65, 80, 81, 91, 93–4, 102, 107, 116, 127, 150, 152, 177–8
  Germany and 13, 14, 16, 17, 26, 39, 40, 65, 80, 81, 89, 91, 93–4, 102, 116, 150–3, 177–8, 179
  Hague Conferences (1929, 1930) 36, 38, 39, 40–50, 50–5, 74, 125, 161
    preliminary negotiations 41, 45
  Hoover Moratorium 90–1, 93–5, 107, 126, 151, 152
  Lausanne Conference (1932) 149, 177–8, 179
  London Conference (1924) 20–1, 168
  London Conference (1931) 91, 95, 107, 121
  payment in kind 14, 16, 18, 19, 47, 80, 125
  Reparations Commission 15
  sanctions 14, 17–21
  'tribute' 91
  Young Plan 7, 36, 43, 49, 51, 52–4, 56, 77, 78, 97, 152, 177
    referendum (1930) 53
Respondek, Erwin 101
Rethel (Ardennes) 97
Reynaud, Paul 182
Rhineland 97
  Allied evacuation of 21, 26, 36, 42, 46–50, 54, 74–6, 85, 86, 116, 125, 165, 175
  Allied occupation of 12, 14, 21, 37, 180
  demilitarization 75, 93
  France and 11, 12, 15, 74–6, 93
  security agreement 22
  separatism in 20, 97
  Versailles Treaty and 39
Ribbentrop, Joachim von 179
Riesser, Hans 171
Rieth, Kurt 78–9, 85
Rilke, Rainer Maria 31
Ritter, Karl 110, 135, 140, 144, 145, 148, 149
Rödder, Andreas, historian 88
Rollin, Louis 141, 145
Rome 111
Romier, Lucien 44
Roosevelt, Franklin D. 178
Rosenberg, Frederic von 17–18
Ruch, Charles Joseph Eugène 162

Ruelberg, Heinrich 145–6
Ruhr District:
  Allied evacuation of 21, 147
  Allied occupation (1921) 14
  Allied occupation (1923–5) 16–22, 92, 95, 113, 119, 147, 168, 179, 180, 185
    British reaction to 19–20
    passive resistance during 18–19
    US reaction to 19–20
  mining industry wages in 128
Ruhrort 14
Rumbold, Sir Horace 62, 73, 74, 88

Saarland 12, 27, 45, 50, 55, 75, 79, 89, 116, 118, 125, 150, 154, 161
  projected referendum in (1935) 125
  proposed Franco-German cooperation in 43
  return to Germany 26, 42, 97
    British view on 42
Sahm, Heinrich 129–30
  French media and 129
Salter, Sir Arthur 58
Sangnier, Marc 27, 95
  Democratic International 27
  French/German youth and 95
Sauerwein, Jules 43, 60, 65, 115
Schacht, Hjalmar 41–2, 53–4
Schäffer, Hans 174
Schirmann, Sylvain, historian 91, 178
Schleicher, Kurt von 154, 169, 182
Schreiber, Christian 105
Schubert, Carl von 50–1, 52, 62, 63
Schuman, Robert 95, 187
Schwendemann, Karl 30–1
Second World War v, vi, 2, 5, 187
Semaines sociales de France 98
Serruys, Daniel 73, 148
Seydoux, Jacques 21, 24, 43–4
Sievers, Johannes 120
Snowden, Philip 47–9
Société des artistes décorateurs 84
Societé pour l'échange artistique 120
Sohlberg Circle 27
South-East Europe 51, 71–2, 73, 86, 87, 115, 118, 137, 141, 179, 186
Soviet Russia/Union 15–16, 22, 28, 56–7, 61, 63, 64–5, 71, 72, 95, 127, 135, 178
  and trade with Germany 127
  Franco-German collaboration regarding 135, 178
Spanish Civil War 1
SPD 4, 23, 40, 44, 45, 47, 50, 54, 68, 77, 78, 87, 96, 106
  leaves government 53, 177
Stael, Madame Germaine de 130
Stahlhelm 74, 79, 85, 86, 134, 156, 179
  Strasbourg section 156
Steeg, Théodore 72
Stern-Rubarth, Edgar 65, 108
St Gobain 9
Sthamer, Friedrich 59
Stimson, Henry L. 94
Stinnes, Hugo 9, 16
  and Ruhr crisis 19
  in DVP 16
  Stinnes–Lubersac Agreement 16–17, 19
Stocky, Julius 101
Strasbourg 39, 97, 157, 158, 161–4
  post office statues 165
  Straβburg 164
  Straβburger Theater 157
Stresemann, Gustav 11, 57, 155, 161
  and DVP 16–17
  and Nobel Peace Prize 4
  as Chancellor (1923) 18–19, 92
  as Foreign Minister 19–25, 26, 29, 36, 45, 50, 51–2, 68, 86, 87, 97, 108
  Curtius and 7, 51–2, 86
  death of v, 3, 24, 50, 166, 185
  foreign policy of v, vi, 16–17, 148, 179, 182, 185
  French view of 24, 44, 96, 166–76
  historians and 3
  memoirs scandal 166–76, 181
    Crown Prince letter 22–3, 167, 170, 173
  partnership with Briand v, 3, 5, 11, 13, 24–5, 29, 31, 36, 38, 45, 49, 50, 57, 74, 92, 125, 126–7, 148, 166, 167, 173, 175, 176
Stresemann, Wolfgang 170
Stülpnagel, Otto von 154
Suarez, Georges 5
Sulzbach, Herbert 69
Suth, Willi 101
Switzerland 12–13, 63, 69, 81
  Bern 12

Tardieu, André 38, 71, 72, 75, 81–3, 94, 100–1, 141, 146, 151, 154, 166, 171
  relations with political right 171
The Hague 22, 36, 46, 49, 54
Thoiry meeting 24, 26, 40, 174–5
Thyssen 8
  global interest of 8
  Thyssen, August 8–9
  Thyssen, Fritz 8
Tirard, Paul 15
Treaty of Frankfurt (1871) 39
Treitschke, Heinrich von 75
Trendelenburg, Ernst 135
Treviranus, Gottfried 75
Turkey 71, 117, 135
Tyrrell, William Lord 46, 73

UDE 57, 65, 108, 109
Ullstein Verlag 166, 167, 168, 172, 174
United Nations 2
  and League of Nations 2

United Press of America 131
Frederick Kuh, Director of 131
United States of America 47, 90–2, 95, 126, 138
and Briand Plan 70
and Germany 13, 60–1, 66, 94, 131, 177
and Great Depression 54, 56, 90, 131
Smoot–Hawley Tariffs 58, 69
and League of Nations 2, 11
and reparations 20–1, 47, 90–1, 94, 132
and war debt 11–12, 15, 21, 24, 36–7, 55, 56, 90–1, 94, 126, 178
economic predominance of 14, 22, 36, 44–5, 56–8, 95
media in 70
universities/academic exchanges 84, 120, 160

Vallentin-Luchaire, Antonina 175
Vannes 181
Vatican 95, 162
Verdier, Jean 95, 104
Verlag Walther Rothschild 36
Vermeil, Edmond 31
Versailles Settlement 15, 22, 36, 38, 43, 74, 78, 82, 108, 113, 119, 132, 150, 152, 155, 158, 160, 162–3, 171, 175, 181, 183, *see also* Paris Peace Conference/ Settlement
disarmament and 21, 82, 93, 150
sanctions 21
tenth anniversary of 39–40
war guilt question and 38, 39, 40
Viénot, Pierre 28, 91, 108, 183–4, 187
death of 184
Vockel, Heinrich 101
Vogüé, Louis Marquis de 101
and Suez Canal Company 101

Washington 126
Weber, Helene 103–4
Weimar Republic 16, 23, 70, 96, 159, 179, *see also* Germany
Article 48 of constitution 4, 51, 74, 78, 83
banking collapse in 55, 93–4, 139
budgetary/economic crisis in 3–4, 16, 18, 40–1, 77, 79–80, 81, 83, 89, 90, 93–5, 101, 103–4, 107, 128, 130, 151–3
hyperinflation 18, 19, 40
Standstill Agreement 107
collapse of vi, 3–4, 5, 51, 116, 148, 149, 150, 173, 175–6, 182
conservatives/nationalists in 4, 22, 52–3, 76–7, 112, 113, 134, 148
elections (September 1930) 4, 51, 53, 76, 77–8, 81, 83, 96, 106, 116
post-war famine in 16
unemployment 140, 152–3
war debt 12
Weiss, Louise 91, 124, 127
Welczeck, Johannes Count von 173–4
Whaley-Eaton News Service 49
White, Ralph, historian 73
Wiesbaden Agreement (1921) 14–15, 19
Wilhelm, Crown Prince of Prussia 22
letter from Stresemann 22–3, 167, 170, 173
Wilhelm II 9, 179
Wilhelmstraβe, *see* German Foreign Office
Wilson, Woodrow 2, 11
war aims 13
Wirth, Joseph 14, 44, 83
Wolff, Otto 34
Württemberg 159

Young, Owen D. 36

Zaleski, August 87
Zollverein 69
Zuckmeyer, Carl 166
Der Hauptmann von Köpenick 166
Zürich 44

The manufacturer's authorised representative in the EU for product safety is Oxford University Press España S.A. of el Parque Empresarial San Fernando de Henares, Avenida de Castilla, 2 – 28830 Madrid (www.oup.es/en or product.safety@oup.com). OUP España S.A. also acts as importer into Spain of products made by the manufacturer.

www.ingramcontent.com/pod-product-compliance
Lightning Source LLC
LaVergne TN
LVHW011801200926
848484LV00003B/754
* 9 7 8 0 1 9 9 6 7 6 2 9 3 *